Praise for *The New American Spirituality*

"Elizabeth Lesser offers up a rich cornucopia of lessons for the soul in *The New American Spirituality,* a warm and fascinating account of a modern pilgrimage."
　　—Daniel Goleman, Ph.D., author of *Emotional Intelligence*

"Those who are looking for an uncharted way of living their beliefs will find *The New American Spirituality* a guiding light. Elizabeth Lesser's book defines what many have longed to see in print—a new *Varieties of Religious Experience* one hundred years after William James. This is a courageous book in which the author doesn't spare her own leaps of faith and dark moments of the soul, even as she encounters some of the great luminaries of our times. I was moved and affected—and I had a great time—reading her journey of a thousand stories that began with a girl's first halting spiritual steps. Her luminous sense of spirituality bubbles out of every deep pathway described along the way. For the seekers of the nineties and the visionaries of the next century, this book will shake your world too."
　　—Phil Jackson, former coach of the Chicago Bulls and author of *Sacred Hoops*

"A lucid, provocative, and enlightening tour of the American spiritual landscape. Lesser has a storyteller's eye and a philosopher's spirit."
　　—Julia Cameron, author of *The Artist's Way* and *The Vein of Gold*

"I've often been repelled by the flakiness and intellectual vacuity of those who claim to be presenting the world a new spirituality. So it was a delight to read Elizabeth Lesser's deep, serious, and intellectually stimulating portrayal of the range and possibilities of contemporary spiritual discourse and practice. Lesser has a remarkable capacity to highlight that which is most powerful and compelling in the revival of American spirituality. No serious intellectual could reasonably dismiss the lasting significance of the new interest in spirituality after reading Lesser's book."
　　—Rabbi Michael Lerner, editor, *TIKKUN* magazine, and author of *The Politics of Meaning* and *Jewish Renewal: A Path to Healing and Transformation*

"As the cofounder of the internationally known Omega Institute, Elizabeth Lesser has witnessed the search for God in America from a front-row seat. As both an observer and a participant, she is funny, profoundly moving, unpretentious, and simply brilliant. In *The New American Spirituality,* she validates our spiritual hunger, offering us the clarity to separate what will nourish it from what will not. This is a book for anyone who wants to read their own spiritual story more clearly and find the inner compass that can lead them home."

—RACHEL NAOMI REMEN, M.D., author of *Kitchen Table Wisdom*

"A comprehensive guide to what is best in the new spirituality that is delightful to read and will satisfy your mind, heart, and soul."

—SAM KEEN, author of *Fire in the Belly* and *Hymns to an Unknown God*

"*The New American Spirituality: A Seeker's Guide* is a dynamic tale of the search for the true self. As one of the primary founders of growth centers in America, Elizabeth Lesser has had a profound influence on the development of the spiritual movement in this country. Follow her trail to your heart."

—STEPHEN and ONDREA LEVINE, authors of *Who Dies?, Healing into Life and Death,* and *A Year to Live*

"As a founding member of Omega Institute, Elizabeth Lesser has known many of the leaders who have brought their spiritual insights to America over the past twenty years. Her own curiosity, discernment, and intuition have guided her in taking in what is authentically her own, and in letting go what is not for her. She shares this process in a style so honest and personal that readers are continually evaluating their own insights and saying yes or no from their own core. *The New American Spirituality* is a tuning fork for where we ring true."

—MARION WOODMAN, author of *Addiction to Perfection* and *Conscious Femininity,* and coauthor (with Robert Bly) of *The Maiden King*

"In this book, Elizabeth Lesser ranges with a clear mind over a wide field of human spiritual activity—with the added dimension of a woman's heart. She helps us to utilize the transformative ingredients that are available for every person's spiritual development. *The New American Spirituality* is a book to study and to keep handy near your altar. You will always find something in it to raise the ceiling of your awareness."

—RABBI ZALMAN SCHACHTER-SHALOMI, coauthor of *From Age-ing to Sage-ing*

"The great sages of the past taught us all we could ever need to know about spirituality. The problem is their followers created religion, which instead of joining us together has created more problems. Bringing spirituality into modern life is vital and this book can help you do just that. Do not wait for a life-threatening illness to awaken you. Instead, read this book, and find the revelation and transformation to begin a process of spiritual rebirth now."

—BERNIE SIEGEL, M.D., author of *Love, Medicine and Miracles* and
Peace, Love and Healing

"Through her particular vantage point at the Omega Institute, Elizabeth Lesser has been an observer, participant, and evaluator of the rich smorgasbord of teachings and teachers who have had an enormous effect on the spiritual perspective and practices that are now entering the American mainstream. America has historically been known as a melting pot, and as a union of individual states. The new American spirituality of which Elizabeth Lesser writes follows in this tradition, and can be appreciated as a democracy of spiritual perspectives, a freedom to choose to follow that which has personal meaning, an egalitarian sense of valuing body, mind, and spirit, and not elevating one above another.

I appreciated Elizabeth's inclusion of details of her own spiritual journey, because she is like so many whose lives and beliefs have been affected by the civil rights and women's movements, by the influx of Eastern thought and teachers, and by the need to find one's own path. To have authentic spiritual experiences woven throughout a book like this is what the new American spirituality is all about."

—JEAN SHINODA BOLEN, M.D., author of *Goddesses in Every Woman,*
Crossing to Avalon, and *Close to the Bone*

"This beautiful book is a sensitive guide to the inner life as well as a revolutionary text on the new spirituality."

—JOAN HALIFAX, Ph.D., author of *Shamanic Voices* and *The Fruitful Darkness*

The New American Spirituality

The
New American
Spirituality

A SEEKER'S GUIDE

Elizabeth Lesser

Random House New York

RANDOM HOUSE and colophon are registered trademarks of
Random House, Inc.

Owing to limitations of space, acknowledgments of permission
to quote from previously published materials will be found
following the index.

Library of Congress Cataloging-in-Publication Data
Lesser, Elizabeth.
The new American spirituality : a seeker's guide / Elizabeth
Lesser.
p.   cm.
Includes bibliographical references and index.
ISBN 0-375-50010-3
1. Spiritual life.   I. Title.
BL624.L46   1999   291.4—dc21   98-50310

Random House website address: www.atrandom.com
Printed in the United States of America on acid-free paper
9 8 7 6 5 4 3 2
First Edition

Book design by J. K. Lambert

To my parents, Gil and Marcia Lesser,

for seeking and for guiding

Contents

BOOK II / THE LANDSCAPE OF THE MIND

BOOK III / THE LANDSCAPE OF THE HEART

Introduction

Although a book is born of many impulses, and influenced by diverse experiences, authors often speak of a symbolic moment of conception—an "aha" moment when you say to yourself, "I have to tell this story." That moment came for me several summers ago, in the faculty dining room at Omega Institute, the education and retreat center I cofounded in 1977. Over the years I have shared countless meals with conference and workshop leaders in that room, moderating discussions between medical doctors and shamanic healers, Christian monks and Jewish rabbis, Zen teachers and business executives.

On this particular day I was eating lunch with Babatunde Olatunji, the West African drum master and world-music innovator. Seated next to Baba was the American poet Allen Ginsberg, engaged in conversation with Gelek Rinpoche, a Tibetan Buddhist lama, and Joseph Shabalala, a South African musician and freedom fighter. They were talking about their twin passions—politics and spirituality—and how challenging it is to combine the two. At the other end of the table was the onetime heavyweight champion of the world Floyd Patterson, picking over his plate of tofu salad, and discussing his workshop, "The Tao of Boxing," with a Chinese tai chi master, a tiny woman dressed in black pajamas. Next to them sat Huston Smith, the renowned authority on the history of religions, chatting with Ysaye Barnwell of the gospel group Sweet Honey in the Rock, and John Mohawk, a Seneca author and spiritual leader.

Catching bits and pieces of conversations, I turned to Baba Olatunji and asked, "So, what do you make of this—all these traditions meeting and merging?" Baba leaned back in his chair and surveyed the scene. Then, waving his fork at the extraordinary cast of characters seated around us, he announced, "This is a new kind of spirituality. It's American, and one day it will be the world."

An American spirituality—I liked that concept. It described my own spiritual life, something I had never been able to label. I had been actively searching for God since childhood. My path wove through the peaks and valleys of many different traditions: organized religion, disorganized mysticism, psychotherapy, philosophy, mythology, science. My search had all the signs of being an American one: it was diverse, individualistic, open-minded, free. It included ten years of discipleship with an Eastern meditation master; a deep immersion into Christian, Jewish, and Islamic mysticism; extended work with a psychotherapist; study of Jungian psychology and Western schools of philosophy; and exposure, from my work at Omega Institute, to the world's wisdom traditions, from ancient healing systems to modern consciousness research. For more than twenty-five years I had been searching—not to become a Christian or a Jew or a Muslim; a Buddhist or a Sikh or a Hindu—but to become a spiritual person, here in America, at the beginning of the twenty-first century.

After my "aha" moment in the lunchroom with Baba, I set out to research and write about the emerging American spiritual tradition. I had three distinct yet related stories to tell: America's story, my story, and yours—the reader's story. America's story, because each American's spiritual quest is fundamentally marked—for better and worse—by American values, and particularly by democracy, diversity, and individuality. My story, because a book about the spiritual journey is about an individual's most basic questions: Who am I? How should I live? What happens when I die? Without honest, real-life examples to accompany theories and practices, spiritual literature lacks veracity. Since the real-life examples I am most familiar with are my own, I have structured this book around my journey—my blunders and my accomplishments, my dark nights and my luminous awakenings. But in writing about my path, I did not want to betray the most important message of the book, which is that each person's spiritual journey is different, worthy, and unique. Therefore, the third story in the book belongs to the reader. Guidance, directions, and practices are offered here, but it is my hope that you will use them to chart a course all your own.

AMERICA'S STORY

In titling this book *The New American Spirituality,* I realize that some will criticize the use of the words *new* and *American*—*new,* because spirituality has been a universal longing in all people, throughout all of history; *American,* because America's brash materialism and excessive individualism often seem at odds with the spiritual impulse. While I share these concerns, I also believe that the American experiment with democracy and diversity *is* new, and that it is also a profoundly spiritual endeavor. In democratizing the spiritual search, and in diversifying the ways of explaining, expressing, and celebrating the mysteries of life and death, America has indeed created a new tradition, and a wonderful, worthy one at that.

The ways in which humans have searched for and worshiped the divine have changed throughout history. As cultures rise and fall to meet the needs and psyches of the times, religions and philosophies come and go, influencing their successors, acting as building blocks in the evolving human story. The American era has already changed the way people eat, speak, make music and art, and arrange their family and work lives. This book is about how America is changing the way we interpret and practice spirituality. It addresses quintessentially American questions:

- What is gained and what is lost when religious traditions meet and cross-pollinate?
- What structures and practices are emerging to revamp the more autocratic and patriarchal forms of traditional religious paths?
- How do we determine what is helpful and genuine in the crowded array of psychological, spiritual, and healing theories and practices?
- Where do we draw the fine line between wise self-examination and narcissistic selfishness?
- How do we set goals, find teachers, and gauge our own progress on the path?
- How do we merge inner healing with social healing, honoring both our individuality and our interconnection with others and the world?
- How do we develop the habits of faith and hopefulness in a cynical age?
- What exactly does it mean to live a spiritual life?

MY STORY

When I first set out on the spiritual path, I wasn't paying much attention to the meaning of the word *spiritual.* I thought I knew what it meant. Somewhere I had heard that to be spiritual was to behave as God would:

loving, pure, selfless. Therefore, I figured that anything within me and others that was hateful, crude, and selfish was not spiritual. If I could transcend the parts of myself that I didn't like—parts that I thought were antithetical to spirituality—and if I could be loving and forgiving at all times, then I would be walking a spiritual path. I was nineteen when I decided to become a saint.

It took me a long time to decide to become a human being, and to look within my own flawed nature for salvation. It took mistakes, dark nights of the soul, hard work, and help from teachers and friends to fashion a spirituality that respected both my divinity *and* my humanity, my radiance *and* my shadow. It took my own combination of religion and psychology, meditation and physical healing, mysticism and science, to forge a path that felt genuine and effective. Instead of sacrificing a self I hardly knew or loved, I turned my attention to self-understanding and self-forgiveness. Instead of accepting a straight-and-narrow route to someone else's concept of God, I set out to make my own way, using my inner longing as a compass. This is the story I tell throughout the book—not so that you will follow my path, but so that you might follow your own longing for a spiritual life.

A note here about the word *longing,* because I use the word often in this book. Longing is my fuel of choice on the spiritual journey. Spiritual longing is a sort of loneliness for an unknown yet deeply perceived presence. Some call the presence God; some call it peace; some call it consciousness; some call it love. Its source rests in the well of our own hearts. When we slow down, quiet the mind, and allow ourselves to feel hungry for something that we do not understand, we are dipping into the abundant well of spiritual longing. We have grown accustomed to shutting down or blotting out feelings of longing, loneliness, hunger. It's less challenging to feed the hunger with explanations, concepts, or rules (or drugs, food, or drink) than to rest for a while in the depths of the heart's longing. But if we want to open the doors to life's joy and God's peace, we have to learn how to fearlessly explore the full terrain of our human longing.

This exploration does not have to take place in a monastery—the ordinariness of our daily lives provides sacred enough ground for the journey. In this book I have organized the journey into four landscapes: the Landscape of the Mind, the Landscape of the Heart, the Landscape of the Body, and the Landscape of the Soul. In each landscape I use examples from my own life, provide methods and practices I have learned along the way, and offer encouragement for you to chart your own course.

Why should you trust me as a guide through these landscapes? Perhaps because I have been a canary in the mines of the new American spirituality; perhaps because I am a skeptic on a mystical path, open to anything, but wary of those who claim magical powers or irrefutable answers; and perhaps because I have stumbled as much as I have succeeded, and resisted change as much as I have been transformed. I do not claim to have *the* answers. I do claim to have spent almost three decades studying and practicing diverse spiritual traditions. I believe, from my own experience, in the power of these traditions to bring peace of mind and generosity of heart to the seeker. I have distilled what I believe is essential to the spiritual quest, and offer it with a sense of gratitude to those who have taught me, and a sense of camaraderie with those who recognize their own longings, blunders, and transformations in these pages.

YOUR STORY

In some ways, it is easier to live in a country ruled by a king or a tyrant. You know the rules, and you understand the consequences for following and not following them. You have someone to blame when things go wrong, and someone to worship when things go right. It's the same with the spiritual life. A well-worn path, directions for the journey, rules for the followers, roles for the leaders—these can make for a far less demanding journey than the one I am calling the new American spirituality.

In democratizing the spiritual life, the burden is on you, the seeker. You are entitled to your own beliefs and practices, but you are also accountable for your own morality and enlightenment. Your path is your own, but you must walk side by side with others, with compassion and generosity as your beacons. You don't have to join a religion or a school of thought or a community of seekers to be part of the American spiritual tapestry. You can do this, and you may benefit tremendously if you do; but you don't have to. If anything is required it is this: fearlessness in your examination of life and death; willingness to continually grow; and openness to the possibility that the ordinary is extraordinary, and that your joys and your sorrows have meaning and mystery.

In empowering the seeker, this book is not a rebuke of organized religions. Rather, it asks the follower of a particular faith to use discretion and imagination on the path. You can decide which of your religious customs work for you, and which ones may need to be revitalized. For example, if you are a practicing Jew or Christian or Muslim, you may want to examine practices and rules that made sense to ancient nomadic desert communities, but may no longer be relevant to us today. Or, if you are a Buddhist, it's good to remember that what had meaning to a sixth-century B.C. Indian monk may no longer apply to life in twenty-first-century America.

One of humankind's greatest ironies is how throughout history, prophets who have preached genuine, radical experience in place of institutionalized, inflexible dogma become, after death, the central figure in an "ism" they would never have supported. The world's great spiritual personalities—Buddha, the prophets of Israel, Jesus, Mohammed, to name but a few—were considered revolutionaries, and even heretics in their day. They inspired their early followers to break from tradition and update their relationships to God. On his deathbed the Buddha begged his disciples, "Do not accept what you hear by report, do not accept tradition, do not accept a statement because it is found in our books, nor because it is in accord with your belief, nor because it is the saying of your teacher. Be lamps unto yourselves."

America is just the place for spiritual seekers to be lamps unto themselves. Throughout our history, revolutionaries who worshiped God *and* the individual, a higher order *and* democracy, the One *and* diversity, have made America a land of many lamps. There is room enough for everyone on God's mysterious path, and millions of lamps light the way for the benefit of all. Millions of lamps can also kindle confusion and superficiality. Many have disparaged the recent upsurge of nontraditional spirituality for its lack of discipline, and for its apparent shortage of moral fiber and hard-hitting truths. Indeed, some new spiritual and psychological systems have put forth an ethos of ego-friendly fluff and fantasy. But as we move away from the autocracy of religion to the democracy of spirituality, anything that runs counter to a "thou shalt not" theology gets lumped in with the "thou shalt do whatever you want" approaches. My hope is that this book lands in the middle of that pendulum swing, offering the reader a more balanced road map for the spiritual journey—not dogmatic and restrictive on the one hand, but not convenient and self-serving on the other. Like democracy, the kind of spirituality this book addresses asks the seeker to exercise responsibility on the path of freedom.

While this book does offer a wide selection of spiritual lessons and meditative practices that can bring you happiness and peace of mind, it does *not* offer easy answers, miracle cures, or ten ways to get something for nothing. It is not a magic carpet ride back to nonexistent times when indigenous cultures lived in peace and harmony. Nor is it a promise of a dawning age of instantaneous enlightenment when divine intervention will save humanity from itself. Rather, it is a realistic and practical synthesis of the American spiritual traditions of our times—a seeker's guide to forging a personal path that honors who you are as an American, even as it honors your unique religious roots, your need for discipline and morals, and your desire to belong to a community of fellow seekers.

In trying to include the diversity of choices available in American spirituality, I have left out more systems, traditions, books, and teachers than I have included. This is an inherent problem in the kind of book I have written. At the back of the book I offer lists of books, music, and audiotapes that can be used to add other flavors and nutrients to the American feast. I faced tough choices in putting these lists together, and I offer apologies to those authors and disciplines who undeservedly were left out. I encourage you, the seeker, to add your own discoveries to the menu, even as you stay alert to the American predilection for overeating, and to the appeal of fast food and quick fixes. These pitfalls are part of our heritage, and therefore pervasive in each American's consciousness. Remember to go slow; expect mistakes; welcome surprises; let one door open onto another.

When asked about the myriad of choices available to Americans, E. B. White said: "I wake up in the morning torn between the desire to save the world and to enjoy the world. This makes it hard to plan the day." Please don't feel torn as you read this book. You don't have to choose between saving the world and enjoying the world, between loving your self and loving God, between opening your heart and illuminating your mind. If you take your time and keep your wits about you, you can cultivate a wholesome and artful spiritual life that nourishes the whole self—one that will help you enjoy the world, and perhaps even save it.

Book I

The American Landscape

1 ⫶ My Search

Like every other form of human knowledge, religious psychology is built upon expe-
rience. It needs fact. And since the circumstances are such that the facts occur only at
the deepest level of men's consciousness, this branch of knowledge cannot develop until
individuals supply the necessary "confessions." It is entirely with this sort of docu-
mentary purpose in mind that I have tried to pin down, in what follows, the reasons
for my faith. . . . I in no way believe that I am better or more important than any
other man: It simply happens that for a number of accidental reasons my own case is
significant, and on that ground it is worth recording.
—TEILHARD DE CHARDIN

Writing about the spiritual search without writing about oneself is like
writing about a road trip and never mentioning the car. One's self—or the
sum total of one's body, mind, and heart—is our vehicle on the spiritual
path. Parts of it can break down and need repair; it can function with ease
and balance; or it can sit in the garage for years, ignored and rusting. Direct stories of breakdown, healing, and patience are the most helpful
teaching tools we can access as we progress on the spiritual journey.

Therefore, I begin with my own story, and refer throughout this book
to my struggles and awakenings, my teachers and the wisdom they have
shown me. As the great Christian mystic Teilhard de Chardin suggests
above, my own story is no more important than any other person's. But

because it is a story of someone who has been searching her whole life—stumbling along the spiritual path, finding grace, making mistakes, and discovering joy—it has the potential to describe a particularly relevant way of seeking to Americans, here and now. Each bump and every blessing have informed what I have learned and adopted as my own. It is my hope that by revealing all the textures of the road I have traveled, I may help you gain faith and find meaning on your own journey.

Indeed, there is an unbroken golden thread that weaves its way through human history, stitching together the many wise voices that have pointed seekers toward the simple spiritual truth. Yet while the timeless message of spirituality may be simple, the searching is not. Why? Because human beings are complex. By the time we make our spiritual searching a conscious endeavor, we have acquired layers of stubborn misconceptions about ourselves and the nature of life. Not only must we follow the golden thread toward spiritual freedom, but we must also unravel the garden-variety twine that is wrapped tightly around our hearts and minds. The golden thread parts of my own spiritual story are interesting and enlightening—they involve extraordinary teachers and are set in exotic places, like India and Israel. But the most useful stories emanate from the unraveling of the tightly wound twine. Here the characters and sets are ordinary—me, my family, and others who have shared their questions and growth with me. How we unravel the twine—through the hard knocks of daily life and the hard work of self-examination—is just as much a part of the spiritual path as are solitary retreats and meetings with remarkable teachers. In daily life we make real the rarefied wisdom that we can only glean in meditation and in the words of saints and gurus.

Each part of my story—youthful zealousness, marriage, my work as a midwife, mothering, divorce, leadership, loneliness, the death of friends and family members, and periods of cynicism and lack of faith—is a radiant bead on a necklace that is still unfinished. The more jagged beads, including divorce, illness, and struggles at work and with money, are strung nobly beside the smoother ones: my loving family and community, meaningful work, pilgrimages to holy places around the world, silent retreats in the wilderness, and the wise men and women with whom I have studied. I am offering you the whole necklace because I know that yours too is a work in progress with precious gems, simple pebbles, and rough stones.

I start with the first bead: my childhood. When I was a child, God was dead. I was raised in a family and a culture that were hooked on science and progress, and suspicious of spirituality and introspection. *Time* magazine put the nail in the coffin in 1966, when I was fourteen: "Is God Dead?" ran the headline on the cover. Magazines provided the equivalent of scripture in my home, and the magazine rack that my father had built on the kitchen wall came as close to any family altar that we would ever have. Avid readers, my parents subscribed to at least ten magazines, everything from *National Geographic* to *The New Yorker,* as well as the standards of the day—*Life, Time,* and *Woman's Day.* I received my cultural education from their covers, as I passed the rack on my way to school or to play in the neighborhood. Glancing at the glossy photographs, I learned about my world: John-John Kennedy, Marilyn Monroe, the civil rights marches, Dr. Spock's latest on toilet training, or the best table setting for Thanksgiving dinner. Later I'd see pictures of the Beatles, vanishing tribes in Samoa, battlegrounds in Vietnam, the first long hair of the hippies.

But it was the questioning of God's death that stopped me in my tracks at the magazine rack. God was already on shaky ground in my home. My father, a New York City advertising man, had told me that his most religious experience had been when his mother and father finally allowed him to stop attending Hebrew school. He now was free to tramp around the still-wild bogs and streams of Long Island. My mother, raised in a devout Christian Science home, had rejected as an adult its formal spiritual underpinnings, while holding on to some of its more extreme ideas about the body, mind, and health. From my father I received an almost religious appreciation of nature; from my mother, a lover of words, poetry, and enlightened ideas, I absorbed a quest for knowledge and understanding. But both of my parents resented organized religion. My sisters and I were given no spiritual belief system or formal training of any kind. In fact, there existed an unarticulated equation in the family philosophy that if a person was intelligent, he or she would therefore *not* be religious. And it was not just my family putting forth this equation. In school the reigning divinity was science; in society the supreme being was the individual; in daily life automobiles and washing machines were the sacred symbols of fulfillment and value. On top of all of that, the sixties were upon us, and organized anything was being called into question.

And so, while I was not surprised to learn from *Time* magazine that God was feared dead, I was shaken to have my assumptions confirmed. As secular as my upbringing had been, I still longed to believe in *something* that addressed my questions about life and death. At an early age I prayed, although I would have been laughed out of the house if any of my sisters had known about it. I tried to make sense of the Bible stories that my mother read to us along with Greek myths and Grimm's fairy tales. I was aware that some of my friends actually believed that some "mythological figures" (as my mother called Abraham and Moses and Jesus and Mary) were real people who had direct access to God. In the absence of a formal intercessor, I prayed to a picture of the late President Kennedy on my bedroom wall, sure that he had made his home with the God that no one in my family would believe in.

Without some kind of religious institution, my life in the 1950s and 1960s was based almost entirely on material values. Suburbia bred isolation from community and the shared rituals that bring a sense of mythic proportion to life. Age-old rites of passage such as birth, coming of age, and death were no longer part of the fabric of life, but instead were relegated to "experts" in hospitals or institutions. The same society that revered the rational and the scientific held the intuitive, the magical, the unmeasurable, and the wild in disdain. It seemed that every year the natural world was shrinking, as huge housing developments covered remaining tracts of wilderness. When I was twelve my mother experienced a prolonged period of grief when acres of farmland and forests across the street from her hero's birthplace were transformed into the Walt Whitman Shopping Center, one of the country's first malls. Where could one go to hear the voice in the wilderness if the woods were disappearing? In my young mind, the only remaining place was a church.

I recently heard a great writer say that an essential element in the life of a writer is to have been an outsider in childhood, to have been given the "gift" of not belonging. This man's gift had been a father whose job kept the family moving from one Irish town to another. Not having a hometown fueled his longing to belong to a community and made him an acute observer of people. My own childhood predicament of not belonging to any formal religious institution or distinct ethnic group awakened in me an intense yearning to understand the mysterious nature of life. I was given no explanations, no answers to such basic questions as Where do we come from? and Where do we go when we die? In the absence of any shared spiritual ritual, I had no model of individuals searching together, fulfilling their own destinies while being in relationships and community. With no prescribed beliefs, I set out at an early age to create my own.

My town was a curious mix of Italian Catholics, middle- and upper-class Protestants, a few Jewish and African American families, and Unitarians—people like my family, only they had decided to belong to something. We were maddeningly none of the above. I longed for conformity, and not only of the religious kind. This was America in the fifties and sixties. I wanted my school lunch to look like the other kids' lunches: sandwiches on white bread with the crusts cut off, orange slices in little plastic bags. But my mother packed me hunks of homemade bread and hard-boiled eggs. This and other similarly unfair acts made me covet normality. Barbie dolls were out—they were not anatomically correct. Television and movies were strictly limited. I dreamed of my family piling into the station wagon, going to church, and then coming home and sitting together in the family room, watching *The Ed Sullivan Show.* But we didn't belong to a church, nor did we have a family room, or even a TV.

My best friend in the neighborhood was from an Italian Catholic family that most definitely had a family room. They went to Mass at Saint Patrick's church every Sunday, to religious instruction on Fridays, and, best of all, to High Mass at Christmas and Easter and to the mysterious service on Ash Wednesday. After her First Communion, to which she wore white gloves and a hat, she could kneel at the main altar and eat the little wafer, *the body of Christ,* and drink the wine, *his blood,* and then tell her dark secrets to a priest behind a black curtain. I wanted to belong to this religion.

For a while I went to Mass with my friend's family, and once, risking the ridicule of my sisters, received the thumbprint of the priest on my forehead on Ash Wednesday. I loved the drama and ritual and the Latin words and music that filled Saint Patrick's. I fantasized becoming a nun, marrying Jesus, belonging to something mysterious and grand. But, since I wasn't Catholic, I understood that I was only a visitor and therefore doomed to hell. Perhaps there was some other doorway in for me. There was a black gospel church in my town, and once my mother and I went to a civil rights gathering led by the church pastor. The singing and vocal prayer enraptured me, as did the sense of community. Now, this was what I had in mind! I longed to attend church here each Sunday and sing my praises to the sweet Jesus that captivated the hearts of the congregation. But this also was not to be. My introduction to the black gospel tradition coincided with rising racial tension in my town, and eventually with Martin Luther King's assassination. I could only admire the worship from afar. I did buy a record album made by Marian Anderson, the great black singer who featured strongly in my mother's pantheon of heroes. In 1939 the Daughters of the American Revolution denied her access to Washington's

Constitution Hall for a concert. Eleanor Roosevelt then invited her to perform on the steps of the Lincoln Memorial before an audience of seventy-five thousand people. My mother approved of my record choice although she had no idea that when I was alone in the house I would turn up the volume and sing to Jesus as I had seen the church faithful do.

By the time I reached the age of fourteen I still yearned for spiritual community. Therefore, the public questioning of God's existence felt like a great loss—he had apparently died before making formal contact with me. I never read the article. I was too young to understand that it was describing an erosion of values in Western culture that had been gathering speed in America for decades, and in European culture for centuries. Nietzsche had written about the death of God in 1883, but God had been dying a slow death in the Western world long before Nietzsche. The cultural bias in favor of the material, the rational, and the scientific was not new to the twentieth century; Western culture had been leaning in this direction for more than three hundred years. When Descartes, in 1637, said, "I think, therefore I am," he provided the philosophical basis for the scientific revolution and the Enlightenment, movements that would, of course, have started without his famous adage. Yet that one small sentence summed up a radical shift in human consciousness and behavior. Where in the past humankind saw itself as part of a larger, collective scheme, fundamentally linked to creation and the cosmos, now each person was to be governed by his own intellect. Now the *individual's* aptitude and sense of self would receive the kind of sanctification once reserved for the gods, nature, and the community.

Almost thirty years after *Time* magazine asked if God was dead, it published another exposé of American culture in 1993, when one of its journalists wrote, "The most significant thing in the last half-century has been the dramatic expansion in personal freedom and personal mobility, individual rights, the reorienting of culture around individuals. We obviously value that. But like all human gains, it has been purchased with a price." Now, at the start of a new century, we are beginning to understand what this price includes. The judging, parental god died; the autonomous individual was born. In the past, the rights and creativity of the individual were sacrificed for the health and protection of the community. Now it seems that our sense of responsibility and connection to the community—be it a family or a city—has been sacrificed for each person's quest for self-fulfillment. In the swing from one extreme to the other, we have elevated personal progress and materialism to a kind of religion. The emptiness of these pursuits as a social value system has brought on a mass yearning for a sense of the sacred in our lives together.

My own yearning for a spiritual life and the sense of belonging to something greater than my personal world followed me through childhood and grew stronger in adolescence. Around the same time that God was declared dead by *Time,* I began listening to the music of the Beatles, Joan Baez, and Bob Dylan, and taking an interest in the society around me, especially the civil rights and anti–Vietnam War movements. My adventurous older sister went to great pains to introduce me to anything unusual she discovered in college. The first time I saw her in a Volkswagen van filled with long-haired hippies was a watershed moment in my young life; here were people with a belief system that I could embrace. With the intuitive understanding of cultural change that each generation seems to be born with, I identified with what the hippies stood for even before I knew what it was. Something about these people, and their dress and music and books and language, thrilled me just as the dress and music and books and language of the Catholic Church had thrilled me when I was younger. By the time I left high school for college I had done more than admire the hippies. I had wholeheartedly become one.

The phenomenon of the hippies can be understood only in light of the generations that preceded and raised them. My parents came of age in the era of the World Wars and the Depression. Their beliefs had been formed in a time of scarcity and fear, where ours had emerged in a time when America was more prosperous and secure. My generation had the luxury to question the strict boundaries that our parents had constructed in the aftermath of the chaotic war years. Their love of order and hygiene and tidiness, their sacrificial attitude toward their own emotional needs, their prudent ways with money and their respect for material things were in direct response to what they had not had. We, on the other hand, at least those of us in the glory days of the great American middle class, felt confined by the structures put in place by our parents. We wanted expansion, and sought it through new forms of music, dress, drugs, politics, relationships, and lifestyle; everything constructed by our parents' best intentions was up for grabs.

In 1970 I entered Barnard College, across the street from Columbia University in New York City—a haven for intellectuals, feminists, and political activists. It was also my mother's alma mater. Although I had always known that my experience at college was not going to be very similar to my mother's, I was not prepared for what I found at Barnard and Columbia. In high school I had imagined that college was going to be like one long Grateful Dead concert, punctuated by classes. But a few weeks after my first semester began, Columbia University students joined students across the country and went on strike to protest the continuation of the Vietnam War. Since half of my classes were at Columbia, I went on strike too. My first year at Barnard was indeed only punctuated by classes, and dominated by political meetings and protest marches. My boyfriend went to jail for his radical anti-war activities. Part of my first year at college was spent in the legal aid offices of Lower Manhattan, at the courthouse on Wall Street, and finally, in the visitors room of Rikers Island House of Correction, perhaps the most violent jail in the country.

For a while, filled with the passionate desire to be "part of the solution, not the problem," I devoted my days to protesting the war, disrupting Columbia's business-as-usual, and working with disenfranchised people in New York's Upper West Side. My hunger to belong to something greater than myself was temporarily satiated by my wish to see an unjust war ended. Of course, I was also fueled by the typical longings of an eighteen-year-old, and I found plenty of opportunities to participate in the general unraveling of the established order. Those were the days when sexual freedom and drug experimentation were explored with a naiveté that seems inconceivable today. Yet to us, children of middle-class, middle-twentieth-century America, free expression took precedence over conventional mores.

One spring evening in Manhattan, I met my father at the Cornell Club for dinner. Waiting for him in the stuffy lounge, amid gray-suited businessmen and their properly attired wives, I glanced at my own outfit: ripped bell-bottom jeans, a Mexican peasant blouse, no bra, and hair down to the middle of my back. I was suddenly made aware, by the cool stares of the club members, that everything about me, from the sheerness of my blouse to the dirt on my work boots, represented an attack on the values they held sacred. Could they tell that I had come straight from the legal aid office, where I had been discussing my boyfriend's retrial? Did my dirty clothes give away the fact that I had skipped my final in anthropology to help build an illegal "people's park" on a lot owned by Columbia?

By the time my father arrived I was glad to escape the accusatory stares. During dinner I increased the shock value of my conversation by telling my father about a march I had participated in the week before. The Barnard feminists had joined forces with feminists throughout the city to protest the Playboy Club's denigration of women. I watched his face as I told him that women had thrown rocks through the window of the club. I knew this wouldn't please him—my parents had been horrified when I had participated in the May Day march on Washington, one of the final and most violent of the anti-war marches. In response to the massive bombing of North Vietnam and Cambodia, student protesters attempted to shut down Washington, D.C., and therefore the government, by pushing cars off bridges into moving traffic, throwing glass into the streets, and making human barricades to stop traffic.

What I didn't tell my father was that I was scared of the increasing violence emanating from a movement that had started with dreams of harmony and freedom. For all of the real peace and love of the times, an equally real sense of turmoil and intolerance shadowed the years that have become known as the sixties. It was a confusing time to be leaving home and setting out into the world. I had turned to the anti-war movement because my political conscience was too troubled by the war not to stand up and be counted. But now the movement had adopted a harshness that was not my own. I was too proud to tell my father this. The alternative looked like the people sitting around me at the Cornell Club, drinking martinis and talking about the stock market.

By the end of my first year at school it seemed that everything I turned my attention to was exploding into violence. It wasn't just the anti-war movement. Across the country, from black separatists to radical feminists, people's moods had shifted. I experienced this personally when I mistakenly got off the Barnard dorm elevator on the floor that a black students' organization had demanded as their own. Walking down the look-alike hall toward a room I thought was mine, I was confronted by four girls I had seen on campus but had never dared talk to. "What are you doing on our floor?" they demanded. I suddenly realized my blunder and tried to explain it to them. Surrounding me, they pushed me toward the elevator. One of the girls grabbed me by my shirt collar and slapped me hard across the face as the elevator doors were closing.

That slap woke something up within me, something that had been bothering me all year. I was ashamed of the mean-spirited rhetoric that pervaded the anti-war movement. Now the hypocrisy of hatred within some of the peace and freedom groups began to gnaw at my conscience. How were we going to heal the wounds of the country if our own rancor was only intensifying? This question echoed in everything I heard and saw. In the music world the drug of choice was no longer marijuana, but cocaine, even heroin. The raggle-taggle, tie-dyed clothes of the hippies had been replaced by the black leather jackets of the Hell's Angels. The strident resentment toward men and "nonliberated" sisters within the women's movement was escalating. The great hero of nonviolence— Martin Luther King, Jr.—was dead, his message of tolerance and love no longer the unifying element of the civil rights movement. American involvement in the Vietnam War was about to be over, and the issues, never as simple as we had assumed, were even less clear-cut now. We were riding the dying wave of the sixties, about to hit the shore with a painful thud.

I rode the wave to the shore that first year in college and then watched people scatter in different directions. Some of my friends began to pay more attention to their studies. Some involved themselves more seriously with politics and social action; others dropped out of school, moved to another country, or to a farm, or went down the dark path of heavy drug use. I looked around for something to answer the question that my black dorm-sister's slap had awakened.

In my disillusionment with politics I began reading Thomas Merton's autobiography, *The Seven Storey Mountain*. I felt a personal connection with Merton since he had been a student at Columbia when he began his life-long search for spiritual wholeness. His sense of alienation within his own religious order reawakened my childhood hunger for a relevant spiritual path and community. Through his words, and the books of other Christian mystics I found in the Columbia library, I reconnected with my childhood forays into Catholicism, when I went to Mass with my best friend's family. I mimicked a ritual that Merton had secretly performed in college—getting off the subway at random stations, just to sit in a new church. Like Merton, I kept this strange behavior from my friends, who, I imagined, would find my mystical leanings incongruous with radical politics. It was in one of Merton's books that I was led to Zen Buddhism and then to other Eastern religious traditions.

Zen was an appropriate first step into Eastern spirituality for the existentially raised post-war generations. Its lack of pretense and dogma was appealing to the Western mind, and it is no surprise that Zen was one of the first of the Eastern religious practices to take serious hold in America. A fascination with Eastern philosophies had been growing steadily in

America since the late eighteenth century, when different Eastern texts, including the great Hindu masterpiece, the Bhagavad-Gita, were first translated into English. The Transcendentalists in the nineteenth century were profoundly influenced by Eastern thinking. In 1893 the first World Parliament of Religions was convened in Chicago, bringing together noted religious leaders and theologians from around the world. Many of these leaders, in particular Soyen Shaku, a Zen Buddhist, and Vivekananda, a student of the Hindu saint Ramakrishna, would have a lasting effect on American spirituality.

Around the turn of the century, with the advent of easier communication and travel, ideas from around the world began to permeate American thought. Psychotherapy found its way from Europe. New Thought, a religious movement that began in the United States at the dawn of the twentieth century, drew on a variety of sources, including ancient Christianity, Hinduism, Transcendentalism, and the thinking of the American philosopher and psychologist William James. Movements such as Christian Science, founded by Mary Baker Eddy, and Theosophy, founded by Helena Blavatsky, were born in these fertile times. The work of these spiritual pioneers, and of their students, set the stage for the wave of Eastern philosophies and practices that rolled into America in the 1970s.

I was introduced to Zen practice by a medical student I met as I pulled away from radical politics. When I first walked into the New York zendo, or practice hall, I was struck by the smell and the colors and the stillness. Outside the city was a swarming hive of exertion and commotion. Inside the zendo not much was happening. Somber men and women sat on brown cushions (*zafus*), staring at the bare wooden floor. Incense, as subtle as wood smoke on an autumn day, drifted in the stillness. Every now and then a tiny Japanese man in black robes would shuffle behind the meditators and whack them on the shoulders with a long stick. I couldn't imagine what the point of any of this was. But my friend had been sitting at the zendo for a year. I trusted him, and I gave meditation a try.

I remember when I first took my seat on a *zafu* at the Zen Center. The simple gesture of folding my legs beneath the cushion and resting my palms in my lap felt powerfully familiar, as if I had sat like that, in that posture, smelling that same incense for a thousand years. A strange sense of peaceful dignity overcame me. The instructions were simple: Become aware of the breath rising and falling in the stomach; keep a straight back; let thoughts come and go without focusing on them. Merely by following these directions I would experience a novel state of self-containment and inner strength.

The severity of the Zen Center puzzled me, but the power of the practice was undeniable. I started to sit on a daily basis. Throughout my second year at Barnard I developed a great respect for the Zen teachings. I read and sat and participated in *sesshins,* long meditation retreats. I moved in with my friend the medical student, who would eventually become my husband. Together we explored yoga and health food and Indian music. We read Carlos Castaneda's books about the shaman teacher, Don Juan, aloud to each other on the bus, and went to lectures given by anyone who sounded interesting: Krishna Murti, Joseph Campbell, Maharishi Mahesh Yogi. We studied yoga from a Hindu yogi, a small man wrapped in white cotton who didn't speak but wrote his directions on a chalkboard. We meditated under the guidance of Chögyam Trungpa Rinpoche, a Tibetan Buddhist who had led his people over the Himalayas to escape the Chinese Communists. We celebrated Shabbat by singing and dancing on the tables at Rabbi Shlomo Carelbach's shul.

It wasn't long after I began sitting zazen that I heard of a strange-sounding weekly gathering called Sufi dancing, held on the Columbia campus. While Zen stressed a solitary, unsentimental, and orderly progression toward enlightenment, Sufism was at the other end of the spiritual spectrum. At my first gathering I fluctuated between wanting to leave immediately and feeling as though I had come home. Forty young people, dressed in flowing clothes, held hands and danced in circles chanting the names of God from a variety of religious traditions. At the end of each dance the leader would instruct us to look into each other's eyes and to "see through the eyes with which God sees us." That simple act of exchanging glances spoke to me. It challenged me, in a nonaggressive, loving way, to *connect*—with myself, and with my fellow seekers; to see the world—its beauty and its pain—through God's eyes. One evening, gazing into the eyes of a fellow dancer—a young African American woman—I flashed back on the slap I had received in the Barnard dorm. Could this shy exchange of glances be answering my questions about peace in the world? I wanted to know more about the Sufi way.

My boyfriend and I spent hours in a little esoteric bookstore in Greenwich Village. There I came across the writings of Hazrat Inayat Khan, a Sufi from India who had first brought the Sufi message to the West in 1910. As one of his books described it, Sufism was to Islam as Zen was to Buddhism—an esoteric branch of an established religion that appealed to those who wanted direct access to the divine. And like Americanized Zen, the Sufism being practiced by my new friends was considerably altered from its root sources in Turkey, Iran, and other Middle Eastern and Asian countries where Sufism is practiced in its traditional form. The term Sufi comes from *suf,* Arabic for "wool," and refers to the simple clothing worn by Sufi mystics, as well as by the Prophet Mohammed and the Christian mystics whom the early Sufis encountered in the deserts of Syria, Arabia, and Egypt. While decidedly Muslim in their adherence to the Koran and traditional Islamic practice, the Sufis have remained open to many mystical influences since they began their wandering in the seventh century. From their contact with desert hermits they incorporated into their beliefs a mystical variety of Christianity that in turn had been influenced by Gnosticism and Neoplatonism. Traces of Buddhism are woven into Sufi practice; the use of prayer beads and meditation are said to have come from early contact with Buddhist monks in India. Spreading into Turkey, and then Spain and other European countries, around the year 1200, Sufis influenced and were influenced by the troubadour movement and Provençal culture.

Perhaps the best-known Sufi mystic is Jelaluddin Rumi, the thirteenth-century Persian poet responsible for establishing a sect of Sufism referred to in the West as the "whirling dervishes." Rumi's volumes of love poetry and allegorical prose are some of the most beautiful and powerful metaphors of spiritual longing ever written. He uses images of the lover seeking the beloved, and of wine and the intoxication with God, with a passion and a sense of humor rarely found in mystical texts. Rumi's influence on Sufism was significant; his focus on music, word, and dance found its way into other Sufi sects, including the Chisti order, of Pakistan and India, where centuries later the young Sufi musician Hazrat Inayat Khan was given instructions by his teacher to teach Sufism to Westerners. Inayat Khan arrived in Europe, and later the United States, just when interest in Eastern spirituality was growing. His marriage to the American niece of Mary Baker Eddy, the founder of Christian Science, brought him into a large circle of Western seekers, and produced a family of four children, including his son, Vilayat Inayat Khan. Hazrat Inayat Khan died in India in 1927, after having written a number of remarkable books on Sufism in the West.

After World War II, in which Vilayat fought and his sister died at the hands of the Nazis, Vilayat immersed himself in an education that included both Western and Eastern philosophy. He studied classics at Oxford and the Sorbonne in Paris, and cello with the great French music teacher Nadia Boulanger. Leaving Europe he traveled to India, where he undertook several long, solitary meditation retreats, steeping himself in the teachings of different world religions, including Buddhism, Hinduism, Taoism, Christianity, Judaism, and of course, Sufism. When he finally landed in the United States in the early sixties, he had evolved a teaching style that incorporates meditation, chants, and scripture readings taken from a wide variety of spiritual traditions, as well as an erudite understanding of Western philosophy and modern science. Therefore, the eclectic spirituality that he was to introduce to Americans is not considered genuine Sufism by many Muslims.

I met Pir ("revered teacher") Vilayat Inayat Khan in the summer of 1972. The people leading Sufi dancing at Columbia urged me to study with Pir Vilayat, as he was called by his students. They were all planning to caravan out to "Sufi camp" in the golden hills of Northern California. My boyfriend had to stay in medical school that summer, and I was tired of New York City. California sounded like heaven to me; so did a tribal gathering of spiritual seekers. When school was over I crowded into a van and drove for four days straight across the United States.

For a month, a few hundred students camped out in the hills of Mendocino County, ate together, and practiced the wisdom traditions that Pir Vilayat taught. To a nineteen-year-old, sprung from New York and hungry for spiritual teaching, this was indeed a divine adventure. Pir.Vilayat, dressed in flowing robes and with long white hair and a graying beard, fit the part of a guru perfectly. Everything that had struck me as solemn and severe at the Zen Center was dramatically missing from Pir Vilayat's teachings. He taught us to sing and dance, encouraged us to read and learn from the great sacred and mythological texts of the world, and led a variety of meditation exercises. We arose early and meditated as the sun rose over the hills, and stayed up late sharing poetry and chants around the campfire.

There were parts of the experience that troubled me—the blind devotion; the language that excluded anyone not involved; the male-dominated leadership; the expectation on the part of the students of being given enlightenment; the deception on the part of the teacher of being able to give it; the romanticizing of the guru on both sides of the equation—but my examination of these concerns was to come later. That summer I embraced the spiritual path of Sufism and took initiation from Pir

Vilayat. Initiation, a step common in most Eastern spiritual disciplines, is the handing down of the wisdom of the lineage from the teacher to the student, and therefore from one generation of seekers to the next. Initiation is a commitment on the part of the student to safeguard the tradition through study, meditation, prayer, and right behavior. Part of the commitment is to the *sangha,* a word used by both Hindus and Buddhists that means "community of meditators on the path." In return, the student receives the teachings, guidance from the teacher, and the support of the community. To a young person who had not grown up within the similar commitment or support of a Christian or Jewish congregation, this kind of spiritual flock seemed an exotic variation on my childhood dreams.

Although I returned to New York after my first Sufi camp, I continued to study with Pir Vilayat whenever I could. Eventually my boyfriend and I moved to California. The group of people who gathered around Pir Vilayat were talented and creative and he encouraged us to explore all of our interests. He taught musicians Gregorian chant and Eastern scales; he conducted what amounted to a university-style, live-in course in comparative religions; and he pushed us to understand the new theories of chaos science and quantum physics. I was getting my elementary teaching degree at San Francisco State University at the time, and Pir Vilayat started me on a study of the spiritual development of children. My boyfriend was doing his medical internship at a San Francisco hospital and simultaneously learning acupuncture, herbal remedies, and psychic healing techniques.

At a "Meeting of the Ways," a yearly gathering of spiritual groups held in San Francisco, I listened to a variety of teachers speak and realized that my own teacher was giving me a unique spiritual education. Young people from around the country were exploring a variety of Eastern paths including Yoga, Tibetan and Zen Buddhism, Taoism, and Hinduism, as well as hybrid theologies created by charismatic leaders from Europe and the United States. Some of these teachers guided their students to genuine spiritual scholarship and awakening, while others were more shallow or duplicitous in their motivation. A few of the gurus and teachers were behind the well-publicized cults that left followers scarred and unable to function in the world.

Pir Vilayat's idea of guru-ship was to give us a classical education as well as to steep us in the Sufi teachings of his father. Teaching sessions were conducted as "universal worships," where each of the major world religions, and many of the minor ones as well, were honored with scripture and practice. In one Sunday service we might read from the Koran, Hindu and Buddhist texts, Sufi stories, and the Old and New Testaments of the Bible, and then chant mantras, do traditional Jewish dances, and wash each other's feet in the spirit of Jesus washing the feet of his disciples. Always we would meditate, focusing on the breath and silently repeating the ninety-nine beautiful names of Allah, a traditional Islamic practice called dhikr ("remembrance").

This immersion in religious tradition was thrilling to me. My childhood curiosity and hunger were being addressed in ways I had never even imagined. What I had intuited—that it is human nature to hunger for the sacred—was being revealed in a rich tapestry of myth and traditions from around the world. God may have died in mainstream culture, but spirituality was being revived in my life through the traditional and proven practices of world religions. To an outsider, and especially to the American press, *traditional* is not a word that would have been used to describe the spiritual communes of the 1970s. But in contrast to many Americans in those years, from the "radical chic" to the expanding consumer culture, we were busy studying sacred texts, worshiping together each Sunday, and adhering to moral codes set to secure our marriages and families, much as early Americans had done in the founding years of the country.

When Pir Vilayat came to the United States in the sixties he was dismayed by what he believed to be the irresponsible and undisciplined behavior of his students. Their use of drugs, their untidy appearance, and their inability to discipline themselves at work or in meditation struck him as behavior at odds with spiritual advancement. He began to organize summer camps with specified rules of conduct: no drugs of any kind, no lying down during meditation, and scheduled periods of communal work, or karma yoga, a Hindu concept that stresses the holiness of work. It was during one of those camps that Pir Vilayat had the idea of creating a year-round experiment in living. I was at that camp and remember well when he shared the idea with us. A rift developed between his students, between those who wanted to seriously pursue Pir Vilayat's teachings and those who didn't want to abide by the rules. Those of us who were attracted by his vision of straight living, hard work, and daily prayer began to look for land on which to build a community.

Pir Vilayat specifically did not want to be in California. Most of us were living in Northern California at that time, but we started to search in the

Southeast for land. Just as we were about to purchase a few hundred acres in North Carolina, a friend named Wavy Gravy, the celebrated master of ceremonies at the Woodstock festival, put us in touch with some friends of his who needed to sell part of the land they had inherited from their parents. It was the New Lebanon Shaker Village, nestled in the Berkshire mountains of New York State, and charged with the spirit of the devout people who had built it in the 1700s. While the cold winters and the antiquated buildings (that needed more money for repair than we would ever have) were intimidating, the Shaker doctrines of communal sharing of possessions, equality of the sexes, and consecrated labor attracted us to the structures and land.

In their well-organized, self-sufficient communities segregated from the outside world, the Shakers had worshiped in unusual ways—ecstatic dancing and singing that led to direct contact with the Holy Spirit. We were struck by the similarities between the Shakers' manner of worship and our own and by their sincere desire to live a genuine, spiritual life. Before purchasing the land, we went as far as asking for the blessings of the eight remaining Shaker sisters who lived in a remote village in Maine. I can only now, in retrospect, imagine the shock that these elderly, reserved women must have endured when we arrived at their home. At the time I thought it quite reasonable for six young people dressed in hippie garb, traveling with a white-bearded Indian guru, to ask for their permission to carry on the spiritual legacy of the land in New Lebanon.

We arrived in Sabbath Day Lake, Maine, on a gray autumn day. The Shaker sisters listened to Pir Vilayat politely, and with some amazement at his knowledge of Shaker history. Pir explained to them that Mother Ann Lee, their founder, had visited him in his meditations. She asked him to carry on the work of the original New Lebanon settlers. The sisters were careful to point out that they had no way of knowing what Mother Ann would want, and that the Shaker lineage would die with them as foretold by their elders. As they served us tea and made small talk, Eldress Mildred Barker, the remarkably energetic leader of the community, lovingly gave us her own kind of blessing: "Put your hands to work and your hearts to God," she said. "God will give you his blessings, and that is all you will need to succeed." Then, without much fanfare, each sister wished us good luck, and we moved to New Lebanon.

We settled into the Shaker village, renamed it the Abode of the Message, and started families, a school, businesses, a farm, and a loose system of governance. Soon the difficult realities of communal life emerged, like the weeds in our organic gardens. The two hundred remarkable men and women—doctors, businessmen, teachers, artists, builders, farmers, even a pilot—whose combined talents had sounded so promising began to bicker about everything. To debate whether a "family member" could have a dog or to decide how we should divide resources from community-held businesses, we convened endless family meetings. My understanding of political process and my compassion for anyone involved in governance grew in those years.

I took my discipleship with Pir Vilayat seriously. My boyfriend and I were married by Pir Vilayat. My husband, now a medical doctor, became the leader of the Abode. By the time I was twenty-four, I was a mother, a practicing midwife, and a teacher in our elementary school. I had also immersed myself in a deep engagement of spiritual practice that included reading, prayer, solitary retreats, and group worship. I found more similarities between myself and the Shakers than I did between myself and most of my peers out in the world. For six years I did just what the old Shaker adage advised: I put my hands to work and my heart to God.

Work consisted of repairing the austere and functional Shaker buildings, farming, cooking for two hundred, and delivering and caring for babies. While some commune members taught themselves how to repair the plumbing system or balance the books, I and several other women learned from my husband how to care for pregnant women and conduct home births. My nights were often spent in the mysterious and wondrous company of laboring mothers, protective fathers, and innocent newborns. Over and over I relived the rhythmic power of the body, the earthy noises and smells that connect us to the animals, and the awesome moment when a baby, still wrapped in an angelic light, takes its first breath here and joins the human family.

In everything that we did we took each other to task for laziness at work or worship. Pir Vilayat coined the phrase "slugs and heroes," adding it to an already rich Abode vocabulary. Those who gave themselves selflessly to family and community were heroes. Slugs were chastised for thinking only about themselves, resting too much, or not participating in community projects. Selfless service and a dutiful work ethic are not revolutionary concepts. They were, however, at odds with the general tone of the prevailing culture. While out in the big world the "human potential" movement was gaining popularity, within the community we were suspicious of psychology and its focus on emotional expression and individual freedom. We valued what Pir Vilayat taught—that one should rise above human problems to a realm where love, harmony, and beauty prevailed. We worked hard at rising above.

Yet in my attempts to use spiritual teachings to bypass the emotional ups and downs so natural to family and community life, I was not only visiting higher realms, I was also doing harm to myself. What I judged in myself as qualities of selfishness or laziness were often merely predictable psychological stages of growth that anyone in his or her twenties passes through, learns from, and incorporates into a maturing psyche. Budding problems with my husband were put in deep freeze, only to blossom quickly after we left the commune, like dandelions at the end of a long winter. Self-judgment and the effort to rid myself of "ego," which served me well in my attempts at saintliness, turned into an unforgiving attitude toward myself and others when I woke up to the fact that I didn't want to be a saint. Likewise, years of unconscious neglect of my body left me ignorant of how to heal and nurture it when eventually youthful luck gave way to health problems. In the narrow definition of spirituality that we had adopted, there was little room for other forms of self-discovery, ones that would have rounded us out and made us whole.

After the highly publicized Jim Jones massacre, when hundreds of his devotees drank poisoned Kool-Aid and died for the cause, some parents sent deprogrammers to the Abode to save their children from what they assumed was a cult. They were surprised to find a group of modern-day Puritans living out the old American dream. At a recent twenty-year Abode reunion, one of my friends wondered aloud how a group of middle-class kids raised in the sixties had gotten it into their heads to become medieval saints. We all laughed knowingly, mystified by our zealous behavior, but also thankful for an extraordinary experience and for each other.

My husband and I left the community when our second child was born. We wanted things and time for our family that were in conflict with the group mind. One morning, washing dishes in the huge communal sinks, I was overcome with a deep American yearning for my own dishwasher. After years of going without, I coveted things like my own bathroom and dinner for four. I also was tired of the tedious and complicated decision-making process we all labored under. To this day I am grateful not to have to debate among two hundred people how often we should flush the toilet or whether cheese is an appropriate snack for children. Eventually the strain of combining the intensity of communal life with the responsibilities of family life became too difficult. I understood why the Shakers had forbidden nuclear families to exist within their community. They believed that the devotion to one's own family would compete with devotion to God and the community. They were right about the community part; my path to God was now centered around my children, and I felt too divided to do both.

And so I moved, with my little family, to a nearby farm. My husband opened a private medical practice in town. We both continued to work on an interesting idea that Pir Vilayat had put us in charge of—the founding of an adult education center that would teach much of what we had been exploring at the community to people who did not want to live communally. Over the years at the Abode a wonderful and wild parade of teachers and performers from around the world stayed with us, often making their keep through teaching. Guests from India and Afghanistan offered lessons in dance and music; herbalists and doctors exploring alternative medicine visited and helped us change our diet and grow healing herbs; spiritual teachers joined us on Passover and led a Seder, or during Ramadan and instructed us in fasting; and authors of books on the merging of physics and mysticism lectured. Pir Vilayat wanted us to offer a similar experience to people from all walks of life, backgrounds, and occupations.

Omega Institute for Holistic Studies, as Pir Vilayat called his idea, would resurrect a concept of education put forth by the literary and scientific visionaries of ancient Alexandria in Egypt. Under the Ptolemies in the second century B.C., Pir explained, with his customary erudite understanding of history, Alexandria was the enlightened center of the Hellenistic world. Concepts about time, astronomy, healing, medicine, mysticism, and human development that emerged from the schools of Alexandria changed the course of the history of ideas. Pir Vilayat believed that the manner in which subjects were taught in those ancient schools was *holistic,* in that students were instructed to live what they were learning as they were learning it. He imagined a live-in summer institute, modeled after the ancient schools of Alexandria, where the community would support the learning being done through a carefully planned environment of intellectual and spiritual support, physical beauty, and simple and healthy living.

Pir Vilayat chose Omega's name from the writings of the Christian mystic Teilhard de Chardin (1881–1955). The omega point, said Père

Teilhard, was the place where all thought converged. He asserted that humans as they are now known are not the end of the evolutionary process, that every living thing within the cosmos is evolving toward a more enlightened consciousness. "Widely different human cultures around the Earth are now converging toward an *omega point . . . ,*" wrote Père Teilhard. "That seems to me the only possible conversion of the world, and the only form in which a religion of the future can be conceived." This was the genesis of Omega Institute. Its birth coincided with my own need to expand out of what had become a limiting experience for me at the Abode and a troubling one within an organized religious group. The exclusivity of belonging to a particular religion—complete with foreign mantras, spiritual names, and ways of behaving that were endearing only to us—had become unappealing. I no longer wanted to separate myself from the world. Relegating my spirituality only to practice, prayer, and meditation created a split within myself. I needed to find ways to incorporate my sense of the sacred into my family life and my psychological and physical well-being. Was there a way to bring the peace I had found through inner spiritual practice out into my daily life? Were other people already experimenting with this? What about my social and political conscience, which had been slumbering as I meditated and prayed? And why, if God is love, and I had spent so much time searching for God, was I so unhappy in my marriage?

A few of us from the community put our heads together and researched any and everything in which we were interested and that spoke to the combination of spirituality and everyday life. We invited a small faculty of health practitioners, psychologists, artists, and spiritual teachers to join us for Omega Institute's first summer program in 1977. We then rented the campus of a nearby boarding school, sent out a few thousand brochures, and waited to see if anyone would respond. No market research could have prepared us for Omega's immediate success. That first summer one hundred people responded to the brochure. The next summer attendance doubled. Each year after that it doubled again. Our program and faculty and staff grew; suddenly we were running a large organization. Holistic education was an idea whose time had come, and we were in front of the wave.

In 1982, five years after Omega's first summer session, we had grown out of renting prep school or college campuses. We needed our own home where we could create the kind of healing environment that formed the core of Omega's founding purpose. More and more people were coming to study principles of health and wellness. The need to find a place of our own was driven home one day when I stood in line at the cafeteria of Bennington College in Vermont, the last campus that we rented. I was with Ann Wigmore, the grand dame of natural foods, trying to make her feel welcome. Ahead of us were two participants in her class, discussing what they had learned that morning about whole grains and live foods. I winced with embarrassment as they reached for the lunch-meat sandwiches and Jell-O. This was not what we had in mind when we used the word *holistic*.

We found the campus that is now Omega's permanent home in a rushed search, between the end of one summer season and the planning of the next. An abandoned children's camp in the Hudson River Valley, it was a white elephant that needed substantial money and fix-up time, two things we didn't have. But this piece of land had its own rich past, which helped us make the decision to move ahead with our plans. It had been settled in 1919 by the Sholem Aleichem Folk Institute, an organization devoted to the spiritual depth of Jewish education. Concerned by what they saw as a loss of tradition in the generation of children born of Jewish immigrants, the institute founders created schools and a summer camp to teach children the Yiddish language and culture. Camp Boiberick was committed to keeping Yiddish culture alive while giving Jewish children and their parents an opportunity to be in nature and an intellectually and spiritually stimulating environment. The camp flourished in the 1940s and 1950s and then slowly began to diminish in popularity. By the 1970s it had lost its appeal and was forced to shut its doors. Abandoned for ten years, it still had an aura of spiritual study when we inherited it, complete with Yiddish graffiti painted on the dorm walls.

After we moved to the campus, we were surprised to discover that Teilhard de Chardin was buried a few miles down the road, on the grounds of a former Jesuit monastery. A priest and a scientist, Père Teilhard had spent his life attempting to show that the acceptance of evolution does not have to involve the rejection of Christianity. His efforts to convince the Church of this met such powerful resistance that in 1926 he was silenced by his superiors and later was exiled from France and sent to live in New York State. He died in 1955, and was brought to rest far from his home in Paris, in the countryside near Omega.

The interest in Omega grew; each year more than fifteen thousand guests would participate in our programs. I began to understand that God had not died in America, but rather that our culture was in the birth pangs of a new kind of spirituality. My childhood hunger had convinced me of the need for the sacred in one's life. My experience as a disciple of an organized religion was my first step on the spiritual path. It provided me with a meaningful framework and community. But it also narrowed my experience of the sacred and exposed the pitfalls of the group mind. Now I was witnessing something else, something more wide-ranging, inclusive, and humane. Whether people came to Omega to study nutrition or self-awareness, Native American spirituality or African dance, what they were really interested in was a spirituality that could infuse the totality of their daily lives. If Omega's curriculum seemed like a spiritual smorgasbord, we simply were forging new territory and needed all the input we could get. Experimenting with the mistakes and the wisdom of the past, the marriage of East and West, the crossbreeding of religion and psychology, and the alliance of science and mysticism, we were searching for a new American spirituality.

Shadowing the birth and the success of Omega were the crumbling of my marriage and the end of stability in my family life. If each spiritual seeker must go through a dark night of the soul, then my divorce served me well. It took me on a descent into a land that seemed to me as dark and unfamiliar as Dante's hell. My most cherished dream of being the perfect mother with the perfect home was derailed by my own choices. Everything I judged as immoral in others—having an affair, being a single mother, shaming one's parents—was now part of my own identity. I went through a long period of painful reckoning that led me to seek help from a skilled therapist. This part of my spiritual education, although full of sorrow and loss, awoke in me a tenderness toward myself and others. It opened me to other forms of spirituality, including psychological growth, emotional wisdom, and physical and sexual healing. I became interested in Jungian psychology and made a study of world mythology, only to discover that the territory I was slogging through had already been well mapped by the heroes and heroines of ancient times.

From the more settled perspective of my current life—remarried, rooted again in home and community, older and wiser—I can regard my descent into darkness with gratitude and even fondness. But during that time I suffered, made others suffer, and often couldn't see the path beneath my feet. Spiritually, I learned as much in this chapter of my life as I did in the more traditionally religious chapter that preceded it. Through experiencing and weathering crisis I gained some humility and generosity, identified and strengthened the healthy parts of my ego, and solidified my growing trust in the perfection of God's plan. I also became familiar with the predictable stages of loss and grief, so that when the forward march of change visited me over and over, I became more graceful and less dramatic when faced with the inevitable: my sons transformed themselves from sweet little kids into teenagers, and then went off to college; two beloved friends suffered through and died of AIDS; my father suddenly died. These milestones have tested my ability to accept all we are given as opportunities to be more genuine in love and life. They have also reinspired me to make use of the marvelous spiritual teachings and techniques that work so well when darkness and fear overwhelm us.

The following chapters invite each part of the self to venture forth in the heroic pursuit of what Joseph Campbell calls "the rapture of being alive." They include stories, history, techniques, and counsel from a wide variety of wise women and men spanning many faiths, eras, and disciplines. When you meet them, or me, or other characters on the pages of this book, please find yourself there too. No one has *the* answer; only you know the way home.

2 | What Is Spirituality?

Science cannot solve the ultimate mystery of Nature. And it is because in the last analysis we ourselves are part of the mystery we are trying to solve.
—MAX PLANCK

I have been following a path that I call spiritual for most of my life, yet I hesitate when people ask, "What do you mean by *spiritual*?" I would like to give a quick and easy answer; it seems that I should have one. I have certainly met enough people whom I call spiritual beings, and have had many experiences that lifted the veil between my usual consciousness and another, vaster reality. Yet, there is no one-liner that could adequately describe the mysterious nature of these beings or states of consciousness. Besides, the spiritual quest is different for each one of us, and it changes as we change. As the comedian George Carlin says, "Just when I found out the meaning of life, they changed it."

And yet, it is critical to ask, "What is spirituality?" as we venture on the path. The word is so laden with contradictory meanings and confusing traditions that many forgo the one journey in life that brings real happiness and fulfillment. For some, the word *spiritual* is connected to their mistrust of religion. For others, the word spiritual means anti-scientific; as such, it is either a refreshing departure from rational tyranny, or it conjures up the occult, UFOs, and bogus misinformation. Some hear the word spiritual and are encouraged by its whispered promises of grace; others are threatened by it, afraid of looking too deeply at their own behavior, the unlived parts of their lives, and ultimately, death. For most of us, the word spiritual probably activates all of the above associations. We are drawn to it and suspicious of it at the same time.

The first step on the spiritual path is to find a satisfying definition of the word, one that is as free from our conditioning as possible; one that can keep us on track. This is not as hard as it seems. Deconstructing the word *spiritual* is a freeing and an enlightening task, and once we start searching for the word's meaning, we find simple hints all along the way. A good thing to remember as we search for our own definition of spirituality is that no one has *the* definition or *the* answers to the most basic spiritual questions of how to live, love, and die. If such unequivocal answers existed they would be as universally accepted as how to make fire. As I began researching this book, I sent a questionnaire to two hundred spiritual leaders from a variety of faiths and backgrounds. The first question I posed was: What does the word *spiritual* mean to you? Reading through the answers to this seemingly simple question, from the eloquent and generous people who responded, verified for me that no spiritual leader, no brilliant intellectual, no scientist—no one—has *the* answer. After hearing from some of the world's wisest hearts and brightest minds, I must report that all of us, from the unusually sage to the normally confused, can add only our own bits of wisdom to the poetry of mystical conjecture. So right at the get-go we can let ourselves off the hook, accept our confusion as par for the course, and relax a little as we search. We can feel part of an ancient and ongoing community of seekers.

As you search, keep in mind that religion and spirituality are not necessarily synonymous. Religions are like cookbooks and guidebooks: they are not the food or the foreign country; rather, they suggest ingredients and point us in the right direction. "Do not be idolatrous or bound to any doctrine, theory, or ideology," says Thich Nhat Hanh, a Vietnamese Zen monk. "All systems of thought are guiding means; they are not absolute truth." Many people are so turned off by religions—their seemingly arbitrary moral codes, the boundless hypocrisies between word and deed, the arcane rituals—that they have acquired a resistance to spirituality itself. I sympathize with those intellectuals who equate spirituality with sanctimoniousness or sentimental nonsense, and who turn a disgusted back on the whole topic. Many who call themselves spiritual seekers are so irrational and hold so rigidly to their beliefs that, if their way is the only way, count me out as well. But in truth, spirituality and intelligence are not in competition. They are one and the same if we affix a definition to spirituality that is inclusive and forgiving enough to hold the full human condition. As we search to define spirituality for ourselves, let's put aside the misconception that spirituality excludes things like rational thought, intellectual rigor, literacy, learning, science, and other great advances of the human mind.

You can walk a wonderful spiritual path with or without adhering to a religion. All paths are available; none are exclusively right or wrong or even required. As you search for your own definition of spirituality, set aside your religious beliefs and/or resistances. You can come back to them later on. For now, respect your resistances as acquired opinions, not sacred truths, and turn your attention to whatever it is within you that made you pick up this book in the first place. Ask yourself what draws you to consider the spiritual side of life. Are you questioning how to live your daily life? Are you facing a critical choice? Do you sense that there is more to life than meets the eye? Are you unhappy? Do you fear life or death or both? While some lucky people approach the spiritual path with a light and sure step, most of us stumble upon it led by a vague sense of longing for something *more,* an anxiousness for meaning, a basic intuition informing our modern minds.

A formidable resistance that arises when modern people approach the spiritual path is a cultural bias in favor of intellectualism, as well as a devaluing of other human modes of perception: emotions, intuition, sensation. An unnatural divide between intellectual development and the development of our other capacities has evolved in the twentieth century to the point where many who consider themselves thinking people will have nothing to do with anything that smacks of mysticism. Intellectuals scorn spirituality, as if pondering our very existence is not as valid as researching science or history. The modern reverence for the mind has obscured a profoundly natural yearning—one that is as basic as hunger and as near to us as our breath.

Another misconceived notion about spirituality that alienates the modern seeker is the association of sacredness with saintliness. It is erroneous to separate spirituality from everyday life. To equate holiness only with celibacy, or solitude, or poverty is to deny most of us a spiritual life. Enlightenment can be nurtured in a monastery or in a family, alone or in a relationship, in prayer or at work. The bliss of the world is no less spiritual than the bliss of transcendence. We can indeed "follow our bliss" as we follow the spiritual path, whether that bliss is raising our consciousness or raising children, reading a holy text or running a marathon. But be warned! There's a fine line between bliss and narcissism. I remember the first time I came across Joseph Campbell's now famous line about "following your bliss." I was in college, in the stodgy library at Columbia, using one of Campbell's texts on mythology to research a paper. There, in a section called "Sacrifice and Bliss," I received confirmation that my dream of dropping out of college and driving across country was the spiritually correct thing to do. Of course I neglected to read further, to where Campbell put bliss in the context of sacrifice. Many have made the same mistake, going for the goodies of spirituality without grounding the search in reality.

While spirituality *is* about bliss, it also is about balance. Without some degree of sacrifice for the greater good, spiritual self-discovery eventually leads to plain old self-indulgence. When we witness people using wise teachings to justify unwise and selfish behavior, spirituality seems like a game people are playing to get what they want. Spirituality is not the abdication of responsibility; it's not a magic carpet ride to la-la land; and it's not sunny, easy answers to life's complexity.

Rather, spirituality is a long, slow process—a patient growing into wisdom. It is no wonder that this kind of spirituality seems foreign to many Americans. It is much more like cooking a fine meal of many courses—picking the fresh herbs from the garden, waiting for the yeasted rolls to rise, marinating the meat, rolling the pie crust—than like driving up to the fast food window and drumming your fingers for two minutes while a stranger wraps your burger.

Inviting spirituality into your life is like packing for a long journey. As you search for your own definition, here are some of the most important things to pack: an openness to things you may have been conditioned to reject, a comfortableness with the unknown, and fearlessness.

FEARLESSNESS

If spirituality is *not* religion or cynicism or sentimentality or narcissism, then what is it? One thing that we can confidently say is that spirituality is fearlessness. It is a way of looking boldly at the life we have been given, here, now, on earth, as this human being. Who am I? How should I live my life? What happens when I die? Spirituality is nothing more than a brave search for the truth about existence. Nothing more, but nothing less as well.

We are born with a body that experiences pain and comfort, a heart that suffers and feels joy, a mind that strives and is peaceful, a spirit that yearns for both solitude and communion with others, and a contract on earth that has a beginning and an end. Each one of us knows this, and yet, each one of us spends much of our time swimming against the current of life's reality. The spiritual path teaches us how to float on our backs, relaxed and aware, in the waters of reality. The Buddhists define spirituality as *shamatha,* or "tranquil abiding."

We are drawn to a spiritual path out of a desire for tranquil abiding. Just saying the words feels wonderful, like an antidote to the fear, unhappiness, and anxiety with which we often approach life. Fear of what? Fear of our basic human condition. If we stop long enough to take a quiet look at our situation, we'll hear the tick-tick-ticking of time's impersonal progress. For each of us, time's march breeds a different fear: for some it is the terror of death; for others it is the worry of a life unlived; for some it signifies the loss of what we hold dear and familiar. These are not thoughts on which we usually enjoy lingering. Spirituality invites us to linger. It gives us a way of standing naked in the truth of the human condition, meeting it head-on with curiosity and openness. This is serious work, but the mysterious outcome of the work is a lightness of heart—what we call happiness.

Fearlessness sows the seeds of happiness. First comes a loosening of fear; from this relaxation comes a growing acceptance of life on its own terms; then a sense of wonder awakens, one that is large enough to contain the many ups and downs that are natural to our physical, mental, and emotional makeups. All around us are the ingredients for happiness—happiness, but not perfection. Perfection is an idea; imperfection is reality. Happiness within the field of imperfection is a promise of the spiritual quest.

"The purpose of the spiritual life," writes the Sufi master Hazrat Inayat Khan, "is to be happy. . . . The reason why man seeks for happiness is not because happiness is his sustenance, but because happiness is his own being; therefore, in seeking for happiness, man is seeking for himself."

Spirituality is the search for the kind of happiness that Inayat Khan is speaking of, a happiness born from fearlessness.

BEGINNER'S MIND

I once overheard my oldest son, Rahm, then six, speaking with his best friend. They were in the bathtub together, the only place I knew to put the two of them after a sad and trying day. This was the day that my own best friend, whose little boy was now in the bath, had finally given in to a long battle with cancer and died.

"Where's your mom?" I heard my son ask his friend.

"She's dead."

"I *know*, but where is she?"

"I don't know. I'm gonna ask my dad tomorrow."

I imagine that religions sprung from this kind of exchange. In my mind's eye I can see two cave people, as in a "Far Side" cartoon, standing over the body of a friend and pantomiming a similar conversation. Children and early peoples share a purity in their search for the meaning of our existence. Indeed, in their original intent all spiritual traditions aimed to answer bare-bones questions about birth and death. As we search for the meaning of spirituality in our own lives, it is best to begin very, very simply, in the same wide-open manner as children, or cave people.

Children learn because they have no shame about being bare beginners. They ask, "Does the sky stop?" and "What does God look like?" When Jesus said, "Lest ye become as little children, ye shall not enter the Kingdom of Heaven," he was referring to this kind of guileless questioning. In their unaffected, optimistic curiosity little children are models for spiritual seekers. The Zen master Shunryu Suzuki called this unaffected curiosity "Beginner's Mind." If we want to fashion a spiritual path for ourselves it is best to begin at the beginning with Beginner's Mind.

If you drew a long line and put modern cynicism at the start and Beginner's Mind at the end, you'd have a map for the contemporary spiritual pilgrim. Somehow our culture has evolved to the point where pessimism has become synonymous with intelligence, and where an overload of information is mistaken for knowledge. Admitting that we don't know something doesn't come easily to the modern person. Voicing innocence and a sense of wonder is difficult for many of us; it can only mean that we've read too many Hallmark cards. But children are not sentimental, nor are they lacking in intelligence. Rather, they are unafraid to admit their status as a beginner, to say to the world, "I don't know. Please show me." This doesn't mean that to be spiritual is to remain a child or to take on the trappings of indigenous, less industrialized cultures. Beginner's Mind is about discovering the *essence* of our humanness—the pure water of the inner heart, before it was clouded by conditioning.

On a recent trip to France, I visited an area of the country called Le Pays de l'Homme—the "Land of Man." Halfway between the north pole and the equator, its climate is among the most temperate in the world. The landscape is varied, with wide plateaus and fertile valleys, chalky sandstone cliffs and swiftly flowing rivers. It is no mere chance that Cro-Magnon man was born here some 25,000 years ago. This is the area in France where archaeologists have discovered caves with the densest concentrations of Neanderthal and Cro-Magnon paintings and carvings in the world. They have been called the "Sistine chapels of prehistory." Panthers, bison, woolly mammoth and rhinoceros, horses and cows, as well as female symbols of fertility, and even mythical unicorns, adorn the caves' surfaces. The paintings are believed to be remnants of a religion that centered on the earth, the mother of all forms of life. Their purpose is seen as ritualistic, perhaps as a way to initiate their young, expressing the wonder and reverence felt by prehistoric man for the forces of nature and life.

It is quite an experience to visit the caves. Some are located high above the riverbanks in enormous cliffs near ancient towns built in the Middle Ages. Others can be found in hillsides adjoining farmers' fields where truffles, walnuts, and grapes have been harvested since the first century A.D. Emerging from the darkness of a cave, after an immersion into Cro-Magnon consciousness, one is aware of the seamless flow of history. All around are architectural artifacts of the human story. Signs of the ancient Celts, Gauls, and Romans are visible in the oldest buildings. Evidence of the wars of religion and the peasant revolts can be seen in the layering of towns along the riverbanks. Ice ages, plagues, foreign invasions, and famines have all left their marks, as have religion, art, and periods of renaissance and enlightenment. Next to a towering castle, fortified to protect against invasion, is a simple stone church with a statue of the Virgin and her child. Along a centuries-old pilgrimage route, one passes stone outcroppings left by various ice ages; towns where the populations were decreased 60 percent by the Black Plague; mustard fields that have been cultivated for thousands of years; woodlands that once were sheep pastures and before that were swamps that once were dense forests.

The effect of such a display of history on an American, whose concept of old is a pre–Civil War house, is profound and, in a certain way, comforting. I came away from my visit to Le Pays de l'Homme with a sense that the essential human condition has changed little over time. Our earliest ancestors were grappling with our own longings and questions. They responded to their vulnerable position in the world with both awe and fear, reverence and violence. Far from being brutes dressed in animal hides, Cro-Magnon people had complex thoughts and deep feelings. Over the centuries the tools that humans have developed to help them survive and to express their desires have changed. But the core human experience has remained the same: We wonder where we come from and where we will go after we die. We love and fear each other and the natural world. We express our intelligence and gratitude in art, religion, and civilization; our ignorance and intolerance in brutality, war, and destruction. At the heart of the human story is our search for understanding within the mystery of creation.

I have always been attracted to places of antiquity, and to people who radiate "Beginner's Mind." I find them more inspiring than those who profess to know everything. When I was twenty I started voice lessons with a master of North Indian classical singing, Pandit Pranath. Pranath was, at that time, in his late fifties, but to me he seemed like a very old man. He would greet me at his home in his slippers and his loose Indian cotton clothing, his long white hair wrapped in a little bun. Shuffling around the practice room as he taught, he would mumble at seemingly odd moments several phrases that I heard him repeat during all the years I studied with him. "Ram, Ram, Ram" was one, and "Allah knows; I do not know" was another. I would be practicing an Indian scale, playing the tamboura, a drone instrument used to enhance the singing, and Pranath would look up and say, "Allah knows; I do not know." I found this puzzling and amusing. At twenty, my goal was to know as much as I could. In this case I wanted to learn this complex system of music and become a great singer.

Now, years later, it is his little phrases I remember when I think fondly of Pandit Pranath, while I would be hard pressed to sing the Indian scale. In fact, I find myself repeating "Ram, Ram, Ram" and "Allah knows; I do not know" in my music teacher's Indian accent when I get tired of trying to figure everything out. Now I know that Pandit Pranath was also. His mutterings were abbreviated prayers for Beginner's Mind. "Ram, Ram, Ram" was his way of calling to Ram, the Hindu godhead, for the kind of understanding that surpasses our mind's limited abilities and neurotic attachments. There are some things that are better left alone, some questions that can be answered only by patience and faith. "Allah knows; I do not know" kept Pranath on the path of humility. Often we *don't* know what is really going on. Our perspective can barely accommodate another person's point of view, no less the forward march of evolution or the eternal mind of God. Better to admit not knowing and to relax in the mystery of life than to try to force our minds where they can't go.

The poet Rainer Maria Rilke described Beginner's Mind like this: "Be patient to all that is unsolved in your heart and try to love the questions themselves like locked rooms and like books that are written in a very foreign tongue. Do not seek the answers, which cannot be given you because you would not be able to live them. And the point is, to live everything. Live the questions now. Perhaps you will then gradually, without noticing it, live along some distant day into the answer. Resolve to be always beginning—to be a beginner!"

I like to think of Beginner's Mind as the crouch position runners take when they start a race. Alert yet poised, the runner embodies in that moment the kind of readiness necessary for the spiritual path. There is nothing blasé in the racer, nor is there anything arrogant. Rather there is a wise eagerness, a trained openness. The crouch position is not the whole race, but it is necessary to the race, and within its readiness are all possibilities. Likewise, Beginner's Mind is not the whole spiritual path, but it is a necessary attitude to bring to every step along the path, and contains within it the possibilities for freedom, peace, and joyful living.

SPIRITUAL LONGING: THE OPEN SECRET

Each one of us is a complex stew of changing emotions and thoughts; a mortal being, unsure of our place in the universe, longing for something that we cannot even name. Sometimes we experience joy and strength; sometimes we are sad and confused. None of this is cause for dismay. It is who we are and has been so since the first humans found themselves under the night sky with a desire to understand as vast as the sky itself. Yet then, as now, our capacity to fathom the limitless universe is bound by the laws of a limited world. Human history is the story of abundant longing and insufficient answers.

To long for peace, or God, or spirituality is quite natural. To feel a certain loneliness for a nameless friend or an emptiness that cannot be filled with the ways of the world is instinctive. Especially today, with the accelerated pace of human activity and technology, we may feel a deep spiritual hunger. Yet many of us don't know what to do when a longing for spirituality settles briefly in our hearts. We may not even know what it is. With the first pangs of hunger we rush to fill the empty space with something, anything, rather than float quietly on our backs in the mysterious waters where our souls live.

To give voice to our spiritual longing is to reveal a side of ourselves that we have become skilled at hiding. We may be ashamed to admit that we feel a kind of helplessness—a need for something that we cannot even describe. We may have grown up thinking that we should always be smart or happy or strong, consistently able to deal with the vagaries of life. Therefore, revealing our mysterious longings is unsettling. We don't want to be seen stumbling around in the wilderness of our own ignorance and meagerness. Nor do we want to come across as innocent or eager in a world that has elevated cynicism to an art form. Instead, we pretend to be fine, strong, smart, hip, amused, or disinterested even when we are not. Most of us have become habituated to hiding our weakness and wonder from each other. We construct brilliant masks to wear over our humanness, until we forget the authentic nature of our own true face.

Jelaluddin Rumi, the twelfth-century Sufi poet, called this phenomenon the "Open Secret." In his poetry and prose Rumi writes of the secrets we keep and the veils we wear so others won't see our foolishness, our pain, our tenderness. Because the big secret we keep is none other than the condition of our humanness—the "full catastrophe," as Nikos Kazantzakis's fictional character Zorba the Greek called it—it is really no secret at all; it is an Open Secret. Visitors from another planet would be baffled by the way humans behave. Our daily interactions would look to them as a Halloween party does to us: people hiding their true faces in order to look like someone else.

I have found that no matter where my searching has taken me, it always leads me back to my need to face my own true nature, and since I am a human being, my human nature. We may choose a beautiful and moral way to know God, replete with an interesting theology, an engaging community, and a well-conceived set of practices. We may look far from our own culture and adopt a path that includes ancient wisdom, meditation, and foreign mantras and dress. Perhaps we look closer to home, and embrace a religious tradition that teaches more familiar prayers and concepts. It doesn't matter what path we take toward spiritual realization. If we bypass our humanness, each path leads back to the same question: What are we hiding from in ourselves and in each other?

Opening up the secret of our human nature, revealing to ourselves and to each other our deep and soulful longings, our fear and sadness, our joy and wonder, is *the* critical step on the spiritual path. It is the step that makes the difference between living our own, real spirituality and just acquiring someone else's beliefs. Particularly in our own times, when guarded cynicism is seen as a sign of intelligence, revealing our spiritual longing is a brave act.

We could say that the history of human suffering is our inability to come to terms with spiritual hunger. Like one big cosmic joke, humans were born yearning for a home of tranquil abiding, yet without the map to get there. In every age some people seem to know more than others about the way home. They have been called shamans, prophets, and messiahs, monks and gurus, poets and philosophers, scientists and psychologists. They spend their time contemplating the way home and reporting their findings. Religions and big bang theories are attributed to their wisdom. Yet when all is said and done, each one of us is left abiding in the mystery, longing for the tranquillity that is whispered about in the depths of our own hearts. Thus a critical step on the spiritual path, and one that we will take over and over, is to let ourselves experience spiritual hunger long enough and deep enough to follow it to its source. Unless we do that, we will never get the chance to taste the true nourishment that is indeed available, closer to us than we think.

Take a minute now to make contact with your own spiritual hunger. Put your hand on the spot at the center of your chest where your ribs join together. It is the same spot called the heart center in some spiritual traditions. It's the place in your body you can feel when you quickly inhale in fear, or when you speak of an aching heart or a heart overflowing with joy. When you gently touch that spot and breathe quietly, concentrating with eyes closed for a few minutes, what do you sense? If we allow ourselves to rest in the quiet recesses of the heart, most of us will feel a gentle tugging, a sense of *longing.* Humming softly in the background of our daily life, this is the call we answer when we journey on a spiritual path.

What is this longing? Neither a feeling nor a thought, it is more like a gravitational pull in the direction of wholeness, enlightenment, truth— what some call God. There are some people who know from an early age how to follow their heart's longing with grace and sureness. Others feel it as strongly and fill it with anything they can to dull the longing. Alcohol, drugs, materialism, work—many of our excesses can be traced to the spiritual longing that dwells in our hearts.

Unchanneled spiritual longing is a powerful force. It has been successfully manipulated throughout history in ways so hypocritical and repressive that religion has earned a bad name. But spiritual longing came before religion. Step into a limestone cave in France where Cro-Magnon people left their paintings and ritual markings, and you will find your own questions and yearnings engraved on the walls. The need to understand our place within the mystery of the universe is as ancient and instinctual as our other basic human needs. Creation stories, religions, prophetic philosophies, and scientific explanations rise and fall within cultures and throughout eras. Spiritual longing remains constant in the human heart.

The source of our spiritual longing resides in a place deep within us. It is a quiet and faithful place and if we learn how to access its powerful wisdom, it can become our most dependable friend. The following meditation exercise is designed to help us open to our longing and therefore to the fullness of the human experience. It is a practice that if done on a regular basis helps us to relax into the mystery of life.

CONNECTING WITH YOUR SPIRITUAL LONGING

Sit quietly right where you are, and close your eyes. Feel yourself breathing. Follow the breath on its journey into and out of your body. Sit feeling yourself breathe for a few minutes. Place your hand over your heart and feel the warmth of your hand connect with the steady beat of your heart. Then put your hand or fingertips lightly on the spot in the center of your rib cage, to the right of your physical heart. It is the spot you can feel when you are startled and draw your breath sharply inward. Move your hand gently, and breathe slowly and softly into that spot until you are focusing intently on what many traditions call the spiritual heart or the heart center.

Imagine that the spot you are touching is the top of a deep, deep well. Follow your breath on a journey into the spacious interior of your own heart. Breathe slowly in and out. Let yourself be pulled ever more deeply into the well of your heart. As you meet thoughts and emotions on the journey, do not push them away. They are part of you, but not all of you. Greet what you find and move on, ever deeper into the well of your spiritual heart.

Be aware of what you do when feelings or thoughts arise. Be like an explorer, using your breath as you would a high-beam flashlight. Observe yourself as you get lost in, reject, avoid, try to change, or judge thoughts and emotions as they arise. Use your breath to help you stay open to whatever you meet on your journey, without judgment or rejection. If a sense of sadness or grief appears, do not turn away or fight it. Gently observe your feelings as you let yourself be pulled ever onward. If anxiousness or boredom overcomes you, use your breath to return to the journey. If a sense of pleasure or joy envelops you, observe it as well. Welcome whatever you discover, without judgment, as part of yourself, but not all of yourself. Sit in this state, letting yourself be pulled by your longing into the well of your heart, observing your breath, for as long as you feel comfortable and then slowly remove your hand, return to normal breathing, and open your eyes.

RELAXING INTO THE MYSTERY

Late in his life, Max Planck, the Nobel laureate and father of quantum physics, wrote, "Science cannot solve the ultimate mystery of Nature. And it is because in the last analysis we ourselves are part of the mystery we are trying to solve." Planck had mastered every aspect of physics when he wrote this, from thermodynamics and electrodynamics to relativity. Albert Einstein echoed Planck when he wrote, "The most beautiful experience we can have is the mysterious. It is the fundamental emotion which stands at the cradle of true art and true science. . . . I am satisfied with the mystery of the eternity of life and with the awareness and a glimpse of the marvelous structure of the existing world."

Here, then, is another way to define spirituality. It is a mystery, the mystery behind the "marvelous structure of the existing world." Through my work and travels, I have met many of the Eastern gurus of our times, those who have brought Buddhism, Yoga, Taoism, and ancient shamanic wisdom to the West. I have studied with Christian, Jewish, and Islamic mystics, worked with the founders of new psychological schools of thought, and experimented with the methods of maverick American spiritual teachers who combine Eastern mysticism with psychology. The wisest, sanest, and happiest of these people are not those who profess a complicated and rigid spiritual doctrine. Rather, I have gained the most from those whose paths lead them and their students gently, humorously, and fearlessly into the very mystery that Planck and Einstein are talking about. The most useful spiritual techniques are those that have taught me how to relax into the mystery. Once there, the path home lights up from within.

The spiritual path is the process of fearlessly peering into the mysterious nature of life and relaxing our mental and emotional grip on our own place within it. Learning how to do this opens the way to a kind of wisdom that answers our own questions and touches the deepest strands of our longing. This kind of spirituality makes it marvelously OK to long for something that we do not fully understand; to be aware of its presence, even if we cannot describe what it is; to merge with its powerful truth without having to buy into an "ism" that demands we dress a certain way, talk a certain way, behave a certain way.

Ultimately, you are the only one who can answer the question, "What is spirituality?" All of the suggestions made so far should be used only if they ring true to you. If fearlessness, Beginner's Mind, and Open Secret move you closer to a working definition of spirituality, then make them your own. Zen master Thich Nhat Hanh gives us yet another clue: "All spiritual seeking is aimed at awakening us in order to know one and only one thing: birth and death can never touch us in any way whatsoever." When we ask the question "Who is the *us* that cannot be touched by birth and death?" we invite spirituality to define itself. How we search for this place or this being, how we learn to relax into its mystery, and how we share its gifts of peace, love, and fearlessness is as good a definition of the spiritual path as I have found. God's name and ways may be different in different religions, but this human longing—to know and revere the "us that cannot be touched by birth and death"—is shared by all of us.

THE BIGGIES AND THE DAILIES

What should we include within the scope of our definition of spirituality? Some religious traditions are quite clear about what parts of life are spiritual and what parts are not. You have your daily life, Monday through Friday, and then, depending on your faith, you get spiritual for a few hours on the weekend.

Other traditions say that God is everything. It's hard to argue with that definition, but also hard to wrap our minds around such a concept. Rather, I prefer to experience spirituality as an attitude toward everything—a daily choosing of a way to approach the different textures of my life. I can choose a fearless, relaxed, and open-hearted attitude toward how I deal with a problem at work, or how I make sense of suffering in the world, or how I approach my own death. In this way, spirituality *is* everything.

I always begin the spiritual retreats I lead by asking people why they are there. The variety of the answers, from a group who share a stated intent of pursuing their spirituality, reveals just how much of the human experience we bring with us on the spiritual path. The following are actual responses culled from years of teaching:

"I need peace and quiet."
"I am yearning for connection."
"What is my passion?"
"I don't know how to relax."
"I want to find my inner voice."
"I have lost my job (my child, my lover, my husband, my wife)."
"I love the sense of sacredness."
"I am up against an important choice and I don't know which way to go."
"I had an out-of-body experience (near-death experience, visitation)."
"I want to wake up and stop spacing out."
"I am sick of my own mental chatter."
"I want to rediscover an inner strength I had when I was younger."
"How do I link the spiritual path to everyday life?"
"I am afraid of the unknown."
"I have anxiety attacks."
"I want to dwell in the present moment more, and in the past or the future less."
"I no longer know what I believe in."
"I long for beauty."
"I am always tired."
"The wounds of my childhood are haunting me."
"I regret the joy I have missed, the unlived parts of my life."
"My fear of death is ever-present."

"I am in a new stage of life."

"My relationships don't seem to work out."

"I am addicted to alcohol (drugs, food, sex, work)."

"I am tired of being so cynical."

"I have been diagnosed with a terminal illness."

"I am always angry."

"I want to have fun."

"I've lived fifty years as a caterpillar."

"How can I let go of my armor?"

"I have nostalgia for something I cannot name."

All of these are good reasons to walk the spiritual path. Together they create the tapestry of human experience, from the mundane to the most mysterious. They include our mind, body, heart, psyche, and spirit—the "biggies" and the "dailies." I didn't come up with that phrase; my youngest son, Daniel, did when he was five and having trouble falling asleep at night. Night after night I would lie next to him in his little bed, scrunched in a corner against the wall, massaging his back, waiting for his eyes to close. After a few months of resting each night in this uncomfortable position, I tried to get to the bottom of his sleeplessness.

"Sometimes, if you say what is happening to you," I said to him in his bed, "then it will go away."

"Really?"

"Sometimes."

"OK," he said, as eager to be released from his evening ritual as I was. "I'm afraid."

"Afraid of what?" I asked.

No answer.

"The dark?"

"No."

"School?" He had recently started kindergarten and the whole process overwhelmed him, from taking the bus to remembering to bring home his lunch box.

"No."

"Spending the night at Grandma's?"

"No."

"Then what?"

He rolled away from me and whispered something into his pillow.

"What?"

"I'm afraid of the big things," he squeaked in a tiny voice.

"What big things?" I asked, looking around the room.

"You know, the really big things."

"Monsters?"

"No," he said, disgusted, "I don't believe in monsters. I mean big things, like . . . dying."

I was stunned, and sorry that I had suggested that by naming his fear it would go away.

"Well, honey," I said, "join the crowd. Lots of people are afraid of dying. It's one of the biggies."

After that conversation, and over many years of bedtime chats, my son and I came up with a list of "biggies" and of what he called "dailies," or smaller worries and concerns that weren't big enough to keep him up at night but that still needed to be lit up from behind with a spiritual searchlight. The biggies include life purpose, love, human suffering, higher consciousness, death, and beyond. The dailies are closer to home: physical and mental health, feelings, relationships, work, and family.

A spiritual path traverses the landscapes of both the biggies and the dailies. If we regard spirituality as a fearless investigation of reality, then we'll find that all of our experiences fit within its boundaries. The rest of this book is a guide to shining the light of spirituality on the biggies and the dailies—how to create a practice within each realm, how to gauge our progress, pitfalls to beware of, and gifts to expect.

3 ┊ Hiding Somewhere Near Us

In all ten directions of the universe,
there is only one truth.
When we see clearly, the great teachings are the same.
What can ever be lost? What can be attained?
If we attain something, it was there from the beginning of time.
If we lose something, it is hiding somewhere near us.
    —RYOKAN

There is a sense these days that we have lost something. Watch the faces of people in the streets of any American town or city. Look below the surface of how we live—past the strain and speed of our daily routines—and consider how we relate to our friends and family; where we live and the health of our communities and environment; what we eat every day; how our children spend their time. American culture, and those of us who live within it, seems to have lost a certain quality of life: a graciousness, a spiritual value system, a peace of mind.

Yet what we sense is missing is only hiding. It is hiding somewhere near us, resting in the depths of our own bodies, minds, and hearts. Spirituality is waiting for us, as it has waited for people in every age and every culture. A culture cannot destroy the soul; it can try to evict it, but the soul waits around in the shadows. Shining a spotlight on the whole of American life is a helpful part of any one American's spiritual search. For as much as it is an individual journey, the spiritual search is also a collective one. And just as we are influenced by our family of origin, so are we formed by our larger family—our culture, with its articulated ethics and rules, as well as its unspoken expectations and images. We may disagree forcefully with certain American values, but nonetheless we are stamped by them, and the mark goes deep.

We live in a culture that is seriously split off from the nourishing pace and values of soul. What exactly are these values? We call some African American food or music or worship "soulful," but what do we mean? We go to Italy or rural France and there's this *je ne sais quoi* about the food and the markets and the way that everyone closes up shop at noon and heads home for lunch and a nap. What is this? And what is soulless about fast food, shopping malls, our excessive work schedules, and the mechanistic pace of daily life? These are good questions for an American interested in spirituality to consider.

"Start where you are," says Pema Chödrön, an American Buddhist teacher. As Americans in the twenty-first century, "where you are" looks like this: after living out our first hundred years as a *relatively* cohesive and religious society, Americans spent the next one hundred years steeped in the Age of the Individual. Our focus on materialism, science, and the separation of Church and State led to a steady decline in the spiritual influence on individuals and communities. We have been fully secularized. This is not bad or good. It is just a fact that stacks up with other facts of American life and fills in the story line about each one of us who has grown up in America. The "loss of soul," as writers like Thomas Moore and James Hillman call the casualty of modernity, is a fact of our lives, and the sooner we feel deeply into the reality of this fact, the sooner we will be able to know how we want to deal with it.

The reason I stress that loss of soul is neither bad nor good is because with every loss there is a gain, and much has been gained in America over the past one hundred years, even as we have lost our way spiritually. As industry and technology have disconnected us from nature and accelerated the pace of daily life, so have they freed many more people than ever before to explore dimensions of the human experience other than survival. While the focus on the worth of each individual has eroded the health of communities and families, this same focus has empowered previously disenfranchised individuals to exercise their God-given rights. As patriarchal authority structures have been questioned and overturned, more than just lawlessness and moral torpor have replaced them. Voices that were silenced years and years ago—including the voices of women and of the earth itself—are claiming their legitimacy and changing American society. Rising from the ashes of the old ways is the steady growth of the inner authority of the individual—any individual—and in the end, that will be the most important foundation of a real democracy.

And finally, the loss of a majority population, the melting pot alchemy that literally changed the face of the country during the twentieth century, has created a cacophony of competing traditions. No longer is there one way to speak, to learn, to celebrate, to eat, to worship. On the surface, the conflicts and confusions of diversity look overwhelming. Some may long for the more traditional days when one people celebrated the seasonal round with known rituals and shared beliefs. But American diversity is also a gift of profound proportion. The challenge of unifying many different peoples into one cohesive people may seem like an impossible task. It is also a sacred task. It mimics the journey each one of us takes individually as we seek to integrate the many, often conflicting parts of the self. It asks us to meet within ourselves "the other," or what C. G. Jung called "the shadow." It mirrors nature, where diversity equals life. Ultimately, striving for harmony within diversity is akin to the mystical marriage—the reconciling of the unreconcilable, the discovery of unity within duality. American diversity points us in this direction. And it is the direction of soul.

We can indeed find our way back to soul. It *is* hiding somewhere near us. But before we go looking for it, let's look clearly at what we have lost and what we have gained. And let's look with open, unsentimental eyes. Yes, there's often more safety and civility in hierarchical societies. Yes, we have lost that. But there's more room for communication and creativity in free societies. And we have gained that. Where there's a soulful simplicity to nonindustrialized societies, there's frequently more empowerment and opportunity for a wider range of individuals in industrialized societies. We may have lost the sense of unity and tradition of a homogenous society, but by mixing it up we have gained the aliveness and the potential for a higher unity that is inherent in diversity.

Our charge now is to find a middle way, to do what the American philosopher Ken Wilber calls "transcend and include"—pull the depth of the American soul with us as we transcend the casualties of our times. We can mine for the simple treasures that we have lost to the horrible excesses of modern culture, while at the same time enjoying the fruits of our advancements—our liberties, our inventions, our variety. We can *transcend* those parts of our past that were exclusionary and rigid, and *include* those parts that celebrated community, civility, and authenticity. We can do the same with modern America: *transcend* the hollow values and obsessive individuality of the times, and *include* the freedom and diversity—our sacred trust as Americans.

TRANSCEND AND INCLUDE

"Evolution always *transcends* and *includes,* incorporates and goes beyond," writes Ken Wilber in *A Brief History of Everything,* his synthesis of scientific and spiritual thought. Wilber uses the evolutionary concept of "transcend and include" to describe both the personal and societal movement toward wholeness. A healthy person grows into individuality, incorporating the best of inherited and taught behavior and beliefs, and transcending those parts that no longer serve the mature self. If we try to transcend only, in a compulsion to separate from the past, we end up damaging parts of ourselves—root parts that keep us connected to our basic nature and our place in the world. Yet if we reject the natural urge toward transcendence and turn around, grabbing on to the past with nostalgia, we also do violence to life, because life is also movement, creativity, evolution.

To walk the spiritual path is to transcend and include. For the person this means evolving beyond the limits of the past, while honoring the wisdom of those who came before; incorporating the voices and traditions of one's ancestors, while claiming a unique identity. I believe that Americans are well suited for this task, having inherited from the Puritans the idea that one can make oneself anew through hard work and honest self-examination. The new American spirituality includes the Puritan idea of personal transformation, and transcends it, expanding its realm to embrace psychological, physical, creative, and spiritual transformation. The next chapters of this book map a course for the individual through the varied terrain along the path of transcendence and inclusion.

Nations must also transcend and include if they are to mature. The new American spirituality that is now emerging in the culture reflects an impulse toward transcendence and inclusion. Which of our collective attributes should we transcend? Which should we include? If a vote were being held, I would choose the following American traits to move beyond, to transcend: First, an unforgiving piety that negates our full humanness; next, our blind faith in so-called scientific progress; our compulsive striving for material gain; the lack of community and civility in our daily life; the agitated pace of modern life; and the silenced voices of the powerless.

On the inclusion side of the ballot, I would vote first for the promise made to Americans: life, liberty, and the pursuit of happiness for each individual; I would certainly vote for the Puritan legacy of personal transformation; next, I would include into America's maturing psyche our celebration of diversity, and then our faith in democracy, our healthy mistrust of authority, and our roots in wilderness. These are unique aspects of America that deserve preservation. In particular, the radical promise of life, liberty, and the pursuit of happiness demands not only inclusion, but a whole new way of viewing the spiritual life of a nation and its people.

THE PROMISE: LIFE, LIBERTY, AND THE PURSUIT OF HAPPINESS

After returning from France, Thomas Jefferson said of his new nation, "We can no longer say there is nothing new under the sun. For the whole history of man is new. The great extent of our republic is new." The Europe that the early Americans had left behind found its inspiration and integrity in honoring the old traditions, the pedigreed families, the noble past. America was to be distinctly different. Now each person would be given a fresh start. The future would not be determined by a past that the individual had inherited. The "self-made man" was born in America when each citizen was promised life, liberty, and the pursuit of happiness.

The great strengths of America can be traced to this revolutionary promise. But the weakened soul of the nation can also be traced to the promise. John Adams warned of the dangers of the promise when he wrote, "Our Constitution was made only for a moral and religious people. It is wholly inadequate to the government of any other." The drafters of the Declaration of Independence were well aware of the risks they were taking when they signed off on such a radical promise. Thomas Jefferson took the greatest risk when he substituted the words "the pursuit of happiness" for the original word, "property," in the trinity of inalienable rights. And while he pointed out that "happiness is attainable only by dili-gent cultivation of civic virtue," he was unclear on how, or even if, that civic virtue could be legislated.

When the Constitution was first conceived, the Founding Fathers granted the rights of personal happiness only to a most homogenous group—for the most part, white, European, Christian men. Whether this decision of exclusivity was based on a prescient knowledge that to do otherwise was to court chaos, or simply on patriarchal prejudice, I do not know. Most likely, both. It was much easier to grant freedom to a group who adhered to a similar religious belief system; much less likely that freedoms would be misused with a strong moral code firmly in place; much easier to trust in such an egalitarian system when those involved were already of equal status. It was one thing to promise life, liberty, and the pursuit of happiness to a homogenous people who practiced self-restraint because if they didn't they would be held accountable by their re-ligious community. It was quite another thing to imagine those freedoms in the hands of the unwieldy concoction that America was to become.

In retrospect we can see that our founding fathers opened a Pandora's box by molding a government around individual freedom and happiness. Even as the American Constitution was being crafted, debate raged around the possibility of its lofty ideals being distorted by self-serving in-terpretations. The correspondence between Thomas Jefferson and John Adams in their later years is full of concerns of what could happen to America if its citizens took advantage of the sacred promise of life, liberty, and the pursuit of happiness.

It didn't take long for the promise to be put to the test. In less than one hundred years, women, African Americans, and immigrants demanded to be the masters of *their* lives, and to enjoy the same liberty and happiness heretofore reserved for an elite minority. It took a civil war, the abolition of slavery, the suffragette movement, and the industrialization of the country to legally secure the rights granted in America's Constitution to all of its people. (It would take one hundred more years and counting to psycholog-ically and spiritually integrate those rights into the American way of life.) In the process, the European ethics and Christian religious morality that had been the backbone of the country lost their grip on the American psyche.

When "Give me your tired, your poor / Your huddled masses yearning to breathe free" joined America's purpose statement, and people from all over the world rushed to join the nation, Judeo-Christian values got blended right into the melting pot. At the same time, Americans were in the process of shifting their definition of happiness from the procurement of *rights* to the acquisition of *things*. Industry, mobility, and communication technology all contributed to the rise of consumerism as an American passion. To have more was to be happy.

Jefferson and Adams would no longer have recognized their country. Would they have been brave enough to draft their Constitution if the "inalienable rights" of liberty and happiness were to be granted to a patchwork of temperaments, colors, and beliefs? Would they have been as radical without the container of a religious code? Could the Constitution's spiritual generosity be granted to a people whose values were increasingly materialistic?

Certainly, the Judeo-Christian foundation of America's early years is an essential part of our spiritual identity. But even more so, the uniquely American promise of happiness and liberty for every person—regardless of class or color or gender—forms the backbone of an evolving American spiritual tradition. That promise set in motion the ongoing dialogue between the old value system of Puritan restraint and civic duty and the new hankering for self-expression and individual advancement. Could anyone assume, therefore, that American spirituality would not change? In the same ways that American literature, or music, or food has changed to transcend and include the old and the new, American spirituality is also changing. It was bound to happen. Given enough time, a new society harvests a unique spiritual tradition. A study of the world's religions reveals each new tradition as a response to, and an inclusion of, outdated theories and mores. In *A History of God,* Karen Armstrong writes, "The human idea of God has a history, since it has always meant something slightly different to each group of people who have used it at various points of time. The idea of God formed in one generation by one set of human beings could be meaningless in another."

Each of the world's spiritual traditions is built on the foundation of previous religious traditions. Buddhism and Hinduism are linked in this way, sharing concepts and gods. The Romans diverged from the Greeks, transcending, yet including, much of their mythology and culture. Judaism, Christianity, and Islam are branches of the same tree. Therefore, what is happening in American spirituality is not a departure from history, but a further flowering of the cultural crossbreeding that human evolution has always engendered.

THE NEW AMERICAN SPIRITUALITY

We are witnessing the birth of a wisdom tradition that is uniquely American. Within traditional organized religions, as well as in the hybrid creations of our times, the stamp of American thinking is plain. We see the American spirit in the proliferation of nonaffiliated Christian, Jewish, Buddhist, and Islamic churches, and also in the profound changes within sanctioned denominations. This spirit values independence from religious hierarchy. It crosses religious and social boundaries, telling the tale of a diverse people, gathered in close proximity, and absorbing each other's ways of worshiping, ritualizing, and mythologizing the great mysteries of life. It contains the nature-centered traditions of the original peoples of the Americas. It is part science, which has underscored, for most of the twentieth century, our unspoken collective philosophy. It respects both a mistrust of heavy-handed authority and the willing surrender to a greater power. It draws from the religious teachings of the past: from the biblical traditions; from the spiritual roots of Africa; from the meditative schools of Asia; and from other diverse mythic and religious worldviews. And it draws from our own times, from the wisdom of psychology, democracy, and feminism.

The following lists are a somewhat oversimplified outline of how spirituality is changing in America. In the spirit of transcendence and inclusion, the "old" list notes those aspects of American spirituality that we have outgrown. The "new" list leans in the direction of the most positive aspects of the emerging spiritual traditions. What is missing is the best of the old that we must safeguard, and the worst of the new that we can be aware of and work to overcome. Both of these are explored later.

OLD SPIRITUALITY

1. *Who Has Authority?* The hierarchy has the authority. Church authorities tell you how to worship in church and how to behave outside of church.

2. *What Is Spirituality?* God, and the path to worship Him, have already been defined. All you need to do is follow the directions.

3. *What Is the Path to God?* There is only one path. It is the right way and all other ways are wrong.

4. *What Is Sacred?* Parts of yourself—like the body, or ego, or emotions—are evil. Deny or transcend or sublimate them or they will lead you astray.

5. *What Is the Truth?* The truth is like a rock. Your understanding of it should never waver. Therefore ask the same questions and receive the same answers at all stages of life.

NEW AMERICAN SPIRITUALITY

1. *Who Has Authority?* You are your own best authority. As you work to know and love yourself, you discover how to live a spiritual life.

2. *What Is Spirituality?* You listen within for your own definition of spirituality. Your deeper longings are your compass on the search.

3. *What Is the Path to God?* Many paths lead to spiritual freedom and peace. You have a rich array of gems from which to draw illumination: the world's religious traditions; mythology; philosophy; psychology; healing methods; scientific wisdom; your own experience. String a necklace all your own.

4. *What Is Sacred?* Everything is sacred—your body, mind, psyche, heart, and soul. The world is sacred, too, with all of its light and darkness. Bring the exiled and unloved parts of yourself back into the fold.

5. *What Is the Truth?* The truth is like the horizon—forever ahead of you, forever changing its shape and color. Let your spiritual path change and diverge as you journey toward it. You live many lives in one lifetime. The truth accommodates your growth.

What was needed to uphold the old spirituality and to educate its followers is quite different from what we need now to guide us on a spiritual path. To forge our own way through life's deeper terrain requires different perceptions and skills than what it took to follow someone else's directives. To pursue personal happiness here on earth, and to sanctify the human body, is a different sort of quest than the search for redemption in an afterlife. And to understand and heal the troublesome parts of our own self and the world, as opposed to punishing or repressing the darker parts of human nature, asks us to do something for which few of us have been trained.

While the new American spirituality traverses much of the same territory that spiritual pilgrims have crossed throughout the ages, it also brings us into uncharted lands and presents each of us with disturbing paradoxes: If I focus too much on the self, won't I end up drowning in Narcissus' pool? But if I neglect myself, what will I really have of value to give to others? If I turn my attention to my body, what will keep me from becoming vain, or materialistic, or obsessed with the body's inevitable demise? But isn't the body the temple of the soul? If I work on opening my heart, what's to stop me from becoming an emotional mess? Conversely, won't I dry up if I concentrate exclusively on spirit? With so many ways to worship, seek, and heal, what will prevent me from flitting like a butterfly from fad to fad to fad, never landing long enough to settle into wisdom and health?

It's important to swing back and forth between these questions. Somewhere, in the middle, between the old homogenized, autocratic ways, and the new diverse and individualistic ways, is a clear path through the paradoxes. The goal, as we move from the old ways to the new, is not to replace one set of "isms" with another. Rather, the goal is to become more and more genuine, fearless, and free. Therefore, one of the most valuable skills we can develop as we travel the spiritual path is the ability to know the difference between genuine spirituality and "spiritual materialism," a phrase coined by the Tibetan scholar and meditation teacher Chögyam Trungpa.

SPIRITUAL MATERIALISM: AMERICAN STYLE

Chögyam Trungpa was one of the first teachers to bring Tibetan Buddhism to the West, in the late 1960s. A young monk and scholar, born and trained in the seclusion of Tibet, he found the American fascination with diversity and newness both refreshing and alarming. Imagine the shock of a Tibetan, handpicked by his people to carry to the West their ancient and pure tradition, in confronting the freedom-loving, happiness-pursuing, and materialistic people of America. He used the phrase *spiritual materialism* to warn his students about abusing the richness of spiritual material available to those in the West. He observed that Americans had a way of avoiding the disciplined work of real spirituality through an unrealistic and wasteful pursuit of shallow happiness. In his classic book on meditation and the spiritual path, *Cutting Through Spiritual Materialism,* he wrote that we are often "deceiving ourselves into thinking we are developing spiritually when instead we are strengthening our egocentricity through spiritual techniques."

This tendency is, of course, not new. Spiritual materialism has shadowed religious traditions throughout history. But Americans, being materialistic in general, and having a sense of entitlement to happiness, would be wise to be on the lookout for spiritual materialism. There's a disturbing underbelly of spiritual materialism in the plethora of self-help literature and spiritual-growth programs available today, so much so that it can appear that Americans' spiritual inclinations mimic our love of fast food and superhighways.

I have a personal investment in weighing this suspicion against the real benefits of the new spirituality, since my daily work, as well as my personal history, reads like a who's who in the New Age Hall of Fame: a child of the sixties; a feminist and anti-war activist; a disciple of an Eastern guru in California; a resident of a rural commune who had her babies at home in a log cabin; a home-birth midwife; a participant in several forms of psychotherapy; an environmentalist; and a founder of a learning center that has hosted a grab bag of innovative thinkers, healers, and spiritual teachers.

My critical eye has often made me doubt my work on the spiritual front. As moved as I have been by the genuine spiritual teachers I have met through my work, I have also watched, with a mixture of horror and humor, as a parade of pretenders and downright oddballs sold their wares to people looking for quick fixes, magical cures, or eternal youth. In moments of cynicism, especially in its early years, I would look around Omega Institute and wonder if we had created a monster of spiritual pretense. I remember years ago standing in a circle at Omega with more than a hundred people who had come to study with a man who taught Native American spirituality. Wrapped in a blanket and smelling of soil and sage and smoke, the teacher certainly looked the part. He explained to the group in a gravelly voice that until we knew the direction in which we faced, we would never get where we wanted to go. "Now we will pray to the east," he said, "the direction of beginnings, the sun bearer, the white shell dawn." With one hand he held a drum, with the other he held my hand. Pulling me close, he whispered into my ear, "Hey! Which way is east?"

And I had other experiences, lots of them, that helped me develop a keen sense of discrimination in my quest for genuine and effective spiritual teachers and practices. Once, in the course of evaluating faculty, I sat in on a class where therapists were learning to induce trances to help their patients explore past lives. Putting aside my own lack of certainty regarding reincarnation, I watched the teacher do an expert job of inducing a trance on a volunteer from the group. Soon the participant was speaking in a southern drawl.

"Tell us what you are wearing," said the instructor.

"I'm in a long dress. It's torn. It's dirty. I'm ashamed of it," said the woman.

"Can you tell us your name?"

"Yes," she answered in a soft voice. "Scarlett O'Hara."

Now, clearly this was ridiculous. I waited for the class to realize the mistake—I wanted to call out, "Hey! She cannot be reborn from a fictional character, right?" But I didn't, and the class went on as if any one of them could have once been Tarzan or Jane.

Spiritual materialism is something we all confront on the spiritual path. It refers to a genuine interest in spiritual enlightenment gone awry. I am not talking here only about gross spiritual materialism, like the stories above, or when a revered teacher or therapist sleeps with his students, or when a group raises money for supposedly altruistic purposes and instead feathers its own nest. I am talking about the little ways in which we all deceive ourselves on the spiritual path—the ways that allow us to read about simplicity and freedom as we become more complicated and attached; the ways that let us talk about being "free of the ego," while feeling really special saying it.

As Chögyam Trungpa says, "Ego is able to convert everything to its own use, even spirituality." By ego, Trungpa meant the part of ourselves that feels separate from everything else. It is the part of ourselves that struggles and fears. Ego is not necessarily something bad, nor does it refer only to the aggressive, conceited parts of ourselves. Ego is the part of the self that wants to be unique, unchanging, solid. Ego struggles against reality in an attempt to preserve itself. It is so afraid of looking at the vast, mysterious, untamed, eternal universe that it tries like hell to convince itself and everyone else that it is in control. "The ego tries as hard as it can to shield us from the direct perception of what is," writes Trungpa.

Ego is not just a classically spiritual concern. In our times the word *ego* has dwelt more in the province of psychology. Psychology has given us new insights into the structure of the ego and skillful ways of taming ego's inappropriate and harmful impulses. In the next chapters we explore how spirituality and psychology are merging in the new American spirituality into a powerful way to understand and work with ego. It is through the combined strength of these two disciplines—psychological therapy and spiritual practice—that the seemingly incompatible quests of developing a healthy ego and transcending a separate sense of self actually become one and the same.

Unhealthy ego converts spirituality to its own misguided uses in tricky ways. It reminds me of the woodchuck that ravages my vegetable garden each summer. All spring and into the early part of summer, my garden flourishes, except for the occasional slug infestation. Then, just when the carrots are fat enough to be tasted, and just as the beans are yielding their first thin slivers of fruit, the woodchuck mysteriously enters the garden and levels the crops. No matter how tall or deep or strong the fence surrounding the garden, the woodchuck gets in and undoes my work. Ego works in the same way. It will allow you to pursue genuine spiritual development right up to the moment of harvest. As soon as its territory is seriously threatened, though, ego will appear—hungry and determined. Soon, your tidy spiritual garden will be converted by ego into more material for its survival. This is spiritual materialism. Keeping a lookout for ego in the garden is an essential part of the spiritual path. And the best place to look for the signs of spiritual materialism is in the very places where genuine spiritual progress is being made.

In America, spiritual materialism is lurking in the shadows of democracy, individuality, and diversity. Democracy and individuality are prime targets for ego's trickery. A free individual, lacking the external controls set by an organized religious community, must learn to develop self-control. Otherwise, ego will lead the seeker into illusory waters. At different times I have been adrift in these waters, and I have watched hundreds of people at Omega Institute led astray by their own confused egos. They come to Omega to study with a yogi or a Christian monk or a Jewish mystic whose message stresses simplicity and truth. Instead of focusing on the message, they become enchanted with the messenger. Or they turn simple words into simplistic slogans. Or they misinterpret spiritual freedom as psychological self-indulgence.

I have observed so many seekers arrive at Omega looking for a way to drop their illusions about themselves and the world, and leave with even more baggage: a new set of concepts, a foreign mantra, an ancient set of rules that governs everything from diet to sex. Any of these spiritual tools may indeed be powerful gifts for transforming one's life. But taken out of context or used to impress others, they lose their meaningfulness. Soon what began as a genuine spiritual search becomes a way of dressing up and hiding out behind esoteric explanations. Sometimes this seems almost comical, but really, it is a shame when the possibility of spiritual transformation is traded for spiritual materialism.

American diversity has created one of the most seductive examples of spiritual materialism. With so many paths to choose from, we can deceive ourselves into thinking that the more techniques we acquire, the more spiritual we will become. But as Trungpa warns, "If we do not step out of spiritual materialism, if we in fact practice it, then we may eventually find ourselves possessed of a huge collection of spiritual paths. We may feel these spiritual collections to be very precious. . . . We display them to the world and, in doing so, reassure ourselves that we exist, safe and secure, as 'spiritual' people.

"But we have simply created a shop, an antique shop. We could be specializing in oriental antiques or medieval Christian antiques, or antiques from some other civilization or time, but we are, nonetheless, running a shop. Before we filled our shop with so many things the room was beautiful: whitewashed walls and a very simple floor with a bright lamp burning in the ceiling."

I studied with Chögyam Trungpa in the early 1970s. Today as I read his teachings, I cringe at how I wasted the precious opportunity I had as his student. I was twenty, twenty-one, and twenty-two years old when I was around Trungpa, at his meditation center in New York City, at a retreat center in Vermont, and in Boulder, Colorado, as he was starting Naropa Institute, now an established university. I remember the first and only time I had a private audience with him. As I sat on the bench outside his room, waiting my turn to ask him a question, I worked as hard as I could to find a way to prove myself a worthy and profound student. In those days, it seemed that every one of his students wanted to be his special devotee, to impress him and the other students with their brilliant questions, to out-meditate all the other meditators.

When I finally had the chance to sit in front of him, I was so nervous that I was shaking. I didn't even look into his eyes. I asked him something about the role of women in Buddhism and how could I as a "liberated" American woman reinterpret the Buddha's words for these times. I don't remember exactly what he said. It was short and not to the point, as far as

I was concerned. I do remember stumbling out of the room feeling embarrassed and slightly cheated.

I had cheated myself, which is as good as any description of spiritual materialism. My ego got in the way of real spiritual growth. This is what ego will do. It is more interested in proclaiming its existence than in basking in the limitless energy of real spirituality. I entreat you not to cheat yourself on the spiritual path. There is no one to impress, nothing to "get," nowhere to rush to, nothing to miss out on. The truth is always there, plain and simple, hiding somewhere near you.

As you read this book, please be on the lookout for your own spiritual materialism. Pick one or two beautiful, living teachings and give yourself time and patience in your pursuit of the truth. If you discover that you are unwittingly creating an antique shop, give away most of the junk and start all over. Keep before you always your most unaffected goals: to become fearless; to be at home with your life just as it is; to rest gently on the waters of the mysterious universe.

WISDOM AND FOLLY: WARNING SIGNS ALONG THE PATH

Think of these signs as similar to the warning label on a cigarette package. Caution: These practices may be hazardous to your spiritual health.
—SAM KEEN

We could say that America, having grown out of its infancy and childhood, is now in its adolescence, asserting its independence—*individuating* from its parental influences, as Jung would say. In childhood we need clear-cut rules, boundaries within which we can safely grow. Adolescents must stretch out of those boundaries in order to fulfill their own destiny. Typical adolescent behavior is to stretch too far, and then, if one is fortunate, to learn from mistakes and self-correct. This is where America has been in the recent past. Striving for its own sense of self, American culture may have exceeded the bounds of balanced behavior. But the movement has been toward maturity. If we are fortunate as a culture, we will self-correct and grow into our fullness.

Spiritually speaking, adolescent America's experimentation with all things mystical and magical has opened our eyes to new ways of defining ourselves—as Americans and as human beings. As we develop further into a mature sense of self, we will have to weed out some of the less honorable aspects of the new American spirituality. A magazine once asked me to create a top-ten list of the "weeds" of the new American spirituality. These are weeds that are watered by our own egos. They are the crown jewels of spiritual materialism.

SPIRITUAL MATERIALISM'S TOP-TEN LIST

1. *Narcissism:* The thin line between narcissism and "following your bliss" has become painfully clear to me since I first took Joseph Campbell's directive to heart. Without some degree of sacrifice for the greater good, self-discovery eventually leads to plain old self-indulgence. There is a real danger that we will, even unwittingly, end up using spiritual or psychological teachings to perpetuate our childhoods or to mistakenly conclude that constant fulfillment is a God-given right. Teachers and therapists can also get trapped by narcissism. They become less like wise guides and more like lawyers—advocates of the self, devoted solely to the advancement of their client's self-gratification.

2. *Superficiality:* When spirituality veers from being a calm quest for fearlessness and begins to resemble sentimentality or superstition, then we are in the shallow water of superficiality. America's new forms of spirituality and therapy are often accused of selling superficial and sunny answers to life's complexity and pain. Spirituality does not ultimately work if we use it to protect ourselves from the rough-and-tumble of real life. This tendency—to surround ourselves with pat explanations, special prayers, or ritual objects—is sometimes called spiritual bypass. It can result in a wide array of disorders, from the silly to the serious. How do we know when we are using spirituality to skim the surface of life instead of plunging deeper into reality? The more serious kinds of superficiality are easier to spot, as when a whole group of people substitutes new ways of dressing or speaking for the much less showy work of real transformation, or when a cancer patient believes that daily affirmations will work instead of medicine, and therefore forgoes treatment. Most of us are called to root out much more subtle forms of superficiality: Are we hiding behind the safety of a concept instead of going deeper into our own fears or ignorance? Are we using fancy terms to explain away the need for a simple behavior change? Have we bought into a system that allows us to tread

water? Any worldview that suggests that thinking positively always protects you from harm, or that there is something wrong with you if you suffer or fail, or that healing isn't often complex is offering unrealistic promises for daily life.

3. *The Never-Ending Process of Self-Improvement:* There is an insatiability to the quest for self-improvement. It can become life's main activity and that presents a few problems. First, you can become obsessed with your own story—your victimization, your faults, your fears. Second, it's a myth that we can ever change ourselves enough to escape from the gene pool. If we expect a tidy wrap-up to our childhood wounds then our therapy and spiritual practice will become exercises in futility. And last, but certainly not least, a myopic focus on the self leads to social apathy. It just isn't true that your self-empowerment and self-healing will necessarily lead to the health and happiness of others and of society. We have to participate in the improvement of more than just ourselves.

4. *Instant Transformation:* Just as some people get seduced by the never-ending process of self-examination, some are disappointed when they don't achieve understanding and inner peace after reading a book, or in a daylong workshop, or even after two years of weekly therapy. The poet-philosopher Paul Valéry wrote, "Long years must pass before the truths we have made for ourselves become our very flesh." Spiritual awakening takes patience, hard work, and the grace of God.

5. *Desire for Magic:* Perhaps in direct reaction to the Western reign of rational thinking, some of the new American spirituality throws common sense out the window and pursues a search for magic cures and miraculous people. The need to believe in all-powerful teachers, angelic visitations, UFOs, and other unexplained mysteries can obscure the ordinary magic of everyday life, proof enough of God and the miracle of life. It can also allow spiritual teachers who claim magical powers to justify abusive behavior.

6. *Grandiosity:* One of the best aspects of the new American spirituality is also one of its dangers. In democratizing spirituality and bringing it to the daily life of each person, each one of us risks becoming a messianic little pope, or a humorless saint, or just an unbearably profound person, grander or better than others.

7. *Romanticizing Indigenous Cultures:* There exists a kind of reverse prejudice in our politically correct times that just because something or someone is from another culture, especially an indigenous or minority culture,

that it/he/she is somehow more valuable, spiritual, or wise. Some spiritual teachings rewrite history by harking back to mythic eras when human beings lived in peace and harmony on lost continents under the wise counsel of native shamans. "Whenever teachings come to a country from abroad the problem of spiritual materialism is intensified," writes Chögyam Trungpa.

8. *The Inner Child Tantrum:* As the writer Nelia Gardner White says, "Some people just don't seem to realize, when they're moaning about not getting prayers answered, that *no* is the answer." Some spiritual and therapeutic schools of thought teach that if you learn to pray to God (or to ask another person) for what you need, you will necessarily get it. It just doesn't work that way. Learning to know what we want and then to honestly ask for it is a monumental achievement. But so is learning to gracefully accept all that is given and taken away. Spirituality should awaken within us both the wondrous child and the mature adult. Tom Robbins wrote, "It's never too late to have a happy childhood." But I don't think he wanted to be taken literally.

9. *Ripping Off the Traditions:* I have a lot of sympathy for devout followers of established religions, from Christians to Native Americans to Tibetan Buddhists, who feel that the renewed interest in their teachings is insincere. Many modern seekers skim off the ritual trappings of a tradition with little respect for the depth behind it. This trivializes powerful and elegant systems of spiritual growth. The same can be said for the way people pick and choose elements of a complex healing or therapeutic method and fashion a piece of the whole to fit the needs of the moment. There is a difference between carefully creating a spiritual path that includes genuine practices from a variety of traditions, and flitting from flower to flower like a drunk honeybee.

10. *The Guru Trip:* Harry S. Truman lamented: "Memories are short; appetites for power and glory are insatiable. Old tyrants depart. New ones take their place. It is all very baffling and trying." Perhaps the most baffling and trying aspect of the new American spirituality is the disparity between spiritual teachings and the behavior of teachers. While I am aware that inconsistencies abound in what I say and what I do, and while I have compassion for the conflicts inherent in leadership, I have been appalled by the ironic behavior disorders that have shadowed spiritual leaders. Men, women, Western, Eastern, fundamentalist, New Age, modern, or indigenous—none have escaped the temptation to abuse power. Things to be

wary of: extravagant claims of enlightenment or healing; the minimizing of the hard work that accompanies any true spiritual or healing path; the excessive commercialism that betrays the deeper spiritual message; and the blind adherence of followers to charlatans (be they gurus, therapists, preachers, healers, or teachers). With their deceitful double standards, some gurus, therapists, and teachers have given mentorship a bad name and tarnished the image of humbling oneself to a wiser and more experienced guide.

There is both wisdom and folly in American spirituality. Soon enough you will stumble upon the folly, even as you become wiser and happier. Your best guides through the morass will be your own alert mind and sensitive heart, and perhaps most important, your sense of humor. Being awake to the folly is quite different from being a cynic. A healthy blend of skepticism, humor, and mysticism is the best brew for the journey.

4 | Humanizing Spirituality

The first part of the spiritual journey should properly be called psychological rather than spiritual because it involves peeling away the myths and illusions that have misinformed us.
—SAM KEEN

Religious traditions speak of a sacred realm that we can enter through prayer, meditation, and right living. Mystics tell us that such a realm already exists within our own hearts. They assure us that the human being's essential self is one of contentment and security; that we need only to uncover our naturally deep feelings of exhilaration, enthusiasm, and joy; that we do indeed have the capability of meeting life and death without fear; and that the unique blend of excitement and peace which connotes spiritual wholeness is our birthright.

Skeptics, and the skeptic within me, ask the question, "If my essential self is so peaceful, expansive, and free, then why don't I usually feel like that? Why am I, and everyone else, so often anxious, fearful, and confused?" The cynical answer is "Because the mystics are wrong. Life is hard and then you die." A traditional religious answer might be "Because you do not love enough; because you are a sinner; because only in heaven will you know peace and freedom."

In the old model of spirituality this left us with a choice: take the cynic's path and live until you die with a bitter taste in your mouth, or be good and fear God. Perhaps then the door to heaven will crack open wide enough for you to slip through.

There is another choice. Between us and the promised sacred land are obstacles of our own making, the very human "myths and illusions that have misinformed us," as philosopher Sam Keen says in the quote above. But instead of damning or avoiding our humanness, we can actually use each myth and illusion as a stepping stone toward the sacred land. What are these myths and illusions? They are the wrong conclusions we have formed about who we are, about the purpose of our lives, about mortality, love, ego, self-importance, self-responsibility, security, suffering. Our wrong conclusions lead to unhappiness, unkindness, greed, loneliness, fear. Instead of shrugging our shoulders with the skeptics and agreeing, "That's just the way it is. Life's a bitch and then you die," or walking with the religious purists around the whole mess, we can blaze a trail through the swampy territory. We can use our humanness as fuel for the journey. We can humanize spirituality.

The best tools for humanizing spirituality can be found within the body of work we call psychology. The emerging systems of psychotherapy (a term I am using here to include the many schools and theories of psychological healing work) are some of the most hopeful and creative human disciplines to have arisen in our times. Basically (and much more is devoted to this subject in the next chapters), psychotherapy addresses the formation and the transformation of the personality. Psychotherapy helps us uncover the defensive mechanisms of our own mind, body, and emotions, showing us how and why we acquired certain behaviors and belief structures, and ways in which those parts of our personality may no longer serve us. While many, many forms of therapy exist, most psychological schools of thought share the understanding that each individual carries into adulthood aspects of childhood that either serve or retard the maturing process. Going back and reviewing how we formed our basic attitudes helps us identify what parts of our conditioning contribute to our mental health and our spiritual search, and what parts haunt us and obscure our ability to enjoy life and discover peace.

PSYCHE AND SPIRIT:
AN UNNATURAL SEPARATION

It is no coincidence that psychology arose in the late nineteenth century in Europe and the United States. It was then and there that the worth of the individual was gaining ground. Before then there had been little need for a practical science dedicated to helping each person understand how he or she ticked. When one's focus was on survival within an autocracy, then it would be counterproductive to try to understand and fortify the self. Of course, philosophers throughout the ages had pondered the human psyche. Yet unlike medicine or religion, philosophical musings were seen as lofty ideas, reserved for university discourse.

Perhaps the lesson of Socrates being executed for encouraging his students to ponder "What is a 'self'?" sufficiently scared philosophers into their ivory towers. If Socrates could be tried and found guilty for "impiety and corrupting the youth of Athens" just by advocating psychological self-reflection, then it was better to leave the whole business in the hands of religious leaders. And for centuries that is where psychological reflection primarily remained. Human behavior was viewed through the lens of faith in God on the one hand, and surrender to the devil on the other.

With the dawning of the modern era in the seventeenth century, René Descartes and other philosophers broke from tradition and began to conceive of human reason and behavior outside the realm of the Church. Descartes separated human motivation into involuntary and voluntary behaviors. Involuntary behavior linked men to the animal kingdom and was the proper study of physiologists. Voluntary behavior separated man from animal and elevated him to the lofty realm of reason, the domain of philosophy and theology. Descartes's ideas were indeed revolutionary, and yet they were still descriptions of mental structures with little functional value for the common man or woman.

The first psychological laboratory was founded in Germany in 1879, but it was in the United States that psychology was first stressed as a discipline to be used by real people. William James, who rejected many of the early German psychological schools of thought, is often referred to as the father of American psychology. He championed functionalism (also known as pragmatism), a psychological system consistent with the American emphasis on utility as opposed to mere description of mental structures and pathologies. Functionalism was influenced by the American "can do" philosophy, as well as the rising acceptance of Darwin's theory of evolution.

In *The Principles of Psychology,* James's groundbreaking work published in 1890, James turned psychology away from abstract theory in favor of concrete actions that could be measured in terms of their influence on human experience. In his later years James sought to unify psychology, philosophy, and religion, affirming that a belief in God is pragmatically justified if the believer's inner life is changed for the better.

Sigmund Freud was a contemporary of James. He opened the area of medicine to psychological study. A physician and neurologist, Freud borrowed heavily from turn-of-the-century physics. While William James brought his theories to bear on the spiritual search, Freud remained convinced of the need to separate what he considered superstitious religious thinking from any serious psychological healing process. When Romain Rolland, Freud's close friend and a French writer and Nobel laureate, wrote to Freud from India, where he was studying with the Hindu philosopher Vivekananda, Freud rejected Rolland's spiritual musings. Rolland had written of his experience of "something limitless, unbounded—as it were, 'oceanic.' " He shared with Freud his felt sense of being "one with the world," and his belief that this sense emanated from the same source from which religions had sprung. Freud disagreed with Rolland's mystical interpretations. Instead he relegated them to a remnant of the infant's memory of being within the womb. So-called religious, transcendental states of consciousness were merely a regression to infantile states of mind that were primarily motivated by infant sexuality.

Given that Freud was just one of many of the founding visionaries of psychology, it is interesting that his theories were given such primacy, often to the exclusion of those of other thinkers and practitioners. Pioneers in the field of psychology like Carl Jung and Alfred Adler split with Freud over what they perceived as his obsession with the role of sexuality in human behavior. Jung rejected Freud's persistent refusal to grant mythology or religion psychological relevance. William James had earlier warned about separating religion and the study of human behavior, fearing what he called "medical materialism," or the tendency to pathologize—and therefore treat as medical problems—states of mind that may indeed be important dark nights of the soul or transcendental flights of the spirit. James wrote that "medical materialism snuffs out St. Teresa as an hysteric, St. Francis of Assisi as an hereditary degenerate."

Yet despite the complaints of these psychologists and many others, Freud's medical materialism prevailed in most psychological circles. This is one reason why spirituality and psychology have, until very recently, been separated across a huge divide. There are other reasons as well. As the nineteenth century gave way to the twentieth, much was changing that threatened the religious status quo of America. Charles Darwin's theories were challenging commonly held beliefs about the origin of the human species. Feminism, which chiseled at the foundations of the male-dominated Church, was on the rise. And little by little, twentieth-century Western thought became dominated by science to the point where anything that could not be proved by empirical research was viewed as superstitious dogma. Perhaps psychology needed to stand alone in its formative years, separate from religious thought and practice. To become an accepted science it needed to prove itself as one, and that required a complete break from spirituality.

It was in the 1960s that psychological work began to show signs of a reunion with spirituality. "Freudian psychology," wrote Abraham Maslow, a founder in the late 1960s of humanistic psychology, "is largely a psychology of cripples and sick people . . . based upon the study of men at their worst. . . . Under such circumstances, how could it possibly be discovered that man had capabilities higher than . . . the neurotic?" Maslow developed a theory he called the "hierarchy of needs" in human motivations. In his classic book, *Toward a Psychology of Being,* Maslow described the human being as a "wanting animal," who moves from the satisfaction of one desire to another in a progression that actually has a sense and order to it. Maslow observed that individuals he considered to be unusually healthy, psychologically and spiritually speaking, had first satisfied their "lower motivations"—shelter, food, a source of income, etc.—and moved up along the hierarchy of needs to a new motivation—the drive for "self-actualization." He noted that these people shared similar characteristics: the ability to free oneself from stereotypes; the aptitude to perceive everyday life realistically and to accept it without defensiveness; and the responsiveness to frequent "peak experiences" of insight, joy, or intense spiritual awareness.

THE SACRED SELF: INTEGRATING PSYCHOLOGY AND SPIRITUALITY

Maslow was just one of the early pioneers who sought to unite the disciplines of spirituality and psychology. Psychology has now been sufficiently accepted as a science in mainstream culture for many thinkers and practitioners to reconsider its links with spirituality. Reuniting the two disciplines is a boon to the seeker. I love the way Jungian psychologist James Hillman speaks of the need for both psychological and spiritual work: "When we realize that our psychic malaise points to a spiritual hunger beyond what psychology offers and that our spiritual dryness points to a need for psychic waters beyond what spiritual discipline offers, then we are beginning to move both therapy and discipline."

I came by my own understanding of the need for both psychological therapy and spiritual discipline through the crucible of a failing marriage. By the late 1970s my husband and I had been together for close to a decade. We had met in college when I was nineteen. Since then, we had been involved together in spiritual practice—meditation, study, prayer— and assumed that was all anyone needed to strengthen a marriage. The answer to all of our problems—with anger, communication, sex, power— was in the teachings, so what was there to do but study harder, meditate more, rise above the insatiable needs of the ego?

I vaguely understood that the problems we were having were not that unique, and that they probably had something to do with my childhood, and his childhood, as well as repressed emotions and a lot of other pop psychology terms that were beginning to surface in American culture. And yet I was clueless about how to heal wounds that I couldn't even name. The only psychological book that I had read was *The Road Less Traveled,* by M. Scott Peck. It just so happened that Dr. Peck was a friend of a friend, and had not yet reached the world-renowned stature that he has today. My husband and I asked if we could see him for a consultation, assuming that one visit would be enough to fix what was wrong.

At the time we had two very young children; my husband was in a crisis about his career; I was struggling with the almost impossible task of simultaneous mothering and working; and neither of us had looked very closely at our patterns of relationship with the opposite sex. Looking back from my vantage point now, understanding what I do about the delicate and skillful work of unraveling and rebuilding the ego structure, I see the futility in that one session. But the story illustrates an important point: like spiritual wisdom, psychological health is not something you can get quickly through a book or a pill or a shrink. The search for the self is as mysterious and rewarding as the search for God, and as demanding of devotion and patience.

Dr. Peck agreed to see us. He warned us that he did not have time to take us on as patients, that this would not be therapy, but that perhaps one two-hour session might steer us toward a better relationship. So we ventured to Dr. Peck's office, in his beautiful home in Connecticut, where he had struggled and grown wise with his wife of many years. For an hour we talked and he listened patiently to our revelations of betrayal, dissatisfactions, and misunderstandings. He then sent us out into his garden, where we sat for half an hour in the ruinous aftermath of what had been said.

When we went back into the office, he explained that the first part of the session could be seen as the necessary first step of honestly confronting life's problems. Now it was time to deal with them. He then reiterated what I had read in his book. "All relationships are difficult," he said. "Both partners long for the being-in-love stage to go on forever. Women expect a kind of communication from men that is rarely possible." The solution? Resolve our childhood issues and expectations, grow up, and practice disciplined love and acceptance. And that was it. Our two hours with him were up.

That was my introduction to psychotherapy. Of course, we had asked Dr. Peck to do the impossible—to fix us in an hour. He responded in kind. He gave us directions that were meant for people who had already done the long and hard work of self-examination. We left his office stunned but determined to try harder to be good and loving people. What he had said to us made sense. But what *we* had said to each other was what our hearts had really heard. Our first experience with therapy was the tipping point for a marriage that was teetering on the edge of dissolution.

Now, in my second marriage, many years down the road of self-understanding, my husband and I can more readily use Dr. Peck's advice for a loving marriage. Because of the therapeutic work each of us has done, we are familiar with many of our childhood issues and expectations; we have indeed grown up; and we practice a more disciplined and accepting kind of love than either of us was able to do in our first marriages. We have been able to peel away some of "the myths and illusions that have misinformed us": cultural myths about men and women, love and responsibility, repression and expression; and personal illusions forged in childhood about intimacy, sexuality, anger, and passion.

Perhaps one day, when psychological methods have been refined and incorporated into the education process, the spiritual journey will be a balanced blend of psychology, religion, and mysticism. Just as learning to read comes after learning the alphabet, learning about the eternal self will come after learning about the basic, human self. But psychology is a new art and science, and its articulated relationship to spirituality is even newer. Therefore, those of us on the spiritual path today are undoing as we are doing, peeling away the illusions as we discover the truth.

To me, the unique and most positive aspect of the new American spirituality is its emphasis on self-authority. The movement away from a central, hierarchal authority figure to a democracy of individual seekers is the democratizing of spirituality. Democracy is about trusting the authority of one's own beliefs and then voicing those beliefs through the just structures of a democratic system. With democratic spirituality it no longer makes sense for an authority to describe to you the sacred truth and the path to discover it. Now *you* map the journey. And this is where psychology comes in: How do I learn to separate the conflicting urges and identities within myself and establish my own true voice? Which are my real beliefs, and which ones were primarily adopted from my familial and cultural conditioning? What matters most to me? How do I make wise choices? In the next chapters we explore how to blend therapy and spiritual practice into a path all our own.

GENDER AND SELF: GODS AND GODDESSES WITHIN

The motif of the return of the Great Goddess and her consort is encountered over and over again in the dreams and unconscious fantasies of people who seek psychological help to overcome the deadness of their lives. Arts, films, literature, and political upheavals also reflect increasingly the same dynamics. The changes they demand entail new understanding of masculinity and femininity in both men and women and the relations between the sexes as well as new views of reality.
—EDWARD C. WHITMONT

When psychology and spirituality are used in tandem on the spiritual path, sooner or later we are called into the puzzling and productive territory of gender. As we use psychological wisdom to peel away the myths and illusions that have misinformed us, we inevitably confront our place in the world as a man or a woman. So many of our misconstrued notions about our selves are rooted in gender. It helps to explore this territory if we want to uncover our essential, spiritual nature.

It wasn't clear to me when I first set out on the spiritual path how my natural affinity for feminism could be compatible with my interest in spirituality. In fact it seemed that the basic foundations of most traditional spiritual paths were in direct conflict with the women's movement, which I had been a part of in college. When I became a formal student of my spiritual teacher Pir Vilayat, in the 1970s, I moved down a few rungs on the evolutionary ladder, as far as I was concerned as a woman. The leadership of his organization was mostly male, the gender of the prayers was masculine, some of the traditional Islamic practices were segregated, and the subtle and not-so-subtle messages about daily life elevated the male perspective and negated women's ways of seeing the world. Even though the type of spiritual organization I joined was influenced by the "liberated" sixties, the experience remained for me vastly similar to the experiences women have always had within the patriarchal systems of religious institutions.

I use the word *patriarchal* with hesitancy. Its common usage implies a black-and-white situation in which brutal men rule the world and innocent women suffer the consequences. I am more comfortable with another kind of definition: "By patriarchy," writes the Jungian scholar Marion Woodman, "I mean a culture whose driving force is power. Individuals within that culture are driven to seek control over others and themselves in an inhuman desire for perfection."

I often turn to Jungian psychology to better understand issues of gender. Jung separated personalities not so much into male and female, but into unique blends of masculine and feminine qualities, which he believed were found in all human psyches in varying degrees of potency. The masculine principle, or archetype, as Jung called it, celebrates rational thinking, heroic power, goal-oriented achievement, and independence. It is transcendent, visionary, mindful. The feminine principle loves to feel; it compels us to nurture; it links sexuality with relationship; and it reveres life and death as natural cycles of nature. It is embodied, intuitive, heartful.

The feminine is that part of the self that is vulnerable, receptive, open; the part that values connection and communication. It likes to put all the cards on the table and doesn't want to hold back or keep secrets. It is the part that is comfortable right here on earth with all of its pain and messiness, the part that does not want to run away from life or try to change nature's rules. This is the feminine archetype. The masculine archetype sees beyond this life, looks outside of itself, identifies with the eternal, and wants to move ever forward. It plans and negotiates, is reasonable and rational. It is on a mission to achieve, invent, build, make a mark. It is the part of the self that is determined, loyal, judicious, and steady.

A great pair, the feminine and the masculine. A person who cultivates his or her masculine and feminine qualities is able to balance power with love, inventiveness with sustainability, brilliance with wisdom. Of course, most of us are not naturally balanced within ourselves. We usually have more of one archetype than the other, and it usually is true that women are much more heavily endowed with the feminine principle and men with the masculine principle. The point of working to balance our masculine and feminine energies is not to move toward androgyny. It is to become aware of the inner forces at play within each one of us and within the culture. Even as we strive for inner and outer balance, we still can depend on each other to fill in the missing pieces. In fact, the more we value both archetypes, the less pulled each one of us will feel to be "perfect," and the less likely we will be to misunderstand the basic nature of our counterparts. We will be able to stand in for each other as we all grow toward wholeness.

Most of recorded human history is the story of one archetype—the masculine—not merely dominating, but also discounting the values of the other—the feminine. It's particularly ironic to note the suppression of the feminine in religious history, given that the basis for most religions is God's all-embracing inclusion and love of all creation. As the poet Jane Hirshfield says about God's egalitarian spirit, "The numinous does not discriminate . . . infinitude and oneness do not exclude anyone." But indeed, the feminine voice has been excluded in most religious traditions to the point where spiritual myths, images, and structures are primarily masculine. Even more harmful than their mere exclusion, feminine values have also been deemed inferior, even dangerous, in patriarchal cultures. Backed up by our earliest religious myths, from Adam and Eve to Prometheus and Pandora, the message has been insidiously clear: feminine values are manipulative and untrustworthy, bound by the suffering of the earth, controlled by the dark side of the moon, and more related to the animals than to the angels.

It is the masculine principle within humans that is attracted to transcendent spirituality—always moving forward, intent on self-improvement, compelled by the light of truth beyond the horizon. The feminine principle is more at home with the way things already are. Feminine energy moves in a circle, longing to know all by embracing all. In valuing one archetype and rejecting the other, as opposed to enjoying the fruits of the marriage of both, we have denied many people, not just women, their natural way of finding God.

Religions have perpetrated the myth of masculine superiority as much as any social system has; in fact, I think that until we rewrite our spiritual mythology, societal structures will continue to empower men and mistrust women. The first step of the women's movement has been the demanding of equal status for women within the patriarchy. This has been a critically important step. But it has also masked other, equally important steps: the celebration of feminine values in the world; the granting of respect, money, and power to the kind of work that nurtures families, teaches the young, connects communities, and cares for the earth; and the acceptance that while men's and women's wisdom may be different, each is real, precious, and necessary.

It's not enough to say that spirituality transcends gender, even if it ultimately does. Spirituality is the human search for eternal wisdom. It is not the wisdom itself. To humanize spirituality, we must look not only outside of ourselves to the limitless universe, but also inside of our own personhood—the sum total of our gender, our conditioning, our genes, and our unique challenges and gifts. Obviously, then, different people will respond better to different spiritual concepts and techniques. Some people will use their minds most effectively. Others will find it easier to search for God using the physical body or the emotions. Some people, when they think of the ultimate truth, use language and images of light and glory. Others relate to the stark aloofness of the ascetic's search. Still others discover truth right here on earth, inspired by the interconnection of all life and through service to others.

Both genders are capable of tapping into the masculine and feminine wisdom streams. But first we must question the patriarchal obsession with power and control in the culture, and widen the definition of reality to include the feminine principle. To some extent, this has been the role of feminism in our times. When feminism and spirituality combine forces, the feminine face of God will illuminate the path for all of us.

MOTHERHOOD, MIDWIFERY, AND MY OWN AWAKENING

It took a long time and intensive training for me to begin to understand, trust, and embolden my own feminine wisdom. I consider this training as important in my spiritual work as learning to meditate and pray, and as educational as studying the great religious traditions. Men and women raised in a culture that disempowers the feminine archetype are denied wholeness. And spirituality is about becoming whole. To become whole we don't get rid of one thing and replace it with another; we don't now negate masculine values and elevate feminine values. The path to human wholeness is the inner marriage of masculine and feminine values. When each value system is held in equal esteem, when we love and respect both, harmony within the individual, health in the culture, and peace on the planet become attainable.

The feminine is awakened in different people in different ways. The story of my awakening traverses two distinct territories. First I visited childbirth, motherhood, and midwifery—outposts in the territory of the Great Mother. Then I apprenticed with the Wild Woman and learned about power, voice, and leadership. I share my story for what it is—one person's blunders and victories as she sought wholeness.

I became a mother at the ripe old age of twenty-three. I think that part of the brain must go dormant during full-fledged mothering. When you're in the mother zone, the rest of the world becomes fuzzy, while the most mundane priorities become very clear and all-consuming. And if you give an unqualified "yes" to the task, just as a great athlete or a devoted artist or a skilled worker must, then you choose to develop some parts of yourself at the expense of others. I am glad that I gave myself so fully to mothering in my twenties and early thirties. I had to develop qualities that I may not have been able to without the crucible of parenting. I consider these to be my most feminine qualities. Being a mother awoke within me greater compassion, earthiness, fierceness, and patience.

During my mothering years I was also a midwife. I had the chance to work with women and men who wanted to fully participate in the birth of their children. I taught weekly childbirth classes that focused on female anatomy, cycles, and moods. Surrounded by my midwife friends and birthing women, I entered a world that honored the dark womb, the shifting emotions, and the animal noises, smells, and urges of physical creation. I witnessed the courage and power of women in labor and also the sweetness and vulnerability of men in a supportive role.

The world passed me by as I lived in the mother zone by day and the midwife realm by night. I now know that the time I spent with my own babies and with pregnant women and their families was an apprenticeship with the Great Mother, the ancient archetype of feminine spirituality. But as far as the modern world was concerned, I had entered a backwater, an archaic experience of womanhood. Many in the women's movement would have agreed with this. While some women my age were getting their MBAs and entering corporate America, I was learning about the wonders of the female body, and teaching women how to bear down, birth a baby, and breast-feed. I was saving my entry into the conventional work world for later.

Ten years as a mother and midwife deeply changed the way I saw the world. It also eroded my tolerance for our patriarchal culture. Any culture that recognized only man to be the strong, able warrior and reduced woman to the fickle follower was perpetuating a lie. Any power base that silenced the voices of more than 50 percent of its constituency was dubious at best, dangerous at worst. And any individual who, out of fear, ignorance, or arrogance, could not or would not listen to the perspective of another was not deserving of power. We all know this. But it took a total immersion in the female archetype for me to feel strong enough to do something about it. The greatest gift that I received from my days and nights away from the workaday world is a bedrock belief in my own experience of what it means to be human.

The next part of my journey—my apprenticeship with the Wild Woman—took me into territories where the feminine value system was not appreciated. My apprenticeship with the Great Mother had taught me that I didn't need to be like a man to be powerful, courageous, and intelligent. The Wild Woman taught me the difficult lesson of speaking for feminine values in a masculine world. Clarissa Pinkola Estés, author of *Women Who Run with the Wolves,* calls this kind of speaking singing. She writes, " 'To sing' means to use one's soul voice. It means to say on the breath the truth of one's power and one's need." I learned to sing—and am still learning to sing—from my apprenticeship with the Wild Woman.

FEMININE SPIRITUALITY IN
A MASCULINE WORLD

Carol Gilligan, the author and researcher who brings one of the most balanced voices to feminist circles, speaks about how hard it is to represent the feminine in a culture that has always denied its legitimacy. "The gap between what women know through experience and what for years was socially constructed as reality explains why so many women have experienced difficulty in saying what they wanted to say or being listened to or heard, or believing that what they know through experience is true." When your reality is questioned—whether you are a woman or a man whose values differ from patriarchal values—it's hard to stand firm in what you believe. The feminine principle values emotional wisdom: deep feelings of connectedness, compassion, and empathy. Our culture was born out of the minds of the rational men of the Western world. Emotional wisdom, not a forte of rational men, has been at best ignored and mostly disdained as a second-rate, wimpy way of approaching life.

You won't find the language of deep feelings in the primer for patriarchal power. Emotions—both the wise ones and the not-so-wise ones—do not respond well to the patriarchal urges to predict and control. By their nature, emotions are unpredictable, sometimes out of control, and as changeable as the weather. Patriarchal cultures fear emotion. It is no coincidence that cultures with contempt for emotions also treat women and nature as objects to be contained and controlled. An interesting book about this phenomenon is *News of the Universe* by the poet Robert Bly. He uses poetry written over hundreds of years and from a variety of cultures to explore how the Western pride in human reason was elevated over the centuries to exclude other human attributes. When the inclination to be rational and dominating is untempered by the inclination to be intuitive and wild, a serious gap grows between reason-centered human beings and the rest of nature. And when human reason becomes the dominating force, "nature is to be watched, pitied, and taken care of if it behaves," writes Bly. Patriarchal culture then excuses its excesses—war, greed, exploitation—as normal and natural, as the way it just *is*. Bly writes: "We say to ourselves that this *is* true of the human world; yet once more by omission the entire non-human world has been denied consciousness."

It is not only the entire nonhuman world that has been omitted from having its say in our culture. Those humans who are governed by the feminine heart, women and men, have also been left out and denied expression. The keepers of the heart, those beings who are sensitive to the shades and textures of feelings, have been so maligned and misunderstood over centuries of rational dominance that we have few examples to model our own emotional development upon. Much of the art and literature of the modern world reflects a point of view that excludes feminine values. Western culture values control and a stiff upper lip. Our movies lionize the soldier. Our literature keeps its language in check for fear of being branded sentimental or a "woman's novel." What we sometimes dismiss as the ranting of high-strung women or the fantasy of foolish lovers is emotional wisdom leaking out of the patriarchy's seams.

Not all cultures are like ours. I saw a documentary film about the Brazilian rain forest and its native peoples that clearly demonstrates this. A tribe whose habitat of ancient trees and rivers was being destroyed marched to the capital city to protest. They had never before been out of the forest. The men were dressed only in loincloths and ritual face paint. The women were bare chested, wearing skirts made of shaggy bark. The men went up the steps of the enormous stone capital building with their spears and their interpreter. They formed a circle around the Brazilian officials—men wearing suits and carrying briefcases. The women circled the two groups of men. As the men conversed, the women started to cry softly and then raise their voices, until finally they were wailing and yelling. Their cries were fierce. An interpreter yelled to the Brazilian officials what the women were screaming: "You are destroying our world and our children! Stop! You are ignorant! You are evil! Listen to us! We know something that you don't." The native men stopped talking and bowed their heads as the women yelled. The women were speaking—or singing, as Clarissa Pinkola Estés would say—for the heart of the community.

The government officials, trapped within the circle of native men and women, looked about nervously. They wore frozen smiles that mocked the native people. They looked like naughty little boys who had just been caught. I was amazed at the courage of the women and the primacy of their voices, and I was touched by the respect the men showed their tribeswomen. I had nothing to compare the scene with in my own life. I knew what the native women knew, but had never trusted my heart enough to speak out with similar passion and conviction.

Certainly I had wanted to. When I left my ten-year Great Mother apprenticeship and entered the demanding work world of a growing nonprofit organization, my frustration would reach levels where I wanted to stand on a desk and beat my chest and wail. The only woman in power, I would sit in meetings tongue-tied, with no common language for what I knew to be true. If I did try to represent my point of view, my colleagues wouldn't listen. They were more like the nervous and mocking Brazilian officials than the respectful tribesmen. I yearned to speak from the depth of my heart, to educate, to fill in the missing parts of the story—to *sing*. I held back my songs and my tears many times.

Slowly I began to learn how to function in a masculine work environment. I learned things—like how to think more clearly, how to say no, how to plan, and compute, and negotiate—that have helped me in all areas of my life. I am grateful for those skills. But the learning was one-way. I knew that I had a thing or two to teach my male colleagues as well. I was scared to do it. I didn't know how. I didn't even have the words. As I backed up my budget requests with numbers and graphs, I left out equally important information culled from my own experience, intuition, and feelings. When I tried to express these feelings, my lack of confidence and my colleagues' lack of listening made my singing sound like whining. Or, if I used masculine communication to express feminine values, what I said rang untrue. I *felt* and *intuited;* they wanted proof. They *thought* and *calculated;* I wanted depth. They were rational. I was emotional. I thought we were different and could learn from each other. They thought they were right and I should change. They had the power.

My frustration began to turn to rage. For a while I let myself be angry, very angry. I let the Wild Woman have her way. Instead of secretly imagining myself standing on the table and pounding my chest, I exploded in meetings. I yelled and cried and demanded. I did get heard, it was a necessary step for me, but I also lost touch with my "soul voice." I sensed personally how the dynamic of power and powerlessness had spiraled down into hateful frustration throughout history. I understood that my rage would, in the end, be my downfall. It would be my final succumbing to the kind of power-brokering I wanted to avoid.

Was there some way to express feminine values with positive strength? Some way to sing without screaming? Was there a way to take the feminine values I had learned to trust during my Great Mother apprenticeship and combine them with the masculine qualities I was honing at work? Could the Wild Woman and the Cowboys sit down at the table? Was this the "sacred marriage" talked about in the myths, where the gods and goddesses—the masculine and feminine archetypes—meet and mate?

Often it takes someone who has already made the journey to show us our own way. I looked around for models of women and men who were radical examples of the sacred marriage—people who were both powerful and loving, clearheaded and openhearted—and could find very few. Those people who were even *trying* struck me as heroic. They were not perfect, their lives were works in progress, but they were trying to move against the tide in the world and within themselves. They knew that as a culture, we had reached the end of the patriarchal road, and that for the sake of all human and nonhuman beings and the planet itself, they had to find a new way.

I had the good fortune of meeting and studying with several such people whose work is devoted to the sacred marriage: the Jungian analysts and authors Marion Woodman and Maureen Murdock; the poet Robert Bly; the feminist Carol Gilligan; the spiritual teachers Stephen and Ondrea Levine; and the poet Maya Angelou were among the most influential models on my own journey. Meeting Maya Angelou was like being on the receiving end of a feminine thunderbolt of the same magnitude as the native Brazilian women. It was a turning point for me in my ability to speak what I knew to be true.

Maya Angelou's books have been a part of me since I read *I Know Why the Caged Bird Sings* in high school. I heard her speak at a civil rights gathering when I was in college, and although she was just a speck on a faraway platform in front of the Washington Monument, I was overwhelmed by her voice and her bearing. Even at a distance, Maya Angelou was larger than life. Years later, I watched her read her poem "On the Pulse of the Morning" on television at President Bill Clinton's inauguration. Once again, I was struck by her powerful voice and her unusual ability to project that voice from a soft, round place in her body. Surrounded by the leaders of the nation, she, a poet and a black woman, was the authoritative voice of the day. Her imposing figure and her raw emotions elevated and dignified the inauguration ceremony.

Therefore, when she agreed to deliver the keynote address at a conference I was helping to organize in New York City, I looked forward to experiencing her powerful heart at close range. I was also nervous. On the first day of the conference—a cold New York City spring morning—I waited on the curb in Times Square, shivering in my little suit, for a limousine to deliver her to the hotel. The Broadway traffic was heavy and loud in the morning rush. Out of the stream of cars came a long limousine. It pulled up to the curb and the back door opened. I reached in to greet Maya Angelou and she grabbed my hand and shook it warmly. "Welcome, Maya," I stammered.

She continued holding my hand and said in a firm, friendly, and round voice, "Won't you please call me Miss Angelou?"

I was confused and a little put off. "OK," I said. "Welcome, Miss Angelou."

"Do you know why I'd prefer that?" she asked. "Well, did you ever wonder why we say, 'Hello, Miss Bernice,' 'Hello, sister Ruth,' when we greet our sisters and aunts in church? We must dignify our names because in many cases that is all we had." She went on in this way, grasping my hand, pulling me closer into the limousine, telling me a truth that she felt a responsibility to proclaim. She sing-sang a list of names, closing her eyes, calling up the strong ancestral women of her heritage. Some didn't have a last name, she said, only the surname of the slave master. Little white children called them Annie, called them Betsie. "That is why we call ourselves *Miss* Anne, *Miss* Betsie." She was educating me. It didn't matter that we were on a Broadway curb or that she had a speech to deliver.

"I get it," I said.

"Good." She laughed, and got out of the limo. She was very tall, in a flowing dress and red high heels. Miss Angelou took my arm and we marched into the hotel lobby. Inside people walking by stopped in their tracks and came over to her: an African woman who had seen her years ago in Ghana and had never forgotten her; the elevator operator, familiar with her work; a businessman rushing by with a briefcase who just so happened to be carrying one of her books. She held each one's hands and talked softly with the same kind of concentration that she had given me in the limousine. By the time we reached the seventh-floor ballroom she had conversed with a string of admirers.

I sat with her backstage waiting for the cue for her to take the podium. All the while she was asking me about myself. What was the favorite thing I had done with my life? she wanted to know.

I'd never been asked that question, so I let the first thing that popped into my mind be the answer.

"Being a midwife, I guess."

"Did it disturb your soul and call you to grow?"

"Oh, yes," I answered.

"Tell me about it. Tell me about the smells and sounds." She closed her eyes and hunkered down for a story.

Right up to the time of the applause that called her to the stage, I told Miss Angelou about the smells and sounds of laboring women and newborn babies. I recalled the awful hour when I would inevitably be roused from sleep and called onto the empty road, and then into the family's house, hovering with expectation in the blue-black night. The sweet concern of the father, the fierce demands of the mother, the slow descent of the baby against the bones and muscle of the woman's insides. The miracle of birth was repeated once again: the surprising head, the slippery body, the braided cord, the first breath. I kept checking to see if Miss Angelou was really interested in this, my favorite thing. Her amazing face stayed fixed on my words. She was catching them. She was adding them to herself. She had given me a teaching and now she was receiving one back. When she finally was called to speak I was exhilarated and humbled, as if I had just completed a river trip through awesome and dangerous territory.

Miss Angelou went on to deliver a rousing speech. She put her whole body into her words. She was fierce and gentle, funny and deadly serious, outrageous and touching. She moved the crowd like few people I had ever seen. But what struck me most was how she was purposefully moving people away from her words, into their own experience, and then out into the world. She was not using her power to focus on herself. Instead she was weaving a web of inclusiveness while at the same time teaching a lesson.

Later I discovered a new word that perfectly represented what I had seen in the women of the Amazon Indian tribe and experienced in Miss Angelou. The word is *womanist,* coined by Alice Walker in her book *In Search of Our Mother's Gardens:* "Womanist 1. From *womanish* (Opp. of 'girlish,' i.e., frivolous, irresponsible, not serious.) A black feminist or feminist of color. From the black folk expression of mothers to female children, 'You acting womanish,' i.e., like a woman. Usually referring to outrageous, audacious, courageous, or *willful* behavior. Wanting to know more and in greater depth than is considered 'good' for one. Interested in grown-up doings. Acting grown up. Being grown up. Interchangeable with another black folk expression: 'You trying to be grown.' Responsible. In charge. *Serious.*"

TOWARD A SPIRITUALITY OF WHOLENESS

We're going to have to be *serious* to add enough of the feminine into the patriarchy so that what emerges is neither a patriarchy nor a matriarchy, but a human-archy. And not even that. What we need is a being-archy, where all beings are granted mutual respect and where decisions are made with the whole circle of life in mind.

In their book on feminine psychology, *The Goddess Within,* Jennifer Barker Woolger and Roger Woolger speak to the loss of the feminine in the culture: "Jung once described a neurotic person as one-sided, by which he meant someone who overemphasizes one side of his personality to avoid dealing with the other. . . . What is true of individual neurotics is also true of whole cultures. This is where archetypal and feminine thinking converge. They are in agreement that our whole culture—with its endless violence, homeless people on the streets, colossal nuclear arsenals, and global pollution is sick. It is sick because it is out of harmony with itself; it suffers from what the Hopi Indians call *koyaanisqatsi,* which is rendered in English, 'crazy life, life in turmoil, life out of balance.' What is missing is the feminine dimension in our spiritual and psychological lives; that deep mystical sense of the earth and her cycles and of the very cosmos as a living mystery. We have lost our inner connection to that momentous power that used to be called the Great Mother of us all."

And so, empowering the feminine dimension is more than a matter of raising woman's position within the status quo. It is much more upsetting than that. It questions some of the founding myths of the Judeo-Christian worldview and therefore changes our definition of what is real. In allowing the feminine principle to enlarge and change the way we define reality, our very way of life changes.

Recognition of the harm that patriarchy has caused to people and the planet does not mean that men are wrong and women are right; rather it is a call for new organizational forms and for relishing gender differences within a context of equality. We are in the first stages of this difficult process and are already making mistakes: sacrificing the care of children because we haven't figured out how both men and women can work and lead and raise healthy children at the same time, failing to understand that female leadership styles may look different from what we habitually assume "real" leadership looks like, and neglecting to train boys and girls from the earliest age to value and trust their emotional instincts.

It's going to take a long time to rectify hundreds of years of masculine domination within the culture. Some of the work needed is political; some is social; some is personal. And a lot of the work is already being undertaken. At major divinity schools throughout the country women now outnumber men, and their presence is transforming both the curriculum and the culture of American seminaries. Women are making similar inroads in law and medicine, as well as in business, education, psychology, journalism, and the arts. Their participation in large numbers in the institutions that define cultural reality will tip the scales in the direction of wholeness.

But the hardest and the most significant work is going to be the work each one of us does on ourselves, mining the psyche to make conscious our feminine and masculine natures. In a spiritual democracy it is an individual's responsibility to move toward wholeness—to think clearly, to feel fully, to cultivate physical health, and to develop spiritual compassion and peace. If we are whole within ourselves, comfortable with both our feminine and our masculine identities, then we will project that wholeness onto the world. If we are blameful and imbalanced, responding to the world through the lens of an internal split, then the outer victories will ring hollow and will only replace one erroneous ethos with another.

The next chapters map a course through a spirituality of wholeness. Wholeness is not an easy path. It's always easier to address the most familiar parts of our nature. If we are at home in the thinking realm, then meditation will probably attract us as a comfortable spiritual practice. If we are naturally intrigued with our psychological makeup, then the realm of the heart will call. If our body already feels like the soul's home, then we will resonate with the kind of spiritual work that involves movement, sensuality, and nature. It is good to find practices where our soul feels at home. It is a delight. And it is also good to push ourselves into new territory, to take risks and to reach toward wholeness. When we undertake the journey toward wholeness, we need to be on the lookout for that neurotic person that Jung described as one-sided—"someone who overemphasizes one side of his personality to avoid dealing with the other." That person is us.

While it may not be easy, the path of spiritual wholeness ultimately leads to deep happiness and fuller aliveness. Probably the most difficult part of such a path is knowing the difference between superficial dabbling and a well-rounded search. It's important to stay awake to the seductions of spiritual materialism as you read the next chapters. You do not have to do everything. There is no time frame. Move slowly and patiently, with a sense of humor and an attitude of compassion. You can focus for a while on meditation, or on therapy, or on body awareness, and balance things out later with other kinds of techniques and disciplines. In doing so, the sum total of your endeavors will affect each part of the self with the kind of transformation that an exclusive fixation on the body, or the mind, or the emotions, or the soul would never bring.

Book II

The Landscape of the Mind

5 | Mindfulness

Only awareness is at peace with the eternal repetitions that the mind projects.
—RAM DASS

In the course of each day, at home and when we travel, in every season of every year, we witness the ceaseless repetition of weather—rain, sunshine, fog, high clouds, wind, snow. Stormy mornings, dark nights, becalmed afternoons. Cold, rainy spells, blue-sky days, glorious sunsets. Weather rolls in and out, repeating itself in a myriad of combinations, all within the high embrace of the sky.

The mind is like the sky: clear and crisp at one moment, cloud-covered and confused at the next. Full of hopeful thoughts now, despairing of the future later. Angry and agitated, and then kindly, calm. It is a landscape of changing, shifting thoughts. The mind is not our thoughts, just as the sky is not the weather. Mind and sky are both spacious containers for life's continual, creative impulses. If you were to examine your thoughts—really examine them, as they roll across the landscape of your mind—you would begin to notice how repetitious they are, and how you are tricked, over and over, into believing that each new combination of mental stuff is a solid picture of reality. Sit quietly for sixty seconds if you need to be convinced of this, and watch the way your mental weather continually changes.

Just as we would love to be able to control the weather so that it didn't rain on our party, we look for ways to control our thoughts. We take a pill to calm our anxious thoughts, or have a cup of coffee to stimulate creative ones. When clouds of depression blow in, we try to break them up and move them out. Sometimes we work with our mental weather constructively: we go into therapy, change our diet, exercise, work carefully with herbs or medication. Sometimes we are self-destructive and become addicted to anything that will blur our worries, conquer boredom, or cheer us up.

Sometimes it is indeed a wise move to work with the mind's weather through medication, or a glass of wine, or a strong cup of coffee. Sometimes the best medicine is to laugh about our neuroses, or ignore our inner turmoil, or dance around our unhappiness—what I call creative denial. But there is something we can do that is more lasting and trustworthy than all of the above—something that gets to the root of our most stormy mental weather, be it stress, depression, anxiety, or frustration. That something is the ancient practice of meditation.

Meditation does not make things miraculously different. It doesn't give us control over the weather. It doesn't get rid of a stormy mood and replace it with a sunny one. Meditation does something much more subtle and even more magical. It wakes us up and leaves us standing tall in any weather.

WHY MEDITATE?

M. Scott Peck started his famously popular book, *The Road Less Traveled,* with a simple line: "Life is difficult." Almost three million people have purchased the book, which remained on the *New York Times* best-seller list for more than ten years. During those years, my husband and I performed an informal ritual every Sunday: I would turn to the book review section of the *Times,* open it to the best-seller list, and proclaim (with genuine astonishment), "I can't believe it! *The Road Less Traveled* is still on the list." My husband (amused by my astonishment) would feign disbelief, and then reply, "Well, I guess life is still difficult."

Obviously, the opening line appealed to the millions of people who bought *The Road Less Traveled.* They didn't go into a bookstore, open to the first page, read "Life is difficult," and say to themselves, "No, it's not. This guy doesn't know what he's talking about." Rather, they found in that line a kind of comfort. They recognized themselves in those few words. Someone else's life was also difficult. They were not alone.

Life *is* difficult for human beings. Sometimes it seems as if we are half-baked experiments, poorly equipped to function in a world that can look like paradise, but often feel like a wasteland. It's always been like this for humans. We may blame our personal problems or our collective anxiety on modern life, but one need not be a historian to understand that in every time and every culture, life has been difficult. All the way back to the garden of Eden, the earth has been a paradise, and life has been difficult.

In Book I we defined spirituality as the development of a fearless relationship to ourselves and the world around us. An essential step in this process is facing what Buddha called the First Noble Truth: "Life is suffering." This may seem like a morose basis for a religion, but as M. Scott Peck says, after delivering his famous one-liner, "Once we truly know that life is difficult—once we truly understand and accept it—then life is no longer difficult."

Knowing, understanding, and accepting that life is difficult is spiritual work of the tallest order. While we all most certainly have experienced our share of problems, we don't want to accept the inevitability of life's difficulties. We extend a fierce energy in the direction of comfort and safety. In other words, we don't want to embrace the Buddha's First Noble Truth. We want to reject it. We rear up when suffering crosses our path. Accepting suffering seems to go against our instincts, even if we vaguely understand that acceptance is the currency that will procure our freedom.

An ocean of ignorance, misunderstanding, and fear lies between our rejection of suffering and our acceptance of it. Crossing that ocean is the spiritual journey. It leads us from the shore of bewilderment to the shore of understanding, from fear to freedom. We need a boat for this journey—a snug and elegant craft. Meditation is such a boat. Whatever form our life's difficulties take—be it stress, anxiety, grief, pain, confusion, anger, loneliness, or depression—meditation, and the mindful attitude it cultivates, provides a vehicle that will take us to the other shore.

Different people come to meditation for different reasons. And at different times in our lives meditation serves different purposes. But basically, most people are attracted to meditation for these reasons:

> To relax, physically and mentally.
> To let go of the excessive need to control life.
> To accept life on its own terms.

To feel more alive and connected.
To be more content and at peace.
To make contact with other realms of consciousness,
  what some call the divine, or God.

Indeed, meditation can help us achieve all of the above—but slowly, over time, and with dedication and hard work. We come to meditation feeling that our lives are difficult and that perhaps spiritual practice will make them less so. We want relief now. That's not how meditation works. The desire for peace and happiness is noble; the expectation for instant results is unreasonable. Patience is our most cherished companion in the Landscape of the Mind.

Describing meditation is difficult, and it can make one sound like a moron, or a phony, or a shyster. "There's a 2,000-year tradition of finding it impossible to describe," writes Mark Epstein, M.D., a psychiatrist and the author of *Thoughts Without a Thinker,* an excellent book on Buddhist meditation and psychotherapy. The difficulty lies not only in the experiential nature of meditation, but also in the fact that the meditative experience takes us deeper and deeper into realms where language and even thought lose their potency. This is why the great meditation masters have often relied on stories as their major teaching tools.

Perhaps this story, from my own experience, will serve as a good introduction to the practice of meditation. Once, in the midst of a stressful project, tired from the nitpicky work of editing hundreds of workshop descriptions for the Omega catalog, and frustrated by the harder work of dealing with the politics of an organization, I faxed the spiritual teacher Ram Dass his edited workshop description. A long-standing Omega faculty member, Ram Dass was also on Omega's board of directors at the time. He was aware of a contentious struggle within the organization. At the bottom of the fax I scrawled, "Do you think I am retarded? I keep dealing with the same stuff, with the same people, year after year. You'd think I'd make some progress. How is this edit? Please approve or make further suggestions."

He faxed his response later that day: *We all seem retarded—in that we live again and again the phenomenal realities our minds project. Only awareness is at peace with these eternal repetitions. Hang in there and be gentle with yourself. Your rewrite looks great. Thanks.*

I still have that note tacked on my office wall. It catches my attention often, especially the sentence, *Only awareness is at peace with these eternal repetitions.* The starkness and strength of the word *awareness,* balanced by the oceanic rhythm of "at peace with these eternal repetitions," creates a picture in my mind's eye: I am sitting snugly in a small boat, the boat of awareness. Surrounding me is an immensity of water, stretching in all directions. Small ripples, gentle waves, choppy water, enormous crests move the boat, rocking it at one moment, crashing over it at another.

And so it is with my life. The periods of peace or joy come and go, flowing into and out of the times of struggle or sadness. Holding on to the sweetness only makes the bitter feel like a betrayal of some promise that was never made. Rejecting the bitter makes the sweetness seem less sweet, more fleeting. Sitting upright in the sturdy boat of awareness is my only salvation—watching the waves move through my life, instead of believing that each one is the full picture of reality, brings me peace, humor, wisdom. *Only awareness is at peace with these eternal repetitions.* Meditation is a way of promoting this kind of awareness. It is the snug boat—the boat of awareness. It shows us how to avoid getting flustered by the changeable weather of the mind. It gives us tools to access the mind's brilliance, and the patience to yield to its confusion without losing ground.

Meditation helps us "reconcile the unreconcilable," as my Sufi teacher Pir Vilayat used to say. As we practice meditation, we learn to walk the middle path between every one of life's extremes. We actually experience a balanced and flexible state of mind. Our consciousness becomes vast enough to embrace the complexities and contradictions of existence. Things that seemed impossible begin to be very possible: we can withhold judgment even as we develop a keen sense of discernment; we can be soft and open to other people, yet strong and self-possessed; we can be unsure of the final outcome yet brave in the process. The practice of meditation teaches us how to do these things. It sharpens the ability of the mind to stay awake and aware in all kinds of weather.

I love the way Ram Dass ended his note to me: *Hang in there and be gentle with yourself.* This is another essential part of meditation—the cultivation of compassion toward one's self. This chapter focuses on *mindfulness* meditation—the practice of awakening clear, spacious awareness. Chapter Six explores using mindfulness meditation to work with stress, anxiety, and confusion. Chapter Nine adds the dimension of *heartfulness,* the other aspect of meditation practice that Ram Dass is referring to at the end of his note. Heartfulness aims to cultivate compassion and loving-kindness.

When the sharp-edged sword of mindfulness meets the graceful openness of heartfulness, we have an excellent spiritual practice.

MINDFULNESS MEDITATION

Meditation is the centerpiece of the new American spirituality—not a meditation system rooted in any one religious practice, but the pure teachings of mindfulness. Meditation has been around a long time and exists in almost every religious and philosophical tradition. In fact there are so many different forms that one could lose sight of the goal of meditation and dabble endlessly in line at the smorgasbord. So it is best to dig down to the root of all meditation systems, to their one common element. That root element is the direct, personal experience of God, Truth, the Universe, or whatever word is used to describe ultimate reality.

Meditation is a matter of experience. It is not a set of moral values. It is not a definition of the sacred. It is a *way*—a way to be fully present, a way to be genuinely who you are, a way to look deeply at the nature of things, a way to discover the peace you already possess. It does not aim to get rid of anything bad, nor to create anything good. It is an attitude of openness. The term for this attitude is mindfulness.

If you make a study of the world's meditative traditions, you will quickly discover how similar they are. Once you get past the surface words and rituals, the heart of each practice is reassuringly familiar: it's your self, your genuine self. Whether you are in a cave in India chanting a mantra, or in a church deep in prayer, or in your own home, sitting in a chair quietly observing your breath, meditation brings you into direct contact with your own genuine nature. Genuineness is the wisdom stream that is always flowing through you, through others, through the world. Mindfulness meditation is the best way I have found to part the branches, slip down the banks, and float peacefully, relaxed and aware, on that stream.

I have studied a variety of meditative forms. From a Japanese master I learned Zen meditation, and from Tibetan teachers, traditional and ancient Tibetan Buddhist practices. I studied a Christian form of meditation called Centering Prayer, from brothers at a Benedictine monastery. I entered deeply into the meditative practices of the Islamic Sufi tradition, engaging in all-night chanting and whirling sessions with Turkish dervishes.

My fascination with meditation practice brought me all over the world and exposed me to other schools of thought: davenen prayer at the Wailing Wall in Jerusalem, yoga in India, Native American practices in Hopiland.

I have gone through periods when meditation was a relaxed part of my weekly routine, times when I was ruled by a sense of guilt if I didn't meditate twice a day, and times when I never meditated and felt just fine. I once tried to do a monthlong meditation retreat in a little hut high in the New Mexico Rockies, but gave up after one week of discomfort and struggle. Then I *did* do a monthlong retreat at a Buddhist Vipassana meditation center in Massachusetts that was powerful, restful, and enlightening.

One would think that from all of these techniques I would have developed a highly ritualized and complicated meditation practice. But no, my meditation practice is simple. While it is surely informed by all of my study and experiences, I would be mocking the real meaning of meditation if I represented it as an exotic journey. Immersion into so many forms of meditation has led me deeper and deeper into the most essential core of all of them: mindfulness—a nondenominational form of practice that teaches moment-to-moment awareness, a kind of falling in love with naked reality.

TO BE HERE NOW,
OR NOT TO BE HERE NOW

My first introduction to meditation was Zen Buddhism. Like formative childhood experiences, my first forays into meditation in the austere silence of the zendo stuck to my spiritual ribs. When things get tough and I'm tired of my own explanations, I sit down and return to my Zen "roots." And there I am, meditating for the very first time. I can almost smell the same musty Japanese incense, as if a stick lit twenty-five years ago were still burning. I do what I learned to do as a bare beginner: I straighten my back, rest my palms in my lap, and become aware of my breath rising and falling in the belly. I let my thoughts come and go like clouds in the sky.

But I also had another, equally strong influence on my early spiritual journey. I discovered the mystical teachings of Sufism not long after my introduction to Zen meditation. My mind came home at the zendo; my heart found its kin among the Sufis. From my Buddhist teachers I learned a form of meditation that led me into the freshness of pure consciousness, where an open sort of emptiness reigned supreme. From my Sufi teachers I learned to use meditation to connect with God, spiritual guides, and higher planes of consciousness. Pir Vilayat told his students that the purpose of meditation was to "tune into and then remember the divine status of your being, to uphold the dignity with which you have been invested." I was Pir Vilayat's student for more than twenty years; there is no one else whose teachings have affected me more. Yet I am hard-pressed to describe exactly what I learned, and how I learned it. I can give a much more unequivocal explanation of the methods and benefits of Buddhist mindfulness meditation. Mindfulness has served as a powerful compass pointing me in a very clear and simple direction. Sufism, at least the Sufi philosophy and meditation techniques as taught by Pir Vilayat, took me on a cosmic adventure beyond the ordinary modes of perception, and into the grandeur of the universe. Aldous Huxley described this form of meditation as a lamp for the mind: "the lamp by which it finds the way to go beyond itself."

The combined uses of meditation for simply "being here now" and for going on an adventure beyond the self, have served me well. I call these two different meditative themes *mindfulness* meditation and *mystical* meditation. Mindfulness meditation could also be called Beginner's Mind meditation. As described in Chapter Two, Beginner's Mind is the stated goal of Zen meditation and of many other Buddhist meditative traditions. It is described as original sky-mind: the sky before there was weather, the mind before there were thoughts. "If your mind is empty," writes Shunryu Suzuki in his classic manual for meditation, *Zen Mind, Beginner's Mind,* "it is always ready for anything; it is open to everything. In the beginner's mind there are many possibilities, in the expert's mind there are few." Chögyam Trungpa describes mindfulness meditation like this: "By meditation here we mean something very basic and simple that is not tied to any one culture. We're talking about a very basic act: sitting on the ground, assuming a good posture, and developing a sense of our spot, our place on this earth. This is the means of rediscovering ourselves and our basic goodness, the means to tune ourselves to genuine reality, without any expectations or preconceptions. . . . Through the practice of meditation, we can learn to be without deception, to be fully genuine and alive."

Cultivating the fresh open-mindedness of a beginner; becoming genuinely alive in the here and now: these are the promises of mindfulness meditation.

Mindfulness meditation and mystical meditation are not really at odds with each other, yet they are different in form and results. Some people may find mindfulness meditation more to their liking and never want to explore mystical meditation. Others may feel put off by the lack of overt spirituality in mindfulness meditation and long for a more sacred path. Pir Vilayat has spent his life practicing, studying, teaching, and writing about meditation. He is an authority on comparative religion, fluent in five languages, and a serious student of physics, psychology, and music. For all of his expertise in Asian theology and philosophy, he could never relate to the Buddhist goal of empty sky-mind. In fact, he was puzzled by the popularity of one of the best-selling spiritual books of the 1970s, *Be Here Now,* by Ram Dass. Ram Dass introduced a whole generation of seekers to Buddhist concepts. He coined the phrase "be here now"—another way of describing Beginner's Mind.

At one of Omega's first programs Ram Dass joined Pir Vilayat and other spiritual teachers to lead a meditation retreat. I recall a conversation around the dinner table between Ram Dass and Pir Vilayat that I call the "to be here now or not to be here now" debate. In his erudite British accent, Pir Vilayat wondered aloud why anyone would want to only "be here now."

"There are so many glorious planes of existence. The angelic realms are refreshingly different from the one *here,* and they are available to us at all times," he argued. "Why not leave *here,* and go *there*? That's what meditation is for."

"That's not why I meditate," said Ram Dass.

"Well, I meditate to transcend the experiences of pain and separation of the here and now. Why remain in our stale, fossilized state of being, when we could dance in cosmic ecstasy?"

Ram Dass, always ready with an answer, said, "Pain and separation occur when we regret the past or worry about the future. Here and now *is* ecstasy. And about those 'glorious planes of existence'? Those 'angelic realms'? I'm afraid I'm not familiar with them."

Yet meditation has indeed been used throughout the ages to pierce the veil between our ordinary consciousness and the "angelic realms." I was drawn to this landscape and followed Pir Vilayat's directions as best as I

could. I vaguely understood, even remembered, the hosts of angelic beings and mystical places that Pir Vilayat described in his meditations. And
while I don't feel qualified to lead others into the experiences I had as a
student of Pir Vilayat, I am grateful for all those times when I felt overcome with a sense of the sacred, when I bowed in submission to the
grandeur. Book V addresses this aspect of spirituality—mysticism and the
landscape of the soul. The next chapters describe the hows and whys of
mindfulness meditation.

6 · Daily Practice

Our life is an endless journey; it is like a broad highway that extends infinitely into the distance. The practice of meditation provides a vehicle to travel on that road. Our journey consists of constant ups and downs, hope and fear, but it is a good journey. The practice of meditation allows us to experience all the textures of the roadway, which is what the journey is all about.

—CHÖGYAM TRUNGPA

As an acquired habit, mindfulness meditation fosters an exquisite attitude toward the whole of life. It helps us to get through the rough times with more grace. It teaches us to resist attachment to the wonderful times, but to enjoy them fully and with gratitude in the moment. These are the fruits of mindfulness meditation, but the practice part of meditation is like the practice part of anything we want to learn. Meditation practice is like piano scales, basketball drills, ballroom dance class. Practice requires discipline; it can be tedious; it is necessary. After you have practiced enough, you become more skilled at the art form itself. You do not practice to become a great scale player or drill champion. You practice to become a musician or athlete. Likewise, one does not practice meditation to become a great meditator. We meditate to wake up and live, to become skilled at the art of living. And like any art form, the need to practice continues at every level of achievement.

Before I get into the nitty-gritty of actual instruction, I want to address the frequently asked question, "Do I need a teacher to learn how to meditate?" While books and tapes are wonderful introductions to meditation, I believe that they are not as powerful as working with a teacher. A teacher keeps us on track, models behavior, and answers questions along the way. Finding a good teacher is no easy matter, although sometimes we stumble upon exactly the teacher we need without even looking. The topic of teachers, leaders, and therapists is so important, and fraught with so many pitfalls, that I devote a part of Book V to it. There I suggest ways of determining if a teacher is effective, and if he or she is sincerely motivated. I also provide a sort of litmus test for gauging our progress in meditation, in case we don't work with a teacher.

If you are not going to work with a teacher, it is best to choose one specific meditation discipline and adhere to it for a while. Then, once you have a base, you can experiment with other forms, and begin to create a system of your own. The mindfulness meditation instructions in this chapter are excerpted from whole systems. I suggest that if one appeals to you, you read more about that particular system, attend workshops or retreats with qualified leaders, and practice patiently. It takes a while—a couple of years, often—to get used to meditation and to learn what it is really about. But if you stick with it, meditation will yield results. It will make a difference in your life.

In this chapter I give actual instructions in mindfulness meditation, gathered from my own study with several different teachers. In the next chapter I help you apply meditation to the different kinds of stress in your life. And in the last chapter of Book II, I provide a toolbox for dealing with the common resistances and difficulties experienced during meditation. This is an arbitrary separation since the minute you sit down to meditate, you will surely meet with stress, anxiety, resistance, and difficulty. Use these chapters, then, as companions.

Certainly there are many more ways of articulating mindfulness meditation than the few selections I offer here. Yet I feel comfortable recommending only those practices that have worked for me. Some of the instructions offered are in the words of teachers with whom I have studied: Roshi Philip Kapleau, an American Zen teacher; Chögyam Trungpa and Pema Chödrön, Tibetan Buddhist teachers; Thich Nhat Hanh, a Vietnamese Zen teacher; and Jack Kornfield and Jon Kabat-Zinn, American meditation teachers. Some of the instructions are my own and offer a hybrid form of meditation practice. In the context of the new American spirituality, I have combined diverse outlooks and techniques to create a meditation practice geared to my temperament and needs. Please keep in mind as you read and practice that your own path may take you down different roads, into areas not mentioned here. I offer my experience as a guidebook offers suggested excursions, fully expecting the reader to discover his own back roads and special vistas.

There are a few elements common to all of the forms of meditation that I have studied. I use these five elements—*breath, posture, thoughts, time,* and *place*—to provide a template for developing a meditation practice.

BREATH

Most meditation systems use the simple act of breathing in and out as a focus for meditation practice. I have heard many explanations as to why the breath is so universally used in meditation. Some traditions say it's because breathing is the most basic act we do. It connects us to life in an immediate way. While one could go without food for months and without water for days, one can survive only for minutes without breath. Awareness of breathing makes us aware of the precious nature of life; it sweeps away the clutter that gets in the way of a basic appreciation for being alive. Others say that the breath serves as a purifier and has the ability to cleanse our senses and thoughts on a moment-to-moment basis. Zen refers to breath practice as "cleansing the heart-mind." According to many schools of yoga and meditation, breath is the rhythmic mediator between body and mind. Awareness of breath synchronizes the body and mind, one of the great benefits of a meditation practice.

In *Foundations of Tibetan Mysticism,* Lama Govinda writes that breath is "the connecting link between conscious and subconscious, gross-material and fine-material, volitional and non-volitional functions, and therefore the most perfect expression of the nature of all life." For a moment, put down this book to experience the simple power of breath observation. Close your eyes, take a deep breath in and then exhale with an audible sigh. As you breathe out, let your body fully relax. Take a deep breath in, sigh out. Expand as you breathe in, relax as you sigh. Let your breath tell your body what to do. Do this five times, return to normal breathing, and then pick up the book again.

Notice how even a short exercise like this can illustrate how the breath is the "connecting link" between body and mind. The following instructions use the simple act of breathing as the focus for meditation. It is recommended in most meditation systems to breathe through your nose and to fully fill your lungs. Don't force the breath, especially if you experience discomfort or pain. To get the most out of this meditation and the ones that follow in this chapter and the next, you may want to have a friend read the instructions aloud, or make a tape of yourself reading them. If you do read the meditations silently, first read them for content and then use them experientially.

INSTRUCTIONS ON THE BREATH
From Full Catastrophe Living,
by Jon Kabat-Zinn
(To be read slowly to a friend or silently to yourself)

1. Assume a comfortable posture lying on your back or sitting. If you are sitting, keep the spine straight and let your shoulders drop.
2. Close your eyes if it feels comfortable.
3. Bring your attention to your belly, feeling it rise or expand gently on the in-breath and fall or recede on the out-breath.
4. Keep the focus on your breathing, "being with" each in-breath for its full duration and with each out-breath for its full duration, as if you were riding the waves of your own breathing.
5. Every time you notice that your mind has wandered off the breath, notice what it was that took you away and then gently bring your attention back to your belly and the feeling of the breath coming in and out.
6. If your mind wanders away from the breath a thousand times, then your "job" is simply to bring it back to the breath every time, no matter what it becomes preoccupied with.
7. Practice this exercise for fifteen minutes at a convenient time every day, whether you feel like it or not, for one week and see how it feels to incorporate a disciplined meditation practice into your life. Be aware of how it feels to spend some time each day just being with your breath without having to *do* anything.

The "job" of bringing your awareness back to the breath can be facilitated by silently counting each inhalation and exhalation, as described in this next meditation by Thich Nhat Hanh.

INSTRUCTIONS ON COUNTING THE BREATH
From The Miracle of Mindfulness,
by Thich Nhat Hanh
(To be read slowly to a friend or silently to yourself)

Your breath should be light, even, and flowing, like a thin stream of water running through the sand. Your breath should be very quiet, so quiet that a person sitting next to you cannot hear it. Your breathing should flow gracefully, like a river, like a water snake crossing the water, and not like a chain of rugged mountains or the gallop of a horse. To master our breath is to be in control of our bodies and minds. Each time we find ourselves dispersed and find it difficult to gain control of ourselves by different means, the method of watching the breath should always be used.

The instant you sit down to meditate, begin watching your breath. At first breathe normally, gradually letting your breathing slow down until it is quiet, even, and the lengths of the breaths fairly long. From the moment you sit down to the moment your breathing has become deep and silent, be conscious of everything that is happening in yourself. . . .

Making your breath calm and even is called the method of following one's breath. If it seems hard at first, you can substitute the method of counting your breath. As you breathe in, count 1 in your mind, and as you breathe out, count 1. Breath in, count 2. Breath out, count 2. Continue through 10, then return to 1 again. This counting is like a string which attaches your mindfulness to your breath. This exercise is the beginning point in the process of becoming continually conscious of your breath. Without mindfulness, however, you will quickly lose count. When the count is lost, simply return to 1 and keep trying until you can keep the count correctly. Once you can truly focus your attention on the counts, you have reached the point at which you can begin to abandon the counting method and begin to concentrate solely on the breath itself.

POSTURE

When I first met the Tibetan master Chögyam Trungpa, he had recently arrived in the United States from England. He was such a curious mix of cultures, education, and behavior that I found his teaching intriguing and powerful. Here was a man who had spent his youth in the seclusion of an almost medieval monastic tradition, and now was a full-fledged member of the modern world; a man who had led his people over the Himalayas to escape the Communist Chinese, and then become a scholar at Oxford University. Just as he had fully embraced the life of a Tibetan monk, he now took on Western culture with gusto. Wherever he went, whatever he did, he lived with both a mad sort of intensity and a deep sense of stability. Perhaps from the extremes of his own history, he taught meditation as a twofold process: first, as a way to access stability and dignity in the midst of any situation; and second, as a way to wake up, as if from a dream, into vibrant and genuine aliveness.

Trungpa believed that at the core of life was what he called "basic good-ness," and that each one of us was basically good, and more than that, wonderfully noble. One of my all-time favorite lines I heard him say is "You can transcend your embarrassment and take pride in being a human being." Trungpa stressed good posture in sitting meditation practice as a way of demonstrating our basic goodness. He said that keeping a straight back was a way to overcome your embarrassment of being a human being. He often used the image of riding a horse when he taught meditation pos-ture. Sitting tall in the saddle tells the horse that you are the master. Sitting tall on the meditation cushion or in a chair tells your mind and body that you are the master. Sitting upright in the saddle tells the world that you believe in yourself.

Posture in meditation does not refer only to a straight back. Posture in-cludes the whole body. In fact, the body and mind are inseparable in med-itation, and a relaxed and energetic body creates a beneficial base for meditation practice. Trungpa wrote that by working with posture in med-itation "you begin to feel that by simply being on the spot, your life can become workable and even wonderful. You realize that you are capable of sitting like a king or a queen on a throne. The regalness of that situation shows you the dignity that comes from being still and simple."

I still use Trungpa's checklist of six body parts—seat, legs, torso, hands, eyes, mouth—as I sit down and assume a meditative posture. I elaborate here on each point:

1. *Taking your seat:* It is best to sit on a firm pillow on the floor or on a straight-backed, firm-seated chair. If you sit on a pillow, make sure it is high and firm enough so that your knees can rest on the floor. If you sit on a chair, sit forward enough so that your back does not touch the back of the chair.

2. *Placing your legs:* If you sit on a pillow, cross your legs comfortably in front of you on the ground, with your knees resting on the floor if you can. If you sit in a chair, put your feet flat on the floor, knees and feet a few inches apart.

3. *Torso:* Keep your back comfortably straight, your chest open, and your shoulders relaxed. Roshi Philip Kapleau, in *The Three Pillars of Zen,* writes, "If you are accustomed to letting the chest sink, it does require a conscious effort to keep it up in the beginning. When it becomes natural to walk and sit with the chest open, you begin to realize the many benefits of this ideal posture. The lungs are given additional space in which to expand, thus filling and stretching the air sacs. This in turn permits a greater intake of oxygen and washes the bloodstream, which carries away fatigue accumulated in the body."

A straight back and soft shoulders is a natural position. It does not have to feel forced or painful. In fact, after time, meditation breeds a sense of overall comfort. But often when we first start to meditate, assuming a straight back makes us suddenly aware of great discomfort in the body. Chapter Six gives more instructions on how to deal with pain in the back, neck, shoulders, and legs.

For now, understand that the pain you may feel in your body as you meditate is both physical and psychological in nature. If you experience pain, constriction, restlessness, or all of the above, do not be alarmed and do not take the attitude of "no pain, no gain." Adjust your position slowly and mindfully as many times as you want during a meditation session. The point of meditation is to be relaxed and awake. Therefore make sure you are comfortable, and at the same time, sit in a way that keeps you alert.

At a meditation retreat, I heard Thich Nhat Hanh address a question from a man who said he experienced pain in his shoulders and neck the minute he sat down to meditate. Thich Nhat Hanh asked him if he felt that same pain the minute he sat down to watch television. The man said that he did not.

"How do you sit when you watch television?" Thich Nhat Hanh asked.

"I usually sit on the couch with my feet folded under me," said the man. "But after a while I may switch my position and stretch out my legs."

"How long do you watch television?"

"Oh, about an hour."

"Do you stay awake for the whole hour?" asked Thich Nhat Hanh.

"Yes," said the man.

"Well, then," Thich Nhat Hanh suggested, "take that same position when you meditate and make the same adjustments for an hour and see what happens. Later you can see about straightening your back and stilling your body."

As you sit down to meditate, approach the experience lightly so that your body relaxes, just as it would if you were about to slip into a bath or relax before the television. Then, straighten your back, and at the same time soften your shoulders and expand your chest, so that your posture is also one of gentle openness. One of the best ways to maintain a straight back *and* an open heart in meditation is to silently repeat a phrase whenever you feel back or shoulder tension. For example, if you feel your shoulders tensing as you hold your back straight during meditation, you can silently whisper to yourself, "soften, soften," or "let go, let go." The most effective phrase for me is one I learned from Stephen and Ondrea Levine, meditation teachers who have worked with people suffering from illness and dealing with death. They teach "soft belly" meditation, which I include in Chapter Ten. "Soft belly" meditation directs the breath to the stomach and pelvic area, places where we hold a lot of tension. Allowing your belly to let go, after years of sucking it in, naturally relaxes other parts of your body, even as you maintain a straight back. When I feel my body tense during a meditation session, I silently repeat "soft belly, soft belly."

A straight back, open heart, and soft belly will help your meditation practice immeasurably. A straight back will lead to dignity and courage. An open chest will nurture acceptance of life on its own terms. A soft belly will remind you to go easy on yourself, to treat your meditation practice as a gift instead of a chore.

4. *Hands:* Sometimes, when meditation gets very quiet, our concentration coagulates in the hands. It sounds strange, but you may experience this yourself. It's not uncommon as your exhalation dissolves outward to feel as if all that is left of your body is your hands. Therefore, it is good to position your hands in such a way that is both grounding and meaningful. You will notice in statues from a variety of religious traditions that the deities or saints hold their hands in interesting postures. These hand positions are called mudras in the Tantric Buddhist tradition—physical gestures that help evoke certain states of mind.

One frequently seen position is the forefinger lightly touching the thumb and the other three fingers flexed outward. Another common hand mudra is one hand resting in the palm of the other, the thumbs touching. Many people like to meditate with their hands in the common Christian prayer position. Some people meditate with their hands simply resting, palms down or up, on their knees. Some mudras get pretty intricate, as you can see if you visit a museum with Asian art.

Each mudra evokes a specific quality that you can experience yourself merely by experimenting with different hand positions. For example, resting the palms upward on the knees indicates receptivity, an openness to whatever comes your way. Hands placed downward on the knees produces a grounded feeling in the body, a sense of balance and strength. The traditional Zen mudra is an extremely balancing one to assume. It requires you to hold your elbows up and out, and to place your hands—one palm resting in the other with your thumbs touching—a few inches below the belly button, resting on the body. Then you focus your attention on the energy center that your hands are circling—the *hara,* as Zen Buddhists call it.

My personal favorite hand position is where the thumb and pointer finger touch and create a circle. There is something about the thumb touching the finger that reminds me to be on the spot in my concentration, yet delicately so. I gently extend the other three fingers and rest my hands on my knees. This position keeps me steady and balanced. I attach the words "on the spot" to the mudra and use both the position of my hands and the intention of the mudra to bring my wandering mind back to meditation. I usually use this mudra in meditation, but sometimes I use others. It's a good idea to stick with one position for your hands per meditation session, so as not to get distracted by playing the switching-mudra game. It's very easy to turn anything into yet another way not to do the simple work of meditation.

At the end of a meditation session, many traditions suggest raising the hands palm to palm and bowing. This is a way to indicate to yourself respect and gratitude for having meditated. It is also a way to experience a sense of humility as you bow to the universal forces of wisdom and compassion.

5. *Eyes:* Some meditation traditions recommend closing the eyes during meditation, others suggest keeping them open and directing the gaze slightly downward four to six feet in front of you, and focusing on a point on the floor. Some suggest keeping a soft, unfocused gaze. I meditate with my eyes closed. You can experiment and see which way affords you the best concentration and wakefulness. If you find that closing your eyes makes you sleepy, keep them open. If you find that keeping your eyes open is distracting, close them.

6. *Mouth:* We hold a lot of tension in the jaw. Let your jaw drop right now. Open your mouth wide, stick your tongue out, and then close your mouth. Take your hands and massage your jaw area from your ears to your chin. Notice the difference? You can do this often during the day as a way to release tension. During meditation it is not unusual for tension to gather in the jaw. Thich Nhat Hanh recommends smiling slightly during meditation, a great way to keep the jaw soft. Or, you can drop your jaw and open your mouth several times during meditation.

THOUGHTS

Breath, posture, placement of hands, eyes open or shut: all of these techniques form the container for meditation practice. But none of them eradicate the absurd amount and the aggravating intensity of the thoughts that flood the landscape of the mind when we sit down to meditate. Please expect this. Good thoughts, bad thoughts, pleasurable ones, disturbing ones—they will come and go as we sit in meditation, watching our breath, maintaining our posture. They are the weather of the mind. Our goal in meditation is not to get rid of thoughts. Rather, the goal is to abandon identifying with each thought as it comes and goes; to watch the thoughts as we would watch the weather from an observation tower.

Returning to the breath and returning to posture help us make our way back to the observation tower. Many traditions, both Eastern and Western, recommend the use of a sacred sound—called a mantra in the Hindu tradition—to quiet the thought process. The vibrations in the body have a calming effect and the meaning of the words serve as a reminder. Some systems of meditation advise the practitioner to bypass thinking altogether by directing the focus to different "energy centers" in the body. These are called chakras in Hindu terminology. A very good and very simple way to deal with intrusive thoughts is to label them, as taught here by Chögyam Trungpa:

INSTRUCTIONS ON LABELING THE THOUGHTS
From **Shambhala: The Sacred Path of the Warrior,**
by Chögyam Trungpa

As you sit with a good posture, you pay attention to your breath. When you breathe, you are utterly there, properly there. You go out with the out-breath, your breath dissolves, and then the in-breath happens naturally. Then you go out again. So there is a constant going out with the out-breath. As you breathe out, you dissolve, you diffuse. Then your in-breath occurs naturally; you don't have to follow it in. You simply come back to your posture, and you are ready for another out-breath. Go out and dissolve: tshoo; then come back to your posture; then tshoo, and come back to your posture.

Then there will be an inevitable *bing!*—thought. At that point, you say, "thinking." You don't say it out loud; you say it mentally: "thinking." Labeling your thoughts gives you tremendous leverage to come back to your breath. When one thought takes you away completely from what you are actually doing—when you do not even realize that you are on the cushion, but in your mind you are in San Francisco or New York City—you say "thinking," and you bring yourself back to the breath.

It doesn't really matter what thoughts you have. In the sitting practice of meditation, whether you have monstrous thoughts or benevolent thoughts, all of them are regarded purely as thinking. They are neither virtuous nor sinful. . . . No thought deserves a gold medal or a reprimand. Just label your thoughts "thinking," then go back to your breath. "Thinking," back to the breath; "thinking," back to the breath.

TIME

People often ask how many times a day one should meditate, and for how long. This is a difficult question to answer. If you want to jog to stay in shape, your daily exercise regime will be quite different from someone who is preparing for a marathon. If you are meditating to calm your daily anxiety and become more clearheaded at work, then your practice will differ from someone who wants to "know God's thoughts," as Einstein described the goal of his meditations. Someone whose passion is to awaken a fearless and transcendent attitude toward life and death may want to engage in long meditation retreats and to seek the guidance of a teacher. Someone whose goal is to handle stress with more grace may be satisfied to develop a less intensive practice.

A daily twenty-minute meditation practice is the most frequently recommended time period for anyone who wants to benefit from meditation. Many traditions suggest forty-five. If lack of time is an issue, it is better to meditate for ten minutes—even five—than not to meditate at all. It is usually suggested that you meditate in the morning because you are fresh and alert. But you can meditate any time of day. It's good to establish a routine time to meditate, as well as a routine place. When you sit down to meditate, commit to a certain amount of time, set a timer, or check your watch or clock, and then put any thought of time out of your mind. Allow the issue of time to be one less thing you have to think about.

You don't have to get rigid about any of this. Missing a few days, being flexible about the amount of time, catching a five-minute meditation on the subway or while waiting at the doctor's office—this is your practice. Look at it this way: to give over ten or twenty or forty-five minutes of your day to silence and concentration is one of the kindest gifts you can give yourself.

Longer periods of meditation, including meditation retreats that can last for a week or for as long as several months, become invaluable to the serious meditation student. Not only does being in the company of other practitioners boost your own practice, but the intensity of a retreat can encourage you to continue at home on a regular basis. One of the best aspects of a retreat is the opportunity to be in silence, something that we are not used to and may even fear. The Irish mystic John O'Donahue says, "Silence is a great friend of the soul. The soul adores silence." After a few days of resting the mouth, silence becomes delicious, and a great boon to concentration.

Ultimately, the point of any meditation practice is to do it as well and as long as it takes so that the meditative attitude becomes a natural response to everyday life. I have gone through periods on my journey when I adhered to a strict practice of meditation and exercises given to me by different teachers. I know that I benefited from that kind of commitment to a daily practice. These days I meditate often, although not on a daily basis. I do stop naturally, many, many times during my day, and reconnect with my breath as a way of slowing down and tuning in. Sometimes, when my heart fills with joy, I direct my breath there, and offer a prayer of thanksgiving. I don't think about doing this. Years of meditation practice have habitualized a way of being that brings me more peace, a sharper mind, and a grateful heart. I naturally use my breath as a way of detaching from emotions that are dragging me down familiar dark roads or to clear the path and proceed with more clarity.

PLACE

If you have the space in your house, it is lovely to have a meditation room, a sacred space, reserved only for meditation and prayer. This kind of a sanctuary, where you can shut the door to the rest of the world, offers immeasurable support to a meditation practice. But it is certainly not necessary to have a meditation room. You can meditate anywhere that is relatively quiet and removed from the activity of your home. Even reserving a corner of a room where you place your cushion or chair for regular meditation is helpful. Of course it is best to be able to shut a door so that the sounds of the telephone, doorbell, children, or pets won't distract you. The *purpose* of meditation is to achieve a state of equilibrium within the distractions of daily life, but the *process* of meditation is one that feeds on silence and stability. Therefore, try to meditate in the same place each day and try to make that place free of distractions and noise.

I have set up an altar in a corner of my writing room where I keep pictures and objects that inspire me. My meditation cushion sits in front of the altar and calls to me each time I enter the room. The altar and pillow remind me daily to enter sacred time and space. They support my practice.

CREATING YOUR OWN PRACTICE

The meditation practices I have offered are gates into a more peaceful, expansive reality. Depending on my mood, or a problem I'm wrestling with, or an intuitive hunch, I'll enter into meditation through one or another of my favorite gates—either a mantra that finds itself on my lips, or a breath technique, or a certain way of placing my hands. I have on my altar prayer beads from different traditions, photographs of my teachers, sacred objects from around the world, and bits and pieces from nature that inspire me. One of these might call to me and inform the way I begin a meditation session.

I recommend immersing yourself fully in one or two traditional practices for a couple of years before you start fashioning a hybrid system for yourself. Any of the ones I have mentioned, or others like Transcendental Meditation (TM), Centering Prayer, Yoga-based meditation, mantra meditation, or techniques that can be found in the mystical schools of Islam, Judaism, and Christianity, are all tried-and-true meditation systems.

The following exercise is a hybrid meditation practice that I created from my own experiences. It could be good for you. I repeat it here mostly to illustrate how one can weave together into an integrated whole a variety of practices from different traditions.

MY MEDITATION INSTRUCTIONS

Find a quiet spot, hopefully the kind of place described above, where you will be undisturbed for twenty minutes, without hearing the telephone, or doorbell, or the sounds of your household.

Sit quietly, in an upright position, either in a chair or on the floor on a firm meditation pillow. Let your hands find a comfortable and meaningful mudra. As you choose your mudra, feel directly into the position of your hands and attach to their position a gentle meaningfulness and a word to go along with it, like "balanced," or "receptive," or "on the spot." Now, check your posture. Remember that a straight back should not be strained or uncomfortable. A straight carriage is a way of acknowledging your dignity as a human being. At the same time, your shoulders should be soft, your rib cage open. This allows for the breath to flow smoothly, and for the tension in the neck and back to lessen. It opens the heart to the world.

Take several breaths in through your nose and out through your nose as you check your posture. I go through a mental checklist as I check my posture, based on the posture teachings I have already described. First I check my back, and as I straighten I am reminded of my nobility; next, I say to myself, "soft belly," which by now automatically reminds me to deeply relax; last, I smile for just a brief second, to relax my jaw and to recall Thich Nhat Hanh's advice that "a smile makes you master of yourself."

There is no need to perfect your posture or mudra right now. You can come back to them over and over in your meditation, gently straightening your back, relaxing your shoulders, adjusting your hands. If you attach to those adjustments words of encouragement ("noble human," "on the spot," "open heart," "soft belly," etc.) then each time you gently return to your posture or your hands you will get a boost of help.

After your spot on the ground or chair is established, your back is straight, and your hands are resting in their mudra, close your eyes and bring your attention to the breath. First take a deep breath and release it with a sigh. Do this several times and really get into the sound and the sensations as you sigh. "The breath can remind us that ten or twenty feet below the agitated surface of the ocean there is calmness," writes Jon Kabat-Zinn. Go below the surface as you sigh, all the way to the calm depths.

Now allow yourself to come back to normal breathing. Observe yourself breathing. Follow your in-breath down all the way to the belly, and then release it, gently and fully. Follow the exhalation all the way out of the body and into the space beyond your body. Rest gently for a second in this spacious awareness. Then, breathe in again. I once heard Pema Chödrön give these instructions at a meditation retreat: "As each breath goes out and dissolves, you have the chance to die to all that has gone before and to relax instead of panic."

Do not deliberately breathe deeper or longer. Merely observe the passage of your breath in through the nose, into the body, and then out again. It can be helpful to focus the point of inhalation and exhalation on a specific spot in the body. Sometimes my breath focus is as follows: I breathe in through the heart center, in the middle of my rib cage, reminding myself to soften and expand. I hold the in-breath for a second in the well of the heart and then exhale, dissolving slowly out through the crown of my head, into the spaciousness beyond the human form. I relax into the dissolution, without panic, and then return to the in-breath, to myself as a human being. Breathing in through the heart helps me to open to the human condition just as it is. It is a way of washing myself of tension, the kind of tension that builds because of my refusal to accept life on its own terms. Breathing in through the heart releases my resistance to reality. It is a breath of forgiveness toward myself, toward others, and toward life itself.

Dissolving the out-breath through the top of my head reminds me to relate not only to my humanness but also to my eternal, mysterious, and unformed nature. Out beyond the confines of mind and body is pure consciousness. I focus my out-breath through the top of my head to access this purity.

This is the concentration part of my practice. During most sittings my concentration is disrupted by thoughts and body sensations. If these thoughts and sensations overtake me, I return to the concentration on the breath, the posture, and the hands, over and over. At other times my concentration evaporates into the space beyond the exhalation, and I rest fully in that spacious awareness. I loosen the identification of myself as an individual who is breathing in and out, and come home to a sense of belonging to the universe.

GOALS

Maintaining a meditation practice first requires having personal goals. Anyone who has tried to master an art or a sport knows well about the relationship between goals and practice. Here, I am talking about the kind of goals and practice that we form as willing adults. The difference between being forced to practice the piano because of a parent's dream, and playing because of one's own inner urge to make music, is the difference between rote drudgery and a steady, joyful practice. In the former, you practice the piano because you have to. In the latter, you practice out of longing and love. Perhaps you have heard a great pianist play and it inspires you. Or maybe you want to embody the emotions expressed by your favorite composer. Because of what you love, you want to make music yourself—proficiently, beautifully, and in a style that expresses your own creativity. These are the goals that you hold in front of you. They keep you on track, inspire you to continue.

As you practice, your goals may become more and more like the horizon: alluring, yet ever in the distance. It doesn't matter if your goals are pie-in-the-sky—if you practice your jump shot so that one day you may fly like Michael Jordan, or if you sing in the local choir so that you'll be good enough to do backup for Aretha Franklin. It's enough to know that magic is possible for a human being. "If someone else can do it, so might I," you think. It's this kind of hope that keeps you going, even as you surrender to the more realistic boundaries of your own capacity. As you practice, your commonplace goals and your grand, unattainable goals become your traveling companions. Later on in the journey, you notice that you are indeed reaching some of your goals, and still finding inspiration to continue from the others.

It's like this with meditation too. You may hold before yourself the image of the Buddha who sat for forty days and nights, unwavering in his quest for enlightenment. Or Moses on the mountain, determined to hear the voice of God; Jesus upholding the message of love; Joan of Arc steadfast in her faith; Mother Teresa answering over and over an improbable call. Your goals may be as lofty as "I want to understand the workings of the universe," or "I want to free myself from the fear of death." And your motivation may also be more ordinary: "I want to be happy," or "I want to become more relaxed at letting things go," or "I want to be less rattled by the stresses of everyday life." Goals can change as we progress, but we must have goals, and more important, they must come from within.

Goals that do not arise from within can indeed spur us on and eventually even turn into our own cherished ideals, but usually they lead us astray. In the name of religion many have pursued goals that were not their own—impossible moral standards, self-punishing belief systems, all kinds of "shoulds" and "shouldn'ts." Following goals that do not come from an inner passion can be a wounding experience. Being told that one is bad and that only through prayer and penance will the kingdom of heaven be attained is *not* a healthy spiritual goal. In the name of religious "shoulds," many have inflicted harm on themselves and the world. Feeling an inner pull, or wanting to transform self-defeating behavior, or being curious about the nature of reality is very different from being told what you should do.

How is having goals consistent with being here now? This is the kind of question that the Zen Buddhists call a koan, a sort of unanswerable question whose answer is synonymous with enlightenment. It's the kind of question that must have been asked long ago to the monks modeling for those fat, laughing Buddha statues. Yet while the answer may be a chuckle, the question itself is very important.

If the purpose of meditation is to accept the way things already are, then how do we justify any striving at all? When I was involved in Zen meditation I was very confused by this dilemma. The concept of reaching "enlightenment" is a big part of Zen Buddhism. But so is nonstriving. So, which is it? Striving toward enlightenment? Or doing away with all striving so that enlightenment has a chance? The answer, and this is the answer to many of the Zen koans, is both. I eventually came up with a slogan that put the question to rest for me: "Not either-or, but both, and more." Yes, there is a different way of being that is free, contented, awake. This is what the Zen Buddhists call enlightenment. Yes, we must work to achieve this state of being. And yes, the kind of work that it takes to reach enlightenment looks like a passionate form of doing nothing. So we do both: we are rigorous, yet relaxed; disciplined, yet free. Not either-or, but both, and more. The more part is the mystery that cannot be explained, but can only be experienced. Emily Dickinson gives us a close approximation: "Instead of getting to heaven at last, we're going all along."

It's very important to let your goals rest gently in your mind. Otherwise they have a way of turning into yet another version of the "shoulds." Think of them as fireflies on a dark summer night. Follow them with the same kind of dancing humor that you would the light of a firefly. This way you will avoid the sanctimoniousness and guilt that can plague spiritual practice. And always make sure that your goals are your own, and that they spring from a healthy, loving place.

The best way to do this is to ask yourself, each time you sit down to meditate, "Why am I meditating?" Remind yourself of your innermost goals. You can even say them aloud to yourself, or write them down and place them on your altar table, or find a quote that expresses them well and keep it tacked above your work space. For years I was led by one of my favorite lines from a poem by Jelaluddin Rumi:

Let yourself be silently drawn, by the stronger pull of what you really love.

That worked for me for a long time, as did Trungpa's "Through the practice of meditation we can learn to be without deception, to be fully genuine and alive."

Then, when I was going through a prolonged period of anxiety and unhappiness, I switched to a prayer from the Christian mystic Dame Julian of Norwich:

All shall be well,
and all shall be well,
and all manner of things
shall be well.

"Let go into the mystery," Van Morrison's excellent advice for all seasons of life, has often been my stated goal as I sit down to meditate. I've kept Albert Einstein's brilliant words on my altar, "No problem can be solved from the same consciousness that created it," to blow my mind, and Pythagoras' "Astonishing! Everything is Intelligent!" to wake it up. I use these beautiful sayings to remind me of the purpose of meditation. I make sure each sitting session has a goal that comes from within.

Thich Nhat Hanh's Four Pebbles Meditation uses four stones to remind the meditator of four goals of mindfulness: freshness, stability, clarity, and freedom. He suggests to his students that they find four little stones and invest each one with a different quality: one is the flower stone, for freshness; one is the mountain stone, for solidness, stability; one is the water stone, for clarity, like the reflection in a still, calm pool; and the last is the space stone, for the freedom of limitless space. Thich Nhat Hanh tells his students to carry the stones in a little, pocket-sized pouch. At any point during the day one can take out a stone, hold it in the palm, and reflect on a particular goal of mindfulness.

Having goals that emerge from an inner longing does not mean that practice will always be easy. Practice is practice. Sometimes it will feel like drudgery; sometimes it will awaken painful thoughts or feelings or physical sensations; but always, if our practice arises from a deeply personal goal, it will be a dependable, exceptional friend that will eventually lead us home.

7 | Stress

There is no need to struggle to be free; the absence of struggle is in itself freedom.
—CHÖGYAM TRUNGPA

Many of us will come to meditation to deal with stress, and the anxiety, worry, or depression that often accompany stressful situations. On its own, stress is benign. It is the natural unfolding of life—karma, or the law of cause and effect. Take on a new job and your amount of work increases. Have a baby and your amount of sleep decreases. Fall in love and you're in a relationship. Fall out of love and you're lonely. Buy a house, take a trip, quit your job, accept a promotion—everything we do causes stress, physically, mentally, emotionally. No matter how careful we are, stress happens. We all make mistakes, get hurt, fall ill, lose people we love. Really, one could account for all of the stress in our lives by saying, "Become a human being and take on stress."

Stress is; anxiety doesn't have to be. The problem is that for most of us, anxiety, worry, and depression take on a life of their own. We can tell ourselves over and over that stress is a natural part of life, or that we're making a mountain out of a molehill, but we just can't seem to break the pattern of stress leading to anxiety, which then leads to worry, or anger, or depression. This is where regular meditation practice, done patiently and with a sense of lively commitment, really begins to show positive results.

Meditation helps us separate the fact of stress from our anxious reactions to it.

The most common reaction to a stressful situation is the attempt to control it. Sometimes this works. Sometimes it's even necessary. If your briefcase falls open on a crowded street, it's a good idea to rush about gathering your lost papers. But most of the time when we try to control things, we're wasting our time. We're blocking the very energy flow that could be our best ally. Think right now about the stress in your life causing you the most pain and anxiety: Is it your boss's demanding personality? The seemingly never-ending tasks on the job? The fact that your child is going through a rough period? Is it that your parents are ill? Or your marriage is in trouble?

None of these stressors are like the open briefcase in the street. You cannot fix them right away by running around and gathering up the pieces. The papers are already on the wind, out of hand, out of control. They've landed in the river and are flowing downstream.

When we meditate we stretch out on the river, we relax on our backs, and move with the flow. We don't fight the contents of our lives; rather, we discover a freedom that encompasses the whole dynamic river. We observe ourselves and all others—the phenomenal world itself—from that vantage point of freedom. We do this not by fighting, not by forcing, but by freely being in the world just as it is. "Do you know what astonished me most in the world?" Napoleon asked at the end of his life. "The inability of force to create anything. In the long run, the sword is always beaten by spirit." This from a man who spent his life fighting, forcing, and never giving in.

"We can stop struggling with what occurs and see its true face without calling it the enemy," writes Pema Chödrön in a beautiful book about stress titled *When Things Fall Apart*. She says, "It helps to remember that our practice is not about accomplishing anything—not about winning or losing—but about ceasing to struggle and relaxing as it is. That is what we are doing when we sit down to meditate. That attitude spreads into the rest of our lives."

I want to say here that serious anxiety and depression are not to be taken lightly. Meditation and spiritual practice alone cannot necessarily help those who suffer from chronic, debilitating anxiety and depression. I know people who practiced meditation diligently for years and whose pessimism and nervousness continued to dominate their experience of living.

I also know people who were able to awaken from their misery by combining mindfulness practice with therapy, and sometimes with medication. If you have chronic anxiety, panic attacks, or crippling depression you should still pursue meditation. But you may need to combine it with other methods to interrupt the cycle and make real progress.

For those whose lives have been thrown off course by stress to the extent that they suffer from serious anxiety and depression (as well as from acute physical pain, heart disease, or other stress-induced illnesses), I recommend attending a program that combines medical treatment and meditation. Being around others who share your own brand of suffering, in the presence of a skilled practitioner, is tremendously helpful. In groundbreaking studies done at the Stress Reduction Clinic at the University of Massachusetts Medical Center, clinical psychologist Jon Kabat-Zinn led intensive mindfulness meditation programs for people who suffered from stress-related anxiety and pain. He found that "both anxiety and depression dropped markedly in virtually every person in the study. So did the frequency and severity of their panic attacks. The three-month follow-up showed that they maintained their improvements after completion of the program."

FOUR KINDS OF STRESS

Stress has been around since the big bang, but never before in human history have individuals had so much of it. The pace of modern life is faster, the content unusually full, and the texture varied and changeable. The need to balance and juggle a variety of skills, people, places, and situations often feels daunting. It's an exciting time to be alive, but also a taxing one. The amount of stress-related illnesses—like heart disease, hypertension, and sleep disorders—has been steadily climbing. Obsessive-compulsive disorders, eating disorders, attention deficit disorders, and hyperactivity are common. Studies show that women in their forties and fifties are now experiencing memory loss at unprecedented rates due to the increased amount of data they must process and store.

At the same time, we have nearly forgotten how to slow down and experience life's simple pleasures. Working long hours, rushing home, and pursuing entertainment come more naturally to us than communing with each other around the dinner table or taking a quiet walk in the neighborhood. We're almost addicted to stress. We seek out action, friction, and motion and avoid "doing nothing." For this reason, meditation can be particularly difficult for Americans. To focus with calm awareness on the breath; to relax the body; to find within clarity, stability, and equanimity— these have not been wildly popular American pursuits. In fact, we resist this kind of nondramatic nonactivity.

The word "stress" has become a catchall term for the pressures of daily life, large and small, as well as our reactions to them. That's a lot of meaning for one word to handle. In learning how to use meditation to deal with stress, I divide it into these four categories: *choice-based* stress, or the kind of stress we can consciously choose to eliminate; *unavoidable* stress, or the kind that is innate and therefore out of our control; *reactive* stress, which stems from the ways in which we react to both choice-based and unavoidable stress; and *time* stress, a deep-seated, very human anxiety about the passing of time.

CHOICE-BASED STRESS

Sociologist Barbara Ehrenreich notes that in times of war, ratings for American television news shows rise dramatically, and then fall off the minute the crisis is over. More than that, she writes, "We are unnerved by peace and seem to find it boring." At the root of choice-based stress are our misgivings about peace and our addiction to activity and things. One of the best social commentaries I have heard on choice-based stress is from the stand-up comedian George Carlin. His rap on "stuff," in which he describes the process of filling his home with so many items that he must keep moving to bigger houses and renting more space in storage units, is hilariously apt.

Choice-based stress is not a popular subject in stress literature because it quickly leaves the domain of health care or spirituality or psychology and enters the politically incorrect waters of "values." If you look closely and honestly at the most stressful situations in your life, you will see that some of them fall clearly into the category of choice-based stress, while some are clearly unavoidable. For instance, a family member—your parent or child or mate—becomes ill. This is clearly an unavoidable stress. We all must deal with sick kids, or aging parents, or friends and lovers who need us. This is an unavoidable fact of life. But what about that additional work project you recently took on to pay for the rising costs of living? You would have more time to give to yourself and your family if you came home earlier or didn't have to work once at home. Do you really need that income? Could you make do with less "stuff"?

When we look deeply at the stresses we could choose to walk away from, we are forced to ask questions about our personal values and the values of our society. It may sound simplistic, but I believe it is just plain simple: many of us have too much stress in our lives. You can meditate as much as you like, but meditation alone will not bring peace of mind. If you have a family, a home, a high-pressured job, community commitments, and an active social life, there's a high probability that your life would benefit from some degree of simplification. As helpful as a spiritual outlook or meditation practice can be, it's not enough for those overwhelmed by stress to merely learn how to face it well. It may be time for you to make difficult value judgments about the content and speed of your life.

When my children were all in the height of their teenage years I began to experience a kind of anxiety I had never known before. I was worrying more than I used to, having trouble sleeping, and feeling irritated most of the time. At first I chalked it up to the normal angst parents have when their children suddenly transform themselves from cute kids into sullen aliens who drive cars and stay out late. But as the years went on and my health began to suffer (muscle spasms in my neck, constant low-grade intestinal problems, headaches), I realized that I had to do something. My oldest son was eighteen, my middle was fifteen, and my youngest was fourteen. Six more long years of teen mania stretched in front of me. Deep inside, I knew that it had to be more than my children's growing up that was causing such stress in my body and mind. I had always enjoyed each stage of my kids' development, no matter how maddening or worrisome. Something else was going on here.

And so, in a haphazard sort of way, I made an inventory of my life. I began to deconstruct the content of each day and by doing so, I discovered that I was attempting the impossible. I had three sons and a husband. I wanted to be there for them and to enjoy our life together. Especially in the teen years, when parental involvement is so difficult, yet so critical, I wanted to have time for my boys. I wanted enough creative energy to make our home one that nurtured their bodies and souls. But I also had a full-time job and a demanding one at that. I was in a leadership role at a large, growing organization. Deadlines, budgets, staff issues: I brought these concerns home with me. On top of all of this, I was beginning to write magazine articles for some extra money. Their deadlines constantly loomed over me.

One of those articles caught the attention of a book editor and suddenly I was also writing a book. Perhaps to an outsider, my overextended life was obviously undoable. Yet to me it seemed normal. Most of my friends were in similar situations. Our late-night phone conversations sounded as if we were calling each other from the front lines of a war. We compared notes about our kids, our jobs, our health. We tried to help each other out. We gave each other support even as we colluded in maintaining a group trance of unworkable stress.

I can name the hour and the day when I suddenly woke up from the trance and decided that something had to give. I was driving home from the airport. It was autumn, 9 P.M., two days before Halloween. I had been at a board of directors meeting where my own role within Omega was being discussed. I had spent most of the weekend feeling angry, mistreated, tired. I was tired of being the only woman in power; tired of having to defend my point of view over and over; tired of dividing my life into a zillion different segments. Driving through the dark night at seventy miles per hour, all I wanted to do was go home and sleep. I wasn't looking forward to reentering family life. I just wanted to be left alone. Ahh, that sounded so good. Just as I was forming the thought, I saw something coming toward my car. Out of the darkness, rushing through the night, was the face of a deer. For a split second that felt more like several minutes, I wondered what was going on. Was I imagining things? And then the windshield shattered, the deer's antlers came through the glass, and I lost control of the car.

Minutes later, at the side of the road, I realized what had happened. But during the swirling, glass-shattering moments, as my car miraculously swerved through the heavy traffic on the thruway, I left normal consciousness and felt only an overwhelming sense of composure and peace. I let go of control for those seconds. I put down the awful burden of my overextended life and I floated, totally out of control. I will never forget those moments. Their memory served me well over the next year as I gave up my leadership position at work, trained others to take over many of my tasks, and walked away from the role that had defined my life for fifteen years.

My fateful meeting with the buck killed the animal and totaled my car. On the outside, my body was only bruised and scratched; on the inside my psyche was deeply altered. In my meditations, and in conversations with friends and helpers, I used the imagery of the accident to shed light on the nature of the different stresses in my life. I decided to use the experience as a gift in the form of a warning. I was grateful that the warning I had received hadn't killed me, though sorry that it had killed the deer. I was grateful that I was ready to listen to the accident's messages, grateful that I could use them to make meaningful changes in my life.

I have heard other people speak of their heart attacks or the loss of a relationship or other traumatic events as wake-up calls to make important changes. May I recommend, however, that you analyze the stress in your life before it turns into an illness or accident. This type of analysis brings you up against your self-image, your expectations, your relationships, your fears. As you look clearly at the content of your daily life, you may discover that you are using your high-stress lifestyle to put off making an important decision. You may find that you are afraid to slow down because then you'd have to feel some long-buried pain. Sometimes the only way to let go of "the bone of worry" is to "feel the original pain through and through," writes psychiatrist Edward Hallowell in *Worry.* It's difficult to access deep feelings without slowing down. By constantly running toward something, you may actually be running away from something much more important.

In Book III, "The Landscape of the Heart," we question why we load so much "stuff" into each day. We use mindfulness as a base, and turn to psychology to gain perspective on what we really want. By combining the inner listening skills gained through meditation with the self-knowledge gained through therapy, we can courageously and gracefully make important value-based decisions that will actually eliminate some of the stress in our lives.

UNAVOIDABLE STRESS

But what can we do with the unavoidable stress, the stress that is just part of living, the "death and taxes" kind of stress? Loss, illness, aging; relationships, family, environment: these are obvious stressors over which we have little control. We couldn't give up this kind of stress even if we tried. Unavoidable stress also includes the stress that comes when we consciously choose a challenging job, or have children, or buy a house, or pursue a talent. We don't have to take these on, but they bring meaning to our lives, even as they breed tense moments, ongoing worries, and real responsibilities. There's a difference between excessive activity and an interesting, rich life. The point is not to get rid of so much stress that we become bored and boring. The point is to find our own unique balance and then to learn how to handle the "full catastrophe."

In one of the best books written on stress, *Full Catastrophe Living,* author Jon Kabat-Zinn says, "For me, facing the full catastrophe means finding and coming to terms with what is most human in ourselves. There is not one person on the planet who does not have his or her own version of the full catastrophe. *Catastrophe* here does not mean disaster. Rather it means the poignant enormity of our life experience. It includes crises and disasters but also all the little things that go wrong and that add up. The phrase reminds us that life is always in flux, that everything we think is permanent is actually only temporary and constantly changing. This includes our ideas, our opinions, our relationships, our jobs, our possessions, our creations, our bodies, everything."

It is with the unavoidable kind of stress, the "full catastrophe" of human existence, that meditation can work its wonders. Kabat-Zinn says that "the major avenue available to us as individuals for handling stress effectively is to *understand* what we are going through. We can best do this by cultivating our ability to perceive our experience in its full context. . . . So it can be particularly helpful to keep in mind from moment to moment that it is not so much the stressors in our lives but how we see them and what we do with them that determines how much we are at their mercy. If we can change the way we see, we can change the way we respond." Meditation changes the way we see and therefore respond to the unavoidable stress in life. There are other ways to change the way we see as well. I have created a top-ten list of practical, daily ways to deal with unavoidable stress.

TEN WAYS TO DEAL WITH UNAVOIDABLE STRESS

1. Meditate for twenty minutes. Do this every day or at least a few times a week.
2. When you feel stress creeping up on you, take short meditative "time-outs," even ones that last for a few seconds. Take a deep breath in, and exhale slowly. If there's no one around, sigh. Check your posture, relax your jaw, drop your shoulders, and slowly breathe in and out again. Return again to your inner dignity and peace.

3. Keep mindfulness reminders around you: little quotes tacked on the wall; objects that express spaciousness, or peace, or clarity; pictures of people who inspire you to open your heart and quiet your mind.

4. Walk a little more slowly, a little more mindfully, as you move about during your day.

5. When you are driving, be aware of your breath and your thoughts. Use your time in the car to concentrate fully on driving. If you're stuck in traffic or late for an appointment, use the time to let go of control and accept where you are. Be mindful of your reactions to other drivers. Say, "anger, anger" instead of leaning on the horn; take in a breath of kindness and release a sigh instead of shouting, "You jerk!" to the guy who cuts you off.

6. Don't rush to answer the phone when it first rings. Pretend it's a church bell, ringing to remind you to relax. Soften your belly, relax your jaw, and smile gently. Then answer the phone in a more mindful way.

7. When you don't know what to say or what to do, don't panic. Take a deep breath and slow down. Welcome Beginner's Mind into your muddled mind. If you feel intimidated or jeopardized at work, you can take a long and conscious breath, straighten your shoulders, and say, "I don't know, I'll get back to you on that." If you're alone, you can lighten up for a moment and give yourself a break. You don't have to know everything. You don't have to be perfect.

8. When you feel a sense of dread, or panic, or anxiety, slow down, breathe quietly, and locate the tension in your body. Where do you feel it? Place your hand there and gently pat yourself, as if you were calming a child.

9. Energize your body—move around, take a walk, exercise.

10. Check out if your unavoidable stress is really unavoidable. Take a curious, fearless glance within. Listen deeply, give your feelings room to express themselves, and wait patiently for the truth to be revealed.

REACTIVE STRESS

It's easy intellectually to accept that some stress is unavoidable, out of our control; it's less easy, but certainly doable, to get rid of some of the choice-based stress in our lives. Our most difficult task is to master our reaction to stress. Reactive stress is the way in which the mind takes hold of stress and warps it into anxiety, worry, frustration, anger, or depression. Meditation is custom-made for reactive stress. When we meditate we get to see the difference between a particular situation and our reaction to it. We begin to strip the benign *fact* of stress from the irrational judgments, worries, and anxiety that we attach to it.

To understand how meditation works with reactive stress, it is helpful to understand the physiology of stress in the brain and the body. Research done in stress clinics by doctors like Herbert Benson, of the Harvard Medical School, and Jon Kabat-Zinn, at the University of Massachusetts Medical Center, sheds fascinating light on how stress affects physical health and emotional well-being. I recommend that anyone, from the normally uptight to the seriously overwrought, learn more about the physiology of stress in the body and mind. This kind of understanding lends support to a meditation practice. Benson's book *The Relaxation Response* and Kabat-Zinn's book *Full Catastrophe Living* are excellent, highly readable primers, as are many others in the mind-body genre, including the groundbreaking *Emotional Intelligence,* by Daniel Goleman.

I discuss the physiology of stress in Book IV, "The Landscape of the Body." For now, it is sufficient to know that the body/mind interaction is so seamless and powerful that reactive stress naturally spills over into physical health. So learning how to deal effectively with reactive stress can not only bring us peace of mind, it can also help us heal pain and illness. Likewise, learning how to care for and relax the body can help us with anxiety and depression. Diet and exercise are often the simplest and most effective anti-anxiety agents we can use.

I want to mention another way to handle stress—less of a practice and more of a philosophy. When we find ourselves reacting to a stressful situation—coming out of a meeting with a headache, yelling at our child when she spills her juice, feeling our heart race and our muscles tense when we receive bad news—we can greet our reactions as messages from reality. Instead of trying to change our reactions, we can welcome them as news about ourselves. We can stop for a minute and fully experience the symptoms of stress. "The way of mindfulness is to accept ourselves right now, as we are, symptoms or no symptoms, pain or no pain, fear or no fear," says Jon Kabat-Zinn. "Instead of rejecting our experience as undesirable, we ask, 'What is this symptom saying, what is it telling me about my body and my mind right now?' We allow ourselves, for a moment at least, to go right into the full-blown feeling of the symptom. This takes a certain amount of courage, especially if the symptom involves pain or a chronic illness, or fear of death."

We can break through a ceaseless cycle of worry by remembering that everything that comes our way is workable if we greet life mindfully, moment by moment. "Everything that occurs is not only usable and workable but it is actually the path itself. We can use everything that happens to us as the means for waking up," says Pema Chödrön. I know that it's easier for some of us to do this. Some people's life situations are just plain harder than others'. Some people's constitutions are so fragile that it seems as if they're too sensitive for this world. While I am a world-class worrier, I know that my affliction is nothing compared with the crippling anxiety that many people face. Mindfulness philosophy usually can get me past anxiety's tape loop. It has been my greatest friend in times of trouble and change. But I have also seen it work for people dealing with more serious challenges, tragedies, and obstacles.

A dear friend of mine who already suffered from extreme sensitivity and anxiety lost his seven-year-old daughter in a terrible car accident. Unable to deal with the loss, and with his feelings that he had neglected to protect his beloved daughter, he turned to alcohol. After two years of destructive living and heavy drinking, he ended up in a treatment center that used the philosophy of Alcoholics Anonymous in its daily meetings and groups. I visited him a few days before he was about to leave the center. He was scared about reentering daily life, of getting a job, keeping a job, and being around people who might not understand his problems. He said that the only thing that helped him to deal with his sometimes crushing anxiety was to repeat the AA slogan, "One day at a time," over and over to himself, as a form of prayerful meditation.

I asked him what "One day at a time" meant to him. He explained that the past was over—he had already done what he had done. He had lost his daughter. He had started to drink. He had stopped working and functioning in the world. That was done. That was the past. No need to dwell on it because it was over. The future seemed frightening: How would he resist the urge to drink? What kind of work would he be able to find? Where would he live? How would he find supportive friends? Worrying about these unknown, yet-to-occur events served no purpose. They paralyzed his ability to move forward. So what was left? Only the "now," he said. Only this one day, this one step, this one breath.

As he began to notice that he was fine in the "now" moment, he also began to trust that he would be fine in the next one. This had a profound effect on his life. He slowly started to repair his inner world and take successful steps to work and live again.

"One day at a time" is the backbone of the AA movement, one of America's most successful nondenominational, home-grown spiritual paths. It has enabled millions of people to deal with addiction, find solace and strength, and create spiritual community. At its core is the practice of mindfulness as expressed by that most American mantra, "One day at a time." If it can work for people in as much inner turmoil as my friend, it can work for all of us.

TIME STRESS

The secret in life is enjoying the passage of time.
—RICHIE HAVENS

At the root of most anxiety is the passing of time. The inevitability of change, aging, and death grabs at different people in different ways. Some fear the body's aging; some fear dying itself; some fear not living fully. All of these fears produce an underlying anxiety, whether or not we are aware of its root cause. And we do different things to deal with this anxiety. We fight it, we deny it, we bemoan it, we hate it. Whatever we do, time pays us no heed. It marches onward at a clip that seems to quicken as we age. There should be one of those warning stickers in our date books, like the one on the passenger's side-view mirror: *Warning: Dates in calendar are closer than they appear.*

Meditation and the mindful attitude it cultivates are powerful antidotes to the fear of the passing of time. Through them we become more aware of time being dependent on our own consciousness. Consider this: time seems to exist as a constant, and yet, depending on our state of mind, time can slowly drag its feet or it can race ahead of us. A child wants time to pass quickly. She anxiously awaits her next birthday party, longing for the future. The child's mother crams so much into a day that time whirls around her with no beginning or end. She would like to catch a few moments of time just for herself. This woman's father, the little girl's grandfather, feels as if his granddaughter's birthday parties are strung together like days in a week. He wants time to slow itself, to widen the spaces between spring and summer, autumn and winter. They sit together blowing balloons for the party, sharing the same moment, yet perceiving it quite differently. Is time a constant? Is it a figment of our perspective?

A friend of mine with whom I had worked for years recently switched jobs, left her community, moved across the country, and settled in Seattle. Now, instead of working at a spiritual retreat center, she was writing advertising copy for a cutting-edge computer company. She wrote to me about the radical difference in her daily life—how she rose early, downed some coffee, and spent long days in witty repartee with young, smart people, all of whom had been hired to think big and write fast. She was in a new world and it was exhilarating. "Life isn't short," she wrote me. "They were wrong. Life is long. There's plenty of time for everything."

I shared this startling revelation with another friend of mine, the mother of a young child who also works as a nurse-practitioner at a busy medical office. Her response was "There may be time for everything, but there's no time to experience it." Like most parents, this one's attention was divided from morning to night among a multitude of seemingly insatiable demands.

"Life may be long, but it sure goes fast," I wrote to my friend in Seattle. I was struggling to make sense of the awe-inspiring departure of my sons, who were growing up, leaving home, and becoming men. How could this have happened? I would muse on a daily basis. How could my little boys have morphed overnight into men? Suddenly I had time to reflect on my whirlwind years as a mother. It felt as if I were viewing selected vignettes roughly edited together into a movie about someone else's life. Meanwhile, my friend the mother and nurse was wondering if she would make it through another endless day of early rising, packing lunches, driving her daughter from this to that, caretaking her patients, shopping for groceries, cooking dinner, reading a good-night book, cleaning the house, and catching a conversation with her husband before dropping into bed. Out in Seattle, our mutual friend was probably wearing a little black dress and laughing merrily with her new friends at an art opening, trying to decide whether to go home and enjoy a long bath or to take in a late movie.

Through the practice of mindfulness we learn to stop for brief periods in the midst of our day, whether the texture of our current life is choppy, or steady, or crowded, or lonesome. During that time we observe our relationship with time. Do we want it to speed up, so that we will escape the boredom or pain of the moment? Do we long for the past, when things seemed better, fuller, happier? Or do we fret about the passing of time and the lost opportunities along the way? Whatever our relationship to time, during meditation we suspend our time anxiety long enough to sink deeply into the present moment. We rest gently in the rich expanse of now. We observe the way the mind fights against the steady tide of time.

This kind of practice has a curious effect. One might think that sitting alone in the empty stillness might isolate us from others. But instead, it links us with the world. One might think that by living in the present moment we lose touch with the connections of the past, that we must dwell in our memories in order to preserve meaningfulness. But this is not so. "For a life in the past cannot be shared with the present," writes Alan Lightman in *Einstein's Dreams,* a beautiful book about time. "Each person who gets stuck in time gets stuck alone."

Like it does with all aspects of our lives, meditation puts us in reality about time. We begin to accept that here on planet earth, time seems to march forward, dragging us all on a predictable path toward aging and death. We make peace with that reality. And yet at the same time we become aware of the ways in which the human mind interprets reality in erroneous ways. We sense how our *perception* of time and the *reality* of time may indeed be different. We stay open to this possibility even as we accept the rules of what appears to be a fixed causal world. We begin to live in between two realities: the one our minds believe is so, and the one that whispers to us when our minds are deeply quiet.

8 ░ A Mindfulness Toolbox

We do not see things as they are. We see them as we are.
—THE TALMUD

In the last two chapters, you explored the practice of meditation. You took your seat in the saddle, sat up tall and dignified, and rode off into the wide horizon of mindfulness. In this chapter, you take your seat, sit up tall, and learn what to do when you meet obstacles on the path. By obstacles I do not mean your relationships with people unsympathetic to your interests, or the fact that you don't have the right kind of sitting cushion, or that you live too far away from a Zen center. Since the path of mindfulness is within you, the real obstacles to your practice are within you as well. Therefore, you are both the one who wants to meditate, and the one who gets tired and doubtful and restless the minute you take your seat.

This chapter introduces you to the part of yourself who wants to sabotage mindfulness meditation. There is a name for this character—there are many names, actually, from a variety of traditions. I like to use the name *false ego* when referring to the saboteur who gets in your way as you try to settle down, expand your sense of self, and merge with the way things are. The false ego contrives all sorts of obstacles to get in your way. This chapter gives you tools to get out of the way.

When you meditate you are like Copernicus: you announce that the universe does not revolve around you. You tell your false ego that it is part of something much bigger—bigger than it can even conceive. You tell the truth, and the false ego doesn't like it. Like the Church authorities in Copernicus' times, the ego feels threatened and meets the truth with all sorts of resistances. A rule of thumb for the meditator is that 99 percent of the resistance experienced in meditation is the false ego's attempts to derail the process of entering a more spacious reality. These attempts have been called "foes" in Buddhist traditions and "demons" in mystical Christian traditions. Foes and demons can appear as physical impediments to meditation, like pain in the knees and back, sleepiness, or restlessness. Or they can be more subtle. The foes often appear as free-floating cravings, anger, and fear. They masquerade as boredom, self-judgment, and doubt. They can be as pervasive as our speeded-up, no-time-for-anything lives. They can be as profound as the fear of peace itself.

Albert Einstein said that "no problem can be solved from the same consciousness that created it." The problems created by the false ego cannot be changed by the same aggressive, self-referential strategies we habitually employ when faced with something we don't like. When the foes of meditation arise in our practice—as pain in the body, or restlessness, or doubt—we must meet them with a different kind of consciousness. If we meet pain with struggle, the pain will persist. If we meet restlessness with motion, the restlessness will return. If we meet doubt with arguments, we'll only strengthen our doubts.

So, what do we do when the foes attack our mindfulness practice? We don't attack back. We get out of the way. We step aside to create room for a different consciousness. We discover a consciousness so spacious that problems meet their own solutions and we remain in peace. Solving a problem by discovering a new kind of consciousness is revolutionary. It's akin to the way civil rights activists met angry resistance with loving nonresistance; it's like the famous photograph of the student protester placing a flower in the barrel of a gun. This is the way we meet the foes in meditation. We don't fight back, but we don't disappear. Whatever arises in our practice, we get out of the way and let a new consciousness take over.

Before we explore the most common foes of meditation practice, I want to mention a rather tricky hindrance to practice that pretends to be a friend, but is really just another foe: thinking that just because you read about it or talk about it, you are actually practicing meditation. I was reminded of this foe when I took my mother to visit a doctor shortly after the death of my father. Her chronic digestive problems had become worse. I was in the examining room with my mother when the doctor wondered aloud if perhaps her illness was exacerbated by stress.

"Yes, I could believe that," my mother said.

"Do you know how to consciously relax? To meditate?" asked the doctor.

"Yes, I've read about it. I even took a class once."

Then the doctor said, "You know, sometimes really intelligent people confuse knowing how to do something with actually doing it." My mother laughed. She knew what he was talking about.

Meditation is experience. Instructions, manuals, and inspirational books and tapes are all good and helpful. But they are not meditation itself. The daily act of sitting, breathing, and practicing the art of mindful awareness is a solitary undertaking. Simply put, you just do it.

Please do not be surprised by the ferocity and creativity of the foes. The foes will match in strength the false ego's fear of losing control. We will meet them as soon as we sit down to meditate. And please remember that the purpose of meditation practice is to experience a freedom and fearlessness that can be translated into daily life. The foes that confront us as we sit in meditation will reappear in different forms when we get up and walk into the world. Therefore, the same strategies we learn to use in meditation can be used in real-life situations.

THE FALSE EGO

As soon as we enter the Landscape of the Mind, we smack firmly into our own ego. Right inside the gates of mindfulness meditation, ego awaits us—suspicious, defensive, afraid. We come to meditation looking for peace, or for the ability to concentrate, or for solace, or wisdom. We sit quietly, following the instructions of those veterans who have already traveled the road. Perhaps we think that after a few deep breaths we'll follow the leader straight to heaven or enlightenment, and we'll be free at last—free from anxiety, from confusion, from unhappiness. This is not what happens. Heaven does exist. Enlightenment is a worthy destination. But the ego, like a stubborn child, resists the journey. The ego does not want to quiet down, let go, and awaken into a new reality.

In fact, our egos don't want to know about any reality save the one that focuses on ego itself. Ego does not want to wake up. It does not want to become fully conscious. I once saw a bumper sticker that read, "Consciousness: That annoying time between naps." That's ego's message. "Don't wake me up," ego demands. "Don't question my take on reality. Don't make me change anything." But it is ego's limited vision of reality that keeps us anxious, confused, unhappy. Its fearful, self-preserving mode of behavior confines us in a cage of delusion. The ego's delusion is that each one of us is a separate and finite entity that must fight for self-preservation. Therefore, ego takes a me-against-the-world stance. It tells us that we are at risk, even when we're not, and we believe it. We are like the trapped wild animal accustomed to its cage and afraid of freedom.

There are many variations on the definition of ego from a host of brain scientists, psychologists, philosophers, and religious thinkers. Some get very technical or intellectual or dogmatic. But we don't have to have a Ph.D. to understand the underlying structure of the ego. I like to think of my ego as the psychic equivalent of gravity. Gravity is a force that attracts objects in the universe. Here on earth, gravity is the force responsible for attracting and preserving matter in a form that we call life. Without it, the stuff of life—water and air and soil and rocks—would change their form. Things would come apart; the earth would not exist as a separate entity in the universe.

The gravitational balance that allows life to flourish on earth is a mysterious and awesome phenomenon. From Aristotle to Galileo, and from Newton to Einstein, physical gravity has been the one force in the universe most puzzled over, studied, and theorized. It's easy to imagine what would happen if the force of gravity suddenly became too weak or too strong: we'd spin out into space, like an astronaut cut off from the mother ship; or we'd be crushed along with everything else into a solid, heavy mass.

Your ego is a form of gravity. It holds you together in a pattern that you consider to be yourself. It gives you a sense of self as separate and solid. Psychic gravity—the ego—is poised in the same delicate balance as physical gravity. When the ego's force is too strong it dominates reality, forcing us into a confined, heavy sense of self. We all know what this feels like. Ego's excessive pressure can be experienced as an overidentification with our individuality—a sense of self-importance or of isolation. Conversely, a weak ego is felt as a fearful state of helplessness, no boundaries, a lack of a center. Too much ego identification is no better nor worse than too little. Both are forms of imbalance. To deal with ego imbalance some schools of thought—especially religious traditions—have developed theories that recommend "getting rid of" the ego, as if that were possible! The ego, like gravity, isn't something we're for or against. It's not something we want to get rid of when we're having a bad day.

On the other hand, some systems of psychology overstate the need for a strong, individuated ego. Much of the objectionable self-obsession that has become the hallmark of our overtherapized age can be traced to over-fortified egos. It's better to view the ego as a vehicle given us to navigate life's journey, rather than something to be annihilated on the one hand, or exalted on the other. If we approach its imbalances with patience, under-standing, and compassion, ego becomes another wondrous force of nature. In meditation we witness ego's energy, going this way and that, and in doing so gently harness its power to serve us on our journey. We have no judgments toward the ego when we meditate. We observe the ego, we feel its gravitational pull, and we loosen our solid identification with it.

The British psychoanalyst D. W. Winnicott uses the phrase "imposed coherence" to describe ego's natural effort to hold the self together. "Med-itation," says Buddhist psychiatrist and author Mark Epstein, "is exactly the refusal to impose coherence on yourself. It's about sitting in the chaos." No wonder meditation is often difficult. No wonder we resist it. Meditation, or any spiritual practice that questions the ego's supremacy, can feel as impossible as escaping gravity. But it's not impossible, espe-cially if we give ourselves a break when the going gets tough.

The best way to deal with ego is to get to know it well enough to un-derstand when it is serving you and when it is leading you astray. Sufi phi-losophy identifies two parts of the ego: the false ego, called the *nafs,* and the healthy ego, called the wisdom-mind. The false ego goes far beyond the call of duty in "imposing coherence" in our lives. It overreacts and overprotects, blindly hanging on for dear life, even when letting go would serve life better.

The healthy ego knows when to hold on and when to let go; it has dis-tinct boundaries, as well as a respect for the ways in which all things and all beings are interconnected. Jungian psychology calls a healthy ego an "individuated" self, stressing the difference between egocentricity and in-dividuality. In Chapter Nine we explore pathways that nourish the healthy ego. In this chapter we discuss loosening the grip of the false ego. As you use meditation to still the false ego, don't forget that you also want to en-liven the healthy ego. I cannot stress this enough. Many people mistakenly assume that the purpose of meditation is to bypass the ego altogether.

Even if this were a possibility, it would not be a good idea. Indeed, it can be dangerous.

"You can't be nobody until you are somebody," I once heard a meditation teacher say as a warning about working with the ego. It reminded me of a joke: A rabbi and a priest are praying in the holy city of Jerusalem. Overcome with God's presence, the rabbi falls to his knees and cries out, "Oh, Lord! You are great; I am nobody." The priest, inspired by the rabbi's prayer, falls to his knees and cries, "God, I am nobody!" A street sweeper hears their utterances, stops sweeping, and he too falls to the ground, crying, "God, I am nobody!" The rabbi and the priest look back at the street sweeper and then at each other. "Look who thinks he's nobody," says the rabbi.

We are each somebody and nobody. Spiritual work honors both. Meditation addresses the part of us who is "nobody," who is free, unlimited, spacious, eternal. Psychological and emotional work address the part of us who is "somebody." As "somebody," we go to work, pay the bills, have relationships. We deal with illness, stress, and loss. In moments of enlightened thinking we may understand that there really is no distinction between our "nobodiness" and our "somebodiness." But usually the two feel quite distinct. Our goal should be to unite them—not to deny either one—because we won't get very far if we enter into holy warfare with our own minds.

It does no good to pretend that you are only "nobody"—that everything is an illusion, that only God is real—when you most certainly are somebody in daily life. And it also betrays the truth to deny that there is another, less confined way of being beyond the sphere of ego's gravity. Jung believed that the combined use of psychological and spiritual processes led to the unity of these previously contradictory forces. He called the unified state the Self, with a capital *S*. "When the Self makes its impressive presence felt," writes Eugene Pascal, in *Jung to Live By,* "we cease being as a captive of the petty, hypersensitive, personal sphere of the ego, and rather feel as though we have somehow acquired a freer, broader, more circumspective and more objective view of life." The Self does not negate the ego; it includes it into an expanded, more objective view of our own life and of life itself.

My favorite aspect of the new American spirituality is the respect it gives to both our humanness and our divinity. It instructs us to include our ego as we transcend it. Instead of placing an overlay of "shoulds" on top of the false ego, or trying to banish it altogether, we look squarely at the sum total of who we are. We gather together all the parts of the self and love them into unity. Even the overreactive false ego, the *nafs,* receives our loving awareness.

So the question becomes, how do I lovingly observe the very part of myself that resists my longing for peace and happiness? First of all, one must learn to recognize the *nafs,* and to distinguish it from the healthy part of the ego. This is a crucial part of psychotherapy. The act of meditation is also a skillful way to sniff out the *nafs,* for it has a particular, bitter smell and a relentless and repetitive nature. I know I am in the presence of the *nafs* when I harbor ill-will toward someone else, or when my mind tape-loops negative thoughts, or when my persistent desires blind me to the whole picture of reality. The *nafs* works overtime to preserve the separate self.

For years the *nafs* would visit me around a particular issue, over and over again, as *nafs* are wont to do. As a divorced parent, I shared the care of my children with my ex-husband. I loved my young children; so did my ex-husband. I wanted to be with my children all the time; so did my ex-husband. I wanted the best for my kids. I knew this involved having the love and guidance of their father in their life, whether or not I happened to like him at the moment. I wanted the impossible: happy, healthy children and my own, singular way. I was in the presence of the *nafs.*

My wiser Self, my healthy ego, would urge me not to energize my self-serving needs. I knew that this would only hurt the kids. They needed me, they needed their father, and they needed us to make the transition between homes as easy and guilt-free as possible. And then the *nafs* would take over. My vision of the whole picture would be blurred by the false ego's self-centered vision. I'd lose sight of what was best for the children and hold on tightly to what I desperately wanted. It felt like my very survival was at stake—a sure sign of the *nafs'* presence. In the years when this issue was most pressing, my spiritual practice focused around loosening the grip of my false ego in regard to myself as a mother.

Whenever I could, I would try through meditation to become aware of the *nafs* working me up into a worried, angry knot of aggression. I would sit quietly and feel the full impact of my false ego: its desperate grasping, its compulsive sense of self-importance, its resistance to compromise and harmony. Instead of acting on my impulse to get what I wanted, I would sit still and let my body and mind inform me about what was really going on. I would let my misconceptions, born of the ego's delusions, make themselves known to me. My meditation became a sort of prayer: *Please show me the whole picture. Please let me see things as they are.*

"We do not see things as they are," warn the wise Hebrew scholars in the Talmud. "We see them as we are." It is the false ego that insists on seeing everything and everyone through a self-centered lens. In this case, my false ego desperately sought to define all of reality—my children, my ex-husband, and our lives together—as something concerning only me, and only the smallest part of me. Meditation helped me discover my larger self—the Self, with a capital *S*—one that included my needs, my children's needs, my ex-husband's needs, and the totality that we created. When I used meditation to shine a light on my false ego, I became less self-referential and therefore more in touch with reality and more at peace. And I became suspicious of my self-referential behavior in other areas of my life.

"One of the things we discover in meditation is how self-referential we are in all of our dealings with the world, how we're really operating all the time from the point of view of 'what can this do for me?' " says Mark Epstein. "We can't help but feel that we're the most important person in any given roomful of people. So the major task of meditation is actually to bring that self-referential feeling more into awareness; not take it for granted and let it run away but deeply examine it. . . . The theory is that it's possible to be in the world while being suspicious of the need for self-centeredness."

Through meditation we can get quiet enough to notice the self-referential ways of the false ego. We begin to recognize that it is the act of putting our small selves in the center of our lives that keeps us anxious and unhappy. By noticing the false ego's patterns, we also begin to notice two other phenomena: the habits of the healthy ego, and the existence of an expansive and meaningful reality that includes me, you, and everything. Meditation, especially when used in alliance with psychotherapy, frees us from the pain of the separate, small, false self.

REALITY IS NOT WHAT YOU THINK IT IS

"No-self does not mean nothingness," says Mark Epstein. "It means that the self you imagine yourself to be doesn't exist. . . . You do exist but not in the way you imagined." Beyond the false ego's fearful imagination is another reality, barely perceivable through the filter of the ego structure. Looking deeply into the nature of things through meditation, we begin to see that reality is not as we imagined it to be. We see how the false ego makes false assumptions about reality. Its survival mentality distorts true perception and breeds paranoia. Even if we never can fully perceive the whole picture, just knowing that reality is different from what our false ego assumes is liberating. We can put down a lot of the worry, blame, and arrogance we carry around in our minds and hearts. We can lighten up and admit that we don't know everything—that our fears may be groundless; that our judgments may be wrong; that our understanding may be incomplete.

The Zen master Shunryu Suzuki, when asked to sum up all the teachings of mindfulness, answered, "Not always so." Sitting in meditation I often hear the voice of my music teacher, Pandit Pranath, whom I wrote about in Chapter Two. His muttered phrase—"Allah knows, I do not know"—is another mantra of mindfulness. We *don't* know as much as we think we do, and what we think we know is often the very obstacle to our peace and happiness. What we think we know limits our full potential. It can paint a grim picture when we really live in a grand picture.

I once helped organize a meditation retreat for peace activists. Led by Ram Dass, the retreat's premise was that real peace would be served best by peaceful social activists. After the first day of meditation, an agitated woman asked Ram Dass a question: "How can we all sit here, getting relaxed and happy, when at this very moment nuclear bombs are being built? When bombs are pointed at us right now? When we have bombs pointed at the rest of the world? Shouldn't we be out doing something tangible to end the madness we see all around us?" Her voice took on an edge of panic as she continued to berate herself and all of us in the room for abandoning our work for social change. The energy in the room quickly changed. People shifted on their meditation pillows, some looking annoyed, some nervous, some guilty. Ram Dass sat quietly, letting us all stew in whatever sensations had arisen.

The woman finally turned her full despairing attention on Ram Dass and asked him, "How can you just sit there when at any moment someone could press a button and the human race would disappear, all together, in a fiery mushroom cloud?" Ram Dass sat for a few moments longer, and then said, "Ahh. Maybe that's the moment we're waiting for, when we'll all reach enlightenment together. When we'll all go 'poof!' in a cloud of oneness."

Many people in the room laughed. I don't know if the woman who asked the question laughed. Perhaps her feelings were hurt. But Ram Dass's brief and humorous answer was not meant to hurt; it was meant to shift her perspective. It changed the way I think. Even today, years later, when I feel waves of fear or outrage rising in my belly, I think of Ram Dass's answer, and I calm right down. Ram Dass was, at the time, active in peace and world health organizations, and had for years worked in prisons and with the sick and dying. His answer to the woman's question was not glib. It was not addressed to her real concern for the world. It was aimed at her fear, and at the way her concern arose from her limited understanding of the limitless universe. How could something born of panic breed peace? Ram Dass was asking the woman to allow a breath of "Allah knows, I do not know" into her heart. In that way she could continue to work for what she believed but do so with more grace and humor and love.

The false ego will resist your attempts to widen your perspective. It will pull you in one direction, as your spiritual longing will pull in the other. As you meditate, let yourself feel the pull and also let your defenses down. Relax your mind until you slip by the sentry at the gates of the ego. "In trying to defend itself against its own spiritual longing," writes the noted psychiatrist Gerald May of the false ego, "it becomes its own enemy. . . . If only [it] knew how in the end spirituality would actually affirm it and infuse it with meaning rather than eradicate it, it would not be so defensive . . . if only it knew, it would not be so afraid."

WORKING WITH THE FOES: PAIN, RESTLESSNESS, SLEEPINESS, AND JUDGMENT

The false ego enlists some formidable foes in its defense. In meditation these foes take the form of pain, restlessness, and sleepiness. And not just physical pain, restlessness, and sleepiness. In meditation we can experience mental and emotional agitation too. As if these foes were not enough, the false ego also enlists the aid of judgment—the harsh and cynical inner critic who doubts, berates, and gives up. Working in a nonaggressive way with the foes is an important part of meditation practice.

WORKING WITH PAIN

Physical pain in the shoulders, jaw, neck, back, and knees is common during meditation. If you are injured or ill and already dealing with any sort of pain, sitting still can immediately bring that pain to the forefront of your consciousness. Many people never get past the early stages of meditation because of pain. The first rule in working with pain (and in working with all of the foes) is to stay open and soft. Don't condemn your pain. Don't heap more judgments and shoulds on yourself, like, "If I were stronger, or healthier, or more spiritual, then I wouldn't feel this pain in my back." If you meet physical pain with condemnation, you only add to the pain.

While pain is real, a good portion of what we feel is not the pain itself, but our resistance to it. The false ego uses pain as a defense mechanism, and in doing so magnifies our discomfort tenfold. In fact, we rarely experience the pure sensation of pain. Instead, we layer on top of it fear and anger, judgment and anxiety. When pain arises in meditation, we have a choice to make, over and over. We can resist the pain, or we can soften our resistances, experience the raw sensations, and move through them into an expanded consciousness.

A good way to deal with pain in meditation is to practice "bare attention," a loose interpretation of the Buddhist term *Vipassana*. Mark Epstein describes bare attention as "an exact registering of thoughts, feelings, sensations, sounds—separating out any emotional or mental reactions you might have from the raw event. Bare attention means understanding what the original event is and what your reactions are, and not confusing the two." When physical sensations arise—a feeling of tightness in the belly, a recurring itch, an ache in the back, a sharp pain in the knee—you can gently give a name to the exact sensation. You can silently repeat, "itching," or "heat," or "tightness." Often the process of naming a sensation will separate the "raw event" from your reactions to it. Naming the sensation acts like a broom, sweeping away resistances and exposing the pure sensation. And the pure sensation is always less of a foe than the resistance.

Sometimes the pain we feel in meditation is a message from our bodies about physical illness or emotional wounding. Because many of us rarely stop long enough to listen to the body, the pain we feel in meditation may indeed be worth attending to. Our bodies have stories to tell that require a deep kind of listening. A tight belly that is causing indigestion in daily life may indeed be a wise messenger with information about our emotional woundedness and the ways in which we can heal. A painful knee could be asking us to be more careful and kind to ourselves when we exercise. A tight jaw might be a herald from the heart, trying to tell us, "I have something to say that I just can't get out." In meditation we become quiet enough to hear these messages.

Some physical pain is just too intense for bare attention or deep listening to even make a dent in what we are feeling. Sitting cross-legged for an injured athlete may be impossible. Holding the back up may be out of the question for someone with chronic back pain or a physical disability. Work with your pain in a reasonable, kindly manner. Perhaps you will only be able to meditate stretched out on the floor, or in a chair with your back supported, or leaning against a wall. Learn what you can about yourself from the ways in which you resist pain, but stop short of turning the lesson into a reason to stop meditating.

WORKING WITH RESTLESSNESS

Like physical pain, restlessness visits us regularly in meditation. It is the most aggressive of the foes in my own meditation practice. After all these years, when I sit down to meditate, my first thoughts are of wanting to be somewhere else. So many things to do, so many pressing worries and plans. Sometimes sitting still makes me feel like jumping out of my skin. And then I remind myself that indeed, I do have twenty minutes available to me to be in peace, and that those twenty minutes will spread like honey over the rest of my day. I remember that peace and happiness are right here, right now, in this very moment, if I only give myself the chance to rediscover them, hiding somewhere near me.

I have heard Buddhists refer to the restless mind as "monkey mind." The way the mind jumps from a pleasant memory to a nagging anxiety, and then on to a physical sensation, and back again to the memory, or the anxiety, or to planning or worrying, or wanting to be somewhere else altogether, is just like a restless monkey swinging from branch to branch. If you have ever been around monkeys in the wild you will know how apt the comparison is.

I once spent a week in a national park on the western coast of Costa Rica, relaxing with a few friends. The park is famous for two things: its sunsets and its wildlife, especially monkeys, who gather just as the sun is setting in the trees that line the beach. Every evening my friends and I would sit on the sand and watch the luminous pastel sky slowly deepen and merge with the warm waters of the Pacific. The soft quality of the sky and water created a visual tapestry of such repose that we would fall into a delicious silence. And then, like clockwork, the monkeys would arrive behind us and begin chattering and screaming, jumping like mad acrobats from tree to tree. With my back to the monkeys, and my attention on the pale ocean stretching out before me, I formed a graphic image of mindfulness practice. Try as I might to rest my consciousness on the calm evening water, the monkeys kept interrupting my focus. Their constant movement and shrill chitchat were compelling and annoying at the same time.

Sitting on that beach, I learned something about mindfulness. If I regarded the monkeys as endearing, harmless companions, I could incorporate them into the fullness of the sunset ritual. If I wished they would go away, I felt a vague sense of dissatisfaction. If I turned around and watched them, I missed the sunset. And so, I let them be. I watched the glorious sunset, and I let the monkeys be.

The monkeys will be with you as you meditate. They will arrive in the form of distracting images and feelings, worries and urges. They will disturb your concentration and keep you from settling down. As with pain, if you resist distractions, they will multiply. If you let them be, breathing your way into acceptance, or using the technique of naming thoughts and feelings, just as you named sensations and pain, you can settle your mind. And like pain, restless thoughts can also be greeted as helpful messengers. Often right below the surface of the monkeys' chatter are unfelt feelings and truths we have been avoiding. When we let distractions be, we also let the rest of our inner world be. Suddenly a tapestry of emotions spreads out before us—unresolved desire, repressed grief, secret hopes or regrets. We may have to go through all sorts of troubled waters before we reach the stillness. When feelings distract your concentration, allow them to be. If a feeling of sadness sits heavily in your heart, you can softly name it. By saying "sadness" (or "anger," or "fear") you drop the burden of resistance.

WORKING WITH SLEEPINESS

"What's the difference between napping and meditating?" someone once asked me in a meditation class. The question was asked in jest, but it points to one of the most pervasive foes that we'll encounter. Sleep and meditation are *not* the same states of consciousness, but they are often separated only by a whisper, especially when we're not accustomed to remaining alert while being at rest. Within minutes of sitting down to meditate, you may sense a gigantic wave of sleepiness gathering offshore and rolling in toward your body and mind. Twenty minutes later, when you hear the bell or check the clock, you realize that you've slept through the whole session. Your body, hungry for repose, may naturally assume you are preparing to sleep when you first begin to meditate. That's all it may have ever known about deep relaxation.

Sleepiness in meditation can take many forms and arise for different reasons. Like pain and restlessness, sleepiness may be a simple message from the body—a sign of downright exhaustion. Numerous studies have found that most Americans are not well rested and need more hours of sleep for their physical and mental health. If you find that sleepiness is your most constant visitor when you meditate, consider the possibility that you need more sleep. Getting ample rest will not only help your mindfulness practice, it will bring a wakeful energy into all of your life.

Other reasons for tiredness in meditation, and in daily life, include resistance to unfelt feelings and the fear of what resides within you. You may have had the experience of feeling suddenly sleepy or confused when asked a probing question. When confronted with something I don't want to talk about, I have often felt the presence of sluggish, dark clouds advancing like a storm system in my head. The same phenomenon occurs in meditation. As we invite wakefulness into our consciousness, the false ego reacts. Sleep is an excellent defense against waking up!

When a heaviness of spirit, or a general sense of dullness, or a cloudy, confused state of mind visits you, meditation can feel as if you are slogging through pudding. There are several helpful ways to work with this problem. First of all, pick a time of day to meditate when you are most rested. Mornings, after you have awakened and showered, is a good time, as is before dinner in the evening. Meditating after eating is usually a recipe for falling asleep. A manual for prayer, attributed to the ancient Christian Desert Fathers, warned that "the noonday demon of laziness and sleep will come after lunch each day." It's amazing how little has changed in more than one thousand years.

But often, whether you meditate in the morning or evening, and even if you have had a great night's sleep, drowsiness and dullness will continue to be a problem. When you feel waves of tiredness come over you, recognize and name them, as you do with pain and restlessness. You can say to yourself, "sleepiness," "heaviness," "dullness," or whatever shape tiredness takes in your body and mind. Let yourself feel the place in the body where sleepiness is pooling. As you repeat the word "heaviness," or "dullness," and attach the naming process to a place in the body, you may discover that your heart is heavy with feelings, or that your mind is cloudy and dull. Your belly and pelvis may be thick with a resistance that is taking the form of fatigue. You can notice sleepiness pooling in the body not only when you meditate, but when you are at work and need to concentrate, or any time you find yourself overcome with sleepiness.

Pay attention to your posture and your eyes when tiredness visits your meditation practice. Come back to your straight back and noble carriage as a way of waking up. If you are very tired, open your eyes while you meditate, keeping your gaze a few feet in front of you. As you let yourself fully feel and name your tiredness, invite in another energy. The best antidote to sleepiness is wide-awake energy. You can even get up, stretch, and jump around to demonstrate to yourself that a zestful energy resides within you and is available. Then sit down again, resume your posture and breathing, and discover how you can be radically awake and profoundly relaxed at the same time.

WORKING WITH JUDGMENT

Self-judgment is a formidable foe to mindfulness. In the next chapter we examine the harshness of the internal judge, and explore psychological and spiritual remedies that can help heal the wounds of judgment. These remedies, when used with meditation, are powerful change agents in our lives. We need all the help we can get in this department. The human tendency to blame the self and others for the problems in the world is compounded in the West by the biblical concept of original sin. Built into many Western religious doctrines is the belief that there is something inherently evil about the human being, and that the task of the faithful is to hate the evil in the self and others. At the same time, these same traditions confuse the matter by instructing people to serve and love one another. Religions can bark directives of selfless service and love of neighbor as much and as loudly as they want, but until each one of us understands the roots of our own self-judgment, we will continue to judge others. As trite as it may sound, we will not be able to freely give and receive love to others if we cannot love ourselves.

When we meditate, we get to meet self-judgment right away; we get to feel it, taste it, and eventually understand it—where it comes from and what it creates. Judgment often presents itself as guilt and doubt—guilt for what we have or haven't done, and doubt of our abilities or of mindfulness practice itself. Judgment can take the form of anger toward other people, toward the self, or toward the practice. Sometimes judgment masquerades as fierce opinions, or as a creeping sense of despair. Sitting still and observing the strength of our judgments brings us face-to-face with our own lack of love—toward ourselves and others. Meditation alone is not enough to deal with the ways in which self-judgment gets in the way of our ability to enjoy life and to love others. Psychotherapy and psychological theory give the spiritual seeker additional tools to mine the psyche for self-judgment, self-loathing, self-blindness. They teach us how to have mercy on ourselves, how to heal, and how to open up.

The message of both therapy and meditation is this: If we embrace our darkness with compassion, we miraculously become lighter. But if we chastise ourselves for our sinfulness, or if we repress the energy of negative states of mind, we spiral down into more negativity. When negative states of mind visit you in meditation, allow yourself to fully experience them. This may be difficult. Each one of us has constructed brilliant defense mechanisms to keep us from our own darkness. Experiment with this. As you sit, if you begin to feel angry with yourself for being forgetful—"I'm so stupid! I can't believe I left the telephone plugged in again."—or tired—"I'm a lazy slob. I'll never get this right."—or in pain—"I'm such a wimp."—observe what you do with your feelings. Do you heap more judgments on yourself? Do you project your anger on to someone or something else? Do you sink into a sense of helplessness?

Experiment with naming judgment in all of its many guises. Say, "anger, anger," or "frustration," or "despair," or "sadness." Gently repeat these words with loving-kindness. They are not reprimands; they are benign observations. See what happens as you gently name the ways in which the judging mind beats itself up. Be alert to your desire to ignore or sugar-coat your feelings. Do nothing but name them. Don't exaggerate them, but don't deny them. "The answer to anger or other negative states is not to suppress or to deny them, but to embrace them with mindfulness like a mother with a baby," says Thich Nhat Hanh. Suppressing feelings in meditation, as in daily life, is like blocking a stream with sticks and mud. The water will eventually find its way downstream after pooling and gathering the pressure necessary to forge a new course or to break through the dam. "The energy of anger is very important to human beings, perhaps second only to the energy of mindfulness and compassion," Thich Nhat Hanh says, referring to the danger of blocking the flow of energy in the body, heart, and mind.

Guilt, doubt, anger, despair, and other forms of self-judgment are common visitors in meditation practice. So are our convictions, biases, and beliefs. If the purpose of meditation is to step boldly into reality, just as it is in the here and now, it is helpful to sweep the mind clean of belief systems. Strong opinions can be signs of our passion and intelligence, but sometimes they spring from that part of ourselves that wants to be right, and that holds on tightly to familiar explanations. The ego wants to be a "Republican" or a "liberal," a "New Yorker" or a "Midwesterner." It wants to judge things as right or wrong. It wants to be "for" something or "against" something. It does not want to delve more deeply into the full picture of reality. As such, an opinion about the world can become a foe to mindfulness. When I teach, I bring a box of poems to class and allow people to choose one, sit with it, and then share it and their experience with the group.

Without fail, two lines from a poem by the Chinese sage Seng-ts'an create a big stir:

> Don't keep searching for the truth;
> Just let go of your opinions.

Inevitably some members of the class will take umbrage at the poem. One person will say, "My opinions about injustice in the world are what drive me to do good work." Another will feel insulted by the poet's suggestions that opinions obscure the truth: "If I don't form opinions, how will I know what is true and what it false?" Like many mystic/poets, Seng-ts'an has a sense of humor and likes to overstate the case, just to get a laugh. He knows that opinions are not necessarily evil. He just wants us to loosen the grip of our judgments, even for a few minutes, and give the whole truth a chance to reveal itself.

There is another form of self-judgment that deserves mentioning here because of its sneaky nature. This is when we use the inherent difficulties of spiritual practice as yet another way to feel bad about ourselves. Don't give authority to that nagging voice within that says you're not meditating or praying enough, that you're not spiritual enough. The best way to remedy this kind of self-judgment is to remind yourself often why you meditate or pray in the first place. You do not engage in spiritual practice to become a great meditator or an outstanding religious disciple, or even a well-behaved member of society. You pursue the spiritual path to become a genuine and fearless human being. You cultivate a quiet mind and an open heart in meditation so that you can be peaceful and loving in everyday life. The point is to practice so that the truths you discover in meditation become the way you live your life. After a while, your practice shows up everywhere—from driving the car to shopping for food to reading a bedtime story to your child. Meditation is not separate from life; it is practice for mindful living.

Let your resolve to meditate spring from your longing for freedom, not from enmity toward yourself. Let go of the burden of self-judgment by returning, over and over, to your most basic self, just as you are, with an attitude of self-forgiveness. This leads to forgiveness of others, and of the world itself.

THREE MINDFULNESS MEDITATIONS

The three meditations offered here provide useful ways of approaching the foes. The basic instructions on breath, posture, and attention given in Chapter Six apply to these meditations. Each meditation can be read slowly to a friend or silently to oneself.

TOOLBOX EXERCISE #1

INSTRUCTIONS ON WORKING WITH PAIN

From **A Path with Heart,**
by Jack Kornfield

Sit comfortably and quietly. Let your body rest easily. Breathe gently. Let go of your thoughts, past and future, memories and plans. Just be present. Begin to let your own precious body reveal the places that most need healing. Allow the physical pains, tension, disease, or wounds to show themselves. Bring a careful and kind attention to these painful places. Slowly and carefully feel their physical energy. Notice what is deep inside them, the pulsations, throbbing, tension, needles, fear, contraction, aching, that make up what we call pain. Allow these all to be felt fully, to be held in a receptive and kind attention. Then be aware of the surrounding area of your body. If there is contraction and holding, notice this gently. Breathe softly and let it open. Then, in the same way, be aware of any aversion or resistance in your mind. Notice the thoughts and fears that accompany the pain you are exploring: "It will never go away." "I can't stand it." "I don't deserve this." "It is too hard, too much trouble, too deep," etc.

Let these thoughts rest in your kind attention for a time. Then gently return to your physical body. Let your awareness be deeper and more allowing now. Again, feel the layers of the place of pain, and allow each layer that opens to move, to intensify, or dissolve in its own time. Bring your attention to the pain as if you were gently comforting a child, holding it all in a loving and soothing attention. Breathe softly into it, accepting all that is present with a healing kindness. Continue this meditation until you feel reconnected with whatever part of your body calls you, until you feel at peace.

TOOLBOX EXERCISE #2
INSTRUCTIONS ON LETTING THOUGHTS AND FEELINGS BE
From The Miracle of Mindfulness,
by Thich Nhat Hanh

When a feeling or thought arises, your intention should not be to chase it away, hate it, worry about it, or be frightened by it. So what exactly should you be doing concerning such thoughts and feelings? Simply acknowledge their presence. For example, when a feeling of sadness arises, immediately recognize it: "A feeling of sadness has just arisen in me." If the feeling of sadness continues, continue to recognize it: "A feeling of sadness is still in me." If there is a thought like "It's late but the neighbors are surely making a lot of noise," recognize that the thought has arisen. If the thought continues to exist, continue to recognize it. If a different feeling or thought arises, recognize it in the same manner. The essential thing is not to let any feeling or thought arise without recognizing it in mindfulness, like a palace guard who is aware of every face that passes through the front corridor. If there are no feelings or thoughts present, then recognize that there are no feelings or thoughts present. Practicing like this is to become mindful of your feelings and thoughts. You will soon arrive at taking hold of your mind.

TOOLBOX EXERCISE #3
INSTRUCTIONS ON USING POSTURE TO REMAIN ALERT
From Shambhala: The Sacred Path of the Warrior,
by Chögyam Trungpa

[*While the instructions here specify sitting cross-legged on the ground, you can receive the same results from sitting in a chair, with your feet on the ground, and your back upright, but not resting on the chair's back.*]

In the practice of meditation, an upright posture is extremely important. Having an upright back is not an artificial posture. It is natural to the human body. When you slouch, that is unusual. You can't breathe properly when you slouch, and slouching also is a sign of giving in to neurosis. So when you sit erect, you are proclaiming to yourself and to the rest of the world that you are going to be a warrior, a fully human being.

To have a straight back you do not have to strain yourself by pulling up your shoulders; the uprightness comes naturally from sitting simply but proudly on the ground or on your meditation cushion. Then, because your back is upright, you feel no trace of shyness or embarrassment, so you do not hold your head down. You are not bending to anything. Because of that, your shoulders become straight automatically, so you develop a good sense of head and shoulders. Then you can allow your legs to rest naturally in a cross-legged position; your knees do not have to touch the ground. You can complete your posture by placing your hands lightly, palms down, on your thighs. This provides a further sense of assuming your spot properly. . . . You can see this royal pose in some Egyptian and South American sculptures, as well as in Oriental statues. It is a universal posture, not limited to one culture or time.

In your daily life, you should also be aware of your posture, your head and shoulders, how you walk, and how you look at people. Even when you are not meditating, you can maintain a dignified state of existence. You can transcend your embarrassment and take pride in being a human being. Such pride is acceptable and good.

IS IT WORKING? TWO MINDFULNESS SCENARIOS

When I teach mindfulness meditation, people ask me what it feels like when meditation is "working." I hesitate to tell them, because I imagine that every person's experience of a sustained state of mindfulness feels different. I also hesitate because I don't want it to seem that if meditation is difficult then it is not working. But perhaps if I share two scenarios—one of a meditation session when I struggle, and another when meditation flows easily—you will understand how even when meditation feels like a volley between the foes, you are indeed meditating, and you are indeed making progress.

My observations are the only way I know to describe a state of meditative mindfulness. You can use your observations in the same way I do in the next two toolbox exercises. Speak your own experience of mindfulness, or the lack thereof, into a tape recorder as you meditate, or write it down afterward. It is helpful to affix words to your difficulties as well as to your experiences of grace and boundlessness.

TOOLBOX EXERCISE #4
A DIFFICULT MEDITATION SCENARIO

I set my timer for twenty minutes and settle into my session. I assume a comfortable position, straighten my posture, relax my jaw, place my hands in a meaningful mudra, and begin to observe myself breathing. I remind myself why I am meditating. I tell my body and mind that they can relax, and my heart that it can soften. I invite freedom and spaciousness into my consciousness. I begin to settle down.

Within a few seconds I remember that I should have left a note for the Federal Express pick-up man and that he will probably knock on the door and disturb my meditation. Immediately my ego goes into its self-judging mode: "How could you be so stupid? You never think things through . . ."

A familiar tug at the heart—the one that always happens when I heap judgment on myself—is felt. I bring my attention to the tugging feeling, and breathe quietly. I notice that I've been distracted by my judgments and thoughts. I come back to my posture. "Noble human," I silently say. I let go of tension. "Soft belly." Now I try to separate the actual situation from my reaction to the situation. I don't try to stop myself from judging myself. I just notice both the situation and my reaction to it: what really happened, and how I got in the way. The FedEx man may indeed knock on the door. I decide to continue to sit and if he does come, I'll get up and respond mindfully. No big deal. Exhale, sigh.

The constricted feeling in my chest dissipates. I return to my breath. Within seconds I am thinking about an irritating encounter I had at work yesterday and how I should confront that person today. I blindly follow new feelings and thoughts down the road for a while, until I notice that I'm angry, that my stomach is tight, and my breath is choppy. I inwardly say, "anger, anger," and allow myself to fully feel the tightness in my body, the shape and whereabouts of the anger. Now my attention returns to mindful breathing. Next my shoulders begin to ache, then I feel an itch on my face, and my knee is hurting. I panic a little, wondering if I'll ever be able to relax myself and quiet down. Once again, by checking my posture, hands, and breathing, I remind myself to experience pain as pain, itch as itch. No need to add panic to pain, judgment to an itch. I separate my reaction to pain from the pain itself. I shift my posture a little, and gently scratch my face, and then come back to myself again, sitting tall in my boat made of breath, drifting on the sea of consciousness. For a few blessed minutes, I float aimlessly, at home with the way things are. The timer rings. My session is over.

TOOLBOX EXERCISE #5

A GRACEFUL MEDITATION SCENARIO

I take my seat. My meditation pillow, my little altar table with its pictures and stones and objects of beauty, my shawl wrapped around me for warmth—accoutrements that act as the first gate—fade behind me as I close my eyes, check my posture, arrange my hands on my folded knees, and begin to observe my breath. My breath deepens naturally. I have returned to the well, to the oasis of refreshment. My first few seconds of meditation feel like a homecoming. I settle in. Now I feel the tightness of my jeans around my belly. Within seconds, what was unnoticed just minutes before seems unbearable. I struggle to ignore the sensation; I return to my breath; I repeat "tightness, tightness," but the sensation only grows stronger. I give in. I undo my pants, let out a big sigh, sit tall again, check my hands, and return to my breath.

Now a wave of sadness rolls into my heart. At first it feels like a personal sense of loss. I recoil from it. I watch the urge to push the sadness away become stronger than the feeling of sadness itself. I return to my breath and repeat "sadness, sadness." I relax my jaw and sit quietly and fully right where I am, right with the sensation of sadness. The sadness now feels more like an impersonal nostalgia for something I cannot name. Within a few minutes of watching my breath, this feeling also fades away, as if it too were a gate I was destined to pass through on my mindfulness journey. I begin to sense that *I am not going anywhere;* that I merely am coming home to what has always been. "What an interesting journey, this trip to where we already are," I think.

Other thoughts take over and dominate my mind. They take me away from the sense of homecoming. I label them as they obsessively repeat themselves. "Thinking, thinking, thinking." I come back to my breath and move delicately through the gate of thinking. Now waves of gratitude flow through me. My body receives them. I begin to feel the connection between my body and my mind, a sense of solidarity, of harmony, of unity. I sense the jewel-like quality of each moment. As I breathe in I sense the moment as a drop of water poised at the tip of the faucet—full, round, complete; as I breathe out the moment ripples and expands as if the drop of water has fallen and dispersed into an eternal state of becoming. As I breathe in and out I identify with the fullness of the drop of water and the expansion of the ripple. These are just words; the sensation is more like fullness, rightness, completeness; and then freedom, detachment, connection.

As I sit tall and dignified in meditation, I am aware of a gradual softening of my heart and body, even as my mind is focused and vibrant. I sense that I could get up now and walk wide-eyed into the world, free from fear, connected to everything and everyone, yet detached from a need to control anything. I am touched by the world, in love with its darkness and its light, and curious about what will happen next. I am "at play in the fields of the Lord," a willing participant in the eternal dance. There is a sense of magic—I taste it—and also a sense of deep ordinariness. Extra-ordinary. Extraordinary.

Twenty minutes have passed. I return to my breathing, check my posture again, bring my hands together, and bow. My meditation session is over.

RETURN AGAIN: A MINDFULNESS REVIEW

Most spiritual traditions stress the theme of return in meditation. To return is to forgive; to give yourself and the world another chance. Saint Francis de Sales gave his students these meditation instructions: "Bring yourself back to the point quite intently. And even if you do nothing during the whole of your hour but bring your heart back a thousand times, though it went away every time you brought it back, your hour would be very well employed." The following review of Book II serves as a ten-step guide to returning, again and again, to mindfulness.

TOOLBOX EXERCISE #6
A MINDFULNESS REVIEW

1. *Quiet the mind:* Thoughts and dreams, fears and anxieties, all move through your mind like weather through the sky. Use meditation to gain some distance from your thoughts, as if you were observing clouds from an observation tower. Hold the contents of your mind in a wide, friendly embrace, and let your sense of self expand.

2. *Sit tall in the saddle:* In meditation, and in daily life, carry yourself with wide-awake dignity. Straighten your bearing, like a king or queen riding a powerful horse.

3. *Soften the belly/heart:* As you straighten your back, also soften your front. Keep your heart open and your belly soft. A quiet mind, noble bearing, and open heart will make you calm, strong, and gentle. Cultivate on-the-spot awakeness *and* tender relaxation.

4. *Breathe:* Let the act of breathing be the connecting link between body and mind, yourself and all of life, nowness and eternity. Breathe in and feel fully, genuinely yourself. Breathe out and expand into formless, boundaryless awareness. With each exhalation you have the chance to dissolve and let go. With each inhalation you begin again, fresh and curious.

5. *Accept suffering:* You don't have to enjoy the painful parts of life, but you can accept them as part of the human experience. To accept pain is to end suffering: this is the Buddha's First Noble Truth. Practice meeting life on its own terms instead of straining to make everything manageable, or familiar, or safe.

6. *Develop a daily practice:* Create a meditation practice for yourself that is simple yet rigorous, informed by tradition yet suited to your personal needs. Find a teacher if you can, or choose a path and stick to it long enough to learn the directions. Practice regularly and with a sense of purpose. Establish goals but follow them like you would fireflies on a dark summer night. Don't get too rigid. Maintain a sense of humor and openness.

7. *Expect resistance:* The monkeys will visit you as you meditate and as you try to live mindfully in everyday life. They will swing from tree to tree, in the guise of distractions, pain, restlessness, sleepiness, doubts, and self-criticism. Don't resist resistance. Instead, observe the fluid nature of your mind, the rising and falling of your feelings, the pain and restlessness of your body—without judgment, irritation, or panic. Why? So that you can do the same thing in daily life: meet painful situations with grace, difficult people with patience, persistent problems with perspective.

8. *Stress is; anxiety doesn't have to be:* Take a deep breath and look squarely at the stress in your life. Try to divide what's bothering you into choice-based stress, unavoidable stress, and reactive stress. Consider simplifying your life. Where you can't simplify, work with your reaction to stress: instead of control, choose curiosity; instead of struggle, move in the direction that the river is flowing. By letting go of the compulsion to control, your anxiety about stress lessens. You free up creative energy that before you were expending on fighting and forcing.

9. *Reality is not what you think it is:* It's bigger; it's more; it's inclusive. Your

false ego wants to keep things small and under its control. But you are bigger than your little self, with all of its attachments, and anxieties, and opinions. When the false ego starts to panic and demand supremacy, when you think you are right, or that you know everything, practice saying, "I don't know; Allah knows," or "Not either/or, but both, and more." Walk outside of your limited perspective; step into the open air of the big picture.

10. *The secret in life is enjoying the passage of time:* Instead of clutching on to the past or fearing the future, experiment with letting go into the mystery of life. Float on the river of time, curious about its direction, open to its changing nature. You don't really know where it's going, so why not relax and experience the ride?

Book III

The Landscape
of the Heart

9 ⫶ Heartfulness

People say that what we're seeking is a meaning for life. I don't think that's what we're really seeking. I think that what we're seeking is an experience of being alive, so that we actually feel the rapture of being alive.
—JOSEPH CAMPBELL

When we direct spiritual attention to the heart, we take our practice to the next step. In the Landscape of the Mind we sit boldly in reality, just as it is, with no judgment or fear, no likes or dislikes—just awareness. In the Landscape of the Heart we keep on going and open so fully to the phenomenal world that we are touched by it. We allow ourselves to *feel* with the same superawareness that we developed in mindfulness practice. The goal is an awakened heart, one that feels everything there is to feel: joy and hope, enchantment and aliveness; and also longing, sadness, anger, and pain. We feel how wonderful it is to be alive, how funny, how tragic. We don't shut down when the feelings get troublesome; we stay awake even when it hurts. This is the path of the heart: to develop tenderness toward the self and each other by opening wider and wider to the wonders and the woes of the world.

As we enter the heart's domain, it's good to carry with us the fruits of our mindfulness work: a sense of inner dignity, an ability to ease worry and fear, and a broader view of the self. The work of the heart—what I call "heartfulness"—promises a highly developed feeling function. It involves emotional healing and psychological revelation, and as such may lead us into troubled waters where the high waves of emotions can throw us off balance, or where backwaters of sentimentality can lull us to sleep. Without the clarifying and balancing effects of mindfulness, heartfulness work can put us at the mercy of the seas.

In the Landscape of the Heart we meet up with parts of the self that we both desire and fear. The heart longs to feel fully alive; it craves connection and happiness. If allowed to follow its cravings, the heart feels everything: love and loneliness, contentment and gloom, passion and apathy. Like waves on the shore, our hearts normally rush toward joy, then pull back, afraid of pain and loss. Heartfulness is the willingness and the ability not to pull back. If we want to "feel the rapture of being alive," as Joseph Campbell describes the object of the spiritual search, we have to experience the whole ocean of emotions.

Heartfulness work is like swimming lessons: it teaches a skill that very few people seem to naturally possess. But unlike swimming lessons, which can be easily obtained at any YMCA pool or local beach, heartfulness skills are not usually taught in our culture. Most of us didn't learn as children that sadness is sister to happiness and that to deny one is to suppress the other. We weren't given specific tools to handle grief, to deal with crisis, to welcome loss as a natural part of being alive. It was not suggested that in order to understand ourselves we should look to the ways in which our parents cared for us and for each other. No one said, "Here is the best way to communicate when you are angry so that your relationships can flourish in honesty and love." Instead, the whole subject of emotions and psychological development was ignored at best and usually was sentimentalized, or ridiculed, or corked.

"Emotional intelligence," as psychologist Daniel Goleman calls the wisdom of the heart, needs to be nurtured and developed, just like any kind of intelligence. We've put more emphasis on math and history and language than on the skills needed to love our lives and to interact well with each other as mates, families, friends, and communities. Elementary schools don't include honest communication or compassionate listening in the curriculum. High schools don't require students to know how to develop healthy emotional boundaries, how to be strong and gentle at the same time, how to make wise decisions based on what we really want—or how to know what we want in the first place.

Society devises laws to keep domestic and public order, but rules for moral behavior are different from tools for heartful living. They may point us in the same direction—toward kindness, compassion, and decency—but heartfulness is not about being told what to do. Heartfulness warns us not to "grin and bear it," not just to settle for what religions talk about, not to follow rules for the sake of obedience—but to find out for ourselves what we love and what we want. If values don't come from what we love, they become doctrine. Heartfulness leads us away from a rote doctrine of love to loving behavior through self-love, to forgiveness of others through self-forgiveness, to understanding human nature through self-understanding.

By the time most of us have reached adulthood we find ourselves in a curious situation: we have an emotional life but we don't really know how to manage it. The luckiest among us have happy marriages and loving families, deal gracefully with loss and pain, and feel deeply into the pleasures of daily life. The most unfortunate are crippled by depression, unable to make lasting bonds with others, and dulled to the ordinary magic of being alive. In the middle are the rest of us, bobbing in our own emotional oceans, sometimes on top of the water, and often under waves of depression or anger or confusion. You may recognize in yourself the most common emotional coping strategy: in order not to feel the darker emotions—sadness, or pain, or hatred—we turn off the heart's capacity to feel at all. And then we are puzzled by why it is so hard to love, to enjoy, and even to know what we feel or want.

It makes sense that if we don't want to feel unhappy, and we don't know how to cultivate happiness, that we would just turn off the part of ourselves that feels. This is something that we learn to do early on. If our childhood pain was great, we learn all too well how to shut down feelings. The heart then becomes the locked repository for childhood wounds and confusion. The lessons of repression and avoidance learned long ago become trusted habits.

If the purpose of life is to "feel the rapture of being alive," and if our capacity to feel is crippled by old wounds and a lack of emotional education, then it follows that an important part of the spiritual path is to heal the heart and to become emotionally intelligent. Then why is it that the territory of the heart is so rarely explored on the classical spiritual journey? One answer is that the heart's contradictory, messy, and passionate nature seems at odds with some religions. Sin-based religions especially have made it their mission to control the world, not to love it for what it is. The less controllable aspects of our humanness—erotic love, rage and anger, beauty and sadness—have been labeled too passionate or irrational to be trusted. Better to leave passion out of a "spiritual" person's life altogether.

To bring the heart along on the spiritual path is to open Pandora's box. Once opened, the heart wants to feel the rapture of being alive. It longs to know love; it remembers pain; it feels rage; *it demands change.* It wants to know joy in the here and now, in the body, with other people, through the senses. No wonder our culture—with its Puritanical roots and its patriarchal power structure—has made sure the box has stayed locked. But the lack of heartfulness in life is a tragedy, because an enlightened heart delivers what we expect from the spiritual search: wisdom, peace, and a life of miracles.

In this chapter and the next we explore how to cultivate an open heart, one that can help us experience the rapture of being alive. We use psychology to open our minds to our hearts, to educate us in the value of feelings. We peer into the fullness of the human situation and consider ways of handling emotional states like sadness, depression, and grief. We also explore ways to know what we feel, forgive ourselves and others, set boundaries, and rediscover the pleasures of everyday life. Directly related to this process is the journey into the Landscape of the Body, which we explore in Book IV.

Just as meditation is a practice to engage in diligently over time, psychological, emotional, and physical healing work also take commitment and time. I believe that psychotherapy and bodywork provide essential skills for the spiritual journey. A good therapist—and one who values spirituality as well as psychology—can be as important as a spiritual teacher, a trusted philosophy, or a holy book.

As we work on opening the heart, we will confront, over and over, our fearful habit of closing to pain. This is where mindfulness meditation practice can be such a powerful ally and a wonderful companion as we sail the seas of the heart. It keeps us focused and less likely to be swept away by waves of elation or despair. Mindfulness and heartfulness are a powerful duo on the spiritual path: a quiet mind without an open heart is a pretty brittle and boring proposition. But an open heart that doesn't have the support of a quiet and tamed mind is equally unhelpful. Without spirituality, therapy can turn into a never-ending search for self-fulfillment. Without heartfulness, spiritual practice can lead us away from the gifts of life.

Don't worry if you have already been flailing around in emotional waters without being buoyed by a mindfulness practice, or if you have lived primarily in your head, avoiding the feelings and hungers of the heart. Remember to "start where you are." The human journey is rarely orderly; we don't chart a linear route as we set out in life. Each one of us stumbles upon elements of personal development in a haphazard way. We overdo some things. We ignore others. We make mistakes.

My big mistake was to focus myopically for too many years on the Landscape of the Mind without giving voice to the longings of my heart or the hungers of my body. I would have been well served by adding to my meditation practice other forms of spirituality that nurture an open and trusting heart, and a grounded, sensual body. Many make opposite mistakes, ignoring the Landscape of the Mind and concentrating primarily on their psychological development, or their emotional expression, or their sexual and physical fulfillment. All of these are equally important facets of a balanced spiritual path. Of course, it would be best to explore and develop each part equally and simultaneously as we proceed through life. But we don't. Usually we stick around too long in areas where we have already learned the lessons, and avoid moving out of the safe and familiar into new territory.

At some point, if we pay attention, a crisis or a transition will shed light on sleeping giants in the psyche. If we have ignored our body for many years, it will try to awaken us through illness. Or if we've skimmed the surface of our deeper feelings, the heart will call to us through failed relationships, or addictions, or depression. If we are bold enough, we will wake up the giant, feel its fire, and do battle if we must. These battles become what shamanic traditions call "thresholds." Should we choose to cross them, our lives change forever.

I crossed over the heart's threshold when I was thirty years old—later than some people, earlier than others. At the time, I didn't know that a giant was slumbering in my psyche, bedded down in my heart. I had been meditating, studying, chanting, praying, and following prescribed modes of behavior for more than ten years when the giant, whose name was *happiness,* began to stir. While I had developed real capacities to access inner calm and transcendence, I was not a very happy person. In fact, it seemed that ten years' worth of "rising above" the conflict and confusion of daily life was about to crash down on me. I was a young mother, unhappily married, and often physically sick. I had trouble enjoying the daily routines of work and parenting, even though I loved my work and my children.

To deal with my problems, I tried harder to "rise above and to see beyond the goals of the body," as my teacher, Pir Vilayat, described the path of the spiritual seeker. But what about that other teaching that Pir Vilayat often quoted from his father's writings? "The purpose of the spiritual life," Hazrat Inayat Khan had said, "is to be happy." Happiness had always seemed such an elusive state of being to me, and the search for happiness such a fruitless quest. I had turned to spirituality out of a belief that life here on earth could never promise true happiness. Its impermanent nature would only disappoint in the long run. And so I chose to focus on the boundless consciousness that we had known before birth, and where we would return after death.

Giants who have been asleep for a long time are hungry when they awaken. When the giant who lived in my heart began to stir, I suddenly felt as though I were starving. I had equated spirituality with a certain way of being—refined, observant, moral. Now I wanted to taste holiness in my own body and heart. My awakening appetite sought new sources for inspiration. I was drawn to read the ancient myths about bewildered men and women driven to quests in the underworld. In my readings, by mythologists and mystics, I came across a passage by the noted psychologist Lawrence LeShan: "Don't worry about what the world wants from you, worry about what makes you come more alive. Because what the world really needs are people who are more alive. Your real job is to increase the color and zest of your life." This man, who had made a lifelong study of the world's religions, and who lectured at theological seminaries, had come to this conclusion? That my real job was to be more alive—full of color and zest? This rang fearfully true. I was longing to be more alive *here and now,* even if it was a dream, an illusion, maya, or whatever earthly existence had been called by the sages. Something was beginning to tell me that the distinction made between eternal life and this life was fundamentally flawed anyway. I wanted to be happy now. I wanted to feel at home on earth.

Even as it called to me, my new hunger disturbed me. It seemed so self-centered. I had always been puzzled by what I perceived to be conflicting directives in the teachings of Hazrat Inayat Khan. He had said that "real generosity is an unfailing sign of spirituality." And he had also said, "The soul's happiness is in itself; nothing can make the soul fully happy but self-realization." I just couldn't see how centering on the self could lead toward generosity, which was the sign of spirituality. It seemed to me that to be generous one needed to focus on others and to tame the self-serving desires of the ego. Yet my beliefs about self-sacrifice and my moral obedience weren't making me particularly generous. Nor was my unhappiness. Perhaps this "self" that I had worked so hard at subduing and transcending had something to teach me. Perhaps my unhappiness could tell me something if I listened to it.

Around this same time a new breed of teachers was coming to Omega. Instead of talking about higher states of consciousness and ancient religious practices, they were turning to psychology and therapy to help people unlock inner wisdom. While this kind of work had been around for many years, beginning with Freudian analysis, and developing over a century to include a myriad of theories, the concept of using psychological work on the spiritual path was relatively new. Of course I knew about psychology. I had studied it in college. And I had visited Esalen Institute in California, where some of the most innovative therapies were being explored. But I was wary of psychotherapy and cathartic types of group work. Emotional healing work in general struck me as excessive and insatiable, almost embarrassing.

My wariness was fed by a perception I had that people who were involved in therapy focused more and more attention on their own needs, and less and less on their moral upliftment and social responsibilities. The word *process,* which was used by many of the new breed of Omega teachers, annoyed me. It seemed messy and lacking in direction. Did it really ever *get* anywhere? I was afraid that if I began "the process" of exploring my personal past, I would enter a never-ending vortex of self-examination; or if I probed into unfulfilled aspects of my daily life—like my marriage, or my physical health—that the whole structure of my world would unravel. "The rapture of being alive" sounded good on paper, but what if it led me down a hedonistic, self-serving path? And what would really bring me rapture? I wasn't even certain about what my heart longed for. Rumi, the great Sufi poet, said, "Let yourself be silently drawn, by the stronger pull of what you really love." But what did I really love?

Ironically, it was through death that I finally set out to discover the rapture of being alive. The death of one of my dearest friends cracked my heart open, awakened the sleeping giant, and motivated me to do my own emotional healing work. Ellen's story is the story of her death and of my rebirth.

ELLEN'S STORY

Ellen and I met as fellow students of Pir Vilayat. I loved her practicality and her eccentric sense of humor. We had our first babies the same year, and grew into motherhood together. Almost from the beginning of our friendship, Ellen was ill. She was diagnosed with leukemia when we were both twenty-five—when our sons were just a year old. My husband and I helped her through all of her attempts at healing, from carrot juice to chemotherapy, and rejoiced when the cancer went into remission. Her plucky spirit remained strong until six years after remission, when she received the news that the leukemia was back in full force.

Now all she had were questions that no one seemed to be able to answer: Should she go for another round of painful chemotherapy even though the prognosis was poor? Should she tell her son that she was going to die? When would she die? She was tired of fighting, but terrified of leaving her seven-year-old son motherless. What should she do? Would we stand by her and help her die? I had no idea how to do this. I knew about different healing techniques from my husband and from my exposure to holistic health at Omega. I knew about the birth process from my experience as a midwife. But I knew nothing about the dying process, had never even seen an animal die, and had harbored a fear of death since I was a child.

Very little literature existed on the subject. Dr. Elisabeth Kübler-Ross, the now famous pioneer who brought death out of the closet in medical and nursing schools, had first taught at Omega in 1977. She was the only person I had come across who was willing to even broach the subject. So, I called her and asked her who else was exploring death and dying. She recommended Stephen and Ondrea Levine, authors of several books on what they called "conscious dying." This sounded like an oxymoron to me, but after reading one of the Levines' books, I invited them to teach at Omega, hoping that other people wanted to delve into this subject as much as I did.

The Levines' approach to the subject of dying was neither maudlin nor superficial. They had been drawn to work with terminally ill people out of their own bouts with serious illness, and therefore their words carried a refreshing authenticity. In helping others approach terminal illness calmly and even with a sense of joy, the Levines had uncovered a greater capacity in themselves to live fully. Their definition of healing *included* dying, thus releasing people from the guilt-producing New Age philosophy that illness is always conquerable if you have a positive attitude. The Levines had helped people use awareness and intention to reverse an illness, often with seemingly miraculous results. But they had also helped people use healing energy to die with dignity, peace, and spiritual enlightenment. This was exactly the approach I needed to adopt in the next stage of Ellen's healing and/or dying process.

From their work with the dying the Levines developed a set of spiritual practices that began with self-forgiveness. Sitting with people in their final hours, they had seen many achieve moments of transcendent freedom, while others remained locked in fear and grief. The difference between these two final experiences was simple: those who were able to forgive themselves for their own shortcomings—for their failures to love or "measure up"—finally put down a burden they had been carrying for years and rested in a blissful peace. Those who couldn't develop tenderness toward themselves breathed their last breaths with the same sense of confusion and unfulfilled dreams that had plagued them in life. Over and over the Levines noticed how those who accepted themselves just as they were—sick, in pain, afraid—began to feel fully alive even as they were dying.

It was the act of self-forgiveness that made the difference—a dramatic difference—in death and in life. The Levines began leading workshops for people with terminal illnesses like cancer, heart disease, and AIDS, as well as those with the "most common terminal situation," as Stephen Levine called everyday life. What worked for people in their final weeks and hours also worked for those with a long life in front of them. "The beginning of the path of healing," Stephen wrote, "is the end of life unlived."

At the Levines' first retreat at Omega, four hundred people, as many as we could accommodate, crowded into the main hall. Many of these people had cancer or other diseases. Some would die soon after the retreat. Some were people who had just lost a loved one. There were parents of children who had committed suicide; doctors, nurses, and social workers who dealt with death and dying on a daily basis; and others who had come to confront their fear of death and their struggles with life. The amount of suffering in the room was palpable. Introducing the Levines, I felt a panic rising in my organizer's heart. How would they ever be able to handle a crowd as large and emotional as this, no less actually teach anything? What if someone died? And what was the point in languishing in grief and fear for four days?

Within minutes of the retreat I realized that Stephen and Ondrea Levine possessed a rare inner strength. Their very presence had a quality of dignity and humility. Their clarity of purpose and their patience and trust were so obvious that the mood in the room shifted quickly from one of fear to one of openness. After I had introduced them and made my announcements, I joined the group, and over the next days I was drawn to sit in the main hall as much as possible. This may sound like an obvious response to my work. But, actually, over the years of working at Omega, while I have listened to hundreds of teachers speak, I have participated fully in only a few workshops. Like the proprietor of a candy shop who rarely eats the goodies for fear of getting fat or sick, I have chosen just a few teachings to make my own. Something about Stephen and Ondrea, who they were and what they were teaching, pulled me to sit and listen. I thought I was drawn to participate in order to help Ellen; I was to discover that I was also there for myself.

The Levines had asked us to set up the room with microphones in the audience so that people could share their stories and questions. During the retreat I was to witness again and again a subtle magic brought on by the simple acts of sincere storytelling and compassionate listening. As people became more comfortable with each other and with the meditation practices that the Levines were teaching, the honesty and intimacy of the sharing increased. By letting themselves fully experience the very fear and grief that they had hoped to get away from, people who had suffered inconceivable loss were transformed before our eyes. It took some people, especially those who had lost children, longer than others to put down their burdens of guilt and grief. But even those who had spent years in bitter pain began to soften and experience the possibility of a happier life.

How was this happening? The daily routine was not that different from those of other retreats I had observed. We would begin each morning and afternoon with mindfulness meditation—relaxing the body, watching our breath, quieting the mind. The Levines would lecture and answer questions; people would share their stories; in the evening we would meditate again. Yet as the days went on things began to happen in the group meditation sessions that I had never witnessed before in any of the spiritual retreats hosted by Omega. In the deep silence that developed through group meditation, people began to sigh and then sob. Others would get up and gently put their arms around someone in need. Small groups would form and quiet conversations begin. Waves of silence would come and go, mingled with laughter, soft talking, crying. Throughout the session Stephen and Ondrea would remain in meditation, interrupting now and then to remind us to keep breathing softly in the belly—"soft belly" became the code words for opening the heart and feeling whatever was there without judgment or fear. By the end of the meditation session we would all be back in our seats, deep in silence again, purified and opened by the act of putting down our burden with a sense of gentle self-forgiveness.

While some of the meditation techniques that the Levines were teaching were similar to several classic forms I had learned previously, the intent behind them was different. Since many people in the room were dying or in intense states of physical pain and emotional grief, the stated purpose of each practice was to allow healing into the heart. In order to do that it was necessary to direct the meditative awareness to the armoring that protected the heart from feeling pain. The armor that accumulates over years to defend against pain and fear becomes the same armor that keeps us from healing, from experiencing joy, from feeling love. In my notes from that first retreat, I copied the following from one of Stephen and Ondrea's talks: "This armoring around the heart is the accumulation of all the moments we have given ourselves and others so little mercy. *We are so hard on ourselves, so hard on each other.* Healing begins when we soften our stance toward our own tender self."

I was entering the Landscape of the Heart. Where in the Landscape of the Mind attention, equanimity, and peace are the guiding principles, in the heart's abode we aim for forgiveness, openness, and love. The Levines pointed out that the first step in this process, and the most difficult one, is self-forgiveness—letting go of the unforgiving standards of perfection that we heap on ourselves. One common theme ran through all of the sharings I was to witness during the retreat: each one of us seems embarrassed by our very humanness. We fear revealing familiar human traits like ignorance and confusion, or pride and jealousy. We pretend to have it together. We show the world only one side of our face—our happy and confident face—while deep inside we beat ourselves up for our inadequacies and doubts. And we all carry this burden within, this weight of self-embarrassment and self-judgment. It keeps us from knowing each other and from knowing ourselves. The Levines were giving us the opportunity to put the burden down and to find healing in our shared humanity. Encouraged by the honest display of humanness all around me, I started peeling back the layers of my heart. And there, right below the surface, was a solid wall of unhappiness that I had avoided for as long as I could remember. Each time I would get close to really feeling my grief in a meditation or a group sharing, I would be overcome by powerful waves of shame. I had no right to feel sad; my problems were minuscule compared with those of the others in the room; I was here to learn how to help my friend; I would appear weak and self-indulgent if I revealed the nature of my own petty predicaments. What would others think of me if I told them about my unhappy marriage, my unfulfilled longings, my lack of zest for life, my deep sadness? No way, I was not going there.

For the first day of the retreat I sat silently observing others with *real* problems stand before the group and courageously tell their stories. When a man in the group spoke of the deadness he felt at work and allowed us to watch him trace those feelings back to the death of his son, and then farther back to his relationship with his father, I felt great compassion and admiration for him. When a woman stood and through her tears admitted how angry she still was at her ex-husband for years of verbal abuse, I loved her for her honesty. But when I timidly explored my own feelings, in the privacy of meditation, I became a harsh judge of my embarrassing weaknesses, my petty desires, my selfish needs.

One morning, before the retreat started, I had breakfast with the Levines. We sat quietly in the faculty dining room. I ate granola and drank herbal tea. Stephen smoked a cigarette and drank coffee, while Ondrea just sat, wrapped in a blanket, looking like a cross between an angel and a crow. I wanted to know more about these people. How had they learned to create environments that were so refined and gentle, and yet that encouraged such honesty and growth? Across the breakfast table, Stephen looked more like an ex-con than a spiritual teacher, smashing his cigarette butt on the plate, drinking his black coffee.

Eyeing the cigarette, I asked him what in his life had made him able to teach and heal. He told me briefly about his meditation practice, about his work in the California prison system, and how he and Ondrea had run a free consultation telephone line for those confronting serious illness and death. He described his years as a junkie, when he lived on the streets. He spoke candidly about his first marriage, his divorce, and his struggles and joys as a parent and stepparent. Ondrea talked about their devotion to each other and their children, about her own brush with cancer and death, and about the way she and Stephen had stuck together through her healing process. "Now we just live in the high mountains attempting to practice what we preach," Stephen laughed.

I told Stephen and Ondrea about Ellen, and asked for advice about her particular condition. Stephen graciously gave me some basic guidelines to follow should I be with Ellen as she died. Ondrea added a word here and there, but mostly maintained her angelic, no-bullshit silence. Sometimes she reminded me of a boulder, other times she seemed like a bird, poised delicately on a branch, about to fly away. Neither of them was pretending to be anything but the full flowering of exactly who each had been, and therefore was now. Stephen knew how to help others forgive only because he had forgiven himself. Ondrea knew how to help others heal because she had suffered and had healed herself. They brought all of themselves into the retreat. Because of that, people took their words to heart and opened their lives to the group.

As the retreat progressed I began to work deeply with the act of self-forgiveness. The sharings in the room became more and more honest. People stopped trying to impress each other, trying to be someone else, even trying to change. I finally shared with the group, and in doing so I joined the human community with all of its flaws, pain, and limitations. I knew that we were all in this together, "just Bozos on the bus," as Stephen said. We all suffered; we all made mistakes; we all got sick; we all felt anger and sadness. None of us was perfect.

We began to understand how wasteful it was to use life's precious energy on trying to escape the pain of our imperfect lives. "Pain is a given. Suffering comes from our resistance to pain," Stephen said, as he encouraged us to feel whatever our hearts were offering us. The way to joy and freedom was through the pain, not around it. A mother whose only child had been killed by a hit-and-run driver three years previously told her story through a cloud of rage. Each time she would stand to speak she would rail against the driver, or beg for her child to return so that she could begin to live again. Slowly she began to go deeper, as she let herself plainly miss her daughter and experience the unadulterated feelings of sadness. Instead of wanting to punish the driver or get her daughter back, she rested in the reality of what had happened, of how guilty she felt, and how lonely for her little girl she was. At the end of the retreat she shared that while she felt exhausted with grief, she also felt alive for the first time in three years. The energy she had been using not to feel the pain was now freed. Yes, she felt great sadness, but she also felt a river of joy moving in her.

A young man, close to death, had been one of the most vocal members of the retreat. His sharings had been particularly painful for the group to hear. Time after time he would rise and list all of the treatments he had taken, how diligent he had been with his diet and in following his doctor's orders. Why wasn't he healing? Did anyone know another healer or medicine he could take? No one in the room was suffering as much as he, he kept reminding us. He was too young to die. He would do anything, behave better, make up for his past transgressions. It took him longer than most to understand what the Levines were saying—that his healing would be found, whether it be remission or death, when he accepted his disease; that his heart would lighten when he was able to forgive himself for being a human being, full of mistakes and imperfections; and that he would be free when he rested gently in the inevitability of death, whenever that might be. It was an amazing moment when he shared at the end of the retreat, "I realize now that if I die it won't be a sign of failure. I have come to accept myself exactly how I am and now I am free. This is a great gift. I hope everybody can get born before they die."

It was through this process, repeated every time a participant would rise to share his or her story, that I received everything I needed to help Ellen. Whether a person was struggling with a life-and-death situation, or was just troubled by the difficulties of everyday life, I began to understand that pain was pain, no matter how dramatic. Opening to pain, fearlessly confronting the "full catastrophe," and the subsequent freedom that came from that simple act, would benefit the dying person, the grieving person, and anyone trying to make sense out of life. "Treat yourself like your only child," Ondrea had said during one meditation. This is what I saw the people doing in the retreat. For the time being, they had stopped trying to live up to the impossible standards that they had set for themselves. They had forgiven themselves for being imperfect human beings, just as they would their beloved only child. In the process they discovered the life-giving gifts of an open heart. As one of the participants wrote in a letter after the retreat, and right before he died, "An open heart is a much greater blessing than death is a tragedy."

This was what I brought home to Ellen. We spent several weekends together and most of what we did seemed to have nothing to do with the fact that she was living on borrowed time, transfusions, and grace. We cared for our children, cooked, and sat and talked in the window seat, watching the winter sky. I told her, as best as I could, about what Stephen and Ondrea had said: that if she could look openly and tenderly at reality, if she could stop striving for what couldn't be and start participating fully in what was, if she could let go of her burdens of fear and self-blame, then she would be free to discover her own way to healing or to a peaceful death; then she could live fully in whatever amount of time was given to her. I taught her the "soft belly" meditation, which moved her to tears each time we would do it together.

Ellen began to soften. You could see it in her face and in the way she was with her husband, her mother, and her son. As she let herself feel her anger and grief and fear, she realized how much tension she had been holding in her body and how that had been spilling over into her life. This woman who had been such a fighter, whose New England roots were written all over her face, had never been very comfortable with displays of emotion. Now she began to say things to her friends and family that surprised us: "If only people realized what they had in life," she told me one day, "they would not be able to contain their joy!" She tried to clean up old patterns with her husband, told the truth, asked forgiveness from her friends. She spent most of her time with her son, reading to him, holding him, playing with him. She seemed more at peace than I had ever seen her.

One scene comes to mind that I will never forget. A few friends had gathered at her house. I looked around the room. There was her husband, sitting alone in the corner, worn and angry. A couple was arguing about who would pick up their child at the baby-sitter's. I was being short-tempered with my kids and Ellen's son that day, having squeezed this visit into an already full schedule. Then I looked at Ellen, paper thin and wrapped in a blanket in a rocking chair. She was watching the snow fall outside the window. She turned to us and in a small voice said, "Would you all please love each other?"

On a December evening she slipped into a coma. I arrived with my children the next morning, as we had planned weeks before, to take her and her son Christmas shopping. I found Ellen lying on her bed, breathing very lightly, a thin trail of blood coming from her mouth. Her doctors had warned us that at any time her body could reject the blood transfusions that were keeping her alive. The time was now.

Her husband had taken their son to a neighbor's house. I brought my boys there too and then called the hospital to get directions on a journey I had never before taken. I was fortunate to speak to a doctor who was honest and compassionate with me. He knew how much Ellen wanted to die at home. He told me that if we brought her to the hospital they would put her on life-support machines and prolong her life for a while, but that she would probably never regain full consciousness. He guessed that she had suffered a brain hemorrhage.

"What should I do? Should we come to the hospital?" I asked, panicking.

"I can't tell you what to do," the doctor said.

"When is she going to die?"

"I don't know. You will know."

"How?"

"Just watch her breathing. That will tell you what you need to know."

For a few hours I sat with Ellen, her husband, and an old friend who had also chosen this of all days to visit. We were meant to be in this wilderness together. Ellen was leading us now. Tears pushed through her closed eyes and ran down her face. The day seemed to stretch in all directions. It was a circle. It was out of time. Morning moved into afternoon as I held Ellen's hand, breathed with her, and sang to her. Songs that I had never sung found my voice, songs that she had loved. Faces of people whom I had never met, who were dear to her, came into my mind.

Slowly the spaces between Ellen's breaths became longer. Her tears stopped flowing. The night was coming on and the room was getting cold. We sat suspended in time, with only the spaces between Ellen's breaths to guide us. None of us remembers how long we sat like this. Wonderful things happened—visitations, breezes, sudden knowings—things that I feel awkward telling since I hardly believe them myself. And then the space between the breaths got so long, that was all there was—space—huge, abiding space. We sat in the immensity of space with Ellen. We went a little way with her on her eternal journey and then turned back when we noticed that she had not taken a new breath for a long time. She had gone on and we were still here, sitting on her bed, holding on to her cold hands.

Ellen's death changed my life. I had watched someone step boldly into life even as she was dying. It was as if whereas before she had been observing her life—choosing and rejecting, holding back, not giving fully nor receiving—in her final months she had said "Yes" to it all. Like the young man in the Levines' retreat had said, she had been born before she had died. Ellen had stopped worrying what the world wanted from her and had made it her job to become more alive. Would I be able to do this? Could I forge a path to a life fully lived? What was standing in the way? I wanted to find out.

WHAT DO I REALLY LOVE?

Let yourself be silently drawn,
by the stronger pull of what you really love.
    —RUMI

What I discovered standing between me and full aliveness was fear. After the initial impact of the Levines' retreat and of Ellen's death had worn off, I was left with the memory of a wholeness that I had never felt before, but with no way to sustain it within the context of everyday life. It seemed that every time I would try to re-create the experience of opening my heart to life, I would hit a wall of fear. Sometimes the wall felt solid. Sometimes it was vague and shifting, as if it were made of clouds and sadness. Under the Levines' skillful guidance, I had begun to dismantle, stone by stone, cloud by cloud, the structure of my defenses. And I had witnessed other people who had been storing hostility and fear for so long melting before my eyes and emerging with a fresh sense of life. But how many of them, once at home, back at work, had been able to integrate what they had touched on during the retreat?

My biggest fear was that if I freed my heart enough to feel all of my feelings, I would surely want to make some big life changes. If I let myself feel how hungry I was for emotional love, for physical connection, for pleasure, then I would blow up my life as I knew it. I was justified in harboring this fear, because in the end, that is exactly what happened. Other things happened too—wonderful and meaningful things, and ultimately healing things—but it was a phoenix-like experience for me. I ignited my life and a new me arose from the ashes. By no means am I suggesting that this is the only way heartfulness works—that if you shine the light of truth on your emotional core, you will necessarily make volcanic changes. But a word of warning here: the way of the heart is the way of the "sacred warrior," to use a phrase made popular by Chögyam Trungpa. There is danger in asking ourselves what we really love, what we really want. Yet there is a different kind of danger in *not* opening the heart; a darker danger, I believe. Death lives in a closed heart. "Life seems to love the liver of it," says Maya Angelou.

Because we fear the consequences of living from the heart, we try not to listen to its whispers of discontent and longing, its big ideas and wild dreams. "Fear of knowing," writes Abraham Maslow, "is very deeply a fear of doing." How much do we want to know if knowing pulls us out of the safety zone? How much responsibility for our own discontent would we be willing to take? Are we ready to stop projecting our lack of fulfillment onto other people and take our lives into our own hands? A friend of mine who works with corporate managers shared with me what one of his clients admitted: "I knew the work was suffocating my soul but to admit it would be too devastating; it would mean that I had to do something about it!"

The price for staying heart blind is a life unlived. The Dalai Lama has gone as far as saying that "the tendency to avoid problems and the emotional suffering inherent in them is the primary basis of all human mental illness." Heartfulness work is the cessation of avoidance. It is about listening, waiting, and trusting. Here is the key to heartfulness: you can listen deeply to the heart's desires *without having to act on each and every one of them.* In the realm of the heart we learn to separate listening from acting. The action part comes later, after we have learned how to decipher the messages.

The heart is like a bank of messages. Deep in its vault is everything you need to know about yourself: old wounds, misguided conclusions, secret truths, wise guidance. Put together, the messages become the story of who you are and who you aren't; what you really love; decisions you should make; and how you can find lasting happiness. If you don't listen to the heart—if you don't bring your longing to consciousness—you won't find out what you really want, and you will be a slave to your ignorance and denial. Jung said, "What is not brought to consciousness, comes to us as fate," and nowhere is this more true than in the realm of the heart.

After Ellen's death I had felt a new hopefulness rising in my heart, an inner strength, a more open and trusting attitude, less of a need to control others and destiny itself. What was I to do now with this wall separating me from my brief experience of a free heart? Before I had used meditation and other spiritual teachings to walk around the wall and go to some other domain that felt like freedom. Now I understood that kind of freedom was just a hint of what was really available to me if I could bring my whole self along. I didn't want to go around life to find God. I wanted to go *through* it all and emerge whole, connected, fully human. I needed a way through, now that I had experienced what was possible. That way was therapy.

Let me be honest here: I went into therapy because my life was a mess. Yes, I did want to find God in everyday life, but mostly I just wanted to stay functional. I was losing my grip at work and home. The more I allowed myself to know what I felt, the more I wanted to do something about it. Old wounds suffered earlier in my marriage came back to haunt me. I harbored new feelings of resentment and anger toward my husband. As my marriage unraveled, I became a stranger to myself. I had thought that my own needs should always come second to the needs of my husband and children; now I wanted some things for myself. I had prided myself on being such a *good* person; now I fell in love with another man and had an affair. I became the very person I had accused my husband of being. I experienced real guilt and terror—the kind that wakes you up at night as if a knife were at your throat—when I realized how much was at stake for me and my children. I put my job, my stability, my home at risk. These are not easy actions to reveal, nor am I proud of my behavior.

And yet all the while I felt new life stirring in me. It seemed the deeper I went into this underworld, the more alive I felt. I was on a thrilling exploration in a shadowy new world. But something told me I could go too far, that I could pass a point of no return. It was from this premonition that I turned to therapy. What had before sounded like psychobabble now began to make sense.

I had benefited from a teacher in the Landscape of the Mind; I needed a new kind of guide now. I made several stabs at therapy before I found a therapist I trusted enough to help me through the "descent process," the term mythologists use to describe the kind of experience I was having. I worked for three years on a weekly basis with a therapist who had trained in a method called the Pathwork—a system of self-realization that combines spirituality and psychology.

One of the reasons that pop psychology can come across as such drivel is that what actually goes on behind the therapist's door is very difficult to describe. Each time I would emerge from a powerful session and try to explain what had happened or what I had learned, I would hear myself sounding like a bad self-help book. Another reason that therapy can appear shallow is that unless one is willing to work very honestly and very hard, it is all too easy to skim the easy parts off the surface of therapy and pretend that real progress has been made. Self-disclosure without a real desire to change becomes hollow self-apology. Even now, after genuinely benefiting from psychotherapy, I shudder when I hear the process described on talk shows or read about it in magazine articles. There is such a thin line between self-examination and narcissism. It is very easy to cross that line in the Landscape of the Heart. The intimate engagement with a skilled therapist is the best way to stay on the honest side of the line.

The work I did with my therapist focused on three major areas of self-awareness: First, I worked to overcome the shame of having physical and emotional needs. I began to gain respect for the hungers of my body and my heart. I was shown a radically different understanding of self-love and self-forgiveness. I began to see how wanting something for myself was not necessarily a selfish desire, that nurturing myself and caring for others were not mutually exclusive.

The second part of the therapeutic process for me was to learn how to distinguish within myself different voices competing for airspace. I practiced creating boundaries between my own true voice and the voices of my parents, my culture, my husband, and my children.

And third, after I had learned about respecting my feelings and creating boundaries, I embarked on the lifelong journey of living in "conscious relationship" with others. I let the truth of my own needs meet up with the needs of others; I became more honest in my communication and more realistic in my expectations; and I began to replace the fruitless emotion of guilt with the constructive behavior of self-responsibility. I began to make wiser decisions, which took into account the whole picture and not just my side of the story. I hitched my feelings to reality and made peace with this truth: getting what you want does not mean having everything. "From sacrifice comes bliss," says Joseph Campbell, surely not a novel proclamation, but a liberating concept if learned from the real-life experience of following one's heart.

HUNGER

Step number one, allowing myself to be hungry for emotional fulfillment, was the hardest step for me to take. It meant I had to undo a lot of what I believed about human beings. Even though I wasn't formally raised a Christian or a Jew, I still was profoundly influenced by the Old Testament portrait of a punishing, judgmental God, and even more so by the creation story, in which Adam and Eve are happy campers until they give in to their own curiosity and desires. The Christian concept, or at least Augustine's concept, of "original sin" is a very strange basis for a religious worldview. It tells us that to want things for ourselves is bad; to be curious about the workings of the universe is dangerous. And it tells us that obedience to an all-knowing, fearsome father figure is good. It sets up a cycle of self-contempt when we inevitably find ourselves wanting and wondering. Matthew Fox, a former Catholic priest who was silenced by the Vatican for his questioning of the way the Church interpreted the creation myth, believes that "the religious paradigm shift of our time is one from original sin to original blessing."

Fox's "original blessing" theory states that humans are fundamentally good, as are animals, the earth, and all of life. "And God saw that it was good" becomes a more valid biblical worldview than original sin. If mankind is good, then the body is sacred, emotions are valid, sex is holy, and the earth is to be safeguarded. Our hunger for pleasure and connection is not profane. Rather, it is the repression of pleasure that distorts our hunger and leads us to unhealthy sources for satisfaction. Addicts who have thought much about their behavior will tell you that the repression of feelings in their childhood environments led them to their addictions. Because their childhood experiences taught them they were bad to want love and affection, their hunger went underground; it became fierce; they were compelled to seek fulfillment in the darkness.

To some extent, all of us are addicts if we are satisfying our hunger with inappropriate nourishment. When you find yourself standing in front of the refrigerator just an hour after dinner, or mindlessly switching television channels, or dialing the phone number of someone you don't even want to speak with, there's a good chance that you are not in touch with your real hunger. There is a good chance that if you stopped and just sat with your sense of hunger, and let it tell you something about itself, that you would be led to a deeper watering hole. Often we reach for food when what we really want is love; we have a drink or smoke a joint when we long to feel connected; we numb out in front of the television when we're hungering for peace of mind. None of these choices, in and of themselves, is evil. But, usually, if we resist the urge to fill the "God-shaped hole"—

with something, anything—we'd be better off. We'd be better than better off. We would discover a vast reservoir of information, direction, and spiritual nourishment within ourselves.

When I teach, there are usually several people in the class who are suffering from addictions or eating disorders. These people find the following poem, "Feast," by Edna St. Vincent Millay, meaningful and helpful:

> I drank at every vine
>   The last was like the first.
> I came upon no wine
>   So wonderful as thirst.
>
> I gnawed at every root.
>   I ate of every plant.
> I came upon no fruit
>   So wonderful as want.
>
> Feed the grape and bean
>   To the vintner and monger;
> I will lay down lean
>   With my thirst and my hunger.

How many of us could "lay down lean" with our thirst and our hunger, if that meant not giving in to the urge to fill the emptiness with food, or drink, or drugs, or sex, or television? How many of us could sit with our hunger long enough to know what we really hungered for? Many mystical traditions use fasting as a way of bringing this point home. Allowing oneself to feel physically hungry is a powerful exercise if it is done not as a way to deny oneself, but as a way to befriend hunger as a messenger of what we really want.

Think back to the last time you were really hungry or thirsty—maybe after you had exerted your body strenuously, or after you had missed a meal in the busyness of your daily routine. Remember the vivid sensation of thirst after a long hike. You wanted to drink pure, cold water—not a Coke or a cup of coffee, but exactly what your body needed. And when you did, the enjoyment was as vivid as the thirst. You want what you need when you are really hungry. Hazrat Inayat Khan said that "life is an opportunity to satisfy the hunger and thirst of the soul." We'll only know what the soul hungers for if we let ourselves be hungry long enough to feel its presence.

Edna St. Vincent Millay says in her poem that she "came upon no wine so wonderful as thirst" and "no fruit so wonderful as want." If we risk the imaginary dangers of being hungry for a passionate life—if we allow ourselves to feel the emptiness long enough and deep enough to hear the heart's messages—we end up loving the longing itself. We become less apt to want to rush to fill our every desire. We allow ourselves to feel tender and open and even lonely, without having to do anything about it. Hunger becomes a sign of being alive. I want to add here that heartfulness work is closely aligned to the work we explore in Book IV, "The Landscape of the Body." The body doesn't lie about its hungers. Until we connect the heart "to the musculature of the body," says Jungian analyst Marion Woodman, "it lacks the visceral affirmation that says, 'This is of value to me. This is who I am.' " In Book IV we connect the wisdom of the body to the mind and the heart.

THE GENUINE HEART OF SADNESS

A hungry heart is a tender heart. And tenderness contains a certain element of sadness. My favorite writer on the subject of tenderizing the heart is Chögyam Trungpa, the Tibetan scholar whose life and teachings opened the West to Tibetan Buddhism in the 1970s. As described in Chapter Six, Trungpa's youth as a monk in the great monasteries of Eastern Tibet ended abruptly when the Chinese invaded his homeland in 1959. Trungpa's experience—especially leading an escape of his people over the Himalayas into India—led to the development of a unique interpretation of Tibetan Buddhism, what he called "the sacred path of the warrior."

Trungpa taught the Buddhist practice of *bodhicitta,* or awakened heart. His own term for awakened heart was "the genuine heart of sadness," which he explained as a natural and beautiful condition, the result of staying open to the full experience of life. Through the practice of *bodhicitta,* "we can learn to be without deception, to be fully genuine and alive," he wrote in his classic book on the spiritual path, *Shambhala: The Sacred Path of the Warrior.* He used the term *warrior* throughout his writings, to suggest how brave we must be to defeat our own self-deception, while at the same time remaining open, sensitive, tender.

"Tenderness," he wrote, "contains an element of sadness. It is not the sadness of feeling sorry for yourself or feeling deprived, but it is a natural situation of fullness. You feel so full and rich, as if you were about to shed tears. In order to be a good warrior, one has to feel this sad and tender heart. If a person does not feel alone and sad, he cannot be a warrior at all. The warrior is sensitive to every aspect of phenomena—sight, smell, sound, feelings."

Sadness, in this context, is not the opposite of happiness. The opposite of happiness is a closed heart. Happiness is a heart so soft and so expansive that it can hold all of the emotions in a cradle of openness. A happy heart is one that is larger at all times than any one emotion. An open heart feels everything—including anger, grief, and pain—and absorbs it into a bigger and wiser experience of reality. Joseph Campbell calls happiness the "joyful participation in the sorrows of the world."

Many defend against the genuine heart of sadness out of a concern of becoming maudlin, or weak, or a drag to be around. In almost every class I have taught people have expressed the fear that if they let themselves feel the grief or anger within them, they would drown in their tears, or unleash a torrent of rage. Friends would turn away. Things would fall apart. But this is not what happens. Certainly, right below the surface of their emotions, people discover long-repressed grief and anger. Delving into the heart can bring us into contact with feelings and memories we'd rather not have. But underneath the anger and cynicism that dominate many people's moods is a pool of innocent sadness that must be felt. The wounding of purity in childhood can make it feel untrustworthy to venture back into our innocence. An uneasiness with any display of weakness can make us turn tail the minute we sense a rising tide of emotions. We've spent years building protective walls of suspicion and pride.

We may think that by closing the heart we'll protect ourselves from feeling the pain of the world, but instead, we isolate ourselves even more from joy. From my own experience and from observing many others, I have come to believe that the opposite of happiness is a fearful, closed heart. Happiness is ours when we go through our anger, fear, and pain, all the way to our sadness, and then slowly let sadness develop into tenderness.

This is not a quick and easy journey for most people. Our defenses are in place for reasons that made a lot of sense in childhood. That's why we often have to go back into our pasts to retrieve our authentic ability to feel. "As I think back over my last twenty years' work," writes the noted Swiss psychologist Alice Miller, "... I can find no patient whose ability to experience his true feelings was not seriously impaired. Yet without this basic ability, all our work with the patient's conflicts is illusory." Miller believes that it is only through the healing journey into childhood's innocence that a person "regains his long-lost authentic sense of being truly alive."

On my own journey through the landscape of the heart, I went back to my childhood to look for my lost self. On the way, I began hearing the internalized voices of my mother and father, who long ago had unwittingly steered me in directions away from my authentic self. As I learned to differentiate between my own true voice and their voices, I began to put my own voice in charge of my life. Only then was I able to regain my "long-lost authentic sense of being truly alive."

CREATING BOUNDARIES

There is no sense talking about "being true to myself" until you are sure what voice you are being true to. It takes hard work to differentiate the voices of the unconscious.
—MARION WOODMAN

I remember the day I decided to stop obeying my mother's voice. I was thirty-two years old, long gone from my parents' house, with two children of my own. My decision was not an act of defiance. It was an inner awakening and a reckoning with who I was and who she was, and where she stopped and I began.

I had been in therapy for a few months by then, and my therapist was patiently steering me in the direction of "differentiating the voices of my unconscious" (although, at the time, I was ignorant of the host of characters alive and well in my unconscious). My therapy sessions seemed to me storytelling—me telling my therapist about my childhood, my unraveling marriage, my chaotic life. Every time I would chide myself for immature desires or unreasonable behavior, he would ask, "Who says that's unreasonable?" "Who tells you it's immature?" I wouldn't answer. I didn't know what he meant, until one warm autumn day when I found out the hard way.

I was raking leaves in the front yard as I waited for my kids to get off the school bus and run home through the woods. The sweet smell of the rotting foliage awakened my childhood memories, and as I raked, I remembered the mountains of leaves my mother would make for me and my sisters to jump in. Lost in thoughts and feelings—about my mother, about me as a child, me as an adult, about my own children—I raked up huge piles of glowing leaves. Suddenly I realized that the phone was ringing, and running into the house, picking up the phone, I heard my mother's voice. How unusual! My mother rarely called, and never during the day. She was old-fashioned, a letter writer. I did the calling.

"Mom! I was just thinking about you. Is everything all right?" I asked.

"Yes, I was just thinking about you too, and about the kids. I don't want you to go through with this divorce, Elizabeth. I don't want you to do this to the kids," she said, tears in her voice. "They are my grandchildren too."

"Mom, we've been through this already," I pleaded. "Please don't make it harder. The kids will be OK," I said, praying to believe that myself. "In fact, the divorce may be better for them. They may finally have a happy mother and father."

"Oh, nonsense," she said, her voice quivering. "What's the matter with you people? You think you should be happy! Be reasonable. Mature people do not need to be happy. And they don't need to be in love, either. Happiness is for children. Love is for teenagers. Think about your children."

That's when it happened. That's when I knew what my therapist had been getting at. Here was the voice that was keeping me all tied up in confusion and guilt. Here was the voice that used words in my therapy sessions like "mature" and "reasonable." And then I did something I had never done before—I hung up on my mother. It was as if another hand took the phone out of mine and slammed it down. I stood for a moment in stunned silence, and then went back outside and lay facedown in the mountain of leaves.

I let the full force of my mother's words into my heart, as the sun warmed my back and the leaves cradled my body. I let her message ring in my heart, like a bell being rung over and over to announce the end of a war. This time I wanted to hear the sounds for what they really were: her words, not mine; her voice, not mine. I wanted to grasp how unworkable they were, how untrue, and how different from what I really believed. The more deeply I listened to my mother's voice, the clearer my own became. Maybe her words had worked for her. It didn't matter; they did not work for me. I knew she was trying to help in the only way that she knew how. I knew that she was trying to protect my children out of her love for them and for me. But that didn't mean she knew what was best for them or me. Only I knew that.

When I stood up and shook the leaves from my sweater, I was different. All the work I had been doing with my therapist seemed to crystallize in that moment. When the kids ran through the woods and into the leaf mountain, I wanted to yell to them, "Hey, it's me, your mother! Just me, for better or worse, but all of me. I'm giving you all of me from now on." Instead I just jumped in the leaves with them, with a new sense of trust in myself as their mother. I felt strangely alone, more on my own than ever, yet also closer to my boys, and closer to myself.

As I gained more trust in my own values, all of my relationships began to change for the better. My relationship with my mother was never the same. For a long time after that phone call I stayed away from her. I felt too weak in my budding sense of self to allow her voice back in. But over the years our friendship has healed and deepened. My love and gratitude for her—as a woman, a friend, and a mother—are actually stronger now that I have separated some of her beliefs from mine. Our conversations now take place between two women, and we have even been able to help each other grow. Late in her life my mother has started to differentiate the voices of her unconscious, to name some of them—mother, father, husband, Depression, World War II, 1950s—and to come more and more fully into her own, true self. We both have come a long way.

Different psychological schools have different terms for the process I just described. The Jungians call the long journey back to the genuine self *individuation.* Popular psychology calls it *creating boundaries.* I like the image of building a boundary between self and other—not to create alienation, but to secure a healthy ego and a useful identity. Until we learn to separate the conflicting urges and directives within, and establish an authentic voice for ourselves, we don't know which beliefs and values are our own, and which ones were primarily adopted from our familial and cultural conditioning. We can't answer questions like "What matters most to me?" or "What do I really want?" We can't make wise decisions that lead to happy lives when we don't know our own true self. And we can't have healthy relationships when we can't let the other person know what we want, or value, or need.

Once I grasped what my therapist had been leading me toward, I was eager to explore the full cast of characters in my psyche. I began to dialogue with them, and to sort out which voices to make my own, and which ones to hush. I moved from working with my mother's voice, to the voice of my father—an equally powerful influence on my life. I discovered within me demons and angels, saints and sinners. As I began to free myself from the control of the internalized voices of my mother and father, I also stopped blaming them for my problems. Once I stepped up closer to my own true self, I began to take responsibility for both my powerful goodness and my shadowy underside. Over the years I find that the more responsibility I take for my own behavior, the less I project my unhappiness onto others, and the faster I move from confusion to clarity, and from depression to joy.

Taking back projection and *creating healthy boundaries:* these are two psychological concepts that take patience and work to understand and put into action. If they are rushed they can backfire. Taking back projections is the act of seeing yourself truthfully in relationship to others. It involves taking responsibility for your difficulties instead of blaming others. When you take back projections you no longer rush to condemn another, nor do you put people up on pedestals. You see yourself and others clearly. You are more willing to admit your own faults. You are also better able to take credit for your talents and achievements. Therefore you develop an instinct of when to give ground and when to stand firm.

It doesn't work to try and take back projections before you have created healthy boundaries. If you force yourself to take responsibility in relationships before you have sufficiently strengthened your sense of self, you can easily become a guilt-ridden martyr. Likewise, if you think that the end-all and be-all is creating boundaries, you run the risk of becoming self-inflated and unyielding. You want to do both—strengthen your sense of self *and* engage in relationships that respect others and the world.

Both of these important stages of heartfulness work, taking back projection and creating healthy boundaries, can take years to understand and integrate, and, to some extent, are never fully accomplished. This kind of deep psychological work brings us into the shadowy world of the unconscious, where quick fixes and straight paths do not exist. Going into the unconscious may seem too risky or lengthy a process, but we have to go into the hidden places of the psyche before coming into the light. Jung wrote that "one does not become enlightened by imaging figures of light but by making the darkness conscious. The latter procedure, however, is disagreeable and therefore not popular." As "disagreeable" as going into our own darkness may be, the rewards more than make up for the unsettling nature of the journey.

SHADOW-WORK

If you bring forth what is within you, what you bring forth will save you. If you do not bring forth what is within you, what you do not bring forth will destroy you.
—JESUS

Jung called the secret shame and the old voices buried in the dark heart the "shadow." He wrote, "by shadow I mean the 'negative' side of the personality, the sum of all those unpleasant qualities we like to hide. . . ." In their excellent anthology, *Meeting the Shadow: The Hidden Power of the Dark Side of Human Nature,* Connie Zweig and Jeremiah Abrams use the term "shadow-work" to describe "the ongoing inclusion of that which was rejected" in our psyches. "The goal of shadow-work," they write, "cannot be accomplished with a simple method or trick of the mind. Rather, it is a complex, ongoing struggle that calls for great commitment, vigilance, and the loving support of others who are traveling a similar road."

Jung himself warned that shadow-work was a delicate process: "Each piece of the shadow that we realize has a weight, and our consciousness is lowered to that extent when we take it into our boat. Therefore, one might say that the main art of dealing with the shadow consists in the right loading of our boat: if we take too little, we fly away from reality and become, as it were, a fluffy white cloud without substance in the sky, and if we take too much we may sink our boat." We may know people who float around like clouds, unwilling or unable to recognize their own darkness, who consistently try to cover their anger with a smiley-face sticker, or their grief with a joke. And we also may know those whose boats are sinking from the weight of their unconscious emotions—those people who take everything to heart, and then don't know how to handle their feelings. They may be full of rage or despair, or embittered by the trauma and misfortune that have come their way. Shadow-work is a balancing act, a slow process and a stage of growth whereby we fish in the waters for the darkness that leads to the light.

In *A Little Book on the Human Shadow,* my favorite of all the shadow literature, Robert Bly writes a short passage that describes the shadow beautifully:

When we were one or two years old we had what we might visualize as a 360-degree personality. Energy radiated out from all parts of our body and all parts of our psyche. A child running is a living globe of energy. We had a ball of energy, all right; but one day we noticed that our parents didn't like certain parts of that ball. They said things like: "Can't you be still?" Or, "It isn't nice to want to kill your brother." Behind us we have an invisible bag, and the part of us our parents don't like, we, to keep our parents' love, put it in the bag. By the time we go to school our bag is quite large. Then our teachers have their say: "Good children don't get angry over such little things." So we take our anger and put it in the bag. By the time my brother and I were twelve in Madison, Minnesota, we were known as "the nice Bly boys." Our bags were already a mile long.

All of us are dragging a bag of shadows behind us. Being a girl, I put in my bag things like my sexuality, my aggression, and the tidelike ebbs and flows of my emotions. My mother told me girls weren't supposed to be sexual beings; my father expected that women should be sweet and yielding; and the culture maintained that women's moods were way too fickle to be trusted. All that went in the bag. "We spend our life until we're twenty deciding what parts of ourself to put into the bag, and we spend the rest of our lives trying to get them out again," writes Bly. Shadow-work is getting those parts out of the bag in such a way that we heal ourselves and our relationships without causing more harm.

It's helpful to read *about* the shadow, but I cannot stress enough the importance of experiential work in this area of the spiritual path. The beauty, and the terror, of shadow-work is that it demands we make our spirituality real. Noble ideals are put to the test if we take shadow-work to heart. If we just make an intellectual investigation of human darkness and the ideas of the shadow and projection, we'll have done nothing more than add a few more words to our vocabulary. Chapter Ten, A Heartfulness Toolbox, provides several exercises that prod us beyond the vocabulary of the heart and into action.

I had all the right vocabulary for a long time before I was challenged to make my shadow-work real. When my stepson first came from Los Angeles to live with us full-time, he was eleven years old and, as far as I perceived, from another planet. Where my other sons, ages ten and thirteen, were calm and relatively quiet, Michael, quite literally, bounced off the walls. He was so full of energy that he was often out of control—and I was determined to control him. "We see the shadow most indirectly," write Zweig and Abrams, "in distasteful traits and actions of other people, *out there* where it is safer to observe it. When we react intensely to a quality in an individual or group—such as laziness or stupidity, sensuality, or spirituality—and our reaction overtakes us with great loathing or admiration, this may be our shadow showing. We *project* by attributing this quality to the other person in an unconscious effort to banish it from ourselves, to keep ourselves from seeing it within."

Soon after he moved in, we discovered that on top of his natural exuberance, Michael also was suffering from Tourette's syndrome, a neurological disorder that manifests itself in tics and hyperactivity. Although it was mild, and many people never knew about it, Michael's Tourette's was hard on him. It manifested itself in tics and restlessness, which he tried to mask by constant activity.

I felt as if there were two strangers living in my home: one was Michael—a little, wild stranger; the other was myself—a big, controlling stranger. At work I was the one known for her sensitivity and compassion: I listened to coworkers' problems; I championed our scholarship fund; I worked to make our staff more diverse. Now, someone with problems, someone different from the rest of the family, was living with me. Did I greet the "other" with love and compassion? No, I did not. I was horrified to find that I was not the person I thought I was. Michael was just a little boy, suffering not only from a traumatic move from his mother's house to his father's new family, but also from a disorder beyond his control. Instead of trying to love him, I tried to make Michael change. I wanted him to calm down, to sit still, to fit into the mold. We entered into a battle of wills.

"Doing shadow-work," write Zweig and Abrams, "means asking ourselves to examine closely and honestly what it is about a particular individual that irritates us or repels us; what it is about a racial or religious group that horrifies or captivates us; and what it is about a lover that charms us and leads us to idealize him or her. Doing shadow-work means making a gentleman's agreement with one's self to engage in an internal conversation that can, at some time down the road, result in an authentic self-acceptance and a real compassion for others."

The year before Michael had come to live with us, I had wanted to have a Fresh Air kid—a child from a disadvantaged home—spend the summer with our family. Why not share the bounty of our life with a child who needed the kind of love we had to give? I argued to my husband. He argued back that there was already enough chaos in the house and we'd better wait until we were more stable. After Michael had been with us for a year, my resistance to his behavior was becoming a big issue in our marriage. One night, in the middle of a fight, my husband said something that finally got through to me: "Remember that Fresh Air kid you wanted? Well, here he is! He's Michael." That's when my shadow-work began.

For the next few years I made my relationship with Michael my spiritual path. In ways more graphic than I ever would have chosen, I got to see aspects of my shadow self: how desperately, at the expense of other people, I wanted to control life; how arrogant and aggressive I was; how right I thought I was; how conditional my love was. Every time I would spout loving-kindness philosophy at work, and then go home and resist loving Michael, I would feel sick. Did I really want to walk my heartfulness talk? This was as good a chance as any to do it. Over and over I went through the process of shadow-work: feeling my resistance to Michael's inability to sit still and just *be;* beating myself up for it on the one hand, or blaming Michael for it on the other; then going deeper into my feelings—using the ways in which I reacted intensely to aspects of Michael's behavior to learn more about myself; and eventually forgiving myself, forgiving Michael, and accepting the situation; and finally, taking responsibility to make our family work.

In the end, we both made it work. Michael went through his teen years, got a handle on his energy, and became a gifted actor and basketball player. I loosened up and learned how to give more of myself, how to love more fully. Where he would say that I became a second mother to him, I would say that he taught me, firsthand, how love heals and how control doesn't. Michael is my son by choice, which makes our bond rare and precious. Choosing to work on my relationship with Michael was as important a step on my spiritual path as the more glamorous-sounding ones. Pilgrimages to Jerusalem or long meditation retreats might provide a shot of inspiration, but shadow-work creates long-lasting change. I could have remained shut down. Or I could have opened just enough to maintain a cold-war kind of peace in our family. God knows, that's what I would have preferred to do many times. But my shadow was insistent, and thankfully, I listened to it and got a taste of what the Jungian analyst Marion Woodman calls "the dignity of unprojected human love."

I believe in the possibility of psychological change. This kind of faith is helpful during shadow-work because the territory is often dark and full of conflict. Going *through* the darkness may take a long time. Real growth happens in stages, and sometimes a stage may seem to go on and on for-ever. Trust the process. Reach out. Get support and help from friends and healers. Be on the lookout for your own resistance to change. Read the feedback life provides. And don't fear that by bringing your negativity out of the shadows and into the light that it will overpower you or run amok. As Jung says, "Once the negative side of your battle has become conscious, it will lose power."

SELF-RESPONSIBILITY

The goal of heartfulness work is to discover what you really love and want. The process of that discovery will lead you into a rich exploration of your longing, your hunger, your woundedness, and your shadow. The journey promises a wise heart and lasting happiness. But there are some traps along the way that bear noting, some hard truths of the heart that you will encounter sooner rather than later. It would be great if the surgeon general required all therapists to display a list of these truths on their office doors, like the warning on a cigarette package:

1. Warning! There Is a Thin Line Between Narcissism and Following Your Heart
2. Sorry! You Cannot Have Everything You Want
3. Required! A Sense of Humor
4. Stop!

1. *Warning! There Is a Thin Line Between Narcissism and Following Your Heart.* Self-examination of the psychological kind can easily end up as a recurring dip in Narcissus' pool. Without knowing it, you find yourself developing an "inordinate fascination with the self," as the dictionary de-scribes narcissism. What starts out as a genuine desire to find happiness or the answers to some of life's more tricky questions can end up as, Thomas Moore says in *Care of the Soul,* "the habit of focusing attention on oneself rather than the world of objects and of others."

Narcissism can take a variety of guises. The most obvious is when you use your search for the self as an excuse not to show up for others—like your children, or your coworkers, or your mate. Certainly there may be times on the search—stages—when focus on the self becomes primary.

Others may suffer because of our need to make seemingly selfish choices. But when a stage becomes a habit, and when our choices center more and more on our own welfare only, it's time to take a good hard look at ourselves.

Narcissism can also lead us to believe that just because we are pursuing a path of self-examination, therefore everyone else should. The journey through the Landscape of the Heart can be lonely. You may find yourself quite alone in the work you choose to do. Even as you change and become more understanding and heartful, there will continue to be difficult people in your life, people who refuse to join you in the dance steps. Things won't miraculously mend in all your relationships. Heartfulness allows us to go halfway toward harmony with another person. Often the other person doesn't choose to make his or her part of the journey toward you. As you grow you will be able to recognize and take responsibility for your own part of the relationship. And you will also know when the responsibility is not yours. Instead of feeling guilty or blameful, you will be able to make wise decisions based on reality. Sometimes those decisions may involve walking away from someone—not in anger or hatred, but in truth.

2. Sorry! You Cannot Have Everything You Want. Another way of putting this is *Just because you learn how to ask for what you want doesn't mean you are going to get it.* This is something they never tell you about in therapy! I spent a good deal of my first year in therapy becoming less ashamed of my own needs and learning how to express them more honestly. I didn't stop to think what would happen when my own needs conflicted with the needs of others. In the rarefied air of the therapist's office you may begin to think that all you have to do is know what you want, express it, and then sit back and enjoy the goodies. It doesn't happen like this. As a friend once complained to me, "In therapy you only have to deal with your own crazy mind. In relationships you have to deal with two crazies."

It's appropriate to strengthen the self enough to respect your own needs. But heartfulness does not then give you the license to do whatever you want to get your needs met. Rather, it asks you to strike a balance between the quest for personal fulfillment and the need for self-sacrifice in your life with others. In the Landscape of the Heart you hitch your feelings to reality, and life in reality involves sacrifice. When you find out what you really love, whether it's a person, a job, or a place, you must give up something as well. A big part of heartful living involves loving renunciation. "Renunciation," Hazrat Inayat Khan reminds us, "is not something which we must torture ourselves to learn. It is in us, but it is buried and it can only be dug up by our love." Renunciation works only after we have done the work of knowing what we love. To make a sacrifice for what we really love feels natural. We cannot sacrifice something that we have not yet made our own. Inayat Khan says that "to renounce what we cannot gain is not true renunciation; it is weakness."

3. *Required! A Sense of Humor.* If we take ourselves too seriously, the pursuit of happiness can turn into somber business. As we make big choices and take responsibility for our actions, we will experience growing pains. But we also can have fun on the adventure. Herbert Spencer said, "Don't mistake my frivolity for shallowness, and I won't mistake your seriousness for profundity." This is good advice for all of us on the spiritual path.

4. *Stop!* Good therapy should not go on forever. Good therapy helps us recognize and dismantle the inner voices and the avoidance patterns we developed as children. Instead of putting an overlay of techniques or moral judgments on our pain and struggles, therapy helps us lovingly understand the roots of our unhappiness, and therefore the way to our freedom. On the other hand, the task of fully unraveling and restitching our psyches is an endless one, and probably impossible. At some important point in our development, we grasp that we have understood and synthesized the truth adequately, and are ready to move on. How do we know when this is the case? Here are a few clues:

- When the phrase "self-responsibility" no longer sounds like a marching order, but instead like a delightfully sane and optimistic way to live;
- When you naturally find yourself relating to problems and pain as grist for your spiritual mill;
- When you want to apply spiritual and psychological truths to the simple, everyday stuff of life—not to force them on the world for the good of all mankind; and
- When you no longer want to blame others, past or present, but instead are intrigued by your own sneaky psyche, and challenged to become more honest, compassionate, and free.

It is through the subtle combination of spirituality and psychology that we can avoid drowning in narcissism, or spiritual materialism, or whatever you want to call the misguided obsession with the self. Thomas

Moore suggests that the soulful psychological search "expands the boundaries of who we think we are." Then self-love becomes "not the ego loving ego," but rather "ego loving the soul, loving a face the soul presents. We might say that the cure for narcissism is to move from love of self, which always has a hint of narcissism in it, to love of one's deep soul."

Those people who are in touch with the deep soul are the very ones who do real good in the world. Those who are more concerned with "doing good" than with finding and loving their own deep souls end up unable to really help others. The least selfish people are those who know themselves so well, and are so self-confident in their choices, that they don't have to control other people, or manipulate them, or sulk, or whine, or be depressed or angry to get what they want. The rare person who stands naked in the joy and sadness of life—willing to stand for what he really wants, willing to risk real love with another person, willing to give fully and receive fully—radiates a kind of freedom and fearlessness that inspires others.

Your self-knowledge and self-love are the most unselfish gifts you can give to another. Self-knowledge makes you clear, strong, and trustworthy and allows others to know where you stand. Self-love makes love of others more genuine. "He who wants to do good knocks at the gate; he who loves finds the gate open," says the Indian poet Rabindranath Tagore.

When I first started on the path of the heart, I thought that I could become a little happier and perhaps a little kinder. I didn't think that real change on a psychological level was possible. But I have discovered otherwise. It *is* possible to make significant, transformative changes in the way we live each day in the human community. We can find stable happiness; we can learn to have loving and pleasurable relationships; we can be at peace. If we are willing to become warriors—not against others, but against our own dishonesty and defensiveness—then we can indeed grow and change and journey into freedom. It's not enough to aim for pain relief. We can aim for something much more dependable and luminous than that. If we aspire to discover the true self, to know what we love and what we want, to be honest, and to take full responsibility for our strengths and our weaknesses, then we will be on our way.

Its takes an odd combination of backbone and abandon to walk the path of the heart. Jesus told his disciples to be "lights unto the world." A tender heart and a brave soul light up the path for others with the kind of luminosity that heals and enlivens. So don't worry about being good. Instead, discover how both good and bad live within you. Deeply accept the shadows even as you seek the light. Believe in change. Take full responsibility for who you are and what you want. And from such forthright wisdom, your goodness will prevail and your kindness will blossom and your heart will be healed.

10   A Heartfulness Toolbox

Work of the eyes is done, now
go and do heart-work.
    —RAINER MARIA RILKE

Heartfulness is knowing what you love, and having the guts and grace to go for it. It is a balanced blend of wisdom and passion, a way to track the scent of the soul, even if we're not sure of what we're tracking. To track the wisdom and passion of the soul is not only possible, I believe it is the purpose of life. James Hillman, one of America's wisest psychologists, says that the goal of the psychological search should be to dig deep in the soil of life to find our essence, our soul. It's there, just as the original acorn that spawned the mighty oak is still there in the tree's roots, in the bark, in every leaf. Within each one of us is the acorn, the soul seed, the germ of our unique genius and destiny.

    Hillman believes that modern therapy focuses too much on the wounded victim-self and not enough on the creative soul-self—that part of us that is smarter and stronger than any wound. His "acorn theory," as he calls it, regards the problems visited on us in childhood—through cruelty, or neglect, or poverty, or prejudice—as grist for the mill of our destiny. "Despite early injury," he writes, "and all the slings and arrows of outrageous fortune, we bear from the start the image of a definite individual character with some enduring traits. . . . The Romans named it your *genius;* the Greeks, your *daimon;* and the Christians your guardian angel. The Romantics, like Keats, said the call comes from the heart."

Hillman wants therapy to do something different than merely give you coping skills; he wants it to bring you "back to feelings of destiny. For that is what is lost in so many lives, and what must be recovered: a sense of personal calling, that there is a reason I am alive." In this chapter I provide a variety of ways—a toolbox of techniques—for working with psychology in the manner of which Hillman speaks. Our goal here is to uncover the acorn, to reconnect with the inner angel. We don't go looking for what's wrong with us; rather, we go in search of our genius. We investigate how the painful parts and the helpful parts of our lives have revealed or repressed the inner angel. Sometimes, to our surprise, we find that crisis and loss actually fortified the inner angel. Just as surprising, we learn that peace and stability can put our angel to sleep.

This kind of psychological investigation is more like an adventure than a cure. It's less about being safe, and more about taking risks. But don't rush to throw the baby out with the bathwater; the more formal methods of therapy that seek to heal our woundedness are also valuable, especially if our wounds are great. In Chapter Three I talked about the wise choice to "transcend and include" as we create a new American spirituality. It's all too easy to relegate therapeutic psychology to the junk heap now that some of its most important tenets have been absorbed into cultural norms. We don't have to do that. We can transcend the more narcissistic elements of therapy while including the beneficial ones. What I offer in this chapter is not an attack on working one-on-one with a skilled therapist. Here I give you tools of the imagination, mythology, and creativity to help you recover your sense of aliveness and wonder. In therapy (and it is up to you to find the particular brand and therapist that fits your own nature and challenges) you do a different kind of work, the kind we explored in the last chapter.

Both kinds of work are helpful. They keep each other in balance. Too much therapy, or the kind of victim therapy that puts every aspect of your past on trial, is a wasteful, interminable endeavor. Pop psychology's obvious answers to life's complexities lack artfulness and subtlety and can bleed the mystery, humor, and beauty out of our experiences. An excessively therapeutic outlook often pathologizes parts of the self that are actually our greatest assets, like a fighting spirit, or a sensitive intuition, or an eccentric creativity. But that doesn't mean that traditional psychotherapy, undertaken with intelligence and balance, doesn't contribute in unique and important ways to the spiritual path.

THREE HEARTFULNESS MEDITATIONS

Balance in psychotherapy can be fostered by a variety of techniques and outlooks, including the practice of mindfulness meditation. Mindfulness expands therapy's vision. It reminds us that childhood and personality are just parts of the story. It helps us stay open and curious about the contents of the heart. When we want to shut down, or blame our parents, or go to sleep, meditation can help us stay awake to a bigger picture. The following meditations take the core structure and philosophy of mindfulness and tailor them to emotional healing and the search for the inner angel. The inner angel makes his or her home in our hearts. If our hearts are choked from the fear of pain or the shame of disclosure, we'll have a difficult time making contact with our genius.

These three meditations help open and soften the heart. All of the instructions previously given in Book II (regarding breath, posture, and attention) apply to the meditations offered here. As with the meditations offered in the previous chapters, you may want to have a friend read aloud the ones in this chapter, or make a tape of yourself reading them. If you do read the meditations silently, first read them for content and then go back and use them experientially.

This meditation is a journey into the heart center—a place in the body where you can focus healing and enlivening attention. Some people prefer to meditate in silence; I find it helpful to use music with this meditation. (A list of my favorite meditative and inspiring music appears at the end of the book.)

TOOLBOX EXERCISE #1
FINDING THE HEART CENTER

Sit comfortably, with a straight and dignified posture that allows your heart to be opened to the world. Bring your attention to your breath. For a few minutes just sit, breathing softly, finding a solid base for this meditation. Now take a sharp breath in through the mouth, as if you were startled, and use your hand to find the spot where the energy from that breath accumulates. You can do this a few times to help you locate the spot. "There is a point on the chest," writes Stephen Levine, "on the sternum, roughly between the nipples about two or three inches above where the rib cage comes together. It is the focal point for this process. Investigate the breast bone to find this point of sensitivity. It may be extremely sensitive. For many when they find it, it will be unmistakable. For others it may not be as obvious. In this case you sense where it may be, mid-sternum, and work with whatever sensations arise there. This has correlations in many healing technologies. It exists in all traditions which view the body as an energy system. It is the heart center."

Place your hand over the heart center and gently pat or stroke the area. Direct your attention and your body's energy there. At any point in the meditation you may remove your hand, bring it back, rest it gently, or move it softly to bring healing touch to your heart.

As you sit, breathe in and out slowly through the heart center. What are you feeling there? Contraction? Openness? Dullness? Sadness? Nothing? Keep breathing and notice your feelings as they arise. Try not to judge your feelings. Let a river of feelings flow freely through the heart center—each feeling a drop of water in the river. Sit on the bank of the river and observe and name the feelings that flow by, just like you labeled your thoughts in mindfulness meditation. Silently repeat, "hardness, hardness," if you feel closed, or "pain, pain" if painful feelings arise, or "fear," or "sweetness," or "sadness," or "awe," or whatever flows through your heart center. There are no wrong or right things to feel or not feel. Receive whatever flows through as a message from your heart and let it be, just as it is. Stay alert to the fullness of your heart. If emotions arise that make you uncomfortable, take your hand and place it over the heart center as if you were lovingly patting a child's head.

Take time to explore the ebbs and flows of the heart center, as you would get to know a long-lost friend.

The next toolbox exercise continues the process of opening the heart by connecting the heart center to the abdomen—or, as Stephen and Ondrea Levine call it, the belly. "The armoring of the heart," they instruct, "is discovered in the hardness of the belly."

TOOLBOX EXERCISE #2

"SOFT BELLY" MEDITATION

From Embracing the Beloved,
by Stephen and Ondrea Levine

Find a comfortable place to sit and settle in there. And bring your attention into this body in which you sit.

Feel this body. Let awareness come to the level of sensation in the body.

Feel the breath breathing itself in the body. Sensations of body breathing. And gradually focus awareness in the abdomen. Sensations of the breath. Feel the breath breathing itself in the belly.

Sensations of breath coming and going. Each inhalation the belly fills. Each exhalation the belly empties. The belly rising and falling with each breath. Sensation arising with each breath.

And begin to soften the belly. Softening the belly to receive the sensations of the breath. Softening to receive life in the belly. Breath. Sensation in the belly. Received in a new softness.

Softening the hardness, the holding in the belly that resists the breath, that resists sensation, that resists life. Softening that hardness. Sensation floating in mercy and awareness. Softening. Let the breath breathe itself in the softness.

Letting go of the resistance, of the fear, of the holding of hard belly. Letting go of the grief and distrust. Meeting them with mercy. With loving-kindness in soft belly. Letting go of the hardness, breathing it out.

Letting in the mercy, the patience, the kindness, with each inhalation. Soft belly. Merciful belly. Have mercy on you. Softening to the pain. Softening the holding. Breathing it out. Breathing mercy. Breathing in healing. In soft belly. In merciful belly.

Softening. Letting go of years of posturing and hiding. So much holding in the belly. So much fear. So much grief. Softening. Levels and levels of letting go. Levels and levels of healing.

Softening the muscles. Softening the flesh. Softening the holding that resists, that limits life so.

The armoring of the heart is discovered in the hardness of the belly. Meet this pain with mercy, not fear. Meet this grief in softness. In loving-kindness. In soft belly we have room for it all. All the fear, all the anger, all the distrust held so long in the belly. Have mercy on you. Let it go. Let it just be. Gently, in the softness. Met by mercy and awareness moment to moment. Breath to breath . . .

Even a single thought can tighten the belly, can reestablish separation and fear. Let thoughts come. Let thoughts go in soft belly. Expectation, doubt, confusion harden the belly. Soften. Thoughts arise uninvited. Let them float like bubbles in the vast spaciousness of soft belly. Moment to moment letting go. Moment to moment being in soft belly . . .

And gently let your eyes open. Let them open now. As your eyes open, notice at what point the belly tightens once again. Even trying to understand can tighten the belly. Being anything but our own great nature tightens us, removes us from the joy of our essential nature. . . . Soften with the eyes wide open to the world.

Use the next meditation exercise to reach places within that resist softening and opening. This exercise employs creative visualization, a technique that is explained in more detail in an upcoming section of this chapter called "Creative Visualization."

TOOLBOX EXERCISE #3
A MEDITATIVE VISIT TO THE HEALING TEMPLE
From A Path with Heart,
by Jack Kornfield

Imagine you are magically transported to a beautiful healing temple or power spot, a place of great wisdom and love. Take as much time as you need to sense it, feel it, picture it, in any way that feels good to you. Sense yourself sitting there, restfully and attentively meditating in this place. As you sit at this temple, this place of great wisdom, begin to reflect on your own spiritual journey more deeply. Gradually let yourself be aware of the wounds you carry that will require healing in the course of your journey. Breathe softly, and gently feel whatever arises.

As you sit, a wonderful and wise being from this healing temple will gradually approach you. When this being comes quite near, you can picture or imagine or sense who or what they are. They will bow lightly and then come over and put the gentlest hand on a part of your body where you are deeply wounded. With their most loving care, let them touch the part of your body that holds one of your sorrows. Let them teach you their healing touch. If you can't feel their touch, then take your own hand as you sit at that temple and imagine that you bring it to the place of your deepest wound, the place of your sorrow or difficulty, touching it with your hand as if you yourself were that beautiful being. Know that no matter how many times you have buried or resisted your sorrow, no matter how many times you have greeted it with your hatred, you can finally open to it.

Let your attention become like the hand of this wonderful wise being. Touch this place of sorrow with softness and tenderness. As you touch it, explore what is there. Is it warm or cool there? Is it hard, tight, or is it soft? Is it vibrating or moving, or is it still? Let your awareness be like the loving touch of the Buddha or the Goddess of Compassion, of Mother Mary or Jesus. What is the temperature and texture of this sorrow? What color is there to be felt? Let yourself become aware of all your feelings with a very loving and receptive heart. Let them be anything they need to be. Then very gently and softly, as if you were the Goddess of Compassion herself, touch it with pure sweetness. Open yourself to the pain. What is the core of this place that has been wrapped up and held inside you for so long? As you look at it, let yourself see how much you've closed off to it, how much you've suppressed or rejected it, wished that it would go away, wished that you didn't have to feel it, and treated it with fear and aversion. Let yourself sit peacefully, opening yourself to this pain at last.

Rest in this temple, allowing your healing and compassionate attention to suffuse every part of it. Stay as long as you wish. When you are ready to leave, imagine yourself bowing with gratitude. As you leave, remember this temple is inside you. You can always go there.

THE HERO'S JOURNEY

He is a letter to everyone. You open it.
It says, Live.
    —RUMI

I like the image of receiving a letter in the mail, opening it, and finding just one word printed on the page: *Live.* So much in just one word—so much hope and creativity; so much regret and fear. All of the frustrated, unlived parts of the self are crowded under that word. They are begging for attention, some so close to the surface that we can see their shadows, feel their breath. "We want to live too," they clamor. What happens when we open that letter and read the word *Live?* When that which is unlived rushes up to be heard? And what would happen if we gave voice to the hidden and suppressed parts of our being?

We are indeed given many opportunities to choose a life more fully lived. Often these are dramatic moments—an accident, a major loss, a healing, a windfall. Or perhaps we move slowly into a kind of wasteland, and convinced we must make a change, but afraid to make decisions, we stand still, hoping for something as easy as a letter from God to tell us what to do. It would be helpful if the message from God were not just *Live,* but also some indication about *how* to live, especially with those suppressed and unruly parts of ourselves.

Letters of instruction and encouragement do indeed exist. Myths and teaching tales from every human community throughout the ages, whether from Africa or the arctic circle, India or Italy, describe the ups and downs of the human journey with astounding similarity. They chart a path through the life span, complete with warnings, kicks in the butt, healing balms, hints for success, and realistic endings. To read an ancient story is like reading a letter from God, or at least from a wise old woman or man who took the trouble to record his trials, tests, and passages. And while the mail may not be addressed to you or me personally, it is the very universality of the messages that make myths so powerful and ultimately helpful. The point of any myth or fairy tale is not to isolate a few figures as unique heroes and heroines, but rather to map the path of the hero's journey for you and me.

What is the hero's journey? At a certain point—perhaps in our youth, or as we mature, or through a crisis or deadening in our adult life—we feel a hunger for more meaning and aliveness. The journey we take from innocence to wisdom, and from stagnation to new life, is the hero's and heroine's journey.

Joseph Campbell, the mythologist and scholar who gained wide recognition near the end of his long and fruitful life, first introduced me to the hero's journey. Campbell would laugh to hear someone crediting him with the idea. To him, clues about the journey abound everywhere—in common folktales, in the news, in the current cinema. But indeed, Campbell is responsible for reintroducing the function of myth into contemporary culture. His realm of influence started small, as a professor of a few hundred students at Sarah Lawrence College, where he taught mythology and religion in the 1950s and 1960s. It expanded as his classic books were published, and then exploded into the mainstream late in his life when commentator Bill Moyers interviewed him and created a television series and a companion book called *The Power of Myth*.

Campbell refers to myths and fairy tales from the four corners of the earth; to parables from the world's religious traditions; and to modern literature, theater, and movies. He uses the great texts—Buddhist legends, the Hindu Bhagavad-Gita, Native American lore, the Old and New Testaments of the Bible, Greek myths, Celtic tales, the Grail legend, the

Grimms' fairy tales, even the *Star Wars* movies—to reveal how each one of us re-creates ancient legends in our daily lives. At the core of every story about a hero or a heroine is a similar beginning, middle, and end. Campbell says, "The usual hero's adventure begins with someone from whom something has been taken, or who feels there's something lacking in the normal experiences available or permitted. . . . This person then takes off on a series of adventures beyond the ordinary, either to recover what was lost or to discover some life-giving elixir. It's usually a cycle, a going and a returning. . . . That's the basic motif of the universal hero's journey—leaving one condition and finding the source of life to bring you forth into a richer or mature condition.

"The founders of all religions have gone on quests like that," says Campbell. "The Buddha went into solitude and then sat beneath the bo tree, the tree of immortal knowledge, where he received an illumination that has enlightened all of Asia for twenty-five hundred years. After baptism by John the Baptist, Jesus went into the desert for forty days; and it was out of that desert that he came with his message. Moses went to the top of a mountain and came down with the tables of the law. . . . Almost all the old Greek cities were founded by heroes who went off on quests and had surprising adventures, out of which each of them founded a city. You might also say that the founder of a life—your life or mine, if we live our own lives, instead of imitating everybody else's life—comes from a quest as well."

Right now, take a few minutes to bring the idea of the hero's journey down from the mythic mountain and into your own life. Imagine yourself standing at your mailbox, reaching in, finding a mysterious letter, opening it, and reading the following words from the Catholic mystic Thomas Merton:

TOOLBOX EXERCISE #4
WHAT AM I LIVING FOR?

"If you want to identify me, ask me not where I live,
or what I like to eat, or how I comb my hair,
but ask me what I am living for, in detail,
and ask me what I think is keeping me
from living fully for the thing
I want to live for."

Sit quietly with these words, reading them a few times, and meditating on the images and feelings that arise. Then write down your answers to the questions, "What am I living for?" and "What do I think is keeping me from living fully for the thing I want to live for?" If nothing comes, check inside: make contact with your heart center and your "soft belly." Ask your heart and your belly Merton's questions, and see what sensations, resistances, and stories you discover.

You can do this writing exercise several times over a span of a few weeks. See if your answers stay the same or contradict each other over time. Answering these questions without time pressure, and in the privacy of your heart, can inspire your own hero's journey.

Stories of heroes and heroines, gods and goddesses, dragons and witches, and other mythic creatures and themes are really our own stories. Reading them in this context, or watching them come alive in a play or the movies, broadens our perspective and links us to a universal story that gives meaning to our suffering, our mistakes, and our victories. They tell us that we too must enter a dark forest or cross a barren desert or sit alone in confusion and pain if we want to be the hero of our own life. The most useful myths describe a person whose life has lost its inner fire and who can no longer bear to live a half-life. That person must then endure a descent into the underworld—a time of often painful and destructive change. Through the descent process the person gains an inner awakening, a transformation of body and mind, and then reemerges with his or her whole self in tow.

In ancient days it was the role of the alchemically skilled magician or the village shaman or witch to help the journeyer through the underworld. In religious traditions, the person going through a dark night of the soul finds comfort and direction through images and rituals, like the symbol of the cross—death and resurrection—in the Christian faith. In the modern context, the process of descent and reemergence is often facilitated through psychotherapy. In my own process, when I was in a major cycle of descent and reemergence, I chose to regard my therapy sessions as visits to the local shaman. My therapist may not have looked the shaman part—he wore khakis and a button-down shirt—but he was as wise as any native healer, and he helped me spin straw into gold.

During that time, I also found the teachings of Jung, who refers widely to myth and fairy tale in his writings, extremely helpful. While Jung is often academically challenging to read, the books by current Jungians are easier going and uncommonly useful. These authors—who include James

Hillman, Marion Woodman, Jean Shinoda Bolen, Robert A. Johnson, Thomas Moore, Maureen Murdock, Robert Moore, Clarissa Pinkola Estés, and many other fine thinkers and writers—rescue psychology from pure science and cure, and weave potent healing stories and myths into their work.

Maureen Murdock, Marion Woodman, Jean Shinoda Bolen, and Clarissa Pinkola Estés apply the use of myth in psychological work specifically to women. Each mythic figure, hero or heroine, has lessons to impart to each of us, man or woman. But the heroine's journey and the hero's journey are often different enough in their intent and their execution that finding myths to correspond with one's gender can be very important. It is illuminating and empowering to see oneself in the old stories. I have retrieved parts of myself in the stories about goddesses, queens and princesses, witches and healers, and the innocent girl wandering in the forest at night and sleeping in a hollow tree. I have also recognized myself in some of the myths retold by Robert Bly, Robert Johnson, and Robert Moore in their books that outline the masculine quest. Reading about the heroine's journey has helped me understand and respect my own instincts and gifts. Reading about the hero's journey, and about gods, warriors, magicians, and monks, has shed light on the more mysterious ways of my sons and husband and male friends and colleagues.

The use of myth does not mean looking only to the old stories for direction. It also is about turning our daily experiences into living myths. "We dull our lives by the way we conceive them," James Hillman says. "We have stopped imagining them with any sort of romance, any fictional flair." Hillman suggests that instead of conceiving our lives as a chronological series of missteps and successes, we "pick up the romantic theme, daring to envision biography in terms of very large ideas such as beauty, mystery, and myth." One way to do this is to write or tell our own myths, to record dreams and the more unusual events of our lives as living epic tales. If we tell the whole story of what came before, during, and after, on the inside and the outside, we'll create personal myths that can help us make difficult decisions and move more gracefully through transitions.

In Chapter Seven I told a story about hitting a deer on the highway. There are two ways to tell this story. The first way, the plain-Jane version, goes like this: One night in late October, I was returning home from the airport after a stressful weekend meeting. As I drove at seventy miles per hour in heavy traffic on the New York State Thruway, a large deer jumped across the highway median and into my windshield. The deer's horns shattered the glass, and his heavy body bounced from the windshield to the roof to the trunk before being thrown to the side of the road. Fortunately I was able to avoid being hit by other cars before pulling over to safety. A hunter in a pickup truck stopped to help me and to retrieve the deer, who had been killed. My car was totaled, and I was bruised and shaken, but otherwise fine.

Here is another way to tell the story, much as an old grandmother might have told a fairy tale, or a shaman explained the day's events around a fire: On Halloween, when ghosts and demons show us their faces, I took a journey into the night. As I drove at high speed down the highway, little did I know that in the woods alongside the road another being raced in the opposite direction. Our destinies were about to meet in a crashing moment of life for me, and death for him. And other beings were traveling that night too; the ghosts of the past weekend rode along with me. There were three of them: my fear of change, my lack of faith in myself, and my giving over of power to others. Caught in the spell of these ghosts, I drove on with a heavy heart and a confused mind.

And then, quite suddenly, out of the dark came the face of my destiny partner. Not one moment too early or one moment too late, he cut through the ghostly trance with shining eyes and pointed horns—a male deer, a buck, illuminated by the headlights. Our eyes met for what seemed a long time and then the glass shattered into my face and hair. The buck bumped heavily on the car's roof and rear as we swerved and turned round and round, moving in slow motion among the speeding traffic. Then stillness, silence. All the while, from the first moment that I saw his face in the windshield to the final one when I brought the car to a stop, I was aware of a deep inner strength that took over and guided me to safety.

Seconds after the accident, a hunter pulled to the side of the road, pried open the door of my car, took me into his truck, gave me coffee, and called for help. Too stunned to speak, I sat quietly, thinking about the deer: What was his message to me when our eyes met? What was my message to him? As I watched the hunter lash the buck's body onto his truck, and the tow truck man jack up the wrecked body of my car, my eye caught the shadows of the ghosts, fleeing into the night. And I knew then that I would soon make the change I feared and take back the power that was mine.

A couple of months after the accident, Maureen Murdock, author of *The Heroine's Journey,* sent me the following to announce an upcoming workshop at Omega: "Every one of us is living out a personal myth, peopled with allies and adversaries, magical gifts, unhealed wounds, and visions for the future. These myths that unconsciously inform our lives remain largely invisible to us until we give them voice. The heroine's journey entails an initial separation from feminine values, making it in a man's world, experiencing spiritual aridity, and finally turning inward to reclaim the power and spirit of the Sacred Feminine." Here was a perfect description of the accident—before, during, and after. I chose to interpret the story of my fateful meeting with the buck as the moment in my personal myth when I reclaimed the power of the Sacred Feminine. A death was required—not only the death of the deer, but also of a part of myself. My fear and innocence died that night: the fear I had of standing firm in my own values, and the immaturity I still clung to so as not to have to take a stand.

Soon afterward, it came time for me to assert my power at work. The night before I went into a meeting to discuss changes in my job responsibilities and salary, I held a little ritual for myself. I sat quietly and remembered the look I had exchanged with the deer. A sense of strength and peace, the same feelings I had as the car spun around, filled my heart. *This is the gift of the deer, who has sacrificed his life to teach me how to stand firmly and peacefully when my own values are challenged.* I took a small piece of the deer's horn that I had found in my hair after the accident and put it in my briefcase. The next day, in the meeting, I held the deer's horn in my fist. It reminded me to speak from my own values, to listen with respect to others, and not to be swayed.

I can hear all sorts of reactions to this story. Perhaps an animal rights activist finds this a cruel and anthropocentric rendering of yet another incident of humanity's violent imprint on nature. Or a purely rational thinker might find the whole process ridiculous: "She just had an accident, for God's sake!" Of course the story could easily be told as a simple case of hitting a poor, defenseless deer on the highway. But that is too one-dimensional for me. "The basic theme of all mythology [is] that there is an invisible plane supporting the visible one," says Joseph Campbell. This is how I chose to make sense of my meeting with the deer: that behind the obvious—crushed metal, dead deer, bruised face—was a more meaningful and mysterious story. Since the deer and I did run into each other, since it was I and not one of the many other drivers who had ventured into that night on that highway, and since I was on my way home from an important event and in the midst of a major transition, I used the event much in the same way people throughout the ages have spun magic into the mundane to awaken meaning. I committed the accident to a sacred place in my heart, to help me live with more wisdom and passion.

The ancients treated the entire natural world in this sort of way. Every event, large and small, carried a message. Read the African teaching tales and the pantheistic Celtic lore. Study the Bhagavad-Gita and its metaphoric rendering of conflict and war. Read the stories from the Australian aborigines and the Lapland herders. Old Testament stories and Jesus' parables also show a reverence for the reservoir of messages present in nature and everyday events. How will you know which myths to read and use? When a story's invitation into the fire of inner growth pulls at you, and you feel your own fears of change pull back, you know you are in rich territory. At the end of the book I recommend several books that offer a variety of myths and fairy tales and ways of interpreting them.

There is a danger in choosing the mythological life view that should be mentioned. It's easy to overdo the mythic interpretation of events and to grant each moment way too much symbolic meaning. When every encounter begins to weigh down the normal progression of life, when we become unbearably deep, when a simple trip to the grocery store becomes a pilgrimage, then we've probably gone too far. And if we use the hero's journey as a way to evaluate ourselves as somehow different from others—grander, destined for greatness—then we have lost touch with the simple and universal notion of myth and story. "Myths tell us how to confront and bear and interpret suffering," Campbell says, "but they do not say that in life there can or should be no suffering. . . . Thinking in mythological terms helps to put you in accord with the inevitabilities of this vale of tears. You learn to recognize the positive values in what appear to be the negative moments and aspects of your life. The big question is whether you are going to be able to say a hearty 'yes' to your adventure."

USING ART, MUSIC, AND POETRY TO SHAKE YOU UP

In an interview, musician Bruce Springsteen said that "one of the most socially conscious artists in the second half of the twentieth century was Elvis Presley, even if he probably didn't start out with any set of political ideas that he wanted to accomplish. He said 'I'm all shook up and I want to shake you up.' "

The young Elvis shook up an entire country just by the way he turned a phrase and moved his hips. He made millions of people wonder what exactly was going on. Myths and stories, and poems, songs, dances, and art, have the power to shake us up and make us wonder what our lives are all about. The translucence of a poet's words, the soulful rhythm of a great song, the deep colors of a painting create a longing inside of us for beauty and magic. "This longing," wrote the poet Rumi, "tastes like honey to adults and milk to children/It is the last thirty pound bale/When you load it on, the boat tips over." Poets like Rumi always want the boat to tip over. They want us to live from the heart, from the "truth of the imagination," as Keats said.

Poems and music are a sure way to bring us quickly into the Landscape of the Heart, since they speak its native language. The heart speaks in images and metaphors. It makes connections between the visible world and the mysteries beyond the grasp of our mind and senses. Ancient cultures relied on music and dance and the sacred word to stir the soul and create spiritual community. Shamanic traditions deliberately use powerful rhythms and chant to do "soul retrieval" work. The hymns, rituals, and spoken prayers of the modern religious traditions are no different; they add the fertile water of the soul to worship. Rituals like the Christian Eucharist—the sharing of wafer and wine as symbols of the body and blood of Christ—are rooted in the same urge to move from the dry landscape of doctrine into the rich atmosphere of the soul. All over the world, from Jews praying out loud at the Wailing Wall, to Muslims kneeling in the direction of Mecca, to Hindus bathing in the holy Ganges, people turn to symbol and sound and movement to connect them to the truth beyond the rational mind.

Soul retrieval work is something we all can do without getting too fancy about it. Any piece of music or writing—any art form that puts you in touch with your authentic yearning for a deeper spiritual outlook—can work. Music, chant, or drumming can be used to assist solitary meditation, or to facilitate group worship and prayer. At the end of the book I list my favorite collections of mystical poetry, as well as musical selections that move me in the direction of soul retrieval. You can also do what I have done, which is to collect poems and quotes that shake you up, and keep them in a beautiful box. I describe how to make use of the box in this tool-box exercise:

TOOLBOX EXERCISE #5

THE POETRY BAZAAR

An exercise using poetry to stir the soul

A good poem shakes the reader up. I have a box of poems and quotes written by poets, mystics, scientists, and other soul revolutionaries. I use it to lead an exercise called the Poetry Bazaar. I spread the contents of the box on the floor, and invite people to shop for a poem or quote that shakes them up, and makes them say, "Aha!" Later we read our choices aloud and talk about what the poems tell us about ourselves. I've brought the box with me to gatherings where people yearn to express what they are feeling, but may be too shy to speak through their own voice.

Create your own poetry box. Find a handsome box or basket, or build one, or decorate a shoe box with art or wrapping paper. Begin to collect poems, quotes, cartoons, fortune cookie messages, passages from books, etc. Keep adding them to the box. Dip into your poetry box whenever you need inspiration or direction. Bring it with you to parties and family gatherings. Use it to shake things up.

Here is a selection from my box. Take a minute right now and read the following poem by Oriah Mountain Dreamer. After reading it, sit quietly and discover what happened in your body. Did the poem inspire you to throw caution to the wind and follow your dreams? Did it strike you as too dramatic to be trusted? Did it confuse you, or make you angry or afraid? Did it do a little of all of the above? Did it shake you up? Why?

THE INVITATION

It doesn't interest me what you do for a living
I want to know what you ache for
and if you dare to dream of meeting your heart's longing.
It doesn't interest me how old you are
I want to know if you will risk looking like a fool
for love
for your dream
for the adventure of being alive.

It doesn't interest me what planets are squaring your moon . . .
I want to know if you have touched the center of your own sorrow
if you have been opened by life's betrayals
or have become shriveled and closed
from fear of further pain.

I want to know if you can sit with pain
mine or your own
without moving to hide it
or fade it
or fix it.

I want to know if you can be with joy
mine or your own
if you can dance with wildness
and let the ecstasy fill you to the tips of your
fingers and toes
without cautioning us to
be careful
be realistic
to remember the limitations of being human.

It doesn't interest me if the story you are telling me
is true.
I want to know if you can
disappoint another
to be true to yourself.

If you can bear the accusation of betrayal
and not betray your own soul.
If you can be faithless
and therefore trustworthy.

I want to know if you can see Beauty
even when it is not pretty
every day.
And if you can source your own life
from its presence.

I want to know if you can live with failure
yours and mine
and still stand on the edge of the lake
and shout to the silver of the full moon,
"Yes."

It doesn't interest me
to know where you live or how much money you have.

I want to know if you can get up
after a night of grief and despair
weary and bruised to the bone
and do what needs to be done
to feed the children.

It doesn't interest me who you know
or how you came to be here.
I want to know if you will stand
in the center of the fire
with me
and not shrink back.

It doesn't interest me where or what or with whom
you have studied.
I want to know what sustains you
from the inside
when all else falls away.

I want to know if you can be alone
with yourself
and if you truly like the company you keep
in the empty moments.

Our own lives are like the best poetry, art, or music. Really fine art combines many emotions into one masterpiece. Like an Irish jig that bounces along at a jaunty clip yet has an undercurrent of depth and wonder and sadness, our lives are rich expressions of the universe's energy and passion and creativity. I heard Maya Angelou say that "life is pure adventure, and the sooner we realize that, the quicker we will be able to treat life as art. . . . We need to remember that we are created creative and can invent new scenarios as frequently as they are needed." Artists know how to do this in their work. They know how to contact the muse—the inner angel—to enliven their art, to "invent new scenarios." We can learn how to do this in our lives.

Many poets, from the Persian Jelaluddin Rumi, to the French Charles Baudelaire, to the American Emily Dickinson, use the image of being drunk to indicate contact with the inner angel. When mystics and poets speak of intoxication, they are not referring to an addiction to drugs or alcohol. Drunken-angel poems, as I call them, point to an inner ecstasy. They demonstrate how we can be drunk on life, and in love with the world, without being intoxicated. I like to read drunken-angel poems when I need to clear away dullness or find inspiration to live more fully.

TOOLBOX EXERCISE #6
A DRUNKEN ANGEL MEDITATION

Here is one of my favorite drunken-angel prose poems, by Charles Baudelaire. Read it aloud and look within for the answer to his question, "Drunk with what?"

GET DRUNK!

One should always be drunk. That's the great thing; the only question.
Not to feel the horrible burden of Time
weighing on your shoulders and bowing you to the earth,
    you should be drunk without respite.
          Drunk with what?
With wine, with poetry,
      with virtue, as you please.
But get drunk.
And if sometimes you should happen to awake,
on the stairs of a palace,
       on the green grass of a ditch,
   in the dreary solitude of your own room
and find that your drunkenness is ebbing
or has vanished, ask the wind and the wave,
ask star, bird, or clock, ask everything
that flows, everything that sings,
everything that speaks, ask them the time;
and the wind, the wave, the star, the bird
and the clock will all reply:
"It is Time to get drunk! If you are not
to be martyred slaves of Time,
be perpetually Drunk!
With wine, with poetry,
or with virtue, as you please."

CREATIVE VISUALIZATION

One of the most simple and direct ways of bypassing the cut-and-dried and going straight to the imaginal realms is through "creative visualization" or "guided imagery." This is a sort of directed daydreaming that not only connects us to the soul but also has the power to help us heal our bodies and minds. "You may assume that 'imagination' means 'not real,' " write medical researchers David Sobel and Robert Ornstein. "But the thoughts, words, and images that flow from your imagination can have very real physiological consequences for your body. *Your brain often cannot distinguish whether you are imagining something or actually experiencing it.* Perhaps you've had a racing heartbeat, rapid breathing, or tension in your neck muscles while watching a movie thriller. These sensations were all produced by images and sounds on a film. During a dream, maybe your body responded with fear, joy, anger, or sadness—all triggered by your imagination. If you close your eyes and vividly imagine yourself by a still, quiet pool, or relaxing on a warm beach, your body responds to some degree as though you are actually there. Your imagination can be a very powerful resource in relieving stress, pain, and other unwanted symptoms."

The power of creative visualization is easy to test on yourself. Observe what happens to you when you watch an action or horror movie. Notice how your heart races and your body tenses during suspenseful scenes. This is especially revealing when you watch a movie you have already seen, when you know the outcome but still register fear and body tension. Watch a scary scene that you've watched before and be aware of your breath. Breathe slowly and serenely. Don't contract around the film—you know what is going to happen!

This has marvelous applications in your daily life. In many ways you already know what is going to happen with the daily events that you anticipate with anxiety and upset. Somewhere deep within, you know you will be all right. So much of our nervous anticipation is a wasted exercise in worry. Big, bad things do happen, but these are the exception to the rules of ordinary life. You can start each morning, especially if you are anticipating a difficult day, with a creative visualization. Just as you did with the movie, you can relax your tightness and worry by imagining a positive outcome to your day. You can picture the day clearly in your mind, creating vivid pictures of positivity, health, and harmony in your imagination.

At the back of the book I list two excellent books that give instructions on using guided imagery. Here is an exercise from one of those books, *Staying Well with Guided Imagery,* by Belleruth Naparstek. Naparstek's audiotapes and books are used in hospitals and by health professionals to help people heal from a wide variety of physical illnesses and stress-related problems. Her practical blend of the scientific and the imaginal works a sort of magic on all kinds of tension, inner conflict, and hard-to-break habits of the heart. I chose the following exercise—"Imagery to Increase Empathy for Another"—to illustrate the wide range of applications for guided imagery.

Before starting the exercise, think of someone with whom you want to heal or improve your relationship. Don't be surprised if you consciously choose one person, and midway through the exercise, he or she switches to someone else. If this happens, try to go along with it and see what happens.

TOOLBOX EXERCISE #7
IMAGERY TO INCREASE EMPATHY FOR ANOTHER
From Staying Well with Guided Imagery,
by Belleruth Naparstek

[Naparstek uses ellipses when she wants you to pause briefly. Spaces between paragraphs encourage longer pauses. And "(pause)" suggests an even longer one.]

See if you can position yourself as comfortably as you can . . . either sitting upright or lying down . . . shifting your weight so you're allowing your body to be fully supported . . . head, neck, and spine straight . . .

And closing your eyes, or keeping them half shut so as not to fall asleep . . . taking a couple of deep, full, cleansing breaths . . . inhaling as fully as you comfortably can . . . sending the warm energy of your breath to any part of your body that's tense or sore or tight . . . and releasing the discomfort with the exhale . . . so that you can feel your breath going to all the tight, tense places . . . loosening and softening them . . . and then gathering up all the tension and breathing it out . . . so that more and more, you can feel safe and comfortable, relaxed and easy . . . watching the cleansing action of the breath . . . with friendly but detached awareness.

And any distracting thoughts or feelings you might have . . . those, too, are sent out with the breath . . . so that inside, you can be still and quiet . . . like a lake with no ripples . . .

And now . . . imagining a place . . . where you feel safe and peaceful and easy . . . a place either make-believe or real . . . a place from your past . . . or somewhere you've always wanted to go . . . it doesn't matter . . . just so it's a place that feels good and safe and peaceful to you . . . And allowing the place to become real to you, in all of its dimensions . . . looking around you . . . taking the place in with your eyes . . . enjoying the colors . . . the scenery . . . fully appreciating every detail with your eyes . . . looking over to your right . . . and over to your left.

And listening to the sounds of the place . . . the motion of wind or water . . . the music of birds or crickets . . . or a whole blend of sounds . . .

And feeling whatever you are sitting against or lying upon . . . or perhaps feeling the quality of the ground beneath your feet . . . whether it's sand or pine needles or grass . . . or you might be in a cozy armchair . . . or sitting on a nice, warm rock in the sun . . .

And feeling the air on your skin . . . either crisp and dry . . . or balmy or wet . . . perhaps you are inside, feeling the warmth of a cozy fire on your face and hands . . . just enjoying the feel of the place on your skin.

And smelling its rich fragrance . . . whether it's the soft, full scent of flowers . . . or sharp, salt sea air . . . sweet meadow grass . . . or maybe the pungent smell of peat moss in the woods . . .

And as you become more and more attuned to the safety and beauty of this place . . . feeling thankful and happy to be there . . . you might begin to feel a kind of tingling . . . a pleasant, energizing something in the air all around you . . . something that contains expectancy and excitement . . . a sense that something wonderful is just about to happen . . .

And as you look out in front of you . . . just a few feet before you . . . you begin to discern that there is a kind of transparent screen there . . . getting more and more opaque and solid as you look at it . . .

And as you watch the screen with a kind of peaceful curiosity . . . you gradually become aware of a human form beginning to appear on it . . . becoming more and more defined until the three-dimensional image of a person is quite clear . . . Someone you want to understand better . . . or resolve something with . . . appearing on the screen . . . in whatever characteristic posture he (or she) has . . . wearing whatever it is he wears . . . doing whatever it is he does . . . crisp and clear in every dimension . . .

And now . . . in the safe, magical space of the screen . . . for the sake of your own learning . . . somehow, for just a short while . . . sliding past the boundaries and slipping into the body of this other person . . . entering this other awareness . . . and breathing his breath . . . for just a brief while . . .

And if there is any resistance to doing this, just gently noting it, and allowing yourself to soften all around it . . . for the sake of understanding more . . . to learn what you need to know . . . feeling what it is like to be in his body . . . breathing his breath . . . looking down and seeing the hands and the feet . . . the clothing . . .

And feeling what is happening in the heart . . . (pause) . . . the belly . . . (pause) . . . the muscles of the back and the neck . . . (pause) . . . open and curious as to how it is in there . . .

And seeing out from his eyes . . . what the world looks like . . . sounds like . . . feels like . . . as you breathe his breath . . . feel his feelings . . .

(longer pause)

And perhaps even seeing you over there . . . with this pair of eyes . . . what you look like . . . sound like . . . how you seem . . . from this body . . . from this aware-ness . . . feeling what it feels like to be looking over at you, while breathing this breath . . . soft and easy . . . just allowing yourself the space to experience this . . . with friendly but detached awareness . . .

(longer pause)

And now . . . very gently wishing this body good-bye . . . with whatever thoughts and wishes you feel appropriate . . . saying good-bye to this other . . . and gently moving back into your own body . . . reinhabiting your own body, fully and easily . . . breathing deeply into your own belly . . . exhaling fully from your own nose and mouth . . .

And feeling grateful for your ability to move so easily here and there . . . you step out of the magical, translucent screen . . . back into your peaceful environ-ment . . . again taking in the beautiful sights and sounds and smells . . . and watch-ing the shimmering screen fade . . .

Understanding that you have in fact added to your own understanding in a very real way . . . increasing your own well-being as you open your mind and heart in this way . . . and knowing that you can do so again whenever you wish . . .

And so . . . very gently . . . and with soft eyes . . . coming back into the room whenever you are ready . . . knowing that you are better for this . . . and so you are . . .

There are many ways to use your imagination for healing and self-awareness. People use guided imagery (creative visualization) when they are ill or facing a major decision or wanting to change habitual behavior. Look for your own ways to activate the imagination. A psychiatrist friend of mine takes his patients to the roller coaster at an amusement park to help them conquer their everyday worries. First he leads them through a creative visualization of arriving alive and exhilarated at the end of the ride. Sometimes several trips to the park are required before the patient is ready to take the plunge. Afterward (because each person does indeed make it down alive) they discuss the adventure, and the ways in which they first resisted and then enjoyed the ride, as a metaphor for living.

A NECKLACE OF QUALITIES

At the very beginning of this book I likened the spiritual journey to an unfinished necklace—a work in progress—with each bead representing a different stage of growth. The Sufis say that each one of us is like a necklace, made up of beads of different qualities. Qualities are basic human traits, universally similar, unique only in the ways they are artfully combined. Jung called qualities *archetypes*. Just as all human bodies share the same chemistry, our psyches also share the same archetypes. There's something liberating when you cease to think of your state of mind or your behavior as unique to yourself. We are all much more alike than unalike. We are rarely that much better or worse than anyone else. When we are good or smart or lovely or powerful, or likewise, when we are mean or dull or unappealing or weak, we're fooling ourselves if we think we're the only one ever to be so great or so awful. Both self-aggrandizement and self-loathing come from the same twisted place. Viewing the contents of our minds and hearts as the work of archetypal forces depersonalizes much of our most human behavior. It counteracts the tendency we have to heap unnecessary blame on ourselves when we fail, or to get a thick head when we succeed. Thinking archetypally also helps us refrain from passing harsh judgments on others, on the one hand, or placing them on a pedestal, on the other.

When we love and when we hate, when we are powerful and when we are weak, when we are sure and when we are confused: these are archetypal forces at play within us, forces that we can learn to harness, to subdue, or to balance. Jungian analyst Eugene Pascal, and author of the very useful book *Jung to Live By,* writes, "The psychological dilemma plaguing most of humanity is that *the archetypes live us instead of us living them.* Unless we become aware that there are such things as blind forces or archetypes in our unconscious, unless we become cognizant that we are in their grip, we will remain in a state of identity with these blind, unconscious, archetypal forces." In ancient times humans gave the different archetypes the names of gods and goddesses, evil spirits, or helpful animal totems. Then, after giving form to the archetypes, they could work with them in a less abstract way. In modern times we can still use the gods and goddesses of all the various world mythologies to help us get a handle on the archetypal forces at play in our psyches. I highly recommend two books if this kind of work appeals to you: *Goddesses in Everywoman,* by Jean Shinoda Bolen, and *King, Warrior, Magician, Lover,* by Robert Moore.

Sufi traditions use the "ninety-nine names of Allah" to describe the archetypes. These are not just the "nice" names of God. For each lovely quality—like mercy—its opposite exists—like judgment. For "the opener" there's "the constrictor"; for "the first," there's "the last"; for "the giver of life," there's "the creator of death." A common Sufi practice—called *wasifah*—is the repetition of one of the names of Allah, given to the practitioner by the teacher, in order to awaken a particular quality or to balance another. Sufi rosaries have ninety-nine beads; each one holds the essence of a quality. In Islamic art you see the faithful fingering their holy beads, silently repeating the ninety-nine names of Allah.

Repetition of the names was a big part of my practice when I studied with Pir Vilayat. Several times a year I'd meet with him in private, as would each one of his students, to receive a new wasifah. It seemed to me that I would never receive the wasifah I wanted. If I went into my teacher's room hoping to receive a certain name of Allah, I would walk away with its opposite. I remember once even asking for *Al-Quddus,* Arabic for "the Holy One," explaining to Pir Vilayat that I felt a need to focus inward on my most gentle and pure qualities. Pir meditated with me for a few minutes and then shook his head and told me to recite Al-'Aziz, "the Mighty." He sensed that the quality which most wanted expression in me was not the most refined and sacred, but rather the most strong and forthright.

The premise of wasifah practice is that all of the ninety-nine names are within us. If we are working with a certain quality, like *As Sabur,* "the Patient One," we use that name to stimulate the quality of patience which is already within us, borrowed from Allah. We ask that it be awakened and revealed in our thoughts and actions. If we find ourselves becoming too patient—fearful and slow to act—then we can ask for another quality, like *Al Muqaddim,* "the Expediter," to make its presence known. This way, we stop taking all the credit for our strengths and all the blame for our weaknesses. No one of us has the corner on power or ability or beauty or love—they are qualities of God that we have been given to blend and balance wisely. Too much power is arrogance. Too much patience is fear. If our childhoods made us hard—if our gentler qualities had to run for cover—we can artfully invite them back out. They're in there. If our experiences have scarred our confidence and made us weak, we can fortify the noble and powerful qualities that still are part of us. We can play with the qualities within, like an artist at a living canvas.

Wasifah practice also involves repeating all of the ninety-nine names, which is a marvelous way to experience our inner richness and our commonality with others. I carried my prayer beads with me at all times when I was studying with my Sufi teachers, and I still like to pick them up and chant Allah's beautiful names.

THE WORLD BANK

Life in the world is full of pertinent news. Not only news about Washington or Hollywood or Russia or Mars, but news about ourselves—accurate findings and useful statistics about our most personal behavior. In fact, there exists a brilliant feedback system that is working at all times, offering free information about how to—and how not to—function in the world. For every action we take, God leaves little messages about its wisdom or folly. All we have to do is quiet down and listen closely.

Usually we are too opinionated, or defensive, or frightened to hear the messages. We judge our experiences right away as situations we like or don't like, or people as being for or against us, or ideas as being ones we can embrace or fear. But one of the greatest steps we can make on the spiritual path is to learn to stop before we judge experience and give it a chance to tell us something about reality—to impart news about ourselves, about the seeds we have sown, about the changes we can make, about the nature of life. If we can intercept the reactive nature of the mind and the habitual defensiveness of the heart, then we will find ourselves in a world that never runs out of messages.

Chögyam Trungpa describes the message system like this: "If you take steps to accomplish something, that action will have a result—either failure or success. . . . Trust is knowing that there will be a message. When you trust in those messages, the reflections of the phenomenal world, the world begins to seem like a bank, or reservoir, of richness. You feel that you are living in a rich world, one that never runs out of messages. . . . Those messages are regarded neither as punishment nor as congratulations. You trust, not in success, but in reality."

Especially when we've failed and are hurting, it is helpful to approach the world as a bank of messages. It's difficult to stay open to messages during painful times; it requires an act of faith, since the standard reaction to pain is to defend against it. Usually we try to avoid pain at all costs. We blame others right away, or we blame ourselves and wallow in guilt. This kind of defensiveness shuts down the feedback loop of information, the very information we need to get us through the pain. Instead, if we'd stop before we blamed others or ourselves for failure, and quietly listen to our undefended hearts, we would connect with a reservoir of wisdom—our very souls. By standing naked in the truth of a painful situation, we'd know what is actually happening, and therefore how to move through it with grace and growth.

I am not suggesting that by listening deeply to the heart's messages your pain magically disappears. Psychological pain contains information about what is happening; your fear of that pain and your rejection of it only create more suffering. Through the direct, unadulterated feeling of the pain, you can hear what pain is trying to tell you. Listen close enough and you will hear the voice of your inner angel, your wisdom stream, your soul.

One of the problems of contemporary culture is that life moves at such a quick pace, we usually don't give ourselves time to feel and listen deeply. You may have to take deliberate action to nurture the soul. If you want to increase your soul's bank account, you may have to seek out the unfamiliar and do things that at first could feel uncomfortable. Give yourself time as you experiment. How will you know if you're on the right track? I like Rumi's counsel: "When you do something from your soul, you feel a river moving in you, a joy."

TOOLBOX EXERCISE #8
TEN WAYS TO INCREASE YOUR BANK ACCOUNT

Perhaps none of the following sound as thrilling as skydiving or as impressive as a trip to Paris, but if you are looking to contact the soul, you'll often find it hiding in the most basic and intimate ingredients of human life. Consider investing time and attention in any of the following:

1. Get yourself invited to the birth of a baby. Feel the humbling presence of new life.
2. Sit with someone who is very ill or is suffering deeply. Don't try to fix anything. Just be there, heart to heart.
3. Be with a person as he or she dies. Go with him or her a little way into the next world.
4. Spend time with a four- or five- or six-year-old child—one who asks lots of questions.
5. Pee outside in the woods. Watch the steam rise in the winter, the scurrying insects in the summer. Know you are an animal.
6. Have eye contact with strangers. See yourself in another yourself.
7. Don't speak for a whole day. Silence is a friend of the soul.
8. Forgive someone whom you've been holding a grudge against. Forgiveness lubricates the soul.
9. Stand outside in a storm. Let the storm in your head merge with the wind and the rain. You are part of nature.
10. Fast for a day. Enjoy hunger as a sign of being alive.

TOOLBOX EXERCISE #9
LIST OF ESSENTIALS FOR HEARTFUL LIVING

Jack Kerouac created a list of essentials for the modern writer that he circulated among his friends. I have the list hanging above my computer, and when I get stuck I let my eyes rest on one of the essentials. I say the line out loud and let it shake me up.

BELIEF & TECHNIQUE FOR MODERN PROSE
List of Essentials by Jack Kerouac

1. Scribbled secret notebook, and wild typewritten pages, for yr own joy
2. Submissive to everything, open, listening
3. Try never get drunk outside yr own house
4. Be in love with yr life
5. Something that you feel will find its own form
6. Be crazy dumbsaint of the mind
7. Blow as deep as you want to blow

8. Write what you want bottomless from bottom of the mind
9. The unspeakable visions of the individual
10. No time for poetry but exactly what is
11. Visionary tics shivering in the chest
12. In tranced fixation dreaming upon object before you
13. Remove literary, grammatical and syntactical inhibition
14. Like Proust be an old teahead of time
15. Telling the true story of the world in interior monolog
16. The jewel center of interest is the eye within the eye
17. Write in recollection and amazement for yourself
18. Work from pithy middle eye out, swimming in language sea
19. Accept loss forever
20. Believe in the holy contour of life
21. Struggle to sketch the flow that already exists intact in mind
22. Don't think of words when you stop but to see picture better
23. Keep track of every day the date emblazoned in yr morning
24. No fear or shame in the dignity of yr experience, language & knowledge
25. Write for the world to read and see yr exact pictures of it
26. Book movie is the movie in words, the visual American form
27. In Praise of Character in the Bleak inhuman Loneliness
28. Composing wild, undisciplined, pure, coming in from under, crazier the better
29. You're a Genius all the time
30. Writer-Director of Earthly movies Sponsored & Angeled in Heaven

You can create a similar list, a list of essentials for heartful living, updating it every now and then when you learn something new and exceptional. Only you need to understand the style in which you write, the ideas you include, the events or books you mention. My list follows. I keep it in my purse and sometimes pull it out when I'm feeling confused, or lost, or anxious. I let my eyes fall on one of the essentials, breathe in deeply, and exhale refreshed and reminded.

BELIEF & TECHNIQUE FOR HEARTFUL LIVING
List of Essentials

1. Never envy anyone; yr life is the best
2. Make yr life a work of art for all to enjoy

3. Move ever closer to full honesty
4. If you cheat in any way you will pay, sooner or later, with yr own life force
5. Choose passion eyes wide open to the sober truth
6. Shun empty words; test yourself in a field of action
7. Breathing in gratitude, out generosity
8. Try to follow #19 of Jack Kerouac's rules for writers: *Accept loss forever*
9. Joy has many faces: from enchanted melancholy to full throttle body beat
10. Daily practicing loving-kindness and forgiveness because they work

MAKING DECISIONS

It's good to develop a way to access the soul's messages, because life sometimes feels like one long chain of decisions, some so difficult to make that we need all the help we can get. That's one of the big attractions to joining a religion or finding a guru; handing over decision-making to an authority can sound pretty appealing in times of weighty deliberations. There have been many times in my life when I wanted to open the window and yell to a wise someone, "Just tell me what to do!" But big decisions— Should I marry this person? Should we move? Should I walk away from this job? Can I afford to? Can I afford not to?—are best made, ultimately, in the solitude of our own hearts.

Some of the best advice I ever got about decision-making came from the spiritual teacher Ram Dass. I had gone to a meditation retreat to try to get quiet enough to make a decision I had been wrestling with all year. Perhaps in the settled atmosphere of the retreat center I would be able to sort through the obsessive questions dominating my mind: Should I leave my position at work—just give up and leave? How would I help support my family if I left? Should I just accept the place and the people, as is, and stay put? Or should I keep knocking myself out trying to change things that I found intolerable?

At the retreat, the noisy chatter inside my head seemed loud enough to disturb the other meditators around me. In the quiet emptiness of meditation practice, my mind started ganging up on itself. Every thought was like a swiftly moving stream, with little subthoughts veering off in different directions. Like a stick in the river, I went wherever the current took me. The longer I meditated, the more agitated I got. Pretty soon I was caught in a whirlpool, weary and confused.

Ram Dass was also at the retreat center, living there for a month in solitude. I asked him if he'd sit with me and help me with a decision I was try-ing to make about work. He agreed and we met in his little room. Just as I was about to let loose the contents of my mind, he broke in.

"Before you start, I want to warn you that any advice I give will proba-bly lead you in the direction that my own life has taken, because that's all I know. I've never held a job in an organization for any length of time. When things get boring or too political, I leave. I don't have a family to support. I like to keep moving. So if you want to lead a life like mine, take my advice. If you don't, I wouldn't listen to a word I have to say." Then he smiled and said, "Now, what was it you wanted to ask me?"

Hmm. What could I say to that? Nothing. So, I shrugged, and then laughed, and then Ram Dass made some tea, which we sipped together in silence. Later, back on my meditation pillow, I was calmer; I could hear the whispers of my soul. Mysteriously, Ram Dass's little speech had freed my mind from the whirlpool. Knowing that the decision was mine and only mine to make stopped me from flailing around. I sunk deeper, below the surface rapids, and regarded my work-life from a less agitated perspective. I could stay or I could go; I could fight for what I believed in or I could ac-cept things the way they were; I wasn't a victim; someone else wasn't the bad guy. No blame, no guilt, no right or wrong: *just what I wanted.* It came down to that. I had a choice. I could continue to squirm around on the surface, too afraid to move in any one direction, wishing things were dif-ferent, feeling sorry for myself or angry at someone else. Or, I could reroute my energy into the real job at hand: finding out what I wanted. What was calling me to my full aliveness, to my soul's destiny? For this, there was no one but myself to turn to, and suddenly I found the news lib-erating. Pema Chödrön calls this attitude "the wisdom of no escape."

The wisdom of no escape throws decision-making back on ourselves—not in a punitive way, but in a way that is uplifting and meaningful. It in-structs us to take a good, clean look at the reality of the situation we find ourselves in. That's the first step. Instead of wishing things were differ-ent—the "if only" method—we adopt the "no escape" method. We size up the situation with a clear head and an open heart. No fantasy, no blame, no escape.

The "if only" method is a favorite of most of us because it gives us something to fixate on while we avoid making a decision. A friend of mine was trying to decide if he should marry the woman he had been living with. She was pushing for it; he was unclear. If he didn't marry her they would have to separate. This was the ultimatum his girlfriend gave him. My friend's phone calls to me all focused on his anger about being forced to make a decision. He said that ever since his girlfriend had given him the ultimatum, they were fighting constantly. "If only she hadn't pushed me like this," he complained. "Now how will I know if I want to marry her if all we do is fight? Why does she always have to push everything? If she hadn't backed me into a corner I'd probably want to get married." My friend's obsession with the ultimatum allowed him to steer clear of the deeper questions: Who is this person I am considering marrying? Can I love and respect her just as she is? Can she help me on my journey of growth and change? Can I help her? Do I want to?

It's almost easier to circle around the truth and dwell on peripheral issues than to look at a situation from the standpoint of "no escape." Circling around the truth is like having a tantrum. Watch a two-year-old having a tantrum and you'll get a valuable lesson in the wisdom of the "no escape" method versus the folly of the "if only" method. A two-year-old wants what he wants regardless of reality. He doesn't want to squarely look at the situation and he doesn't know what would best serve his inner angel. He just wants what he wants, whether it's possible or not. When my oldest son was two, he went through a period we called the "great banana wars." He loved bananas, and he loved to peel them even more. If an unsuspecting person gave him an already-peeled banana, he would collapse into a helpless, weeping mess. He wanted to peel the banana himself; a new banana wouldn't do. Taping shut the already-peeled banana didn't work. He wanted the original banana returned to its prepeeled state.

Often the pain involved in decision-making comes from banana-war mentality—a refusal to accept the situation for what it is. *If only* my friend's girlfriend hadn't pushed him, then he could decide to marry her. *If only* the organization would change, then maybe I'd want to stay in my job. Before we can make a wise decision, we have to accept the terms of the real situation, not an ideal one. Can you answer the call of the heart within the situation, just as it is? Are you willing to take full responsibility for what you decide? What is your heart calling for? These are the real questions.

My friend did get married. He stopped having tantrums about side issues and got down to figuring out if his soul was calling him to wed the real-life person that his girlfriend was. It took me about a year after my visit with Ram Dass to make my decision and then to follow it through. I revisited the mental whirlpool many times before I was finally able to take a "no escape" approach. When I stopped focusing on blaming other people, feeling like a victim, or wishing things were different, I quietly realized that I no longer wanted to be so identified with an organization—any organization. I wanted to stay at home more, to write, to be a more attentive mother and wife. That didn't make me or the organization wrong or right. I began to understand that I was having tantrums so that I didn't have to feel the fear of change and the pain of leaving a place that I loved. There was no escaping the plain facts: I didn't like some things at work; it would take a struggle to change them; I no longer had the energy to be a revolutionary; and even more significant, my inner angel was calling me into new territory.

TOOLBOX EXERCISE #10
TEN STEPS IN MAKING A DECISION

I mapped the following ten-step strategy after struggling through my own decision-making process and trying to help others resolve important dilemmas.

1. *Quiet the Mind:* Use mindfulness meditation, breathing practice, and spiritual retreat to develop a natural and spontaneous habit of quieting mental chatter, worry, anxiety, and needless clutter.

2. *Open the Heart:* Forgive yourself for being human. Befriend your longing; don't rush to fill it with the things of the world. Instead sit with the emptiness and listen for messages about yourself. Practice being with your feelings just as they are. Give your inner angel room to breathe.

3. *Hitch Thoughts and Feelings to Reality:* Through the clear lens of an open heart and a quiet mind, observe people and things as they really are. Visit the world bank over and over again for messages from reality. Quiet down and open up long enough to begin to see through your own misconceptions.

4. *Identify Your Own True Voice:* Sort out the voices that run you, gently quieting them so that the most essential and healthy ones rise to the surface. You may need some help; therapy is a good tool for this difficult process. Present your decision to the different voices within you and ask each one to make your decision. See if you agree. Ask your inner angel his or her opinion. Listen closely.

5. *Know What You Want:* A truer word for *need* is *want*. Get comfortable with wanting goodness for yourself. Taking care of yourself and being kind to others are not mutually exclusive activities. In fact, the more in touch you are with what you

really love, the more generous you will be with others. Listen within—to the wisdom of your heart and your body—for deeper clues.

6. *Say What You Want:* Respect yourself and other people enough to speak the gentle truth. This takes courage, but if you have quieted your mind, opened your heart, and are speaking from your own true voice, you need not fear that you are making unreasonable or selfish requests. You are merely presenting reality as it is out of respect for yourself and those around you. Most often when you don't say what you really want, you are doing no one a favor. Honesty, offered with tenderness, is a gift to others.

7. *Deal with Conflict Consciously:* Often we shy away from making a decision in order to avoid conflict. But low-grade, terminal conflict is almost always worse than a clean, dignified presentation of the truth. When you know what you want, you can tell the truth with the kind of gentle dignity that respects the other person's feelings and situation. If your intention is truth-telling, and not an act of aggression, then you will lessen the likelihood of out-and-out conflict. No promises here, though. It takes two to get to peace. This is for certain: your willingness to deal with (not run away from) conflict will make decision-making easier.

8. *No Tantrums, No Cheating, No Escape:* With a quiet mind, an open heart, from your own true voice, and with the welfare of yourself and others close at heart, you will be able to know what you want and what you should do. You will be "silently drawn by the stronger pull of what you really love." Pulled where? Into the wisdom of sacrifice. A choice of *one* job, or person, or place takes up a lot of space, shutting doors on other choices. This is reality. If you cheat you won't get there. To choose what you really love—to get what you want—asks for your fullness in return. No tantrums: *You can have what you really love, but you can't have it your way all the time.* No cheating: *You can get what you want, but you can't have everything.* No escape: *Make your decision based in reality.*

9. *Make the Leap:* Have you quieted your mind and softened your heart? Are you willing to take responsibility for what you want, to be genuine in communication, and to deal consciously with conflict? Have you made deep peace with the wisdom of sacrifice? Then at some point—and only you will know when—you must leap. Take a leap of passion and faith. You may feel a little scared and lonely—aware of all the other choices that you passed up, unsure of yourself and the future—but when you commit your whole self to a wise decision, you will also feel abiding peace, incredible strength, and deep happiness. Fun will feel more fun. Pain will feel more painful. Life will feel more alive. You will be, in the words of Chögyam Trungpa, "a king or queen with a broken heart," ruling your world, sobered by reality, exuberant, fearless, and compassionate.

10. *Continue All of These Processes Simultaneously Every Day for the Rest of Your Life:* **The spiritual journey is not technique or luck—it is a long process of discovery. Be patient and, most of all, forgiving of yourself and others. Experience with a sense of wonder the many textures of the journey—the ups and downs, the knowing and not knowing, the light and darkness. Accept help and pray for guidance from your inner angel. Look for humor, beauty, and a trail of bread crumbs in the woods.**

AUTOBIOGRAPHIES OF JOY AND GRIEF

The way to find out about your happiness is to keep your mind on those moments when you feel most happy, when you really are happy—not excited, not just thrilled, but deeply happy. This requires a bit of self-analysis. What is it that makes you happy? Stay with it, no matter what people tell you. This is what I call "following your bliss."

—JOSEPH CAMPBELL

My husband and I were on vacation on a little-visited Caribbean island, one that has no sandy white beaches and therefore few tourists. The island's shoreline is sheer cliff and rocky inlets. Inland, amazing treasures await the adventurous—lush, tropical forests, rare plants and flowers, and more than a hundred rivers that crash fantastically down the mountains, creating waterfalls and deep canyon pools. Hot volcanic springs add weird color to some of the rivers. After a long hike through the jungle, where parrots swoop and call, hikers can swim in a milky-blue mountain stream—the color of a melted crayon—and find pockets of hot, mineral-tinged waters along the banks.

In this Eden we met a group of five adventurous people who were traveling together, and had done so all over the world. They were staying in the same tiny jungle lodge as we were, and over meals we became friendly. Within a day or two the group adopted us, and took us along each day into the mountains, with Robert, their island guide, in the lead.

I gravitated on our hikes to one of our newfound friends, an older man I will call Conrad. There was a sadness in Conrad and a depth that I wanted to understand. As we got to know each other I learned that his wife of forty years had died the year before and Conrad was in a pretty constant state of grief and fear. His own death was staring him in the face and he feared that he would die before he had ever really known happiness. A successful architect, a man who had given his time to a cause he passionately believed in, and someone who had many friends, he had lived a rich and meaningful life. Yet he had been depressed for most of it. He told me that he didn't know what it meant to feel happy.

One day, drifting on our backs down an ink-colored river that cut its way through a narrow ravine, watching parrots dart across the sun-dappled canopy, Conrad told me that he could not imagine living much longer. Here we were in one of the most beautiful spots on earth and this man's sadness gripped his heart so tightly that he was unable to take in any of the bounty. "Were you ever happy, Conrad?" I asked him. He answered, no, he could not remember a time, even as a child, when he had not felt something like a boulder standing between him and joy. I urged him to get some help, to learn to meditate, to see a therapist—anything to help him discover the wonders of living while he still had time.

I stayed in touch with Conrad after our vacation. One day I got a letter from him. He had started seeing a psychiatrist who had put him on anti-depressant medication. Conrad had harbored a condescending attitude toward any such drug for years, thinking it was the "cheater's way." But this time he felt desperate enough to reluctantly start the medication. After a few months on the drug a remarkable thing happened. For the first time in his life, words like "happy" and "content" began to mean something to him. He could almost taste the quality that had eluded him all of these years. A year later, after firmly establishing what it meant to feel happy, and getting used to the natural ebb and flow of happiness in his daily life, Conrad wrote to me again. He had stopped taking the drug. Now when depression would grip his heart he knew that he could head in another direction, one called joy. He knew how to get there now, because he had been there before. This made an extraordinary difference. He told me in a letter, "No wonder I could never fight my depression. I didn't know what it felt like to be happy. It was like going into the jungle without Robert. Now I don't need the drug anymore because I learned the way myself."

Most of us are not as lost as Conrad was. Most people have probably known just as many moments of happiness as moments of sorrow. But humans are a complaining lot. We talk about our problems freely, yet have much less experience sharing our joy. By dwelling more on the painful parts of life, we overlook the sweetness. What we can do, much as Conrad did, is learn how to give joy its due attention, committing its signs to vivid memory. Then, when grief, or sadness, or depression gets the better of us, we won't panic. We'll trust that right around the bend, in equal measure, are happiness, pleasure, and joy.

One of the problems in giving joy its due attention is that we may not really know what joy is. We may have such romantic expectations of "happily ever after" that we miss joy when she comes calling. Joy is actually a more complex emotion than sorrow. I hesitate to talk about it for fear that I will betray its complexities and make others feel as though they are missing the party. A joyful soul often lives in a state of what I call enchanted melancholy. This kind of happiness contains within it many shades of feelings: joy and grief, passion and sobriety, love and longing, innocence and wisdom. It holds the paradoxical nature of existence in a warm and wide embrace. More than anything, it is a sense of wonder.

Too often, because we don't want to appear sentimental or naive, we hide our sense of wonder. If we do experience moments of awe or gratitude merely because we're alive, we're reluctant to express how we feel. We spend very little time basking in the miracles that are given each day— miracles like sensation, beauty, intelligence, humor, love. Perhaps we'd sound melodramatic or trite if we announced that our heart was full of gladness from the smell of rain on the sidewalk, or the taste of red wine, or the sound of an Irish fiddle. I keep a cartoon on my refrigerator of a woman with tears in her eyes, standing before the freezer, exclaiming, "I can't believe it! Perfect ice cubes again!" And I must admit, I often feel overwhelmed by similar magic, yet embarrassed to announce it to the world.

We withhold joyful self-expression for fear of being branded a sap, and for other reasons too: perhaps we're afraid that an exhibition of joy would make those less fortunate than ourselves covet what we have. We've been cautioned not to brag or be self-aggrandizing. But I contend that by stewing in our own simple gladness, and by freely sharing it with others, we spread joy around. Sometimes we're feeling joy and we don't even know it. With a slight shift of perspective, so much of what we take for granted—like not being sick, or not feeling anxious—can become, instead, states of grateful well-being. We can actively choose to regard neutral feelings—like "no headache" or "no worry"—as not neutral, but as full of joy.

When I teach, I have people create "autobiographies of joy" as a way of remembering how much happiness they have had in their lives. Each little story becomes like a shiny fishing lure that we can use later, when we need to be reminded of the way toward the light. It's a wonderful exercise, and far less expensive and serious than taking Prozac. I ask people to go off alone and find images from as far back as they can remember into childhood, or as recently as yesterday, as if remembering dreams. We search for several different incidences when we felt joy. Any kind of joy: feelings of grateful well-being; times when we were at peace with the world; feelings of energy and inspiration; times of pleasure.

Then, during the same exercise, we also create autobiographies of grief, because joy and grief are sides of the same coin. We conjure up different stories of grief: examples of unfulfilled desire; periods of great loss and despair; times when we were overcome by a sense of longing that no one or nothing could fill; or just that familiar, nagging sense that we're missing out on the party. We write little vignettes about those times—short stories of our grief. Anything. I give no limiting ideas of what "should" be considered sad or painful.

Later, when we come together and read our stories aloud, we are always moved. We get to witness the beautiful threads of grief and joy that make up the tapestry of a life. And we begin to sense the presence of the inner angel in our joy as well as in our grief. What never ceases to amaze me is how in a group of people of various ages and walks of life—from successful and powerful men and women, to those in a broken-down state, to young people just starting out—the stories focus on the most simple, raw incidents. Rarely does anyone's autobiography of joy focus on extraordinary events, or lots of money, or fame and status. The stories reveal a core of simple sweetness, a desire for connection, and the ability to grow from the painful events in one's life. Even if a story of grief tells about illness or violence, at the center of the story stands the inner angel, guarding the heart of the teller.

By writing and telling autobiographies of joy and grief, we begin to understand that a flow between grief and joy has been with us throughout our lives. Like the hero's journey, the strength and wisdom gained during our times of grief are as valuable as the pleasure we feel during times of joy. Stirring up our own mythic pot of soup can help us recognize these patterns and trust more in the movement of life.   .

TOOLBOX EXERCISE #11
WRITING AUTOBIOGRAPHIES OF JOY AND GRIEF

Try this exercise for yourself. Choose music that awakens joy and meditate on moments in your personal history when you felt the presence of joy, delight, wonder.

Write your stories down in the way that I illustrate below with a few of my own stories. Do the same with grief: listen to music that softens your heart and meditate on moments in your life when you suffered feelings of grief, pain, sorrow. What you choose to write about might surprise you. Strung together, your autobiographies of grief and joy map the journey of the inner angel.

Grief: Reviewing the griefs of your life brings them out of the closet and makes them seem less burdensome. You may even begin to change your mind about them. A grief may be a joy in drag; how you dealt with it may reveal your greatest strength; how you didn't deal with it may now teach you another way of being.

Joy: Identifying what it is that makes you truly joyful is good practice—it helps you to learn how to distinguish between joy and the kind of false happiness you cannot trust. If you know what you're looking for, it's easier to find it.

MY STORIES OF GRIEF

I am four years old. My mother has gone shopping and left me with my grandmother, who is bedridden, dying of cancer. I take my pillow and lie across the front door threshold, as close to my mother as I can get without leaving the house. "Go and sit with your grandmother," my mother said when she left the house. But I don't want to. I'm scared of my grandmother. She has gnarled fingers and yellow skin and a scratchy voice. I don't want to be with her. I put the pillow over my head so I won't have to hear her call me, and pretend to take a nap. Months later, when my grandmother dies, I think that it is because I wouldn't sit with her.

———

Dinnertime. I am running home through the darkening evening. The clan of neighborhood children disperses. It is summer; I am eight or nine years old. The skies are heavy with the approaching evening and a building storm. I run through the familiar streets, passing houses and trees that form the backdrop of my childhood. The clouds roll by faster than I can run, and the wind begins to move the trees. I stop in the middle of the big lawn by the side of our house and look up at the sky. Emboldened by the presence of my home, yet frightened enough to stop for just a moment, I perform a ritual that I have done many times before: I call out to God to strike me dead as proof of his existence. Nothing happens—no sudden strike of lightning knocks me out. No tornado whisks me away. I bolt to the porch and into the house, feeling both victorious and defeated. Once again, I have been abandoned to a life without God, renewing within my imagination a fear much more profound than an approaching storm. I feel a kind of aloneness that my large family cannot penetrate. I feel a longing for comfort that the safety of my home at dinnertime cannot satisfy.

———

I am in high school, proudly wearing a seven-dollar raccoon coat that I bought over the weekend at a used clothing store. It is 1968, and our school is tense from racial strife that has erupted recently with the assassination of Martin Luther King. I approach my locker to hang my coat and begin the school day, but am blocked by a few black girls. One of them, Edie, whom I have known since kindergarten, demands that I give her the coat. "My mother can't even afford a coat like that," she says with anger. I try to explain that the coat is worth very little, but the girls take it from me and run. My heart sinks. I want my coat; I want Edie to know the truth; I want Martin Luther King not to be dead; I want us all to get along.

———

I am with my spiritual teacher on the road outside the commune's meeting hall. It is a dark, windy night. He is wearing his black woolen cape and it whips about him in the wind. I tell my teacher that my husband may leave me. I am brokenhearted and overwhelmed with a sense of aloneness—that same aloneness I thought I had banished with a spiritual teacher, a husband, a baby, a community. I cry in the arms of my teacher, but there is nothing that he can do for me.

———

I'm at the mall, just before Christmas, buying gifts for my two friends who are dying of AIDS. I walk around in a mall-induced daze, watching parents smack their kids around and people purchase useless items. Outside, huge new stores are being built as others go out of business right down the road. What is the matter with us humans? Sometimes all I see is the world's brutality. Its hopelessness. Its eventual demise. And what does one buy for two young men who probably won't be around for another year?

———

The phone rings very early on Friday morning. My sister's voice tells me that my father has died. It feels like someone has punched me hard in the stomach; I fall back into bed, the wind knocked out of me. There is a huge, empty, grievous gap between what I have just been told and what I can imagine. Like a grave. For the next several months I live in that grave.

MY STORIES OF JOY

It's raining hard outside and I'm playing Monopoly with my sisters. Our father—the weekend taskmaster—is temporarily out of chores. The weather has kept neighborhood friends inside their own homes. There's nothing to do but be four little girls together on a Saturday morning. We lie on our bellies, concentrating on building real estate empires and not landing on Park Place. Our usual sibling rivalry is contained by the rules of the game, and for a few hours we abide in the warmth and safety of our home and our sisterhood.

———

I'm in a car with a group of friends. We're free! No parents around, no teachers, no one to tell us what to do. We just drive around, ridiculously happy for no other reason than being seventeen and together on a Friday night.

———

It's summer; I'm eighteen. For the first time in my life I'm in love and I am beginning to understand that he is in love with me too. Each time I am with him an unspoken acknowledgment passes between us—our fates are about to collide. I know the moment we first kiss will take my breath away, and it does. There's nowhere else I want to be than right here, with him, forever. I could die right now and I would have lived a full life.

———

I am in the final and thoroughly awesome contractions of labor. I can feel the baby's head filling in the contours of the birth canal. The pain is so complete that it begins to feel like something else. For a few minutes I am completely confused. I have never felt anything like this. What is it? asks every cell of my body. And finally in one sensual moment I realize that I want to push. The totality of my body needs to bear down and push, push, push. I grip my husband's hand and quite suddenly I have turned myself inside out and my son is emerging from the watery depth of his home within me. I have let go of my companion of nine months and received my body back. Two who were one are now separate beings! My body rejoices to be one-in-itself again as I offer my breast to the little fishy boy squirming in my arms.

—

I am changing my baby's diapers. He lies naked and smiling on the bed, absurdly perfect and fully alive. I bury my face in the softness of his belly and breathe in the sweetness of his skin. I have never loved like this before, with no holding back, no expectations.

—

I am singing Mozart's "Requiem" in my community choir, waiting for the soprano solo to hit that high note, supposedly one of the last notes written by Mozart. Working together over a few months, we have practiced the art of merging many voices into one voice, the art of choral singing. Although I have sung with these people for years, I do not know any one of them outside of our two-hour weekly rehearsals. Yet when the soprano solo hits that lovely note, supported by the orchestra in exquisite timing and harmony, all of us sigh and share an intimate moment of joy.

—

I am drinking my coffee, lost in my own head, trying to figure out the complex orchestration of my life: parenting teenagers in a stepfamily and a crazy world; dealing with money problems; feeling the anger and guilt of just having fired someone at work. My husband calls me to the window. It is spring and the air is charged with life. A bluebird is at the feeder. Its color shocks me awake. For a moment I let the fullness of my life wash over me—my dearest friend is by my side, our children are in the next room, and the earth has received spring once again. A sense of gratitude and tenderness fills my heart. Everything will work itself out if I just let it.

LOVE IS THE ONLY RATIONAL ACT OF A LIFETIME

True happiness is in the love-stream that springs from one's soul; and he who will allow this stream to run continually in all conditions of life, in all situations, however difficult, will have a happiness which truly belongs to him, whose source is not without, but within.

—HAZRAT INAYAT KHAN

Love is the emotion normally associated with the heart. It may seem odd then that I mention it only now, at the end of this chapter. I do so because love is the fruit of spiritual labor; it is not a technique you try or a dogma you adopt. Love is the secret you unmask yourself to find; it is the foundation of the spiritual life, the destination where all roads of the journey lead. But it does no one any good to rush the process, nor to enforce loving behavior. Loving behavior is unenforceable and herein lies the mystery of the spiritual life and the mistaken role of religions. You cannot legislate forgiveness; you cannot make hate illegal; you cannot require love. Just as you can't pull a shoot out of the ground and demand that it flower then and there, love cannot be forced. Spiritual work prepares the ground. Love will blossom when our egos and our wounds and our fears have been worked with, tilled into the soil of our understanding.

When we do the hard work of stilling the mind and opening the heart, we come into love. First we love within, then we love the world. First we forgive ourselves, then we forgive others and life itself. I don't think it's helpful to tell someone that "There is no way to love; love is the way." I've heard people say that and I don't think it works. You can't force yourself to love others. If you could, the world wouldn't be in the mess it is now. Almost every formal religion has at its core the charge to love one another, to practice compassion, not to covet, not to steal, not to kill. And yet some of the most dreadfully unloving acts have been committed in the name of religion.

Real love of others stems from love of oneself as a soul—not ego loving ego, but soul loving soul. Enforced love activates the false ego. Ego turns love into sentimentality, which is an idea of love. Love is a deep feeling grounded in action. The dictionary defines sentimentality as "resulting from or colored by emotion rather than reason or realism." Love is the combined experience of reality and feelings. It is highly rational, because love is real. But you must find this out for yourself. Love is the fruit of heartfulness. And heartfulness is a lifelong journey.

"Love is the only rational act of a lifetime." That's what Stephen Levine wrote to me on the back of a postcard at the tail end of a hard year—a year in which I lost two of my closest friends, Peter and Tim, to AIDS; the same year that my father suddenly died; and the year that my dear friend and teacher Ram Dass suffered a stroke. Stephen Levine is also a friend of Ram Dass and had been close to my friend Peter, a child psychologist in New York City. Peter had made it a habit of driving Stephen upstate to

Omega whenever he came east to teach. Now, in the wake of Peter's death, Stephen sent me this card:

> Eliz—
>   Heading out your way again—up from NYC to Omega—no Peter at the wheel—Ram Dass in a wheelchair—Life is magic—Life is only now. And love is the only rational act of a lifetime.
>
>   Treasure Yourself,
>   Stephen

TOOLBOX EXERCISE #12
A HEARTFULNESS REVIEW

Here is a review of Chapters Nine and Ten that serves as a ten-step guide in the on-going process of heartfulness. Although the guide is lined up here in a top-to-bottom order, it should really appear as a circle, with no beginning point and no ending. Each section is part of the one before and after, and the process of becoming more heartful extends throughout our lives.

1. *Learn respect for the feeling function:* Become aware of and undo some of your cultural training so that you grant the moods and messages of the heart the same respect that you give the thoughts and ideas of the mind.

2. *Learn how to stay open to feelings without having to act on them:* Apply meditative awareness to all of the feelings you naturally possess. Allow yourself to feel the heart's hunger long enough and fully enough so that you begin to know what you really want. Fear not the darkness; know that if you banish the darker emotions, the more joyful ones will also be beyond your grasp. Sit with the fullness of emotional reality.

3. *Distinguish the voices within yourself:* Use therapy to separate the inner voices that direct your life. Listen closely to and name the voices that say you are bad, that your body is sinful, your needs selfish, your heart not trustworthy, your tenderness a sign of weakness. Find your own true voice.

4. *Overcome your embarrassment at being human:* Allow the heart to be tender and soft. Be gentle and forgiving of your humanness. Forgive yourself. Give yourself a break. Love your own body; release your shame of weakness and imperfection. Join the human community, open your hearts to others, let love arise.

5. *Do shadow-work:* Get to know and accept your own cruelty, ignorance, and rage. Instead of banishing your shadow or projecting it onto others, own up to your

darker emotions. To the degree that you bring your negativity into the light of consciousness, you will be able to transform it into positivity.

6. *Befriend the inner angel:* Dig up the acorn that holds the indestructible seeds of your genius and your joy. Rewrite your victim story. Find the silver thread of your inner angel weaving together every part of your story. Cultivate a sense of wonder.

7. *Learn what you really want:* Trust your basic goodness. Transform the myth of original sin into a belief of original blessing. Know that what you want in your heart of hearts is good and worthy. When you act from basic goodness, the result will be vibrant and constructive aliveness.

8. *Make conscious decisions:* Withdraw information from the world bank. Messages about reality abound in the feedback from your own actions. Take full responsibility for what you want. Say no to blame, no to guilt. Yes to honesty, yes to responsibility. Having what you want does not mean having everything. Life in reality involves sacrifice. When we choose one thing (a person, a job, a home) we must give ourselves fully or else we cheat ourselves and others.

9. *Live a mythic life:* You are the hero or heroine of your own mythic quest. Your crises and achievements echo those of the gods and goddesses of all times. Celebrate your victories; go deep into your dark nights. String the beads of your life necklace with care and compassion, faith and fearlessness.

10. *Head toward love:* Love is not the answer; love is reality. Heartfulness is the answer; it cultivates the ground for love to naturally arise. You will know you are on the right track if your actions toward others become less judgmental, less unforgiving, more spontaneously loving. Keep your eye on love, but don't force it. Cultivate self-love, self-forgiveness, humility, and openness. Love of others and the world will then find a solid footing in your heart.

Book IV

The Landscape
of the Body

11 ⋮ The Missing Body

The soul is happy by nature; the soul is happiness itself. It becomes unhappy when something is the matter with its vehicle, its instrument, its tool through which it ex-periences life. Care of the body, therefore, is the first and most important principle of religion.
—HAZRAT INAYAT KHAN

I journeyed into the Landscape of the Body late; it was the last of all the landscapes for me to consciously explore. I had spent years educating my mind, and then investigating its spiritual powers. I learned to travel the waterways of feelings, and began following them home to my heart. I was more of a stranger in the Landscape of the Soul, the subject of Book V, but always an eager student. Soul's realm—the home of faith, eternal life, and God—had called to me since childhood. But the Landscape of the Body—the most tangible of them all, the one seemingly of the least mystery—remained neglected, even scorned. Physicality, sexuality, health, fitness: it just never crossed my mind that these had much to do with spirituality.

It may have been the misconstrued remnants of my family's Christian Science beliefs that convinced me to bypass my body. Some Christian Scientists view the body, and its needs and disease, as a bad dream, whose symptoms of ill-health are not just illusions, but also signs of religious torpor. "Mind governs" is one of Christian Science's favorite mantras, used to remind the faithful that the mind has the power to awaken from the dream of the body. But Christian Science was just a small part of my anti-body education. Christianity in general, and the Judeo-Christian ethos as a whole, has been banishing the body from the realm of the sacred for hundreds of years.

One of the great tragedies of religious history occurred when the physical body was falsely accused for the sins of mankind, and was rooted out of Western religious traditions. The idea that our most basic bodily functions, our sexual passion, and our sensual pleasure are unclean and unholy is not only a regrettable belief system, it's also a profoundly ignorant one. Deep spirituality is not an out-of-body experience; it's an in-body experience. How could it be otherwise? Here on earth we live in our bodies, and our bodies are as sacred and miraculous as any part of God's creation. The physical creations exalted by saints and poets—stars and gemstones, milk and honey, the waters of life and the flowers of the fields—share our own elemental makeup.

We are not spiritual beings trapped in a carnal existence. Spirit is dancing in our molecular structure and flowing in our bloodstream. Physical form is the way we experience spiritual reality on earth. Our thoughts are electrical impulses; our emotions are fueled by chemistry and biology; our organs pump and breathe in rhythm with the pulse of the tides and the dance of the cosmos. There is nothing in physical creation that is inherently more sacred than anything else. This holds true for nature as it does for space as it does for the human body.

How then can religion instruct us to worship the miracle of life, and at the same time condemn the ways of the body? Why would God make us "in his image," and then want us to live as if that image were rotten with sin? This convoluted concept is a crazy-making theology, and it has indeed made us kind of crazy. It has led to a compulsive desire to control the body and nature; it has created a cultlike adoption of unattainable standards of purity and beauty; and it has separated aspects of the self that are really one and the same. Body and mind are not separate. Body and emotions are not separate. Body and soul are not separate. The self is like a diamond, and each part is a facet of the same essence. The energy of our consciousness is just as precious when it takes the form of skin, or organs, or blood, as when it is revealed through a thought or an emotion. Our bodies are materialized spirit, and therefore, they are as spiritual as anything and everything.

Many of us have disowned our bodies out of the shame and ignorance of our cultural and religious training. One of the best aspects of the new American spirituality is the return of the body to the sacred fold—the questioning of the belief that we were conceived in a physical act of sin, and that therefore the body is indecent, and sexuality is a profanity. Many Western religious scholars believe that the Old and New Testaments were misinterpreted when it comes to sin and the body, and that the prophets and Jesus never meant for us to be so troubled about physical vanity and pleasure and erotic love.

But it's not just religion that exiled the body from spirituality in Western culture. The advance of industrialism in the Western world also spawned negative attitudes toward the human body, and toward our shared body—the earth. Industry, large-scale agriculture, and urban living took away an immediate, physical connection to the natural world, to animals, and to a meaningful relationship between the fruits of physical toil and the fruits of the earth. As the tools to control nature became more and more effective, and as men and women became less identified with the land and the animals, we lost a vital connection to our own bodies. A lack of knowledge and respect for the wilderness marches hand in hand with the disdain for the wild, animal nature of the body. Over centuries of agriculture and industrialism, humans have created a vicious cycle: the more separate one feels from the physical body, the easier it is to control and abuse the natural world, which leads in turn to a further distancing from a caring, loving relationship to the body.

From its beginning, America set out on an industrial quest to control nature, and a Puritan crusade to repress the body. The outcome—the malling of America and the shaming of the body—won't ultimately endure. I don't think they can. Nature will prevail. The question is whether humans will prevail along with nature. I keep a *National Geographic* photograph in my writing room to remind me of nature's restorative powers. The picture shows the aftermath of massive flooding in the Mississippi River watershed area. The river has reclaimed its original streambed, covering an entire town. All one can see are the bright yellow tops of a McDonald's golden arches, surfacing from the muddy waters. I take comfort in this picture and in the victory of wildness over the *excesses* of civilization. I emphasize *excesses,* because surely there is room on this earth for both the tame and the wild, the civilized and the primal. If we can find a way to balance these forces within ourselves, perhaps all of our achievements won't go the way of that delta McDonald's.

Reclaiming the wildness of earth and body is both a spiritual and a political imperative. The journey through the Landscape of the Body is therefore a very important one, one where tangible progress can be made in the form of both personal and social healing. The earth is our home planet; its preservation is something we must do for each other. The body is your vehicle on planet earth; its well-being is a gift you were meant to relish. The body that you inhabit, the one you awoke in this morning, the one you washed and dressed, was designed perfectly to carry you through life. It is a wondrous invention of a mysterious creator, an invention that many of us barely understand, rarely contemplate, and often don't nurture.

For some, the spiritual journey through the Landscape of the Body is merely a shift in attitude. If you already feel at home in your body and enjoy good health, you'll easily be able to envision your body as a sacred vessel. Sensuality as an expression of spirituality will feel natural. But for others, the body is far from feeling like a sacred vessel. It is more like a repository for accumulated shame and abuse. Some people suffered overt abuse in childhood; others are wounded from the culture's distorted images of perfection—ideals of thinness and eternal youth for women, and bulk and invulnerability for men. The poison of self-hate, born of unattainable cultural standards, flows in many men's and women's bodies. Some of us are so afraid to delve into the secrets trapped within the body's memory that we float through life, quite unable to enjoy the strength and earthiness of our human form. Or worse, we punish our body through neglect or self-abusive behavior.

In the Landscape of the Body, we gently turn our attention to healing. We start with the body we have, not the one we want. We come home to the body. We use the same concepts that worked in the landscapes of the mind and heart: start where you are, stay open, and practice fearlessness.

12 ⫶ Ten Laws of Healing

Healing is not forcing the sun to shine, but letting go of that which blocks the light.
—STEPHEN AND ONDREA LEVINE

I have divided the journey through the Landscape of the Body into two sections: healing and dying. As you read this, your body is participating in an ongoing, miraculous process of death and rebirth; it is dying and healing at the same time. Every minute, millions of cells in the human body die. Healthy cells keep dividing, replenishing the body with new cells. Without your conscious awareness, your body continually performs the miracle of healing in an invisible and seamless way. Dr. Andrew Weil, author of the best-selling classic *Spontaneous Healing,* says that "healing is making whole, restoring a state of perfection and balance that has been lost through illness or injury. . . . Everyone has experienced healing. Anytime you cut your finger, you have a wonderful opportunity to observe the body's healing system at work; soon the injured area will be as good as new. What happens on the surface of your body also happens throughout."

Spiritual healing is aligning our consciousness and will with the body's innate ability to mend and regenerate. If spirituality is a fearless, relaxed, and openhearted investigation into life and death, then spiritual healing is a fearless, relaxed, and openhearted investigation into the workings of the body in health and disease, in living and dying. To regard healing through a spiritual lens it is important to take a step back from Western medicine's emphasis on the speedy, by-whatever-means-necessary eradication of pain and disease. This is not to say that Western medicine can't be a legitimate part of one's healing process. But if we rush to cure a symptom before listening to the body's deeper story, we often miss the chance to participate in the kind of healing that is sustainable, meaningful, and whole. Spiritual healing asks that we take the time to listen to our symptoms; to slow down and rest; to accept and love the body in sickness and in health; and to take responsibility when we can and get out of the way when we can't.

The spiritual practices of mindfulness and heartfulness can serve us well in this context. Meditation reminds us to listen before we act; it helps us work with stress, anxiety, and fear. We can use guided visualization to become body educated. Psychological techniques lead to the discovery of meaning in symptoms; to the release of bound memories and bitter attitudes that are toxic to the body; and to the development of strong boundaries and a will to fight. More classical spiritual practices—the kind covered in the Landscape of the Soul, including prayer, ritual, and faith—convince us to give control over to a greater power, even as we take responsibility for our well-being.

To make our way through the Landscape of the Body, I break the healing process into ten laws:

Ten Laws of Healing

1. We Want to Care for the Things We Love
2. The Body Remembers
3. Separate Body Image from Body Reality
4. Come into Animal Presence
5. Listen to the Body
6. Experience the Mind/Body Connection
7. Let Energy Flow
8. Be a Skeptical Explorer
9. Get Support
10. Take Responsibility but Give Up Control

THE FIRST LAW: WE WANT TO CARE
FOR THE THINGS WE LOVE

We live in a confusing time in regards to the Landscape of the Body. Interest in physical fitness is at an all-time high, yet many people are more out of touch with their bodies than ever, with stress-related illness, exhaustion, obesity, and eating disorders on the rise. Personal health is featured on the covers of popular magazines, while toxic environmental conditions get worse. There's no lack of information on how to achieve health—from working out, to yoga, to a myriad of diet regimes and cross-cultural healing techniques. Yet the intuitive self-knowledge of what our own body needs, and the motivation to stick with anything long enough so it can do its magic, is often missing. What's wrong here?

What's wrong is that we have layered a concern about health and fitness on top of a deep-seated distaste for the human body. It is difficult to be motivated to care for something you don't like. Without a basic respect for your body, or better yet, a reverence for it, you won't be instinctually drawn to nurture it. If you have the kind of conditional relationship with your body in which you take care of it *in order* to love it (I'll love my body if it's thinner, if I have strong abs, if my thighs don't jiggle), your care will not run very deep. Think of the way people love their pets, the way parents love a child. You don't take care of your child in order to make him or her lovable. You care for your child because you already love him, because you would do anything for her. *We want to care for the things we love*—this is the first law of the Landscape of the Body. The first work to be done to achieve health and strength and beauty is to fall in love with your body, just as it is now. Then the motivation to exercise, eat well, and seek healing will arise as a natural response, just as loving your baby, or your puppy, or even your new car comes naturally.

When we love something, we instinctively listen to what it needs. Our choices and motivation come from an intuitive understanding and are therefore wiser and more sustainable. It is only through knowing and loving the body, *as it is now,* that we can energize and heal it. *First* we must understand and love the body; *later,* we can work successfully with it. This is just like any relationship: if we try to discipline a child without love, the child recoils and is wounded. If we understand the child, show her love and respect, then she will respond to our direction.

As we travel through the Landscape of the Body, it's good to ground the learning process in experiential exercises. The body responds less to thoughts and ideas and more to care and experience. The exercises offered in this chapter provide valuable information as well as the opportunity to experience your body, as it is now, fully, with openness and love. The purpose behind each exercise is to help you fall in love with the miraculous functioning of your own body so that you develop a spontaneous and genuine desire to care for it. These exercises help us approach any work we want to do with the body—whether it is recovery, getting fit, losing weight, sexual healing, or incorporating the body into a spiritual understanding of the self. You can gain a lot just from reading the exercises, but they are more helpful if you take the time to do them, and even better if done with others, with one person reading the instructions aloud. If you do them alone, first enter a meditative state of awareness (as described at the beginning of each exercise) and then pick up the book again and follow the directions. It is important to be as comfortable as you can—make sure you won't be disturbed and that you have privacy. If your pants or any article of clothing are tight, loosen or unfasten them, or change into less restrictive clothes.

BODY EXERCISE #1

A MEDITATIVE JOURNEY THROUGH THE BODY

Sit comfortably with a straight back, in a chair or on the ground, and close your eyes. Take a few minutes to quiet the mind and open the heart, using any of the mindfulness or heartfulness meditation techniques we've already explored. The "Soft Belly" meditation from the last chapter is a good one to use in the Landscape of the Body. Take a long and deep breath, and follow it all the way down to the bottom of your belly, a spot right below the navel. Hold the breath gently in that place for a second or two and then slowly release your breath. As you breathe in and out, you can repeat, "soft belly, soft belly," to remind you to relax any tightness or holding. Breathe like this until you naturally feel that place, soft and deep in the center of your body. . . .

Sitting up straight and relaxed, imagine yourself on a raft, drifting slowly down the Amazon, or the Nile, or any river that you have *never* visited. Visualize yourself sitting on the raft, seeing the colors of the muddy water and the jungle foliage, feeling the sun on your back, smelling the moist air and vegetation, hearing the sounds

of the river and the calls of the birds. As you sit in meditation, say out loud what you see and hear and smell. Describe the sights and sounds in detail. Visualize river life: fish and alligators and snakes. See the wildlife on the banks: ocelots and monkeys and parrots. Picture the plants in the rain forest: orchids, trumpet plants, rubber trees. Take some time to complete your journey down the river. After you have vividly painted this imaginary landscape, open your eyes, stretch, and then return to your meditation posture.

Sit up tall again, and breathe slowly in and out, letting your breath fill your lungs, feeling your chest expand and contract. Now take even deeper breaths and feel your belly rise and fall. Put your hand on your belly and feel the breath moving deeply within. Close your eyes and picture yourself on a raft again, this time floating through your own bloodstream. Start the journey as if you had entered your body through your mouth. Visualize your teeth and tongue, float down the stream, past the pharynx . . . the tonsils . . . the epiglottis . . . the esophagus . . . the trachea. Take note of the thyroid gland and the thymus gland. Note their shape and size. Now pay attention to the spinal column, the spinal nerves, and the ribs protecting the lungs and heart. Sit on your raft and watch the lungs fill the chest cavity. Listen to the rhythmic beating of your heart as it circulates blood throughout the body. Continue to float through the holes in your diaphragm and observe the major blood vessels on their way to and from the lower body. Pass by the liver . . . the adrenal gland . . . the gallbladder . . . the spleen . . . kidneys . . . the pancreas. See their colors and textures and movement. And finish up by swirling around in the stomach and the large and small intestines. Now journey back up toward the mouth opening, dock your raft by the jawbone, and leave your internal body. Take a few breaths, open your eyes, and stretch . . .

Did you find it easier to visualize the Amazon, a place where you have never visited, than to picture parts of your body? Could you easily imagine an ocelot or an orchid, but had no idea where your epiglottis or pancreas was? Could you see the color of the river water and sense the towering height of a rubber tree, but not the color of your liver, or the size of your spleen? Even though the Amazon lies hidden within the rain forest, remote and far away, most of us can imagine it in detail. But very few people can conjure up a picture of the interior of their own body.

Once, after I led this exercise in a class, I asked the class members why they thought most people chose not to understand the structure and mechanics of their own bodies. "I bet most of us know more about our cars or computers," I said. A woman responded, "I'm afraid to look too close.

Maybe if I knew how everything worked, it would stop working." People in the class laughed, but knowingly. We could all follow this unreasonable line of reasoning. Another person said, "If I really got to know how my body worked, then I'd feel too guilty when I abused it!" Again we all laughed. "But that's the point," I said. "I promise you, if you get to know your body, you'll begin to want to take care of it." But I also reminded the group that even brain surgeons, who can identify parts of the brain down to the smallest receptor cells, don't necessarily take good care of themselves. Knowing how the body works is just one part of the healing process. Becoming body educated is the first step. The next step is to flood the body—the cells and organs and muscles and nerves and bones—with consciousness, forgiveness, gratitude, and love.

I recommend becoming body educated. Include basic anatomy and physiology in your spiritual curriculum. You don't have to go to medical school. The books that I suggest at the back of the book provide straightforward ways to learn more about the way your body functions. Receiving bodywork, like massage, is another way to become more familiar with different parts of the body. Remember that the purpose of becoming body educated is to gain respect for the body's miraculous structure; to fall in love with its elegance and goodness; to activate the first law of the Landscape of the Body: *We want to care for the things we love.*

THE SECOND LAW: THE BODY REMEMBERS

Many people find it troubling, even impossible, to focus on their bodies. If you are ill and in pain, or unhappy about the way you look, you may find it difficult to contemplate the wonders of the body. Your discomfort in being body focused may run even deeper. Your body remembers aspects of personal history that your mental memory doesn't. It has been storing certain tensions, emotions, and memories since childhood. Feelings of shame and inadequacy, and memories of trauma and abuse may be held in the body, even if you are unaware of their presence. You may have been teased as a kid for being uncoordinated, or fat, or skinny, or knock-kneed, or short, or tall. You may have suffered more intense shaming or sexual abuse. These memories linger in your musculature or your gut or in processes as subtle as shallow breathing or as complex as sexual response. It took you a long time to build up physical defenses against childhood wounding. You can't expect that you'll undo those defenses quickly.

So, be gentle on yourself and go slowly. If the body meditations in this chapter bring tears to your eyes, or make you angry and you don't know why, you may want to continue this kind of work with a skilled therapist who combines bodywork with psychotherapy.

Many different forms of mind/body psychotherapies exist, all of them based on the experience of contacting and releasing the emotional memories held in the body. They address the ways we often disassociate from, or form rigid coping patterns to deal with, past trauma—from the most severe to the more common and easily overcome. Accidents, illness, eating disorders, sexual or physical abuse, and unhealthy body image all form "bound memories" within our bodies, a phrase used by Judith Blackstone, an author and psychotherapist known for her work with the body. Blackstone, and others like her in the growing field of mind/body psychotherapy, help people recognize the correlation between tension and pain in the body and deep-seated memories of childhood grief, fear, or pain. "It is not the body itself that is a prison for the spirit, as some religious writing has suggested," writes Blackstone, "but only the binding of pain in the body that confines us. . . . The moments of our life that were too intolerable to experience fully are actually preserved in our field of consciousness, energy, and body." Healer and author Caroline Myss describes this phenomenon as "when biography becomes biology."

Mind/body psychotherapy has been blamed for the "repressed memory" travesties, where irresponsible therapists aggressively encourage clients to "remember" childhood abuses that never happened, and then to accuse and turn away from innocent family members. But these are the exceptions to the rule. Many skilled therapists who work with the body—often through movement, touch, breath, and sound—do so with sensitivity, patience, and intelligence. Less than a way to fish for memories, mind/body psychotherapy offers ways to release unhelpful beliefs and defenses that are trapped in the body—beliefs that were erroneously formed in childhood, and defenses created against the wounding of innocence. "Most methods of psychotherapy treat only the secondary complex of [these] beliefs and defenses," writes Blackstone. "The limitation of this approach is that we may make changes in our beliefs or behavior without releasing the childhood emotions and mentality bound in our body. We will then continue to be haunted by the painful events of our childhood. We are literally trapped in a distorted, contracted relationship with the world as long as our childhood memories are bound in our body."

My own childhood memories trapped in my body were less severe than many people's, but disabling nonetheless. I was a plump kid, while my three sisters were skinny. I wasn't allowed to take ballet with my older sister because the teacher said I didn't have "the right kind of body." I hated gym class and going to the pediatrician, who would wink at the nurse and tell her I was "carrying excess baggage." Growing up as a girl in the 1950s and 1960s required that one join the cult of Barbie-ism. God bless my mother, who wouldn't let her daughters own a Barbie doll because, as she said, "Barbie is anatomically incorrect." But my mother's voice was a lone one in the church choir of Barbie-ism. Although it helped to have a mother tell her little girl that no woman's waist was as thin as Barbie's, and no woman's breasts were as pointy, I still aimed to look like her when I grew up.

I was late to develop physically, and remained innocently childlike longer than many of my friends. In sixth grade I was excluded from a club in which the members were admitted based on bra size. I didn't even wear a bra. I was terribly worried that my body wasn't constructed normally, that I would never make the mysterious transition from girl to woman. But I was much too timid to talk to anyone about my concerns. In eighth grade I still didn't know what in the world kids thought was so funny when they called Mr. Batey (the science teacher) "Master Batey." When I asked my older sister and her friends about it, they collapsed in laughter and chanted, "masturbate, masturbate." "Well, what *does* it mean to masturbate?" I asked them. Again the question was met with more shrieks of laughter, but no information. This is the way I had always learned about my body: I'd wonder and worry, but I'd be too ashamed to seek real answers. And the answers I stumbled upon were often contradictory and puzzling. When I was sick my grandfather would remind me of the Christian Science belief that "mind governs," and then my mother would take me to the pediatrician, who doled out antibiotics. Physical and sexual education in school were a joke. I distinctly remember the day when the girls gathered in our elementary school gym to see a medical film on menstruation, while across the hall in the cafeteria, the boys viewed another film, the subject of which was of great debate among the girls. What was happening to the boys' bodies that needed clinical explanation on film? "None of your business" was the unspoken answer to *that* question.

The messages I received from all corners—my parents, friends, school, doctor—was that my body was a dark and foreign place, almost separate from myself, and certainly not something to love, know, or respect. By the time I left home I was a young woman with a woman's body, a child's naivete, and a spinster's consternation. When I think back to those days, I see two disconnected figures walking into the world: one is lagging behind and floating about a foot above the ground—my body. The other, my psyche—my thoughts and feelings and fears and plans—is leading the way, full of fire but without a container to concentrate and direct its power. I was ungrounded energy, and therefore confused, and lacking in a deep sense of self-confidence.

My noneducation in the mysteries of the body met up with the sexual revolution when I got to college. What I experienced as a puzzling sense of freedom then, I now regard as an unfortunate way to be initiated into sexuality. In high school I had set three goals for myself to reach before graduation: learn to drive; get drunk; lose my virginity. I had reached the first two, but had yet to conquer the third. Once in college, it did not take me long to complete my goals. I was something of an anomaly at Columbia University. Most of the girls were New York City types—brainy, pale, wearing black, reading Virginia Woolf. I had spent the summer working at the beach. I was tan and blond, eager for my college experience. Now I can see that men were attracted to me. Back then I was in a fog. That disconnected part of me—my floating body—was unprepared and lacking in sophistication. I was not ready at all for sex. But that didn't stop me. By age nineteen I had slept with several men (we kept a running list in my dorm—a sort of competition to see who could sleep with the most guys). I made some stupid choices; I got pregnant and had an abortion; and all the while I had no idea how to love a man with my body. How could I know about erotic love if my body was lagging somewhere above and behind me, untethered to the ground and to myself?

The memories bound in my body—memories of feeling not "normal," of not being thin and athletic, of feeling ashamed when I was sick—maintained the distance between my body and my psyche. They remained with me throughout college, as I met my first husband and became a spiritual disciple of Pir Vilayat. When I first approached the spiritual path, I certainly did not look to it for guidance on how to revel in the earthy splendor of the body. The pleasures of movement, touch, sex, or physical strength and beauty were not part of my spiritual study with Pir Vilayat. He combined the Victorian ethics of his European upbringing with his overreliance on his brilliant mind to create a worldview in which the body was practically nonexistent. He wore woolen robes, even in the warmest summer months, and buttoned his Indian-style shirt up to his chin. I remember the first time I saw him without his robes, in his narrow cotton pants, snapped tightly at the ankles, and his prudent long-sleeve top. He was so small and thin! For years he had been big, the flowing folds of his woolen robes giving his chest and shoulders a mighty appearance. But it wasn't his size that surprised me the most; it was that he had a body at all.

When Pir Vilayat performed our marriage, there were four people at the altar: me and my body, and my husband and his body. The four of us stayed married for more than ten years. There were times during those years when it was just the two of us—just me and my husband, both of us merged with our own bodies and with each other—but those times were surprising gifts, and not a way of relating I knew how to nurture or sustain. Perhaps we were most unified during the births of our children, because childbirth had become for me the one place where I could deeply appreciate the miraculous nature of my body.

The first time I attended a birth was with my husband, before we were married, when he was still a medical student. I dressed up in nurse's garb and was allowed to scrub into a cesarean section at the teaching hospital. A cesarean birth is not for the faint of heart. An incision is made in the mother's abdomen. The surgeon then reaches in and swiftly lifts out the entire uterus, cuts it, and pulls out the baby and the placenta—often still in the amniotic sac. Then the surgeon cuts the umbilical cord, delivers the baby to the world, stitches up the uterus, and stuffs it back into the abdominal cavity. All of this happens in a few minutes, but in those minutes an observer can get a good look at the structure, texture, and shape of the female reproductive system. I was enthralled. "So, this is what my uterus looks like!" I marveled. I wanted to see more, to study the working mechanisms of a living body. I scrubbed into a few more surgical procedures, and each time was deeply moved by seeing the flesh and blood of the human body.

When my husband graduated from medical school, he taught me how to assist him in home birth services, which we offered to friends, and then later to the community at large. The more I studied female anatomy, the more I wanted to live more consciously in my own body. When I was pregnant with my first baby I was thrilled to participate fully in the whole process of growing and birthing a child. I relished each stage—even the difficult ones, like morning sickness, discomfort from weight gain, and the intense pain of labor. For the first time in my life I took delight in the power and perfection of my own body. I felt inklings of wholeness. In a way, I became embodied as my children's bodies entered the world. During the labor of both of my sons, my body and my psyche were melded in a way that healed some of my bound memories. More healing was to come later.

I was a practicing midwife and birth instructor for seven years. I attended more than fifty births and taught childbirth classes to mothers-and fathers-to-be. For a while I taught standard Lamaze breathing exercises to help women get through labor. But as I matured as a midwife, and especially after I had my own babies, I began to change what I taught. I noticed that the women who had the easiest time in delivery were those with a visceral understanding of the ways in which their bodies worked during labor. If a woman could picture her uterus and cervix during a contraction, she had a much better chance of relaxing, feeling less pain, and shortening the labor. If instead she felt at the mercy of a scary and agonizing process, her tension would mount and her ability to work with the pain would vanish. Her lack of knowledge would actually work against her in labor.

Another midwife that I worked with began to tell the women and men in our classes that they wouldn't graduate unless they fell in love with the uterus. People always thought this was funny, but they also found out it was true. If a woman could relate to her uterus as a dependable friend, she would have a much easier time trusting the process of labor. The best way to prepare for childbirth, then, was to learn how to visualize, love, and extend messages of appreciation and gratitude to the uterus, so that when it came time for the baby to be born, the woman could consciously work with her body as it relaxed, opened, and let go.

The uterus is really a collection of muscles, closed at its base with a feisty little muscle called the cervix. Throughout pregnancy the muscles in the uterus do a magnificent job of keeping the baby firmly stationed within the mother. The uterus provides a stable home, protecting the amniotic sac and the baby itself, as well as the mother's internal organs. The cervix stays tightly shut, like a fist, sealing off the warm and fertile uterus from infection. And then, after nine months of performing the job of holding things together, the uterus is suddenly flooded with hormones that tell it to loosen its hold and to let the baby out. Responding to these hormones, the muscles in the uterus begin to contract and to push on the baby and the cervix. The walls of the cervix then begin to thin and to stretch open, creating intensely painful contractions in the mother.

If you grip your hand tightly in a fist, you'll have a good idea of what the prelabor cervix looks like. Now take both hands and form a wide circle with your thumbs touching at the bottom and your index fingers touching at the top. This is the size, give or take a few inches, that the cervix must stretch to in order to let the baby's head pass through. That's a lot of stretching in a short amount of time, and to the woman experiencing labor, it feels as if you're being torn inside out. If the mother doesn't understand the physiology behind the pain, she will greet each contraction with resistance. In the same way that you would flinch and draw back if someone threw a punch at you—or screw your face into a tight knot anticipating a shot at the doctor's—so does a laboring woman tighten when the pain of a contraction begins. Yet, as you now know, the uterus's work is to relax, open, and let go. If the body's attempts to loosen and open is met with the mother's tightening, then the progress of labor is slowed and the pain intensified. So the most important lesson a pregnant woman can learn is how to work with the uterus in labor as it does its miraculous job. In order to do this, first she must gain a thorough understanding of her reproductive system and a way to communicate respect and support to her uterus and cervix.

The reason I describe the process of labor here is because it is an apt metaphor for working with the body in any capacity—whether you are ill, or training for a sport, or wanting to lose weight, or trying to release bound memories. You may not be in a physical state as dramatic as childbirth, but the same rules apply to any kind of healing work. To heal, it helps to know and love the body. It helps if you can listen to what your body wants and needs, and appreciate its own wisdom and its miraculous abilities to mend and function.

THE THIRD LAW: SEPARATE BODY IMAGE FROM BODY REALITY

Every part of your body is as miraculous and lovable as the uterus of a pregnant and birthing woman. Those knees that may be failing you after years of strenuous athleticism; those thighs you may judge as being too big; your nose, eyes, ears, mouth—the images you have of these parts and of your body as a whole probably differ dramatically from the beauty and grace with which they function. In fact, we rarely focus on function when we regard and judge our bodies. The next time you are leafing through a magazine, do an informal experiment: study the form of a female model (childlike, heroin-addict thin, and wrinkle free) and the form of a male model (tall, rugged, and supertoned). Now compare their forms with those of any random group of people—on the bus, in your office, at the grocery store. How many people actually resemble the models we all secretly wish to look like? This experiment may not work if you live in Southern California. But elsewhere, with the exception of eighteen-to-twenty-five-year-old models and athletes, the vast majority of humankind does not look like and could never look like the ideal we have been brainwashed to covet.

The saddest part of this fantasy is that each one of us already has something far better than the unattainable image of the "perfect" body. We have been given a remarkably crafted vessel to carry us through life. And regardless of your current state of health and physical fitness, your body is serving you right at this moment with skill and grace. Instead of focusing so fiercely and exclusively on diets, face-lifts, workout programs, and other techniques to ward off illness and aging, we can take some time to appreciate what is working inside our bodies. We can flood our bodies with gratitude and love, and discover, to our surprise, how well the body responds to this kind of treatment.

The next exercise—the body scan—combines an educational tour of a few of the systems and organs of the body with an opportunity to send loving energy to the physical form that has supported you throughout your life. In this exercise we scan different parts of the body and learn about them just as the pregnant women in my childbirth classes got to know the uterus. Of course, the body is far too complex to explore each and every organ and system in one short meditation exercise. The body scan exercise touches on only a fraction of the inner world of the body. It leaves out a myriad of constellations within the body universe, including the nervous system, the brain, the sensory systems, the endocrine system, and the intricacies of the cells and tissue that make up every part of the body. Some of the descriptions used in this exercise are taken directly from a wonderful book, *The Human Body,* by Drs. Ruth and Bertel Bruun. I recommend purchasing this book. You can use its illustrations to help you better visualize the body during this exercise, and to tailor your own body scan exercise to suit your particular interests and needs.

You may be surprised to find how inexperienced you are in showing appreciation and gratitude for your body, or how different parts of the body are better able to receive appreciation than others. When I talk about focusing on your body with gratitude, some of you may have had experiences in your life that make this difficult to do. You may have struggled with negative body images due to eating disorders, physical abuse, religious conditioning, cultural conditioning, or difficult and confusing sexual experiences. You may have never felt healthy or beautiful enough to love your body. You may have focused so exclusively on your mental or emotional bodies that the whole exercise seems foreign. Sending messages of gratitude to the body may take some getting used to, since the messages we usually send are more like: "You're not good enough"; "You're too fat"; "You're out of shape"; "You're a wimp"; "You're getting old." We hold our bodies up to standards of perfection that are impossible to attain. The cultural images of the human form that we receive from the media are really quite ridiculous and, beyond that, detrimental to our mental and physical health.

Please respect whatever arises in this exercise. If you find yourself becoming bored or frustrated or tired, take interest in these states of mind. They may hold messages and provide wisdom. There is no one way to do this exercise—no right and wrong; no "shoulds." Your only mission is to get to know your own body—your real body, not the one you think you should have. Once after I led this exercise in a class, a man said that he felt like he had after his first date. "How so?" I asked. "I feel like I just met someone I'd been longing to meet for so long. And I can't wait to get to know this person better."

BODY EXERCISE #2
A MEDITATION FOR COMING HOME TO THE BODY

Select a piece of music that opens the heart from your own collection or from the list at the end of the book. Music that softens your heart and that evokes a sense of innocence and simplicity helps release emotions bound in the body. Put the music on low and lie down on a rug or mat, comfortable but awake. Feel the top of your head and the tips of your toes and gently stretch your whole body. Roll your head from side to side, until it finds its natural resting place. Breathe slowly and deeply, feeling the weight of your body on the floor. Feel your lower back sink into the floor; sense your buttocks and legs melting into the floor. Now take a few deep breaths and release some audible, deep sighs. Let your breath serve as a broom,

sweeping your body clean from the inside out. Now just rest on the floor, feeling your belly rise and fall with your breath. Listen to the music. Feel yourself relaxing, opening, resting. (If you find yourself drifting off, come back to the breath, directing it gently to the place where your belly rises and falls, a deep and soft place in the body. Use your breath to stay soft yet alert.) When you feel ready, start the body scan process:

Bring your attention to your *feet* and *ankles.* Squeeze your toes together and release them a few times. Tighten the whole foot and relax it, and let your foot roll gently on the heel until it finds its natural place to rest. Your feet and toes and ankles are a wondrous part of the body—small and delicate, yet able to support the weight of the entire body. They have taken you wherever you have gone and done their work humbly, with very little complaining! Here are some facts about the way your feet function. Try to visualize each part as you direct your breath to your feet:

- Your foot has many bones that form an elastic arch which supports your body weight and functions as a shock absorber.
- Tendons stretch from the muscles in your legs to your toes to control movement.
- They are wrapped in fluid-filled sacs that help them slide smoothly when you move your foot.
- When you step down, the bones in the foot spread out a little; when the foot is lifted, the bones spring back into the arch.

Now, send some loving attention to your feet and toes and ankles. Thank them for doing their jobs. Tell them that you have depended on them your whole life. Without much awareness on your part, they have continued to serve you every day. Send them loving, grateful energy.

Move your attention up into your *legs:* your *calves, knees,* and *thighs.* You may think of your legs (if you think of them at all) critically—not strong enough, knee and calf injuries, thighs too fat, etc. Put aside those opinions for now and send your attention to the following:

Follow your Achilles tendons and calf muscles up to the knees. Visualize your thighbone joining the two long bones of your lower leg, the tibia and fibula, at the knee. You can roll your legs a bit and try to feel the way the knee works: the hinge joint, the kneecap bone, and the cushioning sacs and pads of fat protecting this remarkable technology. Become aware of the extraordinary way that your knees allow you to bend and walk and run. Send them respect for their difficult job, and gratitude for their service. If your knees have sustained injuries, take an extra minute to bathe them with love and healing energy.

Now bring your awareness to your thighs, surely not the most beloved part of the body for many people. Feel the strength of the thigh muscles. Your two buttock muscles, attached to the thighbone and pelvis, are remarkably strong. They can pull your body upright from a sitting to a standing position. Think what it would be like not to have use of these muscles. Put your hands on your thighs and gently pat them, sending messages of gratitude for their strength as well as their delicate ability to transfer blood, lymph vessels, and nerves from the abdomen to each leg. Imagine the lymph vessels of your immune system, just beneath the skin of your thighs, transporting your body's defense against illness. Surround your thighs with feelings of love and respect, and ask their forgiveness for any messages of rejection you have sent them in the past.

Now, bring your attention to your *buttocks* and *pelvis*. Breathe slowly and deeply. Squeeze your buttocks muscles together, hold, and release. Do this a few times. Feel the energy in your buttocks and in your pelvis.

Your buttocks are padded to protect the sensitive nerve endings in your tailbone when you bend and sit and lie down. Send this part of your body warm feelings and grateful awareness. Especially if you usually think of your behind as too big or flabby, send it messages right now of appreciation for a job well done.

Lightly place your hands now over your pelvic area, gently touching your genitals. This is an area capable of feeling pleasure, intimacy, and connection, as well as shame, denial, and hurt. Rest quietly here, listening to the music, feeling yourself breathe in and out. Allow whatever bound memories you have to rise gently to the surface. Let any confusion or disappointment make itself aware. There is so much energy in this area of the body, the place where the miracle of life can be created, where feelings of fertility and potency dwell. Let whatever feelings arise fill your awareness. Let sacred, healing energy wash through your pelvis and your reproductive organs. If you have suffered pain from sexual abuse, or if you are experiencing a confusing change in your sexual identity, like infertility, or menopause, or impotency, allow loving, accepting, forgiving energy to flood your whole pelvic area. If you feel great about your sexuality—if you have fathered a child, if you have given birth, if sex is a source of healthy pleasure, thank your pelvis and your reproductive organs for allowing you to feel the creative rhythms of life.

Now move your hands up and let them rest on your *abdomen*, your belly. Stroke your belly, the lower part of your torso that extends from your diaphragm to your pelvis. The chief organs and glands of your digestive system are in this area—the stomach, intestines, liver, gallbladder, kidneys, and pancreas.

Every cell in your body performs work; work requires fuel. Fuel comes from what we eat. In your lifetime, 60,000 to 100,000 pounds of food will pass through the alimentary canal, a long tube (twenty-seven feet long) that begins at the mouth and ends at the anus. Your digestive system is truly a remarkable machine that does its work regardless of the junk food you eat or the stress you endure. As you sleep and work and play, all the parts of the digestive system continue to do their job, processing food into energy that can be used by every part of the body. You may fault your stomach area for its size or flabbiness, but right below the surface, right at this very moment, your stomach is contracting and expanding, churning the food you have eaten, mixing it with digestive juices, and breaking it down into life-giving nutrients. Pat your belly a few times and thank it for continuing to do its job.

Now find your liver on your right side, resting behind the very end of your rib cage. Place your hand on it. This is your largest internal organ. It processes potential poisons for removal from the body, processes nutrients and vitamins, stores fat and glucose, and contributes digestive juices. Appreciate your liver with grateful energy. Thank it for purifying toxins and keeping you healthy.

Now move your focus up to your chest and rib cage, which surrounds and protects your *respiratory* and *circulatory systems,* your lungs and heart. Put your hands over both sides of your rib cage and feel your lungs fill and empty as you breathe.

You could live for weeks without food, and days without water, but only minutes without oxygen. Your lungs, which reach from just above your collarbone down to your diaphragm, supply oxygen to your body. Each time you breathe your lungs exchange gases in a miraculously intricate way so that oxygen enters the bloodstream and carbon dioxide is exhaled. Your respiratory center takes care of all the work without your having to think about it. Take several long deep breaths right now, and visualize your lungs filling with air and then deflating, filling and deflating. Feel how the act of breathing connects you to life.

The lungs work very closely with your heart. Your heart is located in the chest cavity, nestled between the lungs and protected by the breastbone and ribs. Rest your hand there now and visualize this strong and specialized muscle rhythmically beating. See the oxygen-rich blood leaving the lungs, entering the heart, and then being pumped through the largest artery to all parts of the body. Observe the nutrients, antibodies, and hormones traveling rhythmically to every cell, as waste products are carried away from the cells. Feel the way your whole body pulses in rhythm with your breath and your heartbeat.

Both our heart and lungs rely on us to stay in physical shape in order for them to do their jobs well. But more often than not, we make them work overtime by smoking, or breathing polluted air, or our being sedentary or overweight. They deserve some gratitude for the automatic, unconditional work they do. Right now, send your heart and lungs grateful and loving respect.

Now, extend your attention down into the *arms* and *hands*. Form a fist with your hands and release them. Wiggle your fingers and feel the energy of your body radiating out from your fingers. Feel how sensitive your fingertips are to the world around you—like ten finely tuned antennae.

Your hand is beautifully designed for fine movement and dexterity. Your thumb can move across your palm to provide a firm and useful grip. Your fingertips have a large number of nerve endings. They are among the most sensitive parts of your body. Take your hands and rub them together until your hands and fingers are warm, and then cross your arms and hold yourself in an embrace. Feel the power in your arms and the sensitivity in your fingers. Hold yourself tightly in a warm embrace. Rest in this position, holding yourself like you would a beloved friend. Briefly scan through the body again, sending loving and healing energy to the parts of the body we have just explored. Thank your body for the ways in which it serves your life, for doing its job regardless of how you treat it, and for enabling you to be a spiritual being on a human journey.

THE FOURTH LAW: COME INTO ANIMAL PRESENCE

Come into animal presence . . .
What is this joy? That no animal
falters, but knows what it must do?
    —DENISE LEVERTOV

The embodiment process that began for me through the birth of my babies found its full expression through two major life experiences—one quite destructive, and the other healing and life-giving. The first one was a descent into an eating disorder that lasted for several years. The second one was a blessing that will last my whole life: my belated discovery of myself as a sexual being, and therefore as a fully human being. Jung called awakened sexuality—and all kinds of conscious, earthy relatedness—the *Eros* principle. Eros is the principle most devalued in the Western worldview. It is the principle that values the interconnectedness of all life; an ethos that celebrates connection through the pleasure of touch, the sharing of food, the nurturing of relationships, the protection of life. Jung associated Eros with the feminine and the mother. He associated *Logos* with the masculine and the father. In *Jung to Live By,* Eugene Pascal describes Jung's understanding of Logos as "the principle of focused consciousness capable of objectively and clearly differentiating one thing from another, lucidly cutting through ignorance like a sword." He describes Eros as "earthy relatedness to all people, creatures, and things. This relatedness is spontaneous, personal, feeling, and instinctive." Jung knew that "the masculine and the feminine principles desperately need each other; when they cooperate, they show their best faces. The meeting ground for them is the human psyche, irrespective of one's personal gender and sexual orientation," writes Pascal. When Logos is unbalanced or unconscious, it "produces an unrelated kill-joy personality, one-upmanship, competitiveness and the desire to have power over others." When Eros is unbalanced or unconscious, "it produces foggy thinking, co-dependency, lack of self-identity, and vague ego boundaries, as well as extreme passivity in the face of life's challenges."

When the Eros principle is devalued in a person or a culture, it goes underground; it grows sleepy, cranky, dull, or sick. Pascal, and others in his field, believe that at the root of many of our social and environmental ills is the Logos-centered Western worldview that insinuates " 'Father, sky, spirit, Logos' is good and that 'Mother, earth, flesh, Eros' is bad." Often, the only way that an individual's Eros principle can awaken in a culture that has pushed it underground is through a crisis in an area of life where the Eros principle has most been denied. Awakening Eros may take the form of physical illness, relationship problems, or the acute feeling that one must make a big change, coupled with the equally acute inability to make a move. Jungians call this "the descent process." During the descent process Eros' voice rumbles from below, not unlike an earthquake, and if we listen and give way, the ground above begins to shift.

For me, Eros began to awaken during the painful process of separating from my husband. I had been sick for several years with a vague kind of illness that one doctor called chronic fatigue syndrome, and another believed was caused by liver damage from the hepatitis I had contracted in India years earlier. Sometimes I thought my sickness was all in my head, and other times I was sure I was gravely ill. I felt sluggish, heavy, and chronically tired. My liver ached and my mind was fuzzy. I felt as though my body was my enemy, a drain on my energy, "excess baggage." I kept searching for something—some kind of medicine—to cure me. I didn't know yet that my symptoms had something to tell me, that my body knew more than my mind about healing.

And then, to make matters worse, the stress of becoming a single mother and of making a new life outside the safety of my family exacerbated my symptoms. Unbound from my husband, alienated from my parents, and responsible for my sons, I felt very alone, very worried, and very sick. I entered a dark, unfamiliar underworld, where the rules and guideposts that had once served my journey no longer helped. What I didn't know then was that I was sick because the life force—Eros—was blocked. Now, in retrospect, I can see that by breaking down, my body was taking over control from my mind, and leading me out of the darkness and into health, Eros, and embodied spirituality. But when I was so sick and scared—in the depth of the "descent process"—I wondered if maybe I was losing my mind. Now I know I wasn't so much losing anything but, rather, I was regaining my body.

When I look back on that period of my life I am reminded of a fragment of a fairy tale in which a young woman is lost at night in a deep woods. Full of fear and despair that she will never find her way home, she finally gives up searching for the right path, and falls asleep on the back of her beautiful horse. The reins relax in her hands, and left to its own instincts, the horse makes its way through the darkness. All night the horse moves slowly and assuredly through the woods. In the morning, the young woman awakens to find herself back home. Denise Levertov tells us in her poem "Come into Animal Presence" that "no animal falters, but knows what it must do." I first came into the animal presence of my own body through the darkness of illness. Like the horse in the fairy tale, and like the animal that doesn't falter in the poem, my instinctual body knew what it was doing. My job was to loosen the reins of control, and to develop trust that my body knew its way home.

Here is how I tell my own modern fairy tale of being led out of the darkness, the story of how my body took the reins from my worried mind and brought me home. For a few years I had been feeling sick. During those same years I had been using food—and especially sweet food—to compensate for the ways in which I hungered for love and connection. Instead of nourishing the body, this kind of compulsive eating had clogged and burdened my body's ability to process fuel and eliminate toxins. It had taxed my already weakened liver, which led to other symptoms of ill-health. Nothing I read seemed to help—and I read everything I could find. Doctor-prescribed medicines would alleviate some of the symptoms; special diets would work for short periods of time; alternative healing techniques would never get to the root of the problem.

Finally, there was nothing more to try. So I gave up trying to fix the symptoms and trying to control my feelings of helplessness, and I surrendered to being sick. For a few months, alone and ill, I wondered if maybe I was dying. Now I count those months among the most important in my life. But at the time I didn't. At the time I didn't trust that my animal body would make its own way through the woods if I would loosen the reins of control. It took the kind of surrender into helplessness that an illness or trauma can demand for me to let my body find its own healing path. Slowly and quietly like the woman in the woods, my exhausted mind went to sleep, the reins slackened, and my body took over.

The first change I noticed was that I was eating less. Unlike other times, when I had tried to lose weight through dieting, this time there was no decision, no trying, no diets. I just stopped eating as much. And I stopped eating unhealthy food. I began to let my body tell me what it hungered for, and in listening discovered which foods made me feel alive, and which foods made me sick. When I started losing weight I experienced for the first time a pleasurable awareness of the contours of my body. I remember the first time I put my hands on my hips and felt my hip bones. My hands loved the way my hips felt—strong and slender, distinct from my waist, but flowing smoothly from one part of my body to another. It was a sensual feeling to stroke my own flesh and to love what I felt. And it was an entirely new experience for me to love my female form.

I knew *about,* and had great respect for, the female body in general. As a midwife I was intimately involved with the anatomy of women's and babies' bodies. I examined women's bodies during pregnancy—gave them internal vaginal exams, palpated their beautiful bellies, and massaged their nipples to help them prepare for breast-feeding. I loved examining newborn babies, checking every part of their bodies after they were born. I loved their skin, their tiny hands and feet, their perfect ears, their little genitals, their round heads still soft at the crown. My favorite part of the birth process was after I had examined and cleaned the baby. I would wrap it in a receiving blanket and, before handing it to the mother or father, hold it close for a few moments, feeling its purity and warmth.

But I had never given my own body similar attention. I had never enjoyed my own curves, and features, and warmth. At first, being thin—which I quickly became after a few months of healthy eating—served a wonderful purpose. Freed of excess, sluggish weight, my body awoke. While I had never been obese, I had always been about twenty pounds overweight, and I had avoided paying much attention to my body. Now, to my astonishment, I wanted to look at myself in the mirror, and I was aware that men wanted to look at me too. I liked the way my body felt—sleek and trim, like a healthy animal. When I stretched I could feel my muscles; when I breathed deeply I could feel my ribs. When I lay naked in the bathtub I felt like one long, seamless curve. I could sense every part of myself, from my head to my toes, and I liked what I sensed. And even better, because of the elimination of certain foods, I was beginning to regain my health. My exhaustion went away. My head cleared; I became more focused than I had ever been.

Aware of my body, and with a fresh confidence in my physical beauty, I let my body guide me on my new journey alone in the world. I came into the animal presence of my body. "What is this joy?"—asks Levertov in her poem—"That no animal falters, but knows what it must do?" Suddenly my body knew just what it must do, and it led me into love—body and soul—with a man. It was such a joy to come home to the animal presence of my body; such a healing. For the first time, I experienced sex like meditation or prayer. It kept me on my spiritual toes—open, soft, searching, alive, refreshed, mystical. I gave myself over to the experience—fully, with undivided abandon—like a thirsty animal at a watering hole.

Pir Vilayat told his students a story about healing himself by listening to Bach's B Minor Mass after his fiancée died in a car accident. I borrowed this technique and listened to Marvin Gaye's "Sexual Healing" over and over on the Walkman, thanking God for my newfound health. In my naivete, and my desperate dread of what I had left behind, I blindly held on to this first experience of awakened sexuality like a life raft. But the exhilaration of loving sex, of being in love, and of feeling well got all mixed up in my head with being thin. Instead of continuing to listen to the wisdom of my animal body, I see now that I took the reins back, and decided to get thinner and thinner. If everything else was out of control in my life, at least I could control the shape of my body. And if I was to be alone in a culture where thinness equals feminine beauty, and beauty equals feminine worth and power, then I would become thinner than thin.

It was a powerful feeling to be so aware of my body after years of being disconnected from it. But I went overboard. Controlling my weight became compulsive. I associated my new sense of sensual aliveness with not eating. Terrified to go back to feeling the way I did before my physical and sexual awakening, I continued to starve myself.

Fortunately, through the help of friends, and then later through the messy collapse of my love affair, I was eventually able to unhook the misguided association I had concocted between Eros and anorexia. A turning point for me was when the poet Robert Bly, a friend through my work at Omega, took one look at my emaciated face and told me to read some books by the Canadian Jungian analyst Marion Woodman. It was through one of these books, *Addiction to Perfection,* that I began to find the words to describe and make sense of the unfamiliar states of mind and body I was experiencing. When I first purchased three of Marion Woodman's books—*The Owl Was a Baker's Daughter: Anorexia Nervosa and the Repressed Feminine, Addiction to Perfection: The Still Unravished Bride,* and *The Pregnant Virgin: A Process of Psychological Transformation*—I wondered why in the world Robert Bly had suggested such strange titles: *The Owl Was a Baker's Daughter? The Still Unravished Bride? The Pregnant Virgin?* What was she talking about?

And they were not easy books to get through either, laden with images of dark goddesses and demon gods, and stories from dreams, literature, and obscure mythologies. Of all of the people I have studied with, Marion Woodman's work is the most enigmatic. To grasp her ideas, one must digest them slowly and instinctively, like an animal resting on the ground after a meal—a reason why her books and her ideas have not received wider attention. Fortunately, owing in part to my past reading of other Jungians and also to the spiraling down of my personal life into the very darkness that her teaching stories were describing, I understood some of what Marion Woodman was writing about—enough to invite her to Omega, and to ask her to speak about her work with addiction and eating disorders as expressions of the "abandoned soul." Describing her workshop in the Omega catalog I used her own language and hoped that others would be able to relate:

> This workshop is for serious eaters and serious non-eaters, serious drinkers, serious house cleaners, serious anyones. Many of us—men and women—are addicted in one way or another because our patriarchal culture emphasizes seriousness, specialization, and perfection. Driven to do

our best at school, on the job, in our relationships—in every corner of our lives—we try to make ourselves into works of art. Working so hard to create our own perfection we forget that we are human beings.

There is a tremendous sense in our culture of something within being shut off, abandoned. No other era has so totally divorced outer reality from inner reality, the matrix of which is the Great Mother. Never before have we been so cut off from the wisdom of nature and the wisdom of our own instincts. The rise in addiction—to food, alcohol, drugs, work, sex— reveals that our bodies and souls are starving, that we are cut off at the neck, with no ego center in the body, no "I" who senses and feels in the gut. We are terrified of the body and of reality, addicted to control and perfectionism. Sometimes we feel as if we have no *experience* of being alive. But if we listen to the body, we will be guided back to life—its symptoms are the signposts that can reconnect us to our own lost souls.

When she first taught at Omega, Woodman was in her early sixties, a stunningly elegant woman with an unusual speaking voice that compelled me to listen. Even when I could not understand what she was talking about, which was often, her voice swirled through me, touching my heart, waking me up, astonishing me. I had never heard a voice like this, and I had never been in the presence of someone as brilliant, yet humane. She seemed to be speaking not only from the wisdom of her highly educated mind, but also from her heart and her body. The workshop she led switched easily from scholarly lecture to childlike storytelling to freeform dancing and quiet body meditations. "Fear and anxiety block our breathing," she said to the workshop students, in her evocative and soothing voice. "We learn very early in life that any display of archaic or primitive feeling is unacceptable, and we also learn that the way to control intense emotion is to allow as little air as possible to go below the neck. The deep, full breaths that should nourish the vital organs, not only with oxygen but with awareness of emotion, are held tight in the top of the chest, and the round belly that goes with deep breathing is anathema in the fashion world." During the workshop she led breathing exercises much like the "soft belly" meditation of the Levines. All of what she said and the movement and breathing exercises she led stressed the need to experience spirituality *in the body*.

Of the four or five hundred people who came to hear Woodman speak, many were women, attracted to the workshop by Woodman's books on what she calls "conscious femininity." Some of the workshop participants were addicts—women and men—who found her body-based therapeutic theories relevant to their healing process. Woodman made it clear that her work was not just for women, even though she focused on the rise of feminine consciousness in the individual and society.

Woodman's ideas gave meaning to my recent and tumultuous entry into the Landscape of the Body. My sudden urge to starve myself just as I was awakening to sensuality and sexuality no longer seemed so weird. What I had thought to be my uniquely neurotic addiction to not eating was really a reflection of the culture's rejection and hatred of the instinctual body. I was so out of touch with my body's inner wisdom that I swung from obsessive overeating to obsessive undereating. Unable to let my animal body follow its own way home, I had either force-fed my body or starved it. I began to see that in the same way I had rejected the balanced wisdom of the animal body, humanity also rejects the wisdom of the natural world. Always seeking to "improve" nature, or to suppress it, or control it, we destroy that which would be better left to its natural landscapes, rhythms, and cycles.

At the end of her workshop, Marion Woodman said, "In both the East and West, there is a deeply rooted desire or need to transcend who we naturally are. Some higher power, some God, finds us unacceptable as we are. We've spent several thousand years learning the arts of self-transcendence. But life is a matter of incarnation. The soul is an entity that lives within our human body. The problem is too many people in our culture try to skip over this step and go straight up into spirit. Over-spiritualization is a real danger, but usually the body starts to scream. If we can learn to listen to our bodies' symptoms or to our addictions or to the symptoms of the planet, we can start coming down to earth again. If you want to heal—heal your body and your soul—you have to surrender; you have to give up control; you have to stop trying to be perfect, because eventually you have to face that fact that you are not God and you cannot control your life."

DEVELOPING "ANIMAL PRESENCE" RITUALS

Marion Woodman's work is all about the fourth law of healing: Come into Animal Presence. Psychologist Sidney Jourard calls this law "somatic perception." Somatic perception is the capacity each one of us has for knowing what is best for our own body. When we awaken somatic perception, we take the ownership of healing away from an "expert" and give it back to our own body. We let our inner wisdom tell us what and how much to eat, how to exercise, when to rest, how to heal. Healing begins when we release and rediscover our instinctual somatic perception. This can happen only when we stop trying to control or fix or transcend the body, and instead let the animal of the body—the beautiful horse in the dark woods—lead us into healing.

When we follow the body's lead, shamanic cultures say that we enter "dream-time." We court dream-time not only when we sleep, but also when we slow down, rest, retreat, luxuriate, and commune with nature. If we rush through life, skimping on sleep, pushing past our natural capacity for activity and stress, using stimulants and relaxants to make it through the day and night, we won't be able to sense what our body wants and needs. We can't follow the horse home unless we slow down every now and then, loosen up on the reins, and sense a deeper direction. As much as it appreciates good food, good medicine, and exercise, the body also loves to rest, sleep, and dream. When the mind is at rest, the animal presence within moves to its own rhythm and pace.

The most obvious way to move into the slower rhythms of dream-time is to increase your amount of sleep and rest. Beyond that, a good way to "come into animal presence" is to create for yourself time-outs—mini-rituals—that you can use to switch gears and pay attention to the body. I call these momentary gear shifts "animal presence" rituals. Yoga postures (some of which are actually named after different animals) are great for this. Any kind of stretching exercise done with intention can work. Imagine yourself in a tense meeting. Perhaps your anxiety level is building, or your mind is getting foggy, or your mood cranky. Instead of reaching for another cup of coffee, or poring over your notes one more time, take a minute to switch gears completely: Take a deep breath, interlace your fingers, and turn the palms toward the ceiling; raise your hands over your head, look up toward your hands, and stretch like a cat waking up from a nap. For just a second, without having to let on to anyone, you become a cat; you consciously inhabit your animal body. You will be amazed how a simple stretch that includes visualization and intention can help you switch from a cranky or anxious or foggy gear into a more relaxed and grounded one. The image of a cat works for some people, while others prefer to become a bird unfurling its wings, or a bear rumbling in its cave.

You can devise any animal presence ritual for yourself. Find your pulse on your wrist, breathe slowly, close your eyes, and feel the blood pump rhythmically in your body for a minute; or take a few moments before you eat to slow down, feel your hunger, and appreciate your food and your body. How you eat is as important as what you eat; eating a meal in silence and consciously chewing each mouthful can become a weekly ritual that reminds you of your body's connection to the fruits of the earth. Fasting one day a week is another way to give the body a rest and to evoke your animal hunger. Yet another way to quickly reconnect with the body is through the simple practice of "toning." Healers and mystics have used sound and vibration in this way since ancient times. Musician and soundhealer Don Campbell describes toning like this: "Put your hands on your cheeks and hum, lips together—a low hum, so that you feel the vibration—then relax your jaw. This is not vocalizing; the sounds are not meant to be pretty or expressive. You can do this simple practice for just a few minutes—alone in the house, while you are driving, as a brief time-out from a busy schedule. Toning balances breathing, increases skin temperature, balances brain waves. Whatever you do, it puts you in a better place."

Anything that reminds you in a visceral way that you are a walking miracle—embodied spirit, linked to everyone and all matter through chemistry, biology, and mystery—can become your own animal presence ritual. My secret ritual is one that, for obvious reasons, cannot be used in all situations. I like to come into my animal presence by peeing outdoors. I do this whenever I can, in every season, and in different places around the world. When working at home I often pee in the woods behind my office. The sharp contrast of the electrical hum of my computer, printer, heater, lights, telephone, and fax machine with the deep silence of the woods immediately puts me in a more meditative and present state of awareness. If I am tense, I give over, for just a minute, to the peace of wild things. If I am all wrapped up in myself, I lean back on a tree, look up into the sky, and am humbled by a grander reality.

This works for me. It seems to work for animals too. There are places that I pass in the car that I remember sharply only because (much to my family's embarrassment) I have, like an animal, left my mark there. For a few minutes I rested fully in that place, quietly, sensing all that was around me. I watched the land close up, felt my body as an extension of the earth, listened closely for sounds nearby, watched the steam rising from the soil, and for just those moments experienced myself as nothing more or less than a daughter of the earth. There's a spot on the New Jersey Turnpike—where the last stands of forest meet the suburbs—where I once squatted and peed behind a tree. Stopping there, on an early spring day, I watched an ant colony building its village among the roots of an old oak as the traffic roared by on its way to New York City. I am sure that if passersby had seen me, dressed for a meeting in Manhattan, watching ants by the side of the road with my skirt hitched up, they would have wondered what was wrong. I would have told them that I was just fine; that I was preparing for a meeting, asking the earth for depth and humility.

I believe that if you learn to follow your animal body, it will lead you to eat well, to exercise, to rest, and to take care of yourself. Finding a diet plan and an exercise regime that work for you is the easy part. Letting the motivation come from your animal presence is the deeper work, and the work that will make the difference in your health and your life.

THE FIFTH LAW: LISTEN TO THE BODY

The fifth law, Listen to the Body, assumes that you have been working with the first four laws and have begun to develop a trust in the body's inner wisdom. You won't glean much wisdom from listening to your body if you haven't first cultivated the ground through love and attention. There's a line from a Robert Frost poem that beautifully describes the fifth law: "Something we were withholding made us weak / until we found it was ourselves." What exactly are we listening for when we slow down and turn our inner ear to the body's stories? Nothing more or less than *ourselves*—and especially the parts of ourselves that we have withheld. The strength and healing we desire can be found in the secrets that the body holds.

When you fear illness and doggedly try to prevent it, or rush to cure it, you lose touch with the body's capacity to heal itself. The fifth law asks you to first give the body a chance to heal itself, or at least to tell you how to seek treatment. Andrew Weil, one of my favorite spokespeople for a new kind of Western medical practice, says, "My understanding is that the body wants to be healthy and is always trying to restore balance when balance is lost, but that the circumstances of illness or injury can overwhelm its capacity to do so. In such cases, outside help—treatment—can be welcome, even lifesaving. It is important to understand the distinction between treatment and healing: treatment comes from outside, while heal-ing comes from within. Treatment facilitates healing. . . . A man whose re-covery from lymphoma I reported in *Spontaneous Healing* put it this way: 'Most of all I've learned that you are your own physician and have to heal yourself. The trick is to get your ego out of the way, get your concepts out of the way, and just let the body heal itself. It knows how to do this.' "

When you are in pain or feel ill or chronically tired, take a few moments before seeking treatment, and seek healing. Use mindfulness meditation to relax the tension and holding back that usually accompany pain and dis-ease. Resist the urge to tranquilize or avoid pain. Experiment with listen-ing to your body—your organs, your heart center, your muscles. "What we believe is not in our head but in our muscles," writes Sam Keen. "Where there is constriction, repression, denial of the promise that we are, there is dis-ease. Sometimes illness seems to be a voice of conscience call-ing us to listen to our dis-ease, our discomfort with what we have become, how we are living . . . Illness is often a disguise that shame wears, a sym-bolic way of confessing failure. We cannot forget (and, therefore, forgive) what we refuse to remember. Illness is the un/re/membered body. To get on with the future, we must recover the past; to move toward health, we must remember our wounds."

One of the most convincing reasons to develop your inner listening skills is the overwhelming amount of options that exist today for staying healthy and healing from disease. How do you know whom to trust, which medicines to take, or how to eat, when health magazines print in the same issue articles that completely contradict each other:

"Beware! Americans are dying from high-fat, high-protein diets; elim-inate all meat and dairy products. . . . Good news! Your body needs some fat; eat a rich, whole-foods diet."

"Our soil is depleted; take vitamins and mineral supplements. . . . Sup-plements are unnecessary, even harmful; get your nutrients from food."

"Take hormone replacements to save bone mass and prevent heart dis-ease. . . . Hormone replacement causes breast cancer."

"Use homeopathy, energy medicine, acupuncture, chiropractic, herbs, massage, biofeedback, aromatherapy, naturopathy. . . . Don't use alterna-tive therapies; they are quackery, a waste of money, harmful to your health. . . . Combine alternative therapies and traditional medicine; they complement and balance each other."

These contradictory messages confuse the intelligent person. And to make matters worse, when we are ill and already feeling weakened and helpless, too many choices can make us want to just give up. That is why it is so helpful, before you seek actual treatment, to develop an inner ear and a sense of trust in your own body's needs.

THE SIXTH LAW: UNDERSTAND THE MIND/BODY CONNECTION

The research of Dr. Herbert Benson of the Harvard Medical School reveals that 60 to 90 percent of all visits to doctors' offices in the United States are for stress-related conditions and that most stress-related conditions are poorly treated by conventional medicine. Benson, a medical doctor and the founder of Harvard's Mind/Body Medical Institute, is the author of *The Relaxation Response.* Written in 1975, the book is now in its thirty-fifth printing and has sold more than 4 million copies. But in the 1970s, Benson's research at Harvard on the effect of anxiety and stress on blood pressure was considered revolutionary. Human studies were not allowed by the administration, so Benson surreptitiously started working with young people practicing Transcendental Meditation. He discovered that meditation, or any relaxation or prayer technique that uses repetition (of a phrase, or sound, or the breath) to quiet the thinking process, elicited measurable, predictable, and reproducible physiological changes of lowered pulse, respiration, brain-wave activity, and blood pressure. Benson's research opened the way for more research which demonstrated how the "relaxation response" could counter the damaging effect of stress on health. In turn, it led to the current broad-based acceptance of mind-body medicine and stress management in the treatment of a wide variety of diseases.

The term *stress,* as we currently use it, didn't even exist until the 1950s when Dr. Hans Selye first introduced it through his research on animals placed under unusual or extreme conditions. More than thirty years before the medical community would begin to take seriously the interplay of stress and physical illness, writes Jon Kabat-Zinn, Selye developed a theory that "diseases could originate from failed attempts to adapt to stressful conditions." This may sound like old hat to us now, but Selye's findings, combined with the rising time pressure and consumerism in America, changed the way we look at disease and healing. Selye wrote that "significantly, an overwhelming stress (caused by prolonged starvation, worry, fatigue, or cold) can break down the body's protective mechanisms. . . . It is for this reason that so many maladies tend to become rampant during wars and famines. . . . If a microbe is in or around us all the time and yet causes no disease until we are exposed to stress, what is the 'cause' of our illness, the microbe or the stress? I think both are—and equally so. In most instances, disease is due neither to the germ as such, nor to our adaptive reactions as such, but to the inadequacy of our reactions against the disease."

If symptoms are caused by the "inadequacy of our reactions" against disease, how do we develop adequate, even extraordinary reactions? First it's helpful to dissect our own reactions—to understand the inappropriate, unconscious ways in which we deal with stress. In his landmark book *The Wisdom of the Body,* Harvard physiologist Walter Cannon first explained how modern human beings are still in the grips of the ancient "fight or flight" mechanism (the same one that our ancestors used to protect themselves from the woolly mammoth). When you assume the fight or flight attitude, your heart rate accelerates, your blood pressure increases, your digestive process slows, and your mind and body freeze in a vigilant and defended stance. Even though you are not facing a life-threatening situation, even if all you are dealing with is a presentation at work or a parent-teacher conference, your body often reacts as if you were a hunted creature. You can't really blame the body for doing this; thousands of years ago it needed the extra adrenaline and focus that come with the fight or flight response. Back then, you would use the extra surge of power in your body to swiftly run away, or to fight off your adversary with brute strength. Both of these responses would take full physical exertion. Then, you'd fully rest.

Today we're rarely in sudden, grave, life or death situations that call for the fight or flight response. Instead, our lives present us with a steady stream of stressful situations that don't really put us at risk, but that we approach nonetheless as if our survival were at stake. We stay at the edge of reactiveness, ready to do battle or to flee, when what is called for is much less emotionally dramatic and physically taxing. Instead of controlling the fight or flight response, it now controls us.

You can recognize when you're under the spell of this ancient response mechanism when you feel shaky inside, or when you have "butterflies in your stomach." When your heart skips a beat, or when your anger explodes like a sprinter at the start of a race, you can assume that the fight or flight response has the better of you. Over long periods of time, the mis-appropriation of the fight or flight syndrome can manifest as chronic pain or anxiety. And it is this anxiety that is at the root of most of our illnesses—not smoking, or environmental toxins, or obesity, or crime, or the other health risks that we try so hard to avoid. Gavin De Becker, author of *The Gift of Fear,* says that "anxiety kills more Americans each year than the dangers we fear (through high blood pressure, heart disease, depression, and a myriad of other stress-related ailments)."

So, if we don't fight or flee, then how do we deal with stress? Walling off, denying, and masking our anxiety are not helpful alternatives. In fact, they are often worse than the caveman response. We can do two things: we can try to eliminate some of the choice-based stress in our lives (as discussed in "The Landscape of the Mind") and we can become stress-hardy in dealing with unavoidable stress. Mindfulness and heartfulness meditation and philosophy definitely bolster stress-hardiness. "Stress-hardy individuals have greater coping resources than other people under similar circumstances because they view life as a challenge and assume an active role in attempting to exert meaningful control," writes Jon Kabat-Zinn. "Strong internal convictions about the comprehensibility, manageability, and meaningfulness of life experiences are powerful internal resources. People who cultivate such strengths are less likely to feel taxed or threatened by events than someone with fewer resources of this kind." The kind of strong internal convictions that Kabat-Zinn refers to here are the subject of Book V, "The Landscape of the Soul."

BODY EXERCISE #3
ELICITING THE RELAXATION RESPONSE

Before you begin, choose a phrase that you will repeat during this exercise. You can use a word that has meaning for you—like *peace,* or *openness,* or *love.* Or you can choose a phrase from your religious background that evokes peace and faith, like "Hail Mary full of grace," or "Sh'ma Yisroel," or "Om," or "Insha'allah." Or you can pick sounds that are soothing—like *ahh,* or *aum,* or *shhh.*

Sit in a comfortable position in a quiet place on the floor or in a chair. Close your eyes and consciously become aware of your muscles relaxing. You can use any of the relaxation, visualization, or meditation techniques already described in this book to bring yourself into a relaxed, calm state of mind. Now begin to repeat

your word or phrase on the exhalation of each breath, either aloud or silently. As thoughts intrude, gently disregard them and return to your repetition.

Dr. Herbert Benson recommends that you do this practice for fifteen minutes once or twice a day on a regular basis. Benson has found that this kind of regular practice has measurable healing effects for people suffering from headache, back pain, insomnia, infertility, hypertension, depression, and other stress-related conditions. After you become adept at eliciting the relaxation response through regular meditation or relaxation, you can often reduce stress at will, with just a few repetitions of your phrase, or even with a quick change of perspective.

You can also experiment eliciting the relaxation response through other kinds of repetitive activity, like yoga, running, swimming, and other forms of exercise where a repetitive movement can be aligned with a conscious attempt to still the mind and relax.

THE SEVENTH LAW: LET ENERGY FLOW

The seventh law of healing is based on the idea that illness is caused when the body's vital energy system is impeded. This idea permeates most of the world's healing systems. Chinese medicine calls vital energy *qi;* the ancient Indian systems of yoga and Ayurveda call it *prana.* Life energy has been referred to in Western traditions as the breath of life, the universal life energy, and the electromagnetic field. According to Chinese theory, qi is "invisible, formless, and indispensable," circulating through the body, warming us, protecting us against illness, and giving us vitality. Practitioners of Eastern healing traditions, such as yoga, Ayurveda, tai chi, acupuncture, and shiatsu, work to bring the body into balance by finding where the flow of energy has been interrupted, and then using movement, breath, stimulation, or massage to free the vital energy in the body and correct the imbalance in the system.

Working with vital energy in Western medicine is relatively new; systems like Polarity Therapy, Reiki, Therapeutic Touch, and massage techniques that borrow from Eastern medicine are regarded as too new and scientifically unprovable to be accepted by mainstream medicine. Unprovable by science, maybe, but new, no. There is evidence that some form of yoga was practiced as early as 3000 B.C. The first written description was found in the *Yoga Sutra*—parts of which were written in the second century B.C.—a book attributed to Pantajali, an Indian physician. Yoga has developed steadily over thousands of years and is still used successfully by millions of people to keep the life energy, prana, flowing freely, and balancing and vitalizing the body. It is an elegant system that increases the flow of oxygen to the brain and body, which in turn eases stress and fatigue and boosts energy. Yoga strengthens the immune system, relaxes tension, keeps the body strong and limber. There are similar systems to yoga, both Eastern and Western, that are valuable healing techniques. Look around and experiment with different forms of yoga, with body-work systems, with stretching and strengthening techniques: all can be incorporated into your life without having to *become* anything, join a group, or change a belief system.

Whatever you call it—prana, qi, universal life force—life energy does indeed permeate every muscle, bone, organ, and cell of the human body. Neuroscientists and biochemists have their own terminology for the ways in which "information-carrying molecules" move through the body. Current medical research is unlocking fascinating correlations between ancient energy systems and a modern understanding of biology and chemistry in the human body. Suffice it to say here, you can adopt an attitude that healing is assisted by free-flowing energy in the body without becoming either a Yogi or a neuroscientist.

Deepak Chopra, a medical doctor trained in both Western and Eastern science, bases his healing work on the timeless and free flow of energy in the mind-body. "Modern science," he says, "tells us that we live in a universe with no edges in space, with no beginning or ending in time. Eastern wisdom says we have a universe within ourselves as profound, as infinite, as timeless as the world outside. Unbounded freedom permeates everything and yet we continue to live our lives as prisoners of fragmented values—prey to disease, unhappiness, and caught in the web of time." Using energy healing to contact the unbounded freedom that permeates our internal systems is yet another way to heal the split between the spiritual and the physical.

THE EIGHTH LAW: BE A SKEPTICAL EXPLORER

As we seek to bring the body back into the spiritual fold, we run the risk of buying into irrational healing practices that at best are a waste of time, and at worst can be harmful. Succinctly put, the eighth law says, to quote a Sufi saying, "Trust in God, but tie your camel." Stay open to the magical and the mystical, but stay equally open to the practical and scientific. Question quick-fix, invasive Western theories, but be equally suspect of unproven methods that make unrealistic, fantastic promises.

My least favorite aspect of the influx of new healing methodologies is not the methods themselves—it's the fanatical ways in which some people adopt them and exclude other forms of healing that may indeed be more appropriate for certain diseases. I have seen too many friends suffering from serious illnesses turn away from Western medicine in favor of more "natural" forms of healing. I don't think Western medicine is unnatural; rather I think it is more invasive and less subtle than some other forms of healing. Someone suffering from cancer or AIDS or another serious ailment may need Western medicine to stay alive. In these cases, Western medicine is magical and mystical, and to me, the choice not to use it often seems unnatural. Instead of becoming a fanatic in any direction, it is best to stay open, informed, and clear in your intention to heal. From a place of intelligent receptivity, listen to your body, research and explore, and try a wide variety of healing methods.

THE NINTH LAW: GET SUPPORT

One of the most well respected medical researchers working in the field of diet and exercise is Dr. Dean Ornish, best-selling author of several books, including *Dr. Dean Ornish's Program for Reversing Heart Disease* and *Love & Survival*—which presents groundbreaking research on the most important cure Dr. Ornish has found for heart disease: the healing power of human support and intimacy. Many people know Ornish as the doctor who proved that symptoms of heart disease can be reversed with a regimen of a low-fat diet, exercise, and stress reduction. But Ornish also believes, and backs up with extensive research, that support—in the form of groups, friendship, and intimate love relationships—has a powerful effect on our bodies, giving us stronger immune systems, better cardiovascular functioning, and longer life expectancies.

Other medical research backs up Ornish's findings. New studies show that lack of social support is a health risk factor as dangerous as smoking, lack of exercise, and high cholesterol, and that the presence of strong community bonds and extended family in a person's daily life has a direct effect on everything from susceptibility to the common cold to the risk of heart disease. And it's not only love relationships or family bonds that contribute to well-being. In a study of 2,700 residents in Michigan, men who volunteered for community organizations were two and a half times less likely to die from all causes of disease than their noninvolved peers.

There are two ways to seek support in regards to healing. The first is to reach out and ask for help when we need it. This is one of the hardest things for many people to do. Our sense of self is often dependent on our sense of being independent, strong, and healthy. When things fall apart in our lives or our bodies, we may feel too embarrassed or ashamed to reveal our weakness and ask for help. Perhaps the findings outlined above of Dean Ornish and other researchers will convince you to reach beyond your shame and to ask friends and family for help. I have witnessed over and over again the power of friendship and support in the healing process. If I had to isolate the most important aspect of the work done in every healing class at Omega or at similar retreat centers around the country, I would have to pick the intimacy created among the participants. Something truly magical occurs when a group of people let down their emotional defenses, share their stories of pain, and offer each other a compassionate ear. Church members, AA participants, and even on-line chat groupies will attest to the same miracle. It is no coincidence, with the breakdown of the nuclear family, the dispersion of the extended family, and the impersonal, urban lifestyle that many Americans lead, that small, grassroots support groups are now common all over the country.

The second way to seek support is to make your primary love relationships as consciously healing as you can. This is not an easy task, as anyone who has been married for more than a few years knows. But it is a crucial task as we pursue healing. If our relationships don't function, at least some of the time, in an atmosphere of openness, compassion, acceptance, and commitment, they may actually be contributing to stress and disease. Indeed, there is often as much harmful stress within relationships as there is harmful loneliness in a solitary life. The Institute on Family and Health reported from its research into intimacy and healing that those who were most hostile in an interchange with their spouses experienced elevated blood pressure and heart rate and showed a significant drop-off in immune response. The greater the hostility, the greater the immunological changes. Other studies have shown that a spiteful marriage on the one hand, or an ugly divorce on the other, have nearly the impact on heart disease as smoking one or more packs of cigarettes a day.

To get healing support from our mates, friends, family, and groups, we must consciously seek out the kinds of relationships that contribute to well-being. Or we must include in the healing process the healing of our relationships. In Book V, I focus more on this subject—on the importance of forgiveness in relationships, and on the healing power of community.

THE TENTH LAW: TAKE RESPONSIBILITY BUT GIVE UP CONTROL

Taking responsibility and giving up control are the two sides of the healing coin. Healing is at once a process of protection and openness, of boundaries and free-flowing energy, of mastery and surrender. Taking responsibility for the health and healing of one's own body is different from being in control of it. I can take responsibility for my life; I cannot control its twists and turns. I can take responsibility for my health; I cannot control the ultimate outcome. Likewise, I am capable of making healthy choices that will protect and heal my body, but I am not always at fault for my illness, pain, or disease.

Taking full responsibility is different from feeling guilty about the past, or rigid about how to proceed. Sam Keen says that healing "is a complex process that involves a responsible rather than infantile use of doctors, medicine, exercise, food, pleasure, friends, renewal of purpose, redefinition of values, de-mything the body. The point of the process is to change illness and health . . . from mysterious conditions caused by forces over which we have no control to mysterious conditions that are in some large measure the result of our individual and corporate life-choices." The operative word here is *mysterious*. Healing, like happiness, asks us to relax into the mystery, to give up control, even as we take thoughtful care of the body and soul.

To take thoughtful care of your body is to hone the self-healing abilities you already have. Dr. Lawrence LeShan has spent forty years of his celebrated career working to understand how psychology can be used to stimulate the immune systems of severely ill people. His research at Trafalgar Hospital in New York as chief of the department of psychology at the Institute of Applied Biology has made him one of the most respected voices in mind/body medicine. In an interview, he said, "Everyone had self-healing abilities. If I cut myself shaving, it will heal. Depending on age and other factors, this power to heal may be stronger in some persons than in others. But we are all born with it. One thing I've found in my work is that if we can learn to do something, we can also learn to do it better. Whether you're talking about discriminating a fine wine, climbing a rope, giving a speech, making love—we can learn to do it better. We can also learn to more effectively use our self-healing abilities."

Faith in the body's capacity to heal itself must be coupled with patience and perseverance. "Any significant long-term change requires long-term practice, whether that change has to do with learning to play the violin or learning to be a more open, loving person," write George Leonard and Michael Murphy, two of the founding figures in the human potential movement. "Any profound learning requires long stretches of dedicated practice with no seeming progress." Taking responsibility for our health is not as easy as taking a pill and seeing results in a few hours. It requires education, discipline, research, trial and error, and commitment.

But no matter how much we learn about the body from science and medicine, and no matter how well we care for ourselves, the body's ways are still often a mystery—complex, fragile, and uncertain. Why some people heal and others don't cannot definitively be determined. At some point in the healing process, and hopefully at every point, we must give up our compulsion to control the uncontrollable parts of our lives. We even must accept that we don't always know what is ultimately best for our spiritual growth and our daily lives. We must believe in the presence and power of something wiser and vaster than our own grasping sense of self.

The research done by Herbert Benson at Harvard demonstrates that a belief in a greater power, and a faith in that power's benevolent wisdom, is a significant factor in why people heal. He says, "There is something that makes us believers—not everybody, but certainly the vast majority of people, around the world, at all times. From the earliest writing of humans—Gilgamesh, third millennium BC—we have always invoked things beyond us: powers, forces, energies, an after world. This is very comforting to us. I am not saying that God exists or not . . . But what I am saying, from a medical point of view, from a healing point of view, is that we're in a win-win situation. Let's assume you have this profound belief that appears to be wired in us. If you believe in God and God doesn't exist, that belief can heal you. It's something that's good for you because it's playing maximally on your power of belief. Let's assume you believe in God and God does exist. Isn't that wonderful? So we can't lose."

At the end of his book *Timeless Healing: The Power and Biology of Belief,* Benson writes, "I believe in a scientifically describable biology and evolution and in a world that is, nonetheless, divinely influenced. The veracity of the experience of God is undeniable to me." And that is the subject of the following chapters.

13 · The Landscape of Death

And so long as you haven't experienced
this: to die and so to grow,
you are only a troubled guest
on the dark earth.
 —GOETHE

Before we reach the Landscape of the Soul, we journey through the Landscape of Death. Death and rebirth, but first death. The previous chapters traversed terrain familiar and fathomable: our own bodies, minds, and hearts. In the Landscape of Death we feel more like foreigners. We don't know what to expect; we don't speak the language; we can't read the thoughts of God. And yet all roads on the spiritual journey lead here, to death, the soul, and God. How then do we approach the unknowable, especially if we don't want merely to sign on to a belief system out of fear or superstition? Is there a way to make our own peace with death, to peer into the afterlife, to know God's plan, or must we remain, as Goethe says above, "only a troubled guest on the dark earth"?

I feel qualified to tackle these questions, not because I know the answers—I don't—but because I have searched for them since I was a child. My lifelong struggle since birth has been with death—the final death, and all of the "practice deaths" in between. Transitions, change, loss, letting go, moving on—these have not come easily for me. There's a sign tacked on the wall at Esalen Institute in California that reads, *Esalen's Law: (1) You always teach others what you most need to learn yourself. (2) You are your own worst student.* This applies to me most in the Landscape of the Soul. I am my own worst student when it comes to loosening my grip on life and on my desire to control the uncontrollable. I hold on tight to people and places; I make big a deal about little endings and partings, and even a bigger deal about the "biggies"—divorce, the end of a job, the leave-taking of a place, the graduation of a child, the death of a friend or parent. Yet for all of my resistance to death, I seek it out, and I always have. In childhood my fear of death kept me awake at night, and my attraction to it made me the neighborhood ceremonialist for dead birds and animals. Death still keeps me awake; it still unnerves me and it still attracts me. I am drawn to explore up close the process of dying, death, and rebirth. I keep vigil with those who are literally dying, and a vigil with myself as I die the little deaths every day. What I can offer you in this most mysterious of landscapes are my research findings: my many questions, my fewer answers, and my sustaining faith.

I was once asked to teach a class called "Death, Grief, and Healing" at a conference for health practitioners. The class next to mine was called "Humor, Laughter, and Healing," and the walls separating the hotel conference rooms were thin. As I led a meditation to access deeper emotions, my group could hear the people in the other class playing a game. Every time I would say something like "If feelings of grief arise, just let them be," a shriek of laughter would interrupt the meditation. Finally, a woman in my class stood up and announced, "You're bringing me down. I'm going next door where they're having a good time!" She stormed out, leaving the rest of us (especially me) feeling like party poopers.

I dug deep and tried to salvage the class. "Let's pretend that the class next door is life—the big party called your life. This is not a real wall," I said, patting the hotel wall. "It's the wall in your heart that makes you feel separate, cut off from other people and from yourself; it's the barrier that keeps you from showing up fully at the party of life. Who knows what I'm talking about? Who in this room ever feels a barrier between themselves and their daily experiences?" Most people in the class raised their hands. "We're going to spend the rest of our time together examining that wall—which I believe is the fear of death. If that sounds like a drag, you are graciously invited to go join the other class." A few people left. The rest of us settled in and continued to meditate on death, fear, and letting go. We let our hearts crack open as much as we could and welcomed whatever we found beneath the fault line. Later on, we pretended we were at a party and observed ourselves as we talked to each other and ate make-believe finger food. We played with showing up fully at the party of life, and explored what kept us from doing that. We even laughed.

The purpose of focusing on death is not to become a sad sack. Eventually we want to end up at the party. But we can't joyfully participate in life without studying death. "The conquest of the fear of death," says Joseph Campbell, "is the recovery of life's joy." Don't be afraid that by confronting your long-held fear of death, or that by releasing the grief that has accumulated over a lifetime of loss, you will become dour and humorless. In fact, with patience and faith, the opposite will occur. New life is born when the hard shell of our resistance to death cracks. New vistas of understanding open up beyond the border of fear. Our limited abilities to see beyond this life—and sometimes to see just beyond this day—make us resist change. Our hearts tighten, afraid of what we cannot know or control. Opening up, loosening the sense of control, letting go—this is what I mean by studying death.

Jung said that he had never met a patient over forty whose unhappiness did not have its roots in the fear of death. I would widen the age range: I have never met anyone at all, young or old, whose problems with living didn't stem from their fear of dying—whether it's the fear of mortality, or the fear of loss, or the fear of losing control. In the Landscape of Death we confront this primal fear. We dig for the roots—for the deepest source of our unhappiness and anxieties—so that we also can reach for the heavens—for the seeds of our freedom and eternal joy.

Chögyam Trungpa, one of the teachers who helped me most in the Landscape of Death, spoke of spirituality as the perfection of *maitri,* a Buddhist term that he translated as "unconditional friendliness." You could say that all of the meditation instructions and the heartfulness and body exercises in this book are based on developing unconditional friendliness toward the self. In this chapter we explore developing maitri toward death—the death of the body at the end of this life, and the deaths we encounter every day when we lose, when we must give up a sense of control, when we don't get what we want. The work in the Landscape of Death is about developing a friendly attitude toward that which we cannot control. We work to stay open and accepting, even jovial, in the face of uncertainty.

We practice dying while we are alive by making friends with endings, part-ings, and change.

On the journey through the Landscape of Death, we won't get past the first tollbooth unless we confront what, in one way or another, we have put off confronting our whole life. All of what we crave in life—security, beauty, youth, energy, power—is out of our control; all of what we fear—loss, decay, illness, aging, death—will come to pass. Is this bad news? No, but it is important news, and it is news that most of us just won't let into our thick skulls. "Things are always ending and arising and ending," says Pema Chödrön. "But we are strangely conditioned to want to experience just the birth part and not the death part. . . . We have so much fear of not being in control, of not being able to hold on to things. Yet the true nature of life is that we're never in control; we can never hold on to anything. That's how life is. Although we can perhaps accept this intellectually, mo-ment by moment it brings up a lot of panic and fear. So my own path has been learning to relax with this lack of control and the panic that accom-panies it, learning to stay in the space of uncertainty, learning to die con-tinually."

Sometimes it takes a strong blow—a crisis or a major loss—to crack the shell of a frightened heart and set us on a course of "dying continually." What may look to us as a tragedy may indeed be the very thing our soul needs to be liberated from the cage of fear. The mystics speak of the dark night of the soul, a period of time when you go deeply into the despair of abandonment, loss, or grief. Way down in the darkness you find a hidden treasure—your own timeless and eternal soul—and you emerge empow-ered and healed. The journey through the Landscape of Death is this jour-ney into the dark night and the radiant day—death and rebirth, darkness and light, brokenness and wholeness. But first death, and first darkness, and first brokenness.

As Pema Chödrön says, there's a natural tendency to want to skip the death part and go straight to the rebirth. We find such unspeakable joy in birth and in the newness of things—babies, mornings, new love affairs, an original melody, a flower bud—just opening, tender and pure. These things remind us of our own tenderness and purity. We long for their sim-plicity and unadulterated potential, their fresh, new energy. But in order for the new to be born, we must learn how to let the old die. There is no room for the new in a heart that clings to the old. There is no room for growth without death. "And so long as you haven't experienced this: to die and so to grow, you are only a troubled guest on the dark earth." I first was introduced to this line from Goethe's poem "The Holy Longing" by the man who was to become my second husband. Since then I've used the poem like a chain letter from the Landscape of the Soul, passing it on to those in need. In the dark aftermath of my divorce, when I first was getting to know my husband, he sent me the poem:

The Holy Longing

> Tell a wise person, or else keep silent,
> because the massman will mock it right away.
> I praise what is truly alive,
> what longs to be burned to death.
>
> In the calm water of the love-nights,
> where you were begotten, where you have begotten,
> a strange feeling comes over you
> when you see the silent candle burning.
>
> Now you are no longer caught
> in the obsession with darkness,
> and a desire for higher love-making
> sweeps you upward.
>
> Distance does not make you falter,
> now, arriving in magic, flying,
> and finally, insane for the light,
> you are the butterfly and you are gone.
>
> And so long as you haven't experienced
> this: to die and so to grow,
> you are only a troubled guest
> on the dark earth.

At the bottom of the page my future husband, who had recently experienced divorce and the breakup of his family and business, wrote: "I think after what I've just been through I can only be with someone who's insane for the light, someone who is willing to die and to grow." He was sending me the poem as a promise—a promise that he would bring to our relationship a willingness to continually die, and continually grow. This poem is the foundation of our marriage. We return to it often when our marriage gets stale, when we act more like two "troubled guests" in a dark house than like butterflies "insane for the light." We use it when one of us is suffering from an inability to make a necessary change: "What must die within you now, so that you can grow?" we'll finally get around to asking each other. When our frightened egos refuse to get out of the way, and we insist on being right or being in control, we'll also wind our way back to "The Holy Longing." We'll get our priorities straight. "Do you want to be right, or do you want to be happy?" I once heard someone say. Goethe would say, "Do you want to keep trying to be in control, or do you want to die and be truly alive?"

DEATH: LET US WAIT FOR IT EVERYWHERE

The French Renaissance philosopher Michel Eyquem de Montaigne advised that:

> to begin depriving death of its greatest advantage over us . . . let us deprive death of its strangeness, let us frequent it, let us get used to it; let us have nothing more often in mind than death. . . . We do not know where death awaits us: so let us wait for it everywhere. To practice death is to practice freedom. A man who has learned how to die has unlearned how to be a slave.

My friend Joy, whose story I tell later on, frequents death. She tries to deprive death of its strangeness, to "practice freedom." Joy is in the death business: a cancer survivor herself, she works with Hospice and leads support groups for women with breast cancer. She recently lost her close friend Suzanne to cancer. Suzanne and Joy had been diagnosed with breast cancer within a year of each other. They had both gone through mastectomy, chemotherapy, radiation, and reconstruction surgery, with Suzanne always leading the way. They enjoyed some years of remission from the disease together. Joy's remission from cancer eventually hit the five-year mark, and then the ten-year mark; she became a cancer survivor. But Suzanne didn't.

The day after Suzanne died, Joy called a colleague who had been on Suzanne's team of healers and doctors. "Suzanne died yesterday," she said.

"Cool," said the healer. They both laughed.

"Is it OK to say that?" he asked Joy. "I'm beginning to forget what to say.

I know that Suzanne is doing great. She's free; she's soaring. But I guess someone else may not know that. I better be careful what I say!"

People who, as Montaigne says, "frequent death," who "wait for it everywhere," begin to understand, in a visceral way, that death is both an end and a beginning. Some develop such a level of comfort with death that they *do* need to be careful about what they say. Their words can end up confusing those who have not yet learned how to die. "A man who has learned how to die has unlearned how to be a slave," said Montaigne. But a man or woman who clings to the words and ideas of others can become a slave to dogma, no more free from the fear of death than those who pretend not to care. Many religions spoon-feed their flock descriptions of the afterlife and strict instructions on how to get there. They lead followers around the fear and darkness into the promised safety of the light. This is a mistake. People who blindly accept the teachings, who hold on to the wings of someone else's angels, miss out on the peace gained from experience. They still fear death.

Mohammed told his followers to "die while you are alive." The "good news" that Jesus Christ brought was that we could have victory over death while still alive. The story of his death and resurrection is the story of our death and our resurrection. Mohammed and Jesus and all of the great saints and prophets learned how to die while on earth and unlearned how to be slaves to fear and ignorance. They went into the desert; they carried the cross; they suffered, fasted, and learned how to die. Their lives can be examples of what we too can do; their words should not stand between us and our own experiences.

There are lots of ways to make varying degrees of peace with death. We can ignore it, rationalize it, make a truce with it, adopt a belief about it, or we can practice it. If we ignore death, we may indeed freeze our primal anxiety into something we can handle, but we freeze life as well. If we rationalize death, if we make a mental truce with it, we also sacrifice full, joyful aliveness. There's a sense of resignation, even a bitterness, to those who adopt the "life's a bitch and then you die" attitude. And those who make an intellectual peace with death, whose only sense of joy is that their bodies will provide food for the worms and compost for the planet, are selling themselves short. The truth of the matter is that we don't conclusively know anything about death—and not knowing makes most of us uncomfortable. We don't know when we will die, how we will die, or what of the self survives after death. Not knowing this makes death the ultimate stranger. This is why Montaigne counsels us to "deprive death of its strangeness" by getting used to it, by facing it, by seeking out the opportunities life provides every day for practicing dying. "We do not know where death awaits us: so let us wait for it everywhere. To practice death is to practice freedom."

Every day you can practice dying. You can find countless ways to "die before death." Grist for the mill is everywhere: things in your life that seem out of your control; anything that makes you insecure and anxious because of its uncertainty, its "strangeness"; all kinds of change and loss. Do an experiment right now: become aware of something in your life that is making you feel out of control, fearful, worried—some anticipated event or chronic condition that, for better or worse, is in your life right now. Something that your will and your worry can no longer alter. You can't turn back the clock or press the delete button on this one. Perhaps it is the fact that your child is leaving home, or your job is changing, or your body is aging, or your parent is dying. Or maybe it's something less tangible, something that just isn't turning out the way you wanted it to, or the way it was "supposed to be."

Whatever it is that is making you afraid of change, or loss, or death, let it engulf you right now. Imagine it as a swift and broad river, and yourself in the river, floating, traveling, moving along in the waters of change and loss. Tell yourself that you do not know what the outcome of this journey will be. For just a moment, give up thinking you know where the river is taking you or should be taking you. Give up your dread, your worst-case scenarios, your sense of knowing what is going to happen. Because you don't know. You couldn't. The river of your life is too deep and meandering, its currents far too complex and shifting for you to know the course it will take. Instead, just as an experiment, meet the fear of loss and change with openness and relaxed curiosity, as if you are floating on your back, easy about what you'll find around the next bend.

Hazrat Inayat Khan said that "I consider every loss in life as the throwing off of an old garment in order to put on a new one; and the new garment has always been better than the old." Since you don't know how things will turn out, why not have that kind of faith? Why not assume that the new garment will indeed be better than the old? That right around the river bend something new and splendid awaits you. I know that in my life the things I have feared and the losses I have resisted never materialized as I thought they would. In fact, they turned out to be profoundly different in feeling and texture and content than I ever dreamed. When I look back on the losses sustained throughout my life, I see that the outcome rarely, if ever, matched the perceived threat. Even the big threats, like divorce, illness, and death, which knocked me over and shook me up, left me alive and strangely expanded. In retrospect, I can say that each new garment has been better than the old, if better means wiser, stronger, and more free.

To practice dying is to watch yourself carefully and compassionately in the midst of change. Are you gripping tightly to the old garment? Then let go of your grip a little. Are you afraid of the new garment? Try not to anticipate the future. Let the old garment slide off and trust that the new garment will fit you even better. After you have gone through the transition, compare what actually happened with what you feared would happen. Practice this over and over until fear of the unknown slowly transforms into a faith born from experience.

As I practice dying while alive, I gain more and more faith that the final death too has surprises in store for me. As I take the old garments off, I begin to identify less and less with myself as the garments, and more with an eternal soul that survives every change. "Once the soul has been able to feel itself—its own life independently of its garb," says Inayat Khan, "it begins to have confidence in life." After years of spiritual work I am beginning to gain a confidence in life, a confidence that heightens my appreciation of being alive, and makes me less anxious about the death of my body.

It certainly wasn't always like this. My earliest memories are ones of lying in bed consumed by my fear of the words *never* and *forever*. "When I die, I will *never* be alive again. I will be dead *forever*." I hated those words. The thought of an eternal void with no consciousness made my heart ache with fear. In the darkness I would feel my body disappearing, leaving just the sensation of my heart beating. As I lay there, I became the pounding of my heart, and with each beat I became smaller and smaller until I was a pinprick of a rhythm, pulsing closer and closer to a nothingness that was so huge that it swallowed even the words *never* and *forever*. All throughout my childhood, as I fell asleep I would battle this sensation. The harder I tried to avoid the rhythmic nothingness, the more it would pursue me. And so, I began to pursue it.

My need to understand death was the driving force behind my early spiritual explorations. While some people are called to spirituality to learn how to love, or to pray for healing, or to commune with other seekers, I was called by my compelling need to know what happened after death.

Even as a ten-year-old, when I went to Catholic Mass with my friend's family, I was searching in the dark church for a comforting presence that might dispel my fears of eternal nothingness. It came as quite a surprise, then, when I started to meditate, that as soon as I calmed my mind there was the same sensation I knew so intimately from childhood: my heart pounding, my body disappearing, my consciousness becoming one with a rhythm that was very, very small, yet as immense as the void that threatened to consume me. Reading Buddhist and Hindu meditation texts, I even learned that there were terms for and depictions of my experience— maps that detailed what happens when one leaves the body and enters the void either through meditation or death. I found similar descriptions in the ancient Hebrew Kabbalah and in the mystical interpretations for the stations of the cross that Jesus walked on his way to his crucifixion. Later on, reading the literature of the near-death experience (when people who are pronounced clinically dead are then brought back to life), I discovered once again my childhood experience described with spooky precision.

There are many ways to practice dying so that your appreciation in life and fearlessness in death may be nurtured. Reading, meditating, and confronting my tendency to hold on tight when change comes knocking have been key in my own process of making friends with death. I have also benefited tremendously from the opportunity to be with several friends as they left their bodies. I suggest the following ways to practice dying:

If you can, take birth and death back from hospitals and experts. Be with the ones you love as babies are born and the sick or old die. Volunteer to train and work with your local Hospice organization. Witnessing the birth of a child, keeping vigil with a friend as he dies, sharing the last breaths of a parent: these are sacred opportunities to viscerally experience the cycles of birth and death. When the process of birth and death are no longer strangers, our own death seems less alien.

—

Do this practice as taught by Thich Nhat Hanh: "Lie on a bed, or on a mat, or on the grass in a position in which you are comfortable. Begin to take hold of your breath. Imagine all that is left of your body is a white skeleton lying on the face of the earth. . . . Imagine that all your flesh has decomposed and is gone, that your skeleton is now lying in the earth eighty years after burial. See clearly the bones of your head, back, your ribs, your hipbones, leg and arm bones, finger bones . . . breathe very lightly, your heart and mind serene. See that your skeleton is not you. Your bodily form is not you. Be one with life. Live eternally in the trees and

grass, in other people, in the birds and other beasts, in the sky, in the ocean waves. Your skeleton is only one part of you. You are present everywhere and in every moment. You are not only a bodily form, or even feelings, thoughts, actions, and knowledge."

—

The Sufis call the practice of dying *Fana*. It is one of the cornerstones of the Sufi path, and it stems from what the Sufis call the soul's homesickness for God. Whenever you feel the telltale signs of resistance to change, the tugging, grasping feeling of a heart that fears loss and death, rename the feeling "homesickness for God." Understand that the soul wants to feel whole, and pray, like the Sufis do, for your little self to be annihilated, to die, so that you can step into your bigger self. Pray for the surrender of the ego to the bigger picture of reality, of God.

—

Meditate on time as a river carrying you on an eternal journey. Don't regard time as a force that day by day is whittling away your youth, taking you away from yourself toward extinction. Instead, put yourself in the flow of eternal time, which day by day is moving you onward, toward a deeper understanding and expression of who you really are.

—

Study the literature of death, from traditional religious texts to more recent books about the death of the body, like Sherwin Nuland's *How We Die;* books about the dying process, like *Who Dies?,* by Stephen and Ondrea Levine; and books about the near-death experience, like *Heading Toward Omega,* by Kenneth Ring. Find meaningful passages and meditate on them regularly. Read the following selection from Stephen and Ondrea Levine's *A Year to Live,* and then meditate for a few minutes:

> There is some disagreement about when death actually occurs. Physicians insist that it is when their shiny instruments can no longer discern life's presence. They imagine it departs with the last breath. Others say death begins at conception and does not end until that which noisily hurls itself into birth has realized that which remains silently unborn. Still others claim the moment of death occurs when the heart stops. But the heart never stops, for when it is no longer contained between opposing ventricles it expands slowly into its inherent vastness without missing a beat, expressing the truth it has embraced for a lifetime.
>   Death, like birth, is not an emergency but an emergence. Death is akin to a flower opening: It is nearly impossible to tell exactly when the bud starts to be-

come the blossom, or when the seed-laden blossom begins to burst and release its bounty.

Those who know the process directly—from experiences shared with the dying, from decades of meditation, from moments of spontaneous grace, from Eucharists of every description—do not speak of death as a single moment before which you are alive and after which you are not. They refer instead to "a point of remembrance" in which the holding to life transforms into a letting go into death. It is, just a little way into the process, the moment when something is suddenly remembered that it seems impossible to have forgotten. We "remember" how safe death is, we recall the benefits of being free of the limitations of the body, and we ask ourselves somewhat incredulously, "How could I have forgotten something so important, and what was it again that made me want to stay in a body?" Death takes on an entirely new context.

At that moment, just before we feel the lightness lifting us from our body, while we are still trying to capture each molecule of oxygen just to stay alive another instant, we suddenly remember we are not the body, never have been, never will be! Resistance vanishes into a glimpse of our long-migrating spirit. We cut the moorings and dive into the ocean of being, expanding from our body, the mind floating free.

I do not know if this is "the moment of death," but I do know this insight changes everything. No longer holding back, we feel ourselves dissolving safe and sound into an increasingly joyous, even youthful, sense of heading home.

LEARNING TO GRIEVE:
IT'S NOT ALL AS EVIL AS YOU THINK

Let the young rain of tears come.
Let the calm hands of grief come.
It's not all as evil as you think.
　　—ROLF JACOBSEN

"To die is different from what anyone supposed," Walt Whitman wrote, and he is right, as far as I know, this side of death. But to grieve need not be as mysterious. To grieve well the passing away of anyone or anything—a parent, a love, a child, an era, a home, a job—is a spiritual skill worth developing. It helps us make sense of our lives; it reveals to us our deeper feelings; and it encourages us to let go and move on. Instead of freezing up inside and pretending that loss doesn't touch us close to the bone, or instead of squandering our energy, holding tight against the flow of life, full-bodied grieving acts like a tonic. It purifies and revivifies.

Rolf Jacobsen encourages us in the poem above to "let the calm hands of grief come," because "it's not all as evil as you think." If we want to befriend death, the best way to start is to learn how to grieve, how to let the "young rain of tears come." Each one of us has a multitude of opportunities to learn to grieve well. And still, most of us are novices. Fearing the evilness of death, we turn away from facing it and from facing our feelings when death visits us in the form of the loss of loved ones, loved things, loved places. But "it's not all as evil as you think." A loss well grieved can convince you of that.

Grief gets to the bottom of things—to the certainty of death, to our own tenuous grip on life as we know it. When we let grief into our hearts we are doing two things: we are mourning the loss at hand, and we are tipping our hats to the big one. Grief is an expression of helplessness. It is a way of engaging with our existence in its fullness—we are born, we live, we age, we die. But don't despair. Don't buy that bumper sticker, "Life's a bitch and then you die." Let your grief be as full of joy as it is of sorrow. Let it be proof of how much you've loved, how deeply you've allowed life to live in you, how wide the river of your heart has become. Every experience in which you love and lose is excellent practice for learning to face change and to let go. Instead of turning away from love so as not to invite loss, love fully, and learn to grieve.

I have discovered that those who can grieve loss are those who can love life. Those who feign strength or detachment in the face of profound loss restrict the life stream. Those who must satirize or belittle the feelings of sorrow and confusion associated with grief are those who will end up the most sad and the most confused. To the extent that you can find a way to stay open to the movements of change and transition in your life—even the most painful ones—you will be able to find the sweet side of grief. Rumi says it better than I can:

> I saw grief drinking
>   a cup of sorrow.
> It's sweet, isn't it?
>   Grief said, You put
> me out of business.
>   How can I sell grief
> When you know it's sweet?

Grief brings us closest to life's great paradoxes: to live in order to be able to die; to be helpless and therefore to be guided; to surrender to the unknown so as to know. Henri Nouwen, a Catholic priest and monk whose little book *A Letter of Consolation* is one of the most beautiful guides one can use when grieving the loss of a loved one, writes that "a growing surrender to the unknown is a sign of spiritual maturity," and that the ability to grieve "encourages us to give up the illusions of immortality we might still have and to experience in a new way our total dependence on God's love, a dependence that does not take away our free selfhood but purifies and ennobles it. I am constantly struck by the fact that . . . those who have learned through living that there is nothing and nobody in this life to cling to, are the really creative people. They are free to move constantly away from the familiar, safe places and can keep moving forward to new, unexplored areas of life."

I heard Ravi Coltrane, the son of jazz great John Coltrane, speak about the death of his brother when his brother was sixteen and he was eighteen. Ravi Coltrane is now a jazz musician in his own right, but he said that after his brother's death he stopped playing music, dropped out of school, and for four years did nothing but grieve the loss of his brother. His father had died when he was just two, and I imagine that part of the grieving process Ravi entered was for his father as well as his brother. He said that it took him four years to let the pain help him "leave childhood behind." Only then could he move into his own creativity and become the man he was supposed to be. I was moved by Ravi Coltrane's story, and by his courage to let himself take the time his body and soul needed to feel and incorporate loss and grief into his life journey.

People who lose their parents when they are still children, and parents whose children die young, may need the kind of time that Coltrane needed to grieve. Any big loss—like being downsized out of a lifelong job; or experiencing a loss of innocence due to poverty, violence, or abuse; or divorce or betrayal or rejection by the one we love—asks that we grieve in proportion to the love lost. All endings and partings, big and small, are a kind of death. But Jesus said that "love is stronger than death." Grief has shown me that this is true. When I compare the times in my life when I have allowed myself to grieve fully with the times when I have frozen my heart, I see that the other side of grief is a love that can withstand any loss; the other side of resistance is despair—pain frozen in time.

THREE GRIEF STORIES:
KEEPING THE GAP EMPTY

Nothing can make up for the absence of someone whom we love, and it would be wrong to try to find a substitute; we must simply hold out and see it through. That sounds very hard at first, but at the same time, it is a great consolation, for the gap, as long as it remains unfilled, preserves the bonds between us. It is nonsense to say that God fills the gap; God doesn't fill it, but on the contrary, keeps it empty and so helps us to keep alive our former communion with each other, even at the cost of pain.

—Dietrich Bonhoeffer, Lutheran theologian
executed by the Nazis

I want to share with you three stories about "keeping the gap empty"—two of my own attempts and one of a friend. As Bonhoeffer says, it is very hard at first to do this, but if we do, grief allows a space for love to become stronger than death. I suggest you tell yourself your own grief stories. Find out what you do with the "gap." Do you rush to fill it? Do you walk around it? Do you pretend it isn't there at all? As you will see from the following stories, sometimes it helps to have a form into which we can pour our feelings and concerns, while keeping our hearts empty enough to grieve. Ritual, prayer, myth, religion—all of these are helpful tools. In the next chapter we explore the use of prayer and ritual—prescribed ones and ones you can create yourself—as a way of marking rites of passage and honoring times of transition in your life.

GRIEF STORY #1: LETTING A CHILD GROW AND GO

When my firstborn was an infant he let us know that he was displeased to be here: he cried constantly for eight months. We named him Rahmiel, the biblical angel of mercy. How were we to know what it takes to learn mercy? I was twenty-three and unprepared for the self-sacrifice and sheer exhaustion that being a mother entailed. It was a good thing that I had no previous experience with babies; I assumed that they all cried all of the time, and so I walked him around, day and night, until we were both dizzy and wrapped tightly around each other's heart.

When the crying stopped, Rahm turned sweetly sullen. He became a tyrannical toddler, and his father and I his loyal servants. He was a careful, smart, and sensible fellow, not the kind of child who wants a lot of toys or endless television. He always knew his limits. When his grandmother gave him carte blanche at FAO Schwarz, the largest toy store in the world, he chose a ball.

He had strong opinions. His tantrums, although few, are legendary in the family. Once he flew into a rage when a visiting friend, a musician, shared with me her new recording. Unaware of the current household law—that no tape but *The Singing Rabbis* (a collection of folksy Jewish songs that somehow intrigued Rahm) could be played in the home—my friend was foolish enough to put her song in the tape deck and press "play." I was too embarrassed by the control we had granted our little king to stop the tape. The tantrum escalated into the kind of sobbing that resembles choking, and I had to take Rahm outside and put his bare bottom in a snowdrift. My younger sons love this story.

As a kid, Rahm was a little man of few words, and a faithful, kind, and funny friend. When his brother came along, Rahm was just three and a half, but from the start he was protective and eager to love. He was also clear about the pecking order in a benign yet steadfast way. By the time he was seven I was a single mother, and I came to rely on his sharp mind and his navigational skills. In fact, once, when I drove without him, I couldn't find my way home. He seemed relieved when I remarried, and genuinely loved the new family members. He was the child who made sure our stepfamily held together harmoniously, even as he called the shots.

He paved the way for his brother and stepbrother at school, on the soccer field and baseball diamond, and later on the basketball team. He pioneered other teenage territory as well, but it took me an awfully long time to wake up to the alarming fact that kittens do indeed turn into cats. By Rahm's senior year of high school it dawned on me that children *do* leave home, and that I was going to have to live without him in our home in a very short time. I went into a prolonged period of grief that made the college search and senior-itis particularly grueling for everyone. Poor first children! Always a few steps ahead of their parents, they must suffer through being "learned on," while their younger siblings bear the fruit of the first child's involuntary martyrdom.

Rahm's senior year was a rite of passage for both mother and son. Awakening from the trance where my children never grew up and I remained the mommy for ever and ever, I suddenly understood Rahm needed some important directions and warnings. I looked around for the tribal elders—the fathers and grandfathers smeared with frightening face paint, the crones and wise women with knowing smiles—to come and take Rahm into the adult world. Whoops! Wrong culture, wrong century. How could I prepare him for that world, a mother whose instincts were to shield her children from all that is harsh and hard?

I felt as confused now as I had been when I was the mother of an infant. I knew that I had to let Rahm go, but I also wanted him to retain a strong sense of his connection to his family. I wanted to avoid what I had believed could cripple children as they left home: either a sense of being untethered to any home base, or a feeling of guilt about leaving parents and family behind. I wanted to be able to tell Rahm (in a way that I would know he had heard me) that I believed in him, that I took joy in his freedom and self-responsibility, that the road ahead was not always going to be easy, and that he could come to us with both his successes and his failures. I wanted to be able to thank him for our life together thus far without lapsing into the kind of sentimental blather that would turn him off. Beyond writing a letter, which I would never be sure he would read, I wondered how to do this.

I found help in my own community, my village, although not in a form as dramatic as the indigenous rituals I yearned for. I turned to my sister and friends whose sons and daughters were Rahm's age. Together we talked our way down the foggy road. We helped each other gain a sober clarity: there were two transitions going on here—one our children's, the other our own. This time we would primarily be handling our own transition. Unlike other transitions that we had shepherded our children through—like learning to walk, going to kindergarten, joining Little League—now the kids would take over for themselves.

I had several long-overdue talks with Rahm over the course of a month. We talked about his feelings about the divorce of his parents, his anticipation of the future, the transition I was going through, and our love for each other. These were not easy conversations. I had to make them happen. But I prepared for them as one would a ritual because even in their difficulty I could feel a river moving in both of our hearts. I followed the advice of the poet Rumi, who said, "When you do something from your soul, you feel a river moving in you, a joy."

One of the traditions at my children's school is to offer the chance to each member of the senior class to speak at graduation. Since graduating classes are small, usually only twenty or thirty kids, most class members do indeed speak for a few minutes to the friends and family gathered at the ceremony. I had been to previous years' graduations and had been moved by the power of the day. I looked forward to hearing from Rahm although I could not imagine what he would say. A couple of weeks before the ceremony, I asked him what he was planning and he replied, using standard teenage communication, "I don't know. I'll think about it later." This was certainly one of the places for me to practice letting go and giving up responsibility. This was Rahm's gift to give or not to give; it had nothing to do with me.

The day came. Parents and grandparents sat in the audience, proud, happy, sad. The seniors gathered on the stage; teachers and school administrators spoke; the school choir sang. And then the time came for the seniors to speak. One by one they came to the podium and addressed their community. Some were funny, sarcastic, or brief; others were political, symbolic, or long-winded. When Rahm rose to speak I felt my heart pounding: What would he reveal about himself? What would we learn about the essence of this person with whom we had shared our lives for eighteen years? He stood at the podium, a tall young man who looked vaguely like the little boy that he had been only yesterday. "Well, here you go, Rahm," I thought. "Tell us about yourself."

Rahm's speech:

> When I started thinking about what I was going to do when I got up here today, I had a lot of good ideas. I thought that I would get up here and say something inspirational that would be indicative of my high school career. So I started to write about something that I thought was pertinent. But the further I got into my speech, the more I realized that it wasn't what I wanted to say at all. So I started again. I wrote about something completely different. When I started I thought that it was good but again it wasn't what I wanted. I tried again. And again I got nowhere.
>
> Each idea that I wrote just didn't seem to be the perfect closing to my high school career. And then I realized why. It wasn't because none of my ideas were good enough. It was because every one was very good. It was because every emotion that I have for today is so strong that when I was writing about one I felt myself wanting to write about the others.
>
> I have so many emotions and they're all so jumbled. For every emotion that I'm feeling I am also feeling the exact opposite equally strong for something completely different. I am feeling happiness and sadness. I am

feeling nervous and confident. I feel strength and weakness. I am on top of the world, yet at the same time I am overwhelmed by the moment.

Very soon I will be receiving my diploma—a moment that literally ends my secondary education and in some way signifies the end of my childhood, my dependence on my parents, and life as I know it. It's a frightening thought. In fact this could be the scariest moment of my life. And even though at this moment I am scared to death of what the future will hold, I have complete confidence in my ability. Even though I am very sad to be leaving a world that I know so well, I am also extremely happy to be entering a new one. And although I am sorry to be leaving this school with all that it has done for me, I am very glad to be going somewhere new.

I look out on this audience and I see so many people who mean so much to me. I am sad to be leaving all of you and I hope that you are sad to see me go. But at the same time I am proud of myself and my classmates and I hope that you are too. It is rare to be in a place that is filled with so much sadness and at the same time so much joy. Everyone's emotions are split, including mine. I look forward to my future, yet I will miss every one of you dearly.

I was stunned by Rahm's speech. Many people were. One of the parents who knew Rahm's laconic style well said, "Who would have thought that Rahm would speak for the heart of the class?" This young man, who kept so much inside, had been given the rare opportunity to share his soul with his world, and to commit to words his interior landscape as he set out into a bigger world. He was able to get instant feedback and confirmation from his peers and family, his teachers and mentors, that his words had been heard and understood and appreciated. "Yes," we all were saying as we clapped and the kids whooped, "you are on the right track! We respect you. We understand what you are going through. You are not alone." Forever I would know, in moments of wonder or worry, that Rahm had what it takes to make it through the wilderness of life. He was open to his feelings; he was realistic about the contradictions in life; he was self-confident but also self-aware.

I will always have the memories of that day, of our group passage—the parents letting their children go and letting them know of their love and support; of the kids thanking us and expressing their excitement and fear; of the community standing and acknowledging all of its members—kids, teachers, parents, siblings, grandparents—the whole village that it took to raise these people. I will be able to return to the memory, to the speeches of the kids and the teachers, to what was said on sacred ground to remind me of what is real and possible. This is what ritual is for. It anchors us in our highest potential. It symbolizes the best in us and our yearning for harmony and love. It reminds us that there are those who have gone before us and those who will follow and that we remain connected because we cared.

And, like a lighthouse for ships at sea, ritual guides us back when we reenter the same waters to learn our lessons over and over. The letting go did not end on graduation day. But the event showed me the way. I have come back to that day—Rahm's words, my feelings, the group support— many times.

Two months after Rahm graduated, I wrote the following in my journal:

> Early July. Outside each leaf flutters like a flag of youth. I sit inside, stumped by a work project, feeling bogged down by a vague emptiness in the chest. From the corner of my eye, I sense movement and I turn to the window, looking up from my writing to the tops of the tall trees. A high wind is tossing pollen and clouds in the blue afternoon sky. The light changes dramatically as the wind moves the clouds and pale green branches across the afternoon sun. Bees are swarming in the front yard, adding their darting yellow bodies to the swirl of moving colors—wisps of wildflower pollen, blue sky, white clouds, the shockingly green leaves of the younger trees.
>
> How can I be depressed on such a summer day? Inside, things around the house that looked beautiful yesterday seem like projects I am too lazy to tackle today. Outside, the summery day is whirling around in the sky, free of my heavy spirit. I try to work, but instead I keep looking outside, as if my heart might be won over by the same strong wind that is moving the world. No such luck: I fight against the downward gravity of my feelings, telling myself things about my mood, rationalizing, waiting for the wind to enter. Finally, I give up. What happens next is what always happens and it amuses me that after so many years of observing the same patterns—feel pain, resist, feel worse, *or,* feel pain, surrender, heal—I still fight so mightily against letting myself grieve.
>
> And so I sit quietly and let myself sink fully into the feeling. Once again I understand what one would think any simpleton could grasp: go in the direction that the river flows. Enter the sluggish stream of the heavy heart, and ask it to show me the cause of my grief. Trust its messages and its deliverance. "What's wrong?" I ask my heart. Am I worried about work? No an-

swer. That disagreement my husband and I had last night? Nothing. Off-set by the lack of routine in the summer months? "I just hate not having a routine," I hear myself say. "I hate not knowing what the next weeks will bring." My heart stirs a little. Go this way, it suggests. Maybe if I sit with the calendar and get a firmer grasp of my summer plans, I'll feel better.

Studying the little blocks of July and August, I realize I haven't been able to plan anything without knowing when I could visit Rahm at his summer job. He had called the week before and asked me if I would come up on his day off and take him and a friend out to dinner. But he didn't know as of yet when his day off would be and had told me to call him in a few days to find out.

As I think about calling Rahm, my heart lifts, and I feel the life in my body moving. My eyes go back to the window, back to the tree tops. OK, I'll call him now, I decide, buoyed by the quickening. It is lunch time at the summer camp where he is working, and as I wait for him to come to the phone I hear the din of boys' voices in the background. I close my eyes and imagine their faces and bodies, the mess and the energy, the life force of 150 boys. And suddenly the wind fills my sails, the river flows, and finally I know my way: my depression is about missing my son and dealing with the changes of his growing up and leaving home. "Yes," I say to myself as I hear Rahm's voice on the phone, "Yes, this is it."

We share a quick conversation and make a date to meet. Rahm has to get back to his kids, an idea that makes me smile in awe of his new-found maturity. He ends by saying, "I love you, Mom. Can't wait to see you." I put down the phone and let the tears come. I miss him so much now, away for the summer. When he goes off to college in the fall, I will miss him even more—his sense of humor, his intellect, his habits and ways of being that I have intimately known over the past 18 years. He is leaving a big hole in the family structure, changing the nature of our life at home. His brothers will miss him and things will never be the same. I let all of this enter my heart.

To my great surprise, I am suddenly overcome with powerful sobs that I can almost see, building in size and strength, far off the shore of my rational mind. As if sitting on the beach, watching an enormous wave roll in, I let the crying come. Both fearful and curious, I let it come.

With the wave of tears comes images of the years Rahm and I spent together as mother and son. And like those moments before death, when people see their lives played out before them, I relive vignettes of our history that need to be felt and remembered. I see the early years when Rahm was a willful and needy baby, and I was a willful and untrained young mother. I feel into the struggle we went through, as I learned to sacrifice my own youth to the demands of motherhood, and he learned how to live in this world. I cry for my mistakes and ask his forgiveness for being less than a perfect mother. I watch us grow up together through his child-hood—through my maturing into a more confident woman and mother, and his unfolding into the fullness of his personality and gifts. I thank him for the joy he has brought me and forgive him for the trials he has put me through, especially in his uncommunicative teen years. I let my heart know how wounded he had been when his father and I divorced, something I had never wanted to fully feel. I sit with both of our sorrows and grieve for the years of insecurity he had known because of a decision I had made.

And then I see him emerging into his manhood and walking alone into his destiny. I feel the pride of a long job completed, and the sadness of los-ing the daily company of my beloved, first-born son. As my tears wash up onto the shore and then draw back, I sit alone, cleansed and opened to the truth. I know that I am not really losing him, but rather, that I am stepping out of the way so that he can now find his own path. I feel his gratitude and love, and I know that he is taking a piece of my heart with him, for his own good and for mine. Sitting there, alone on the shore, I watch him move away in his own sturdy boat and I silently pray that I have done the best I could to prepare him for his adulthood. I also know that part of the pain I am feeling is the death of one way of being his mother and the birth contractions of another. I pray for the strength to let the old way die and for the patience to let the new way emerge. "How should I be in this new way?" I ask. "What is too much mothering now, and what is too little?" A poem comes to mind, by the 15th century Japanese Zen master, Bunan:

> Die while you're alive
> and be absolutely dead.
> Then do whatever you want:
> it's all good.

Yes, my self as a mother is dying. I will go through this again and again with Rahm, and with my younger sons. I will strive to become "absolutely dead," which in this case means absolutely surrendered to the process of stepping aside and letting my children become adults. And then my prayers will be answered—I will know how to be this new kind of mother and it all will begin to feel natural, genuine: good.

I am writing this book four years after Rahm went away. Last week he graduated from college. Last year my stepson graduated from high school and went to college. Next month my youngest will graduate from high school. I'm on intimate terms now with the process of letting my children go, of keeping the gap empty: "For the gap," as Bonhoeffer says, "as long as it remains unfilled, preserves the bonds between us." Through the process of keeping the gap empty, I've played with the alchemy of loss and grief turning into freedom and connection. It's part science and part magic. There is something that we can do and something that we must let happen. I have learned this before, through divorce, the death of family members and friends, and through changes at work. But being a parent has been my greatest teacher. I know now that grief is a river running through the heart. I know that if I block the way, the water dams up, builds pressure, and spills over, making me sick, or hostile, or tired. Grief turns into joy when we get out of the way, let the river flow, and wait for the water to settle and clear. It's that simple, and that difficult, and that magical.

Years ago my sister gave me a refrigerator magnet that reads, "Insanity is hereditary. You get it from your kids." Yes, and if you can let yourself grieve their leaving, you also inherit the ability to love and to keep on loving as the object of your love grows, changes, and sets sail.

GRIEF STORY #2: JOY'S STORY

My friend Joy, whose work with cancer patients I mentioned earlier, has devoted her career to counseling women with breast cancer and other life-threatening diseases. When we first met, Joy had breast cancer herself, and was filming the process of her treatment. She was doing this not because of some perverse performance-art streak, but because she had discovered her cancer in an odd way. After her sister had died from breast cancer, Joy had decided to do something in her memory that would help other women. She contacted Bernie Siegel, the well-known physician and author, and began with him a video project to educate women on breast cancer prevention. As one of the first segments of the video, Joy filmed her own medical appointment with Dr. Siegel. In an amazing twist of fate, it was during that examination that her own cancer was first detected. With a sense of dedication to her sister, she proceeded to film each step of her diagnosis, treatment, mastectomy, and reconstructive surgery, as well as discussions with friends and her husband and children. The video went on to win several awards and is now shown to women all over the country.

Since her recovery Joy has counseled hundreds of people dealing with cancer and other diseases and sat with many as they died. Some have been her own friends. Her mother died suddenly a few years ago, and her father died from a long illness last year. Through each of these deaths, including her own close encounter, Joy has had to deal with her resistance to the pain of keeping the gap empty. It is one thing to stay open to the departure of children, or other changes and partings in daily life, and quite another to learn how to be graceful and openhearted in the face of one's own death and the death of friends and family. But indeed, it takes the same kind of skills honed through the little deaths to develop an awakened attitude toward death itself. And it takes practice, something that few of us ever have, given how removed we are from the actual dying process.

One of Joy's most recent visits from death has been a testimony to the hard work that she has done befriending transitions and impermanence. After her father died, and as she prepared for her son to leave for college, Joy got a tiny white puppy—a Tibetan temple dog. The family named the dog Zeesa, Yiddish for "sweet." I am not a great dog lover, but it was hard not to love this one. Small and delicate, she was also funny and spirited. She pranced as she walked. She was life itself in the form of a little dog. Joy found that as she let Zeesa into her heart she began to take on more and more of Zeesa's qualities, giving in to her spontaneous decisions to take frequent, bouncy walks.

Zeesa had been with the family for close to a year when Joy followed her on her last walk. Early one winter morning, after driving her kids down the mountain to the school bus stop, Joy noticed that Zeesa wanted to get out of the car. The town cemetery, one of her favorite spots, was directly behind the bus stop. Joy had not planned on taking a walk and didn't have Zeesa's leash. Keeping a close watch, she followed the little dog into the graveyard, once again noting the ironic beauty of Zeesa's white and lively form dancing among the dark gray headstones. Deeper and deeper into the cemetery Zeesa danced until Joy was following her down a path into the woods that led to the back side of town. She ran to catch up, but Zeesa was soon out of her sight.

As she emerged from the woods onto the main street of town, Joy watched, as if in slow motion, a large black car come around the corner and run straight over her little dog. In stunned disbelief she ran into the road, scooped up Zeesa, bleeding and barely breathing, and opened the door of the black car, which had pulled to the curb. She said to the man, a stranger, wearing a dark overcoat and hat, "Bring me to the animal hospital. Now." The man never said a word as Joy directed him to the veterinarian's office.

Zeesa breathed her last breath before they reached the vet's office. Joy sat in that black car in the cold morning stillness, next to the strange man, holding the white bundle, streaked with red blood. All of the deaths, all of the losses of the last few years seemed to be in that little body on her lap. She got out of the car, holding Zeesa, and walked into the animal hospital. Later she told me that she felt as if the stranger in the car was death himself, and in that moment sitting next to him she had made peace with him. He had taken everything that he could take from her in the form of Zeesa, a being who represented all that was sweet and alive. He had taken her sister, her mother, her father, her friends, her clients, her own breasts. He had tried to take her life. But here she was. She was still here. As she slammed the car door it was as if she had discovered something eternally alive in the empty form she carried in her arms.

Zeesa's death was a turning point in Joy's life. Whereas before, when she would meet each death with a period of despair, and then with a new project, she decided this time she would stop fully and live in the gap for a while. And so she went into a period of retreat, pared back her work life as much as she could, and spent more time alone than she ever had. She chose the same route that the ancients did, going into the darkness instead of around it. She imbued her world with mythic dimensions, speaking with the image of the man in the black car, and with the lingering spirit of Zeesa. She took both of their presences as signs of something she needed to learn, changes she wanted to make. Her children would all be gone from home within a few years. She could no longer depend on them for sweetness and energy. She asked Zeesa to live in her heart so that she could *become* what she had relied on in others. She asked the man in the car to help her make peace with change, to guide her in the hard work of letting go. "You have visited me more than most people I know," Joy told death. "Make me wise in your ways."

GRIEF STORY #3: WHEN MY FATHER DIED

I turned to Joy a few years later when my father died, because she has indeed become wise in knowing how to grieve, how to let go, and how to move on. She's growing into her name through her practice with death and dying. The first thing Joy told me to do was to write every night in a journal so that when the process of grieving was over, I would be able to stitch the strange days together into a meaningful experience. Here is how I grieved the death of my father:

February 1

Since the phone call early this morning, when my sister woke me, saying, "Dad died in his sleep last night," everything has changed. It's like I was walking along one road, whistling, kicking a stone, and then bam! I'm on another road altogether. I had heard about this road—that losing a parent is deeper and stronger than one could imagine—but of course, I didn't really understand. When I heard myself on the phone, telling Rahm, in college, "Grandpa died this morning," I thought I was making it up—telling a lie to my son. And when he said, "I'm driving to Grandma's house now," I finally broke down, his noble act of kindness releasing the waters in the dam.

I went with my sister to the funeral home. I wanted to see my father's body. I needed proof. It had been a day of frozen emotions, spiced with sudden thaws of uncontrolled crying. Now I stood in the cold room of the funeral home, again feeling frozen, a foot away from my father's body. The cells of my body that were of my father took over. They had their own private reaction: I was knocked over by their force. I collapsed in a sobbing that came from a far-away region. I really cannot describe it very well. I hope to someday, but not now, since making my fingers move the pen across the page feels like a big deal.

February 5

It seems that along with my father his history is dying too. It makes me want to tell his story, to remember my own story with him. Somehow I thought he would not die for a long, long time. Or, as Rahm said, "I thought Grandpa would never die." My father was 85, but he was in better shape than I was and probably ever will be. He still swam at the local pool a few times a week, down-hill skied, cross-country skied, and hiked the Green and White Mountains. He managed his Vermont property with a nutty fervor that the old Vermont farmers admired and couldn't figure out. He loved tromping in the wilderness, fixing stone walls, chopping and stacking and hauling wood, and mowing the meadow with a rider-mower that was not made to cover such ground.

As the days have gone by and the shock has receded, I have been left with several gifts from my father. First—he was a man who walked his talk like none other that I knew. He believed in, worshiped, really, the glory of the Earth. Therefore, long before it was fashionable, he lived an environmentally conscious life—on Long Island in the fifties and sixties, for God's sake. This was an embarrassment to me and my sisters because it entailed washing and hanging used plastic bags on the line; melting down soap slivers on the stove and making cakes of multi-colored Dial/Camay/Ivory; driving a 1952 Plymouth until 1970; and having a compost pile in a suburban neighborhood. When my parents moved to Vermont full-time, in an act of conservation that may have gotten him into heaven, my father took the Long Island compost in burlap sacks up to his Vermont pile. One of his other famous acts of re-use was the way he built a patio at our Long Island home. Every day on his walk from his Madison Avenue advertising firm in Manhattan to the Long Island Railroad station, he would find a brick at a demolition site and put it in his briefcase. A few years of this daily practice yielded a huge brick patio (that later crumbled to the ground in a hurricane).

The first gift: I love the earth and I try to live like my father did. I am far less committed to preservation than he was. I talk about it a lot, but my father lived it.

He also loved his body—he took good care of it, ate well, exercised, and therefore he lived fully until the minute he died. His hair was thick and brown—no gray, no hair loss. He was strong and healthy and sharp of mind. On the day of his death, he skied until 4 pm, ate dinner, read, went to bed, and died in his sleep. So the second gift: a respect for my body and a desire to take care of it. That's a good gift. I didn't realize until he died that I was doing this so that I could live energetically right up until the day I died. Somehow I thought it was so that I would live a long, long time—maybe forever! Now I realize that I want to take care of my body so that every day will be vibrant, no matter when I die.

My father skied like he was fighting a war. He learned the sport in the army. He joined the famous Tenth Mountain Division—the ski troops. A Jewish guy from Brooklyn found his way to the ski troops because it sounded adventurous to him. A small band of winter enthusiasts, mostly from Colorado and Vermont, made up the Tenth Mountain Division. When they returned from the war many of them ended up creating the ski industry in this country. My father was one of these eccentrics. He dragged us skiing every single weekend of every winter of my childhood, whether we wanted to or not, because he loved to ski and he loved to work—and unlike most people, he had managed to combine his passion with his work. That's the third gift.

In the funeral home the sentimental and slightly suspect director, putting together the obituary, asked us if my father had any hobbies.

I said, "Yes, being a petty tyrant."

"Was he in any clubs?"

"No," my sister answered, "we were in his club." Whatever he wanted to do, we had to do it too. He had four girls but that didn't stop him from climbing Mt. Washington every summer, skiing every weekend, tromping miles and miles of deserted beaches on Long Island, and having huge gardens that required us hired hands to squash Japanese beetles and pull weeds. My dear mother went along with all of his passions and taught us to shut up and buck up when he was around. We were the troops in his own Mountain Division.

He was impatient, selfish, disdainful of feelings. He didn't really have much use for the things that he thought only women did—like, talk, sit down inside a house, cry, feel tired or depressed, or actively nourish relationships. This is another gift—but not a good one. My father gave me his impatience, his fear of weakness, his compulsive work habits. He felt that if a day went by when you hadn't worked hard, produced something, been outside, or exercised then you were BAD. I am saddled with that mindset, as are my mother and my sisters. On the evening after my father died, my mother and two of my sisters and I were sitting in the quiet house, just sitting. The sun was setting, the visitors had left, and a strange peace settled over us. Sitting around is a rare occurrence in our household. My mother had been crying. Then, pulling herself together, she looked around, disgusted, and said, "What a waste of a day." Well, she *had* been married to my father for 50 years. My sisters and I, all fully therapized and trying to break the chain of this addiction to productivity, shot each other knowing glances.

February 6

Dream: I am at a ski resort, in the parking lot, searching for my husband. Suddenly I hear a voice from on top of the mountain. I look up—the mountain is huge and far away—like a distant Rocky mountain range; huge snow fields, strong winter sun. There, way in the distance—a small speck of black on the blinding white slope—is my husband. He calls my name. I can hear him quite clearly even though he is so far away. I look up, and I realize that it's not my husband at all—it's my father. "I'm up here!" he yells with glee. "I'm not coming down! It's great up here." I feel wonderful, no trace of my usual annoyance at his self-centered, impatient behavior. "Well," I think, "that's what he is doing; he's fine without me; in fact he doesn't seem to want me there at all. I'll just do something else." So, I decide to jog instead of ski. I start to run but am having trouble moving my legs. I feel as though I am slogging through mud, awkward and slow. I come to a couple in the road—an old man and woman. They are "walkers," they say, and seem like a happy couple. The man says that I am running incorrectly.

"Would you like some advice on how to run?"

"Sure," I answer, quite happy to be getting some help.

"Run from here," he says, touching my abdomen. "Run from your center." I learn right away, and run off, with a feeling of freedom and connection to the old man, the old woman, my father on the mountain, my husband whom I now know where to find.

This seems to me like a profound letting go of my father and also reminds me of what someone has told me recently: Until you have released your father from old love and hate then he is sharing your bed with you and your husband. The dream begins with my husband, becomes my father, merges the two, and then releases my father in a positive way, leaving me, my husband, and my newfound sense of connection. This bodes well for my ongoing, mud-slogging work around men, impatience, distance.

February 15

For the last two weeks I have had two modes: out-and-out grief, or the sense of being connected by a wisp of light to some other, wide-open, loving place. I have only wanted to speak with my sisters and mother. We have drawn much closer through losing my father. I can't believe I never understood the significance of losing a parent; I've let the milestone pass in my friends' lives without proper acknowledgment. They too probably tried to function in the world through the gauzy haze of feeling unsettled, sad, vulnerable, weird, groggy, disconnected, sluggish, unhappy, and some other states for which I cannot find words. Is there a word that means bathing in some kind of spiritual sea, awash with large emotions? Words like love and mystery come to mind but fall short.

As the shock wears off, what is left is grief. But grief for what? This is what I don't understand. Do I really miss him so much? I don't think that is possible, because while I did love him very much (and respected him and was grateful for him) I also had a complex relationship with him, replete with poor communication, resentment, frustration, and anger. I didn't see him that often, and when I did we mostly ignored each other in a loving, disinterested sort of way. That's what he seemed to do with everyone. He benignly ignored people, unless they got in his way, and then he would grunt some kind of frustrated greeting/conversation/tidbit of information and go his merry/annoyed way outside to do a chore or to tromp into the woods. So, what I must miss is just knowing that he is there, taking care of business and being my mother's protector, and in some sort of subtle way, mine too. Everything has changed now from what I have taken for granted my whole life. Perhaps this is such a profound metaphor for life (how we don't fully appreciate things until they are gone) that I have been stopped in my tracks on a physical level: I cannot seem to function as I usually do.

February 19

I am glad that I got the chance to see my father's body after he died. When I don't believe that he really died, I remember his body on the gurney at the funeral home. I'll never forget seeing his body—his skin so chalky; the heaviness of his form; the lack of any trace of life-force, of spirit—and I shudder, aware indeed that he is no longer here with us. (Where he has gone is another matter altogether.) To see a dead body is to know that death is much, much more than merely "no longer here." A body drained of spirit becomes something new—anti-matter, perhaps, or a shadow that has weight and gravity of a kind we can't fathom. I am swimming around in these shadows, and also in the family secrets and memories that are stirred up when one member dies and the others gather together in a new configuration.

When my friend's brother died she said she wanted to wear a sign around her neck that said, "Warning, person approaching is in grief and is not responsible for her actions." Perhaps that is why the Italian Catholic grandmothers in my childhood town wore black for a year, as a warning, and a protection. I'd like to wear black for a while; and for everyone to know what my dress meant so that I wouldn't need to tell the same story over and over. I need protection. My sister says she needs it too. She told me a funny story on the phone today: a customer shopping in her health food store asked her how she was doing since our father had died. She said she was barely holding on. The customer, a man she had known for years, chided her for not trying some of her own products. "Why don't you take a homeopathic remedy for your grief?" he asked. My sister, often a cynic in a world of true-believers, thought two things: "Yeah, *right*," and "What the hell?" She let the man put a few drops of a remedy on her tongue, and in minutes, the foggy, sluggish feelings lifted and for the first time since our father's death she felt like her old self. She said to me, "So why don't you try one of your own products, like meditation or ritual?"

February 21

A friend said that he got so tired of feeling like this after his mother died that finally, after a month, he staged a ritual for himself where he released her and after that things got better. It helps me to know that others go through the same physical and emotional feelings. There's a good chance that in other cultures grief is not something as foreign and abhorrent as it is here, in modern America. I am worn out from these unfamiliar emotions, and it's only been a few weeks. I imagine that in cultures where grief is shared through ritual, that people know better what to do with themselves, and they allow for a natural engagement with mourning, for as long as it takes. You know when you see those Lebanese women wailing for the dead? I've wondered about that and about what, exactly, they were doing. Now I think it must help to have a prescribed and active way of mourning. I'd like to sit around with the women in my family and wail for a few days. I bet we'd feel purged and better able to carry on.

I did do a ritual of sorts by myself. I was all alone in the house on Monday, and for some reason I had thought that since it was the beginning of a school week for the kids, and a work-week for me, that I'd automatically be "over it." I woke up terrified to discover that I was still feeling so unbalanced that once again I called my colleagues and said I wouldn't be coming in to work. And once again, I just sat at the dining room table, watching the birds at the feeder as a light snow-shower drifted through the sunny winter sky. A female cardinal, with an erotic orange beak, landed on a branch and sang in the sun and the snow. My heart filled with sorrow: What I loved best—nature—was a sudden reminder of all things sacred to my father, and I wondered if I would ever be the same again. I closed my eyes and, for the first time since my father had died, I prayed for strength. I remembered my sister's story and her suggestion of trying one of my own "products."

So, I got a picture of my dad and a bouquet of white roses that I had brought home from my mother's house, and I placed them on the table as the amorous cardinal sang in the snow. I went to my study and took down a few objects given to me by a Native American elder—a white doe-skin pouch, a white feather, and a ceremonial bowl. I filled the bowl with water and placed it by the white roses and the picture of my father. Then I meditated and prayed and spoke with my father. I told him that he didn't have to take care of us anymore, that he had done that well for almost 50 years and that my mother and us girls would be fine. "We're strong, thanks to you!" I told him, and I thanked him for the gifts he had given me. I also told him some things I never had when he was alive: that his selfishness had hurt us; that when I saw men with their daughters now—men who are attentive, kindly, cuddly—I knew that we all had missed out on something important. I felt into his presence and knew that on some level he would now be with me in a better and kinder way than he had known how to be in human form. Then I read a prayer that I had heard Ed Benedict of the Mohawk Nation speak many times before—a prayer used by the Iroquois people at their Condolence Ceremonies. I read this prayer aloud, as the cardinal sang at the bird feeder:

> Some of you may have suffered the loss of a loved one. Perhaps it is something else that has caused you pain. It may be that your eyes have been clouded over by tears and that you can no longer see the beauty of the Creator. Perhaps the soreness of the grief that you have suffered through your eyes now blocks your vision. If this is the case, I offer you in symbolism a white doe skin that I take from the sky of the Creator. The skin of the doe is soft and comforting and with it I wipe the tears of soreness of old wounds from your eyes, so that you may see clearly once again.
>
> I fear that you have suffered the loss of a loved one. Perhaps you may have suffered many losses. It may be that the cries of grief now echo in your ears so that you no longer hear properly. If this is the case, I offer you a white feather—a gift from the Creator—that I take from the sky. I take this feather and in symbolism I will clear the cries of grief from your ears, that the silence may rest and comfort you and that you may hear properly once again.
>
> It may be that you have suffered the loss of a loved one, perhaps something else caused you pain. If this is the case, perhaps you have uttered many cries of grief and done much weeping and that a great sob has become lodged in your throat. This may be keeping you from speaking the truth of the Creator. If this is the case, I will reach into the sky and take for you a bowl of pure water. This water is sweet and pure and comes from the Creator. It will wash the lump of grief from your throat so that once again you may speak clearly and properly.
>
> All of these things are offered you in symbolism so that you may be relieved of the pain of whatever losses you have suffered, that once again we may join hands and with open hearts and minds offer gratitude for this day to the Creator.

As I read the prayer I could feel the sweet water of ritual washing the grief from my body, the feather sweeping the heaviness from my heart, the soft doe skin wiping the worry from my mind. For the rest of the day I felt a sense of release, and a new energy filling the empty space. Late in the winter afternoon, I took a long walk at a clip that would have made my father proud. I looked up at the mountains across the valley, and I heard my father's voice again, reminding me that he was free.

March 1

I've begun to let my father go. A sweet kind of sadness is filling the gap—in fact I cried on the couch last night, listening to some schlocky Kenny G. music on the radio. Tears welled in my eyes and rolled down my face. I found myself saying quietly to myself, "Dad, Dad, Daddy, Dad." Like I was rolling a hard candy around on my tongue, tasting the sour and the sweet as it dissolved slowly in my mouth.

I found this portion of the poem *Song of Myself,* by Walt Whitman. I am beginning to feel this way. I do not want to advertise it. It feels like a secret:

> What do you think has become of the young and old men?
> And what do you think has become of the women and children?
>
> They are alive and well somewhere,
> The smallest sprout shows there is really no death,
> And if ever there was it led forward life, and does not wait at the
>   end to arrest it,
> And ceas'd the moment life appear'd.
> All goes onward and outward, nothing collapses,
> And to die is different from what anyone supposed, and luckier.

April 1

It has been two months since my father died. I awake this morning feeling little rays of light cracking through this long period of shock and sadness. Before opening my eyes, I pray to let go of the weight of my grief. I say a little prayer to my father. I tell him I will remember the best of him and try to live it. I say, "You are free to go on your way now. All of us—all of your family—will keep your earth spirit alive. Now you can go explore the other realms." All day I feel his spirit around me—his love of nature, his exuberance, his humor, his eccentric devotion to the earth. I feel better, lighter, strangely free. One thickness of the big onion peeled away. One layer between me and eternity gone.

AFTER DEATH: I WANT TO KNOW GOD'S THOUGHTS

I want to know God's thoughts. The rest are details.
—ALBERT EINSTEIN

People say, when they hear that my father died suddenly, and in his sleep, "How lucky! That's the way I want to go." I don't think that's the way I want to go. I think I'd rather be awake—really awake—so that I can participate fully with the transition. On the other hand, I don't really know what goes on during the process of dying, what it means to be fully awake during the transition, and what the experience of consciousness is like without the funnel of mind and body. Stephen Levine warns that although "it is said that if you're fully alive before death you will probably be fully alive afterward, it is also said that for some who think of themselves as 'spiritual' the ego wants to attend its own funeral."

Einstein declared that he wanted to know God's thoughts. He also said that "the most beautiful experience we can have is the mysterious." We're all Einsteins, trying to use the brilliance of the mind to fathom a mystery beyond our comprehension. Can we know the thoughts of God—or pure consciousness, the soul, divinity, or whatever word you use to describe the indescribable? I like the way devout Jews will not utter or spell the name of the Lord—nor will they picture the God of Israel with visual images—as a way of indicating their inability to express or even understand the omnipotent, omniscient, and omnipresent source of all being. One of my favorite Jewish mystics, Martin Buber, says, "I know nothing of death, but I know that God is eternity, and I know this, too, that he is my God. Whether what we call time remains to us beyond our death becomes quite unimportant to us next to this knowing, that we are God's—who is not immortal, but eternal. Instead of imagining ourselves living instead of dead, we shall prepare ourselves for a real death, which is perhaps the final limit of time but which, if that is the case, is surely the threshold of eternity."

In Book V we explore the threshold of eternity using the concepts of God, faith, karma, and unity, and tools like prayer, forgiveness, and silence. In this landscape—what I call the Landscape of the Soul—experience is our most trustworthy guide. Concepts and explanations are helpful up to a point. Mother Teresa said that "if it was properly explained that death was nothing but going home to God, then there would be no fear." But who can properly explain such a thing? To date no one has done so in such a way that all humans have faith in God and eternal life. Yet in moments of meditation, states of grace, and times of deep, prayerful silence, we may indeed experience our eternal selves going home to God. For me it has been those experiences that have made me one of the faithful.

Book V

The Landscape of the Soul

14 Soulfulness

Beloved Lord, Almighty God!
Through the rays of the sun,
Through the waves of the air,
Through the All-pervading Life in space,
Purify and revivify me, and, I pray,
Heal my body, heart, and soul. Amen
   —Hazrat Inayat Khan

The work you have done in the previous landscapes has prepared you for this next part of the spiritual journey—the path through the Landscape of the Soul. Through meditation, heartfulness work, and care of the body, your mind is calmer, your heart is more open, and your body is less blocked. The life force is beginning to flow. You are simultaneously more grounded and more sensitive; more sure of who you are, yet less attached to being "somebody." You are learning to die, and to be reborn, over and over. You have done all of this work to become a finely tuned instrument, to hear the song of the soul. Even so, as you enter the Landscape of the Soul, you may feel out of place; you may need to acclimate to the thinner air and the finer atmosphere; you may stumble often as you climb.

I think everyone stumbles in the Landscape of the Soul. At some point on the journey, everyone feels lost, and confused, and discouraged. So, before we begin, I want to offer you two climbing sticks to use when you need some support. One is the prayer printed at the top of the previous page. Prayer is the language of soulfulness. It soothes; it encourages; it works. Whisper this prayer—or any prayer that inspires you—a few times whenever you get discouraged, doubtful, or scared. Or use the second walking stick—the meditation offered below.

The Landscape of the Soul is the least tangible of the spiritual landscapes. Its landmarks are concealed, its messages muted. The main characters on this part of the journey are your soul and God. But how many of us could say for sure that the soul exists or that God is fully known? To enter the Landscape of the Soul requires a leap of faith. I offer the following meditation to help you make that leap. If you can, put aside, for just a minute, your doubts of the soul's existence. Let your questions about God rest for the time being. You can pick them up again, the minute the meditation is over. Just for this moment, come with me to the Landscape of the Soul.

Take your seat, assume your meditation posture, and close your eyes. Let your mind relax and become still. Take a deep breath in through the heart center. Exhale with a few soft sighs. Feel your heart soften . . . open . . . expand. Now, imagine you have been on a long journey, climbing a high mountain through uncharted territory. The cloud cover has been thick and the path covered with underbrush and loose stones. You have been tired, scared, doubtful. But now, as you reach the top, the clouds lift and the way is open and broad. The air is pure. It brightens your mood. Look around: the sunlight is strong and real; the rocks seem lit from within; the clear sky is charged with energy. The atmosphere stirs your emotions, purifying and revivifying you to the core of your being. You feel almost translucent, fully alive, alert. You perceive subtle, spiritual vibrations that communicate to you through the cells of your body and the energetic field around your body. Your mind is at peace; your heart fills with what it has always hungered for. You are in the presence of God. You are in the Landscape of the Soul. You are home.

With an open heart and a quiet mind, sit with dignity on the mountaintop, in the Landscape of the Soul. Feel the solitude, the expansiveness, the crystalline stillness. Now direct your in-breath through the top of your head, as if you are a baby whose skull has yet to completely close. On each inhalation and exhalation, feel an exchange of light moving in and out of your body through the top of your head. Breathe in the "all-pervading Life in space." Feel the Light and the Life pervade your entire body, from the top of your head all the way down to the tips of your toes. As you exhale let your thoughts relax and dissolve back out into space. Become one with the all-pervading Life. All else dissolves—no mountain, no body, no mind, no heart, just the all-pervading Life in space.

Sit like this for as long as you want. If you lose connection with the all-pervading Life in space, return to breathing in and out of the top of the head, allowing light and space to flow in and out of your body, heart, and mind.

And when you are ready, you can call your soul back, leave your perch, come back down the mountain, open your eyes, and return to this body, this mind, this heart. You can always go back to the mountaintop; it is always there, waiting for you.

As you read Book V and consider the Landscape of the Soul, remember to pick up these two walking sticks whenever you need some support.

ASKING QUESTIONS IN AN ECHO CHAMBER

The Landscape of the Soul is like a high plateau stretching out eternally in all directions. If you could be shown a map of this landscape, you'd see yourself—and all selves—as tiny specks in a tiny portion of the vastness. Mountains surround this little area, creating an illusion of separation from the rest of the landscape. The human realm—our little valley in the eternal universe—is an echo chamber: we sense something beyond the mountains, but when we call out our deepest questions, they reverberate against the mountain walls and bounce back to us, changed yet unanswered. We call out, "Who is God?" . . . "What is the soul?" . . . "Who am I?" And instead of answers, we receive back variations of our original questions: "Are we all one with God?" . . . "Then why do we feel so isolated, so separate?" . . . "When I pray, to whom am I speaking?" . . . "Hellooo, is anyone out there?"

In our corner of the universe, we don't get many answers; mostly we hear our own questions, and the echoed questions of our ancestors, reverberating through time. Scientifically speaking, an echo is a repetition of sounds produced by the reflection of sound waves from an obstructing surface. Spiritually speaking, when you send out your deepest questions—like sound waves going forth into the universe—the mountains in your own mind act as the "obstructing surface." The same you that calls out the questions sends them right back. Hazrat Inayat Khan's poem "Why?" describes this predicament:

"Why,—what are you?"
"I am the cry of the hungry mind."
"Why,—what do you signify?"
"I am the knocker on a closed door."
"Why,—what do you represent?"
"The owl which cannot see during the day."
"Why,—what is your complaint?"
"The irritation of the mind."
"Why,—what is your life condition?"
"I am shut up in a dark room."
"Why,—how long will your captivity last?"
"All night long."
"Why,—what are you so eagerly waiting for?"
"The day-break."
"Why,—you are yourself the cover over the answer you want."

Sometimes the spiritual quest feels like knocking, knocking, knocking on a closed door; like a volley of questions bouncing off the walls of our own limited capacity to reach beyond ourselves. It's not difficult to understand why we become weary, or cynical, or make the decision early on that there's nothing to know anyway, no one to answer our questions. "Often enough we think there is nothing to hear," writes the Jewish mystic and philosopher Martin Buber, in *I and Thou,* "but long before we have ourselves put wax in our ears." When asked if his questions about God had been answered, the Christian mystic C. S. Lewis answered with another question: "Can a mortal ask questions which God finds unanswerable? Quite easily, I should think. All nonsense questions are unanswerable. How many hours are there in a mile? Is yellow square or round? Probably half the questions we ask—half our great theological and metaphysical problems—are like that." And yet, if we are curious about life, and especially about the spiritual life, we can't help but call out the "great theological and metaphysical problems," those cosmic riddles that answer themselves with echoes.

Are we stuck? Will we ever get the wax out of our ears? Will our questions escape the echo chamber? Eventually every spiritual seeker arrives at this impasse. All the work done in the previous landscapes have led us to this gate. When Zen masters sense that a student has reached the final barrier, they give the student a koan—an unsolvable, seemingly nonsensical question that is repeated silently during meditation and daily chores, until the mind stops straining and another way of problem-solving takes over. Koans are used, in the words of the American Zen master Philip Kapleau, for "breaking asunder the mind of ignorance and opening the eye of truth." There are many koans, perhaps the most famous being "What is the sound of one hand clapping?"

"To people who cherish the letter above the spirit," writes Kapleau, "koans appear bewildering, for in their phrasing koans deliberately throw sand into the eyes of the intellect to force us to open our Mind's eye and see the world and everything in it undistorted by our concepts and judgments. By wheedling the intellect into attempting solutions impossible for it, koans reveal to us the inherent limitations of the logical mind as an instrument for realizing ultimate Truth."

Zen Buddhists are not the only ones who have concluded that we can't use the logical mind as an instrument for getting beyond the last mountain range. Most mystics and poets and scientists have come to the same conclusion. As Einstein says, "No problem can be solved from the same consciousness that created it." Like great scientific problems, great theological ones ask us to step into a consciousness beyond the one we normally inhabit. Big problems bend the brain; they just can't be tackled using the same two-dimensional way of thinking humans normally use. This is why travel in the Landscape of the Soul is not easily described. Language is a tool of the logical mind. Poetry comes closest to the language of the soul, but even the most gifted poet's words are merely intimations of a reality beyond words.

According to Jewish mysticism, two trees grew in the Garden of Eden: the Tree of Knowledge and the Tree of Life. From the Tree of Knowledge mankind could receive the gifts of thinking, speaking, reasoning. But the Tree of Life offered the most precious fruit: a communion beyond words with the Divine. If you make a study of the ways in which the mystics and poets and sages from all traditions have tried to describe the fruit from the Tree of Life you'll notice that what they have tasted does not translate very well into human concepts. You'll also find startling similarities in the content, the flavor, even the wording of their descriptions—their nonanswers to the big questions. I find proof of a land beyond the mountains by the strange yet similar fruits explorers from every culture and era bring back with them.

I've collected these "nonanswers" for years and share some of them here. Not all religions are represented (but I am sure that all could be) and some of the quotations come not from bona-fide mystics but from poets, scientists, and psychologists. They are arranged in a loose, chronological order, as if the voices from the past are calling out their responses to the great, universal koan: Who is God? Notice how each answer carries with it a thread from the previous one and how even when woven together they still don't definitively answer the "great theological and metaphysical problems." When asked to define God, most wise men and women hedge a little, or answer with a riddle, or at least add a caveat of mystery to their discoveries.

WHO IS GOD?

I pervade the entire universe in my unmanifested form. All creatures find their existence in me, but I am not limited by them. Behold my divine mystery!

—*THE BHAGAVAD-GITA*

Tat tvam asi (translated as "Thou art That," or "The Self in each person is not different from the Godhead").

—*HINDU UPANISHADS*

What is the Buddha after his Nirvana? Does he exist or not exist, or both, or neither? We never will conceive!

—*PATRIARCH NAGARJUNA*

Moses said to God: "If they ask me what your name is, what am I to tell them?" And God said to Moses, "I Am who I Am. This is what you must say to the children of Israel; I AM has sent me to you."

—*EXODUS 3:13–14*

I and the Father are one.

—*JESUS*

Say: "He is the One God;
God, the Eternal, the Uncaused Cause of all being.
He begets not, and neither is he begotten
and there is nothing that could be compared to him."

—*THE KORAN*

Isness is God.

—*MEISTER ECKEHART*

God created . . . so that God's creation, God's splendor, might joyfully declare as it shines back: I subsist, I stand under, I am!

—*DANTE ALIGHIERI*

To be enlightened is to be intimate with all things.

—*ZEN MASTER DOGEN*

And if the earthly no longer knows your name,
whisper to the silent earth: I am flowing
to the flashing water say: I am.

—*RAINER MARIA RILKE*

I hear and behold God in every object, yet I understand God not in the least.

—*WALT WHITMAN*

God is the partner of your most intimate soliloquies.

—*VICTOR FRANKL*

A human being is part of the whole called by us universe, a part limited in time and space. He experiences himself, his thoughts, and feelings as something separated from the rest, a kind of optical delusion of his consciousness. This delusion is a kind of prison for us, restricting us to our personal desires and to affection for a few persons nearest to us. Our task must be to free ourselves from this prison. . . .

—*ALBERT EINSTEIN*

God is the presence that exists.

—*R. D. LAING*

You can call it wisdom, or sanity, or health, or enlightenment. I use the word God as a shortcut. I am comfortable with the word God because I don't have the foggiest idea of what it means.

—*STEPHEN LEVINE*

When you are ultimately truthful with yourself, you will eventually realize and confess that, "I am Buddha, I am Spirit." Anything short of that is a lie, the lie of the ego, the lie of the separate-self sense, the contraction in the face of infinity. The deepest recesses of your consciousness directly intersect Spirit itself, in the supreme identity. This is not a state you are bringing into existence for the first time, but simply a timeless state that you are recognizing and confessing—you are being ultimately truthful when you state, "I am Buddha, the ultimate Beauty."

—KEN WILBER

The common theme running through all spiritual literature in its attempt to define God is the sense of a *relationship* between our limited consciousness—the separate self—and an overarching consciousness—a unified whole. It isn't so much that God is the unified state of consciousness that each of us came from and will return to, but more so that God is the creative energy flowing between all states of consciousness. God is in the land beyond the mountains, but God is also in the mountains and in the valley of illusions cradled within the mountains. God is not one thing or another; rather God flows between and through all things. God connects, relates, weaves all things together as if one. This theme is expressed in surprisingly similar ways from culture to culture. One of the most common poetic devices is the "I am" statements: declarations of an experienced intimacy with God, or Buddha nature, or the Great Spirit, or the Way. They can be found in almost every religion, from the *Tat tvam asi* of the Hindu Upanishads, to the "I am" statements of Jesus ("I am the way, the truth, and the life"; "I am the light of the world"), and in the statements, once considered heretical, of Jewish, Christian, and Sufi mystics who proclaimed that they themselves were God. When a mystic proclaims "I am!" he is saying, "I am myself, yet I am God. We are separate, yet we are one."

But let's not get too esoteric here. "The import of every koan," writes Roshi Philip Kapleau, "is the same: that the world is one interdependent Whole and that each separate one of us is that Whole." Perhaps you can take a break right now from pondering these words and return to the meditation and prayer at the beginning of the chapter. Create an atmosphere within your heart and mind that nurtures your own "I am" experience. Feel your unique self (your soul) in communication with the Whole (God).

I read the words of saints and mystics not to become a religious scholar, but to be led closer and closer to my own experience of God consciousness, to have my own "I am" experience. Experience is the key in the Landscape of the Soul. Language can trip us up. It creates distinctions of gender, culture, species, eras. My friend, who is a divinity student, refuses even to use the word *God*. Instead he says, "He, She, It, Whatever," when referring to the "I am" experience.

But there is great joy in finding friends on the journey, and that's why I read sacred texts—to find soul friends whose shared experiences shed light on and give form to my own journey. Choosing a friend is more a matter of personal taste than a question of right or wrong. At different times in my life I have turned to soul friends within different traditions for different reasons. Early on in my search I felt most at home with the Eastern writings from the Bhagavad-Gita and the Buddhist Mahayana texts. I liked their starkness and the way they were able to captivate my mind. Because I was born in the Western world, the poetry of the Western traditions naturally speaks to me: I have always loved the Koran and the Old and New Testaments of the Bible. Sufi poetry radically bypasses my logical mind and goes straight to the heart. I also find clues about God in the research and writings of biologists and physicists who see proof of a greater intelligence in the handiwork of the material world: nature, planets, the cosmos. The sky- and earth-centered teachings from the Native American traditions are jewels of wisdom that convey the unity of God, nature, and humans.

Perhaps my favorite God poets are the Christian mystics from the Middle Ages, radical thinkers like Mechtild of Magdeburg, a thirteenth-century mystic who could not help but write about her experience of God. Although she had no formal position within the Church (since in her time there were no religious sisters in Roman Catholicism), her journals were translated into Latin and held in high esteem by the Church. Her poetry values experience over concepts and, unless you have had similar experiences, can sound like the rantings of a drug-addled madwoman. I discovered her writings during a long retreat where I felt particularly trapped in the echo chamber. It was Mechtild's words about stones, mountains, and Jesus that, for reasons known only to my nonrational consciousness, finally pushed me over the hump of the mountain:

> One day I saw with the eyes of my eternity
> in bliss and without effort, a stone.
> This stone was like a great mountain
> and was of assorted colors.
> It tasted sweet, like heavenly herbs.
> I asked the sweet stone: Who are you?
> It replied: "I am Jesus."

I cannot tell you why Mechtild's words woke me up. Something about the great mountain being sweet; something about the mountain itself being the Jesus that I sought; something about "eyes of eternity in bliss and without effort" freed my soul to travel forth. Mechtild of Magdeburg stands in a long line of Christian mystics from the Middle Ages—Hildegard of Bingen, Saint Francis, and Thomas Aquinas before her, and Dante, Meister Eckehart, and Dame Julian of Norwich after her—all of whom help me wake up. The words of these soul friends resonate with my experience and have been loyal traveling companions on my journey, and yet they may not work for you. Your choice of soul friends is a truly personal matter. You will find clues about the nature of God and soul everywhere. There's no need to limit your source of wisdom to one tradition or even to religion when the diversity and quantity of sacred inspiration is so rich and so readily available. Let what resonates with your own experience spur you on to discovering the vast and unified and fundamental consciousness called God.

DO NOT SEEK THE ANSWERS:
LIVE THE QUESTIONS

Do not seek the answers, which cannot be given you because you would not be able to live them. And the point is, to live everything. Live the questions now. Perhaps you will then gradually, without noticing it, live along some distant day into the answer.
—RAINER MARIA RILKE

It's not easy for Westerners to "live along some distant day into the answer," as Rilke suggests we do with our big questions. We want answers. We have spent three thousand years looking for them, touching on them, and turning our hunches into intractable "isms" and schisms. On one side of the most modern schism are religious fundamentalists, who seek comfort in rigid doctrines of their own creation, and on the other side are scientific fundamentalists, who demand proof of any answer, using their own intellectual constructs to prove or disprove their own questions. If, as Einstein said, no problem can be solved from the same consciousness that created it, the question of God's existence cannot be solved by the same mind that is doing the questioning. To approach a God or a reality that is ultimately unknowable through thought, we need a different sort of consciousness.

This different sort of consciousness has been sought throughout the ages. Called enlightenment in the East, union with God in the West, and "nonordinary" states of consciousness by the shamanic traditions, seekers have devised a rich variety of practices, prayers, and rituals to nurture the kind of consciousness that welcomes a vision of God. Taken out of context, and especially used out of context, many of these consciousness-altering practices appear bizarre. It is painful for me to see elegantly crafted rituals like the Native American Sun Dance or the whirling practice of the Sufi dervishes presented as exotic entertainment. Unless we have experienced them in their entirety, it is erroneous to judge the means that seekers use to make contact with the divine. The ways of working with consciousness may vary from culture to culture—from charismatic Christians speaking in tongues, to Hasidic Jews rhythmically rocking in prayer, to Brazilian tribal cultures who use psychotropic plants to encourage visions—but there is also common ground. Solitary retreats, long periods of prayer, fasting, repetition of sounds and movements—you can find these in all of the world's wisdom traditions. Done within the protection of the community and the systems created to balance nonordinary states, seemingly strange practices allow one to experiment with other dimensions of reality—different states of consciousness—and enter an experience of the sacred.

Western tradition is just as rich in its means of generating an experience of God as are other traditions. The Jewish, Christian, and Islamic religions were founded by radical seekers who went alone into the wilderness, where they fasted and prayed for visions. They heard the voice of God speaking through natural and archetypal forces, telling them about the secrets of human life and the marvelous structure of the universe. They passed down their revelations in the form of dreams and visions: a burning bush, the parting of the seas, angelic visitations, golden tablets. Perhaps today their transpersonal visions would land them in a psychiatrist's office. In fact, I think that many people in today's materialistic culture try to sedate their visionary tendencies rather than seek creative and meaningful outlets for their sacred hunger. I see the same questions that Moses and Jesus and Mohammed took into the desert in the lost look in many of our young people's eyes. Religion has become so watered down from the original intent of its founders that many people no longer feel it satisfies their spiritual hunger. They seek nourishment elsewhere, often in self-destructive ways.

If we were more open to the legitimate need people have for entering exalted states of consciousness, the destructive drug and alcohol culture that is a hallmark of our society would loosen its grip. If the pursuit of the sacred were valued, we would teach healthy and effective ways of escaping the echo chamber of our limited perspective, and the hunger for God would replace the compulsion for sedation. It's been a slow and steady climb in the Western world away from an *experience of the sacred.* You can't really blame religion. The roots of every religion are in the soil of sacred experience. Rather, it's been the way in which power-hungry people have exploited religion to further their own need for control. Don't throw away the beauty of a religion's original intent because of the ways in which it has been diluted or misused.

One of the ways that has helped me to expand my own consciousness is to study the history of Western philosophy and religion. I do this to get back to the source of the traditions that formed my concept of reality and God. It is useful for me to unravel my own conditioning, to understand that my beliefs are the creation of my culture, that they are not set in stone, and that they are part of an evolving tradition. A good book for this exploration—if your upbringing was influenced by Western thought—is *The Passion of the Western Mind,* by Richard Tarnas. Called "the best intellectual history of the West in one volume I have ever seen" by Huston Smith, and "the most lucid and concise presentation I have read" by Joseph Campbell, the book describes profound philosophical concepts simply (but not simplistically) from Plato to Hegel, from Augustine to Nietzsche, and from Copernicus to Freud. If you would like to understand the roots of Western thought, and therefore the roots of your own philosophical concepts and intellectual habits, this book is worth the read. In five hundred pages you can trace the formation of a culture's belief system, and gain a perspective on what you as a Westerner have accepted as "true" or "real."

Tarnas charts the evolution of Western thought, which he describes as having emerged out of a *participation mystique*—primitive man's undifferentiated identification with God and nature. The book begins with the Greeks, and evolves through Judaic monotheism, the emergence of Christianity, the Renaissance, the scientific revolution, the philosophical revolution, and into the modern and postmodern eras, which have been characterized by existentialism, nihilism, and the triumph of secularism. In the book's epilogue, Tarnas brings us up to date and asks us to continue the quest, to weave the strands of Western tradition into the future, and to move beyond the alienated view of human life that prevails now in our technological and secular world. He writes, "The *telos,* the inner direction and goal, of the Western mind has been to reconnect with the cosmos in a mature *participation mystique,* to surrender itself freely and consciously in the embrace of a larger unity that preserves human autonomy while also transcending human alienation." He answers the perennial question of philosophy—the great Western koan—this way: "How can something come from nothing? I believe there is only one plausible answer to this riddle. . . . The bold conjectures and myths that the human mind produces in its quest for knowledge ultimately come from something far deeper than a purely human source. They come from the wellspring of nature itself, from the universal unconscious that is bringing forth through the human mind and human imagination its own gradually unfolding reality. In this view, the theory of a Copernicus, a Newton, or an Einstein is not simply due to the luck of a stranger; rather, it reflects the human mind's radical kinship with the cosmos."

The human mind's radical kinship with the cosmos. This is a beautiful way to describe the *experience* of God, called enlightenment, or unity, or cosmic consciousness. When we escape from the confines of the echo chamber, we come into kinship with the cosmos. Kinship is more satisfying than knowledge. It is a deep drink. It enchants even as it nurtures. Tarnas uses the word *cosmos.* I use the word *God.* My kinship with God has the same sense of mysterious upliftment I feel when I witness the geese flying south: Why do they go south? How do they know when to start? Why do their honking noises and their perfect flying formation fill me with wonder? Like the geese, God's mystery remains all the more beautiful for my lack of understanding.

Some resist using the word God because they feel it limits their perception of the vast creative energy of the cosmos. Some find that the word God is too patriarchal; others find it personalizes a situation they find highly impersonal. If we grew up with an unhealthy experience of authority in our family or society, the whole notion of "God the Father" may cloud our relationship to the sacred. On the one hand, authority issues can turn one away from relying on any one or thing; on the other hand, they can create childish dependency, where our prayers to God are more like lists to Santa Claus. Thomas Aquinas said that "mistakes about creatures contribute to mistakes about God." This is why it's so important to do the work of the Landscape of the Heart as we search for an experience of God—to clear the psychological path even as we purify the spiritual one.

The Sufis call God "the Friend," bypassing the family or class issues one may have with "God the Father" or the "Lord God." Find what works for you—what brings you most purely into kinship with the cosmos. Hildegard of Bingen described her God like this:

> I am the rain coming from the dew
> that causes the grasses to laugh with the joy of life.
> I call forth tears, the aroma of holy work.
> I am the yearning for good.

And Martin Buber described his God like this: "The *Thou* meets me through grace—it is not found by seeking. . . . The *Thou* meets me. But I step into direct relation with it. . . . All real living is meeting."

"A mystical experience," says Mark Epstein, "is a sense of your not being what you thought you were, an experience of your heart's or mind's true nature. It is a startlingly clear and moving feeling." You will know you have found your own God by the startling and moving nature of your experience.

THE SOUL'S STORY

In *The Handbook for the Soul,* a collection of essays from contemporary spiritual authors, Ram Dass does a great job of describing *his* experience of God and soul. I reprint the essay here because it temporarily satisfies my own impatience as I try to "live the questions." Ram Dass's words are like a rest stop on the climb: I relax in their wisdom for a while, and then continue on my own journey.

THE SOUL'S STORY
As told by Ram Dass

Although the "soul story" has no beginning and no end, I'll arbitrarily start it by saying that in the beginning we are simply pure awareness. It's hard to talk about pure awareness, because there are no words in the English language—or in any language—that can adequately describe it. The best I can do is to say that it is simultaneously everything and nothing; it is nowhere and it is everywhere; it has no form, yet it contains all forms. Pure awareness transcends soul, yet all souls are part of it. It can be called God. It can also be called "the immanent manifest," the thing that has not yet taken form on the physical plane.

At some point, pure awareness begins to divide—and that's when we move into the domain of soul. We could say that, in a sense, a little piece of pure awareness begins to bud off from the larger entity. Although it is preparing to manifest itself on the physical plane, this new entity hasn't yet taken incarnation or physical form. It is unique and separate from pure awareness, and it has, for example, "John-ness" within it, but it is not yet "John." Rather, it is the soul that will soon be identified as "John."

Then, finally, the soul takes incarnation on the physical plane, takes on the body and personality known as "John" . . . But becoming John, reaching the physical plane, isn't the culmination of the story. At the end of John's lifetime—or perhaps at the end of many lifetimes—the soul that was John returns to the pure awareness where it began. All of us souls are on a circular journey, from beginning to beginning. Nourishing the soul helps move us through the physical incarnation—the "John" part of the journey—and bring us back to the state of pure awareness again.

When the soul is part of the pure awareness, it doesn't need any nourishing. But as it buds off and takes form as an individual entity, as it becomes separate from the pure awareness, it develops uniqueness. Along with the uniqueness comes a set of attachments, of clingings and aversions and predispositions, which we call karma. Now the soul is faced with a predicament: the predicament of being an individual who desires to be unique and separate from everyone and everything, and yet who also yearns to return to the undifferentiated pure awareness from which it came. It can only return by increasing its unity with the oneness, yet its very individuality and the separate actions it takes push it further and further away from the unity. And the separation creates suffering. So as we become aware of that predicament, we begin to nourish the soul in ways that help it work through the problems of separation and attachment, so it can move ahead to the beginning. What an interesting journey!

Now, there are many, many different ways to nourish the soul and decrease the separation. Positive experiences, such as compassion, love, and resonance with another soul, decrease our separateness. A moment's meditation into the deeper, undifferentiated awareness in ourselves brings us back into the unity. Anything at all that makes us aware of our identity with the larger consciousness can be positive—even trauma or a near-death experience. Through study and spiritual practices we can overcome the mind's natural desire to be separate and reclaim our connection to pure awareness. But though the intellect can take us to the end of the diving board, it's faith that gives us the courage to leap.

Ram Dass goes on to offer ways of nourishing the soul and decreasing the sense of separation. Here is a list that combines some of his suggestions with others I've gathered from a variety of traditions:

TEN WAYS TO NOURISH THE SOUL

1. *Meditate:* Set aside time each day for meditation, a time when we "loosen the hold of the social identity we've learned for ourselves," as Ram Dass says, and become aware of our unified relationship with life and the eternal journey of the soul.

2. *Integrate:* Through meditation and spiritual study, become aware of the "three stages or aspects of our being—pure awareness, soul, and incarnation" (Ram Dass). You may be more comfortable with other words, but find a way to discover and identify these aspects of yourself. Spend time focusing on yourself as each of these three aspects: unified consciousness; a soul, making its circular journey from and back to unified consciousness; and a human being, with a unique genetic and cultural heritage, who is also a soul on its spiritual journey. Discover yourself as each of these aspects and as all of them. Resist using meditation and spiritual practice to escape your unique human strengths and weaknesses. Make the object of your practice the harmonious and pleasurable integration of all of who you are.

3. *Fall in Love* with your soul. Be like a lover separated from your beloved. Look for your soul everywhere. Make every part of life—the joy and the sorrow, the excitement and the drudgery, the losses and the gains—part of the spiritual search.

4. *Jog Your Spiritual Memory:* Surround yourself with things that jog your spiritual memory—pictures, letters, music, scents, anything that reminds you of your true love. Keep something in your office or by the kitchen sink or in the car that reminds you of your beloved soul. Create an altar, a meditation garden, a sacred space for contemplation. Ram Dass says, "I usually carry a *return* with me—a string of beads. In a checkout line at the supermarket, I'll have my beads going in my hand. The beads are a device for reminding me that I am a soul, at play in a supermarket checkout line. Just feeling the beads in my fingers can change my whole consciousness. Or the breath—often a simple breath will awaken and balance

me. So will seeing the Beloved in other people: suddenly I'll find myself looking through the veil to see what's hidden, to see another soul that's taken incarnation in a different form." Establish your own spiritual memory joggers—singing, moving, cooking, hiking, laughing, serving. Each soul, each incarnation is touched and awakened in different ways.

5. *Take Care of Yourself:* Care of the body and care of the heart are also care of the soul. The soul will more readily come out of hiding if the incarnated self is loved. Physical, mental, and emotional health and well-being nourish the soul. How will you know if you are nourishing your soul? Remember what Rumi says: "When you do things from your soul, you feel a river moving in you, a joy." Put that quote on the refrigerator, on the mirror, in the car—a place where you will see it every day and ask yourself, "Is the river moving?"

6. *Create Rituals:* Ritual is nothing more than a time-out from limited consciousness, a time to reconnect with the all-pervading Life. A ritual can last as long as a week or be as short as a breath. Take time alone and with friends and family to honor the "All-pervading Life in space" and the soul's journey. Say a blessing at meals; meditate on your birthday; gather together to celebrate rites of passage and to mourn loss; pay attention to the seasons; honor your ancestors; give thanks to the Earth.

7. *Slow Down:* Too much speed kills the appreciation of the soul. If your life is crammed with activity, get rid of some of it. Make downtime a priority. Make simple pleasures a requirement. Rest and sleep more. Eat slowly, at the table, with friends and family. The slow, steady journey of the soul is sensed more profoundly in times of peaceful pleasure.

8. *Love Other People:* Hatred, annoyance, and grudges block the energy of the soul. You can try to understand spiritual principles as much as you want, but the most powerful way to open up to the truth of the soul is to love other people, animals, nature, and life itself. Concentration, attention, and intelligence are friends of the soul, but kindness, forgiveness, and generosity are the soul itself.

9. *Gently Remove the Barriers:* Don't force the soul to reveal itself. It can't be done. Soul is already here. Our work is to get out of the way. Work, patience, and faith; work, patience, and faith.

10. *Lean Back into God's Perfect Plan:* The more we identify with the soul, the more spacious and willing we become in our approach to life. When everything is experienced as part of our eternal soul's journey, we can relax. We can let go into the perfection of God's plan for us. Practice leaning on God. Practice being full of faith.

15 ⁞ Inter-Being

God has arranged everything in the universe in consideration of everything else. . . .
Everything that is in the heavens, on the earth, and under the earth, is penetrated
with connectedness, penetrated with relatedness.
—Hildegard of Bingen

In the Landscape of the Soul all roads lead to the question of unity and duality. If we are one with God, then what is this sense of self? If all phenomena exist in wholeness, then why all the conflict, why so much
discrimination, why so much incompatibility? You'll find these questions
broached by every religion and philosophy using words like *discrimination*
and *nondiscrimination, separateness* and *wholeness, diversity* and *oneness.* I use
the words *unity consciousness* to describe the state of harmony where all of
life is seen as a whole, and *duality consciousness* to describe the fractured way
in which we generally conceive of life.

Thich Nhat Hanh uses the phrase "inter-being" to describe unity consciousness. Before exploring this subject further, I'll share with you a
teaching on inter-being that I have witnessed Thich Nhat Hanh offer at
several retreats. As the retreatants sit quietly around him, Thich Nhat
Hanh sits on the ground and holds a piece of paper in one hand and a
match in the other. He asks us to imagine all of the elements that make up
the piece of paper: the pulp from the tree; the soil, the water, and the sunshine that fed the tree; the glue and dye and chemicals that were used to

make the paper. He explains how the piece of paper is the tree; it was in the tree all along; it was in the seed of the tree all along. It was in the soil and the sunlight that nourished the tree. If you could see deeply enough into the nature of things, you would see the piece of paper in the river water that fed the roots of the tree. You would see it in the glue and dye and chemicals that were mixed with the pulp to make the paper. Is the paper soil? Is it the tree? Is it glue, or dye? No, but without any one of these parts of the paper—stretching all the way back to the seed, the rain, the clouds, the sky, the sun—we would not have this sheet of paper. Even the man who ran the machine that mixed the pulp with the glue is in this piece of paper, and his parents, and his family, and his thoughts and feelings.

Then Thich Nhat Hanh lights the match and holds it to the paper. We watch it burn. He asks, "Where is the paper now? Where is the tree? Where is the sunlight? Where is the man? Have they become the smoke? Are they these few ashes?" We sit quietly for a while, pondering these questions. Then he asks, "And now, where is the smoke?" We look around. The air is clear. "Is the smoke those clouds? Is the paper the blue sky? Is the tree the air we are breathing?"

No matter how many times I participate in Thich Nhat Hanh's paper meditation, my consciousness is always altered by it. My usual sense of the world is temporarily suspended. The distinctions I commonly make between things blur; duality consciousness ceases to dominate my perceptions, and unity consciousness takes over. I experience inter-being. Whew! This always feels like such a relief, such a clearing of illusion, such a homecoming.

Once on a meditation retreat where I had been alone and in silence for seven days, I had the experience of a prolonged state of inter-being. I started the retreat with strong resistance. Every time I would sit down to meditate I would feel overcome by two conflicting pulls: one to get up and quit this nonsense, and the other to find my way back to a state of inter-being. After a day or two of struggling I decided to give a name to the two pulls and to just sit still in the middle of their tug-of-war. I called the pull to get up my "separate self"—the one who desired to remain isolated, individual, different; I labeled the other pull my unified self—the one who wanted to inter-be with all phenomena and the universe. As I sat up straight in the midst of this conflict, I experienced my separate self like a wave approaching the ocean shore. I felt perhaps as a wave feels as it asserts its separate self, even as the ocean pulls on it to return. I felt the stronger rhythm of the universe pulling me toward oneness, just as the sea calls to the wave. The more I identified with my separate, wavelike self, the more I resisted the pull. But I still felt it, and it filled me with a familiar kind of longing and loneliness.

As I sat in meditation I experienced each in-breath as a desire to live as a wave—as an individuated soul, a single personality, ME. With each out-breath I gave in to the longing to return to the sea—the immensity of un-differentiated existence, unity, YOU. For a few days I did nothing but engage in a visceral experience of the human dilemma—what Martin Buber calls the I-Thou relationship. I felt my human desire to live and play here on earth, while my eternal consciousness longed to dissolve be-yond form. And for a few blessed days, I existed in a vibrant and peaceful relationship between form and the formless, between the born and the unborn, between my soul and God, between I and Thou.

Granted, we usually do not function on a day-to-day level aware of this creative dialogue going on within ourselves. Instead we experience it as a vague sense of a conflict of interests, one that informs all of the surface conflicts that we engage in each day. Spiritual practice is remembering, over and over, that we are involved in this double life, and that peace and happiness reside in our ability to transcend duality even as we live within it. This is the fulfillment of the spiritual quest—the release from the painful struggle of duality. I use my own homegrown mantra, an abbrevi-ated sort of prayer, to help me deal with duality: *Not either/or, but both, and more.* I use "either/or" to signify the dualistic bind we find ourselves in; "both" is a consciousness that can reconcile duality and hold the opposites in a wide embrace; "more" is God—a peaceful, vibrant, and free state of being where the "ifs and buts" of the dualistic bind cease to exist.

Ultimately, spirituality comes to this: waking up out of the dream of "either/or" into a realization of "both and more." As long as our con-sciousness is trapped on the dualistic plane, our soul feels cramped. The ultimate purpose behind all self-transformation work—psychological, physical, spiritual—is to release our souls from this cramped existence; to cease the struggle of duality and to awaken into the freedom of unity.

DUALITY AND UNITY

In duality consciousness we live in a world of struggle, a world of oppo-sites—light and dark, space and matter, joy and sorrow, life and death. We experience everything—*everything*—as a contradiction or a denial of something else. We filter life through "either/or consciousness." Either a person is a friend or a foe; either we're for or against something; either we're right or wrong, or someone else is right or wrong. This seems to be the way we are wired. Either/or consciousness is a primal response—a life-or-death reaction to the imagined fragility of our very existence. Life on earth as a human being—called the "dualistic plane" by many different spiritual traditions—is experienced as a struggle between opposing forces. We say, "That's the law of nature. That's the law of duality. That's just the way it is."

On the surface, duality consciousness *is* "just the way it is." Things do come in pairs. The pairs appear to be opposites. Opposites create tension and conflict. The law of duality does not describe the world as Hildegard of Bingen does, as "penetrated with connectedness, penetrated with relatedness." Rather, in our normal, dualistic perception we experience life as penetrated with conflict, and other people as penetrated with competition. We are penetrated with separateness. Each one of us sees him- or herself as a separate entity engaged in a life-or-death struggle. We assert our specialness, convinced that we must maintain our edge in order to stay alive. "On the dualistic plane each issue ends with either life or death," writes Eva Pierrakos, the founder of The Pathwork, an elegant self-transformation system that marries spirituality and psychology.

Because we conceive of death as the opposite of life, life on the dualistic plane feels like a continuous problem. Because we don't experience how life and death are just two sides of the same coin—parts of a unified, eternal dance—we cling to life and fear death. And out of this basic misconception of reality, all other misconceptions are born. "Man's struggle," notes Pierrakos, "is in coping with the arbitrary and illusory division of the unified principle; things become opposites and that imposes conflicts. It creates tension and struggle within man and therefore with the outer world. . . . Living trapped in the limited world of duality, there is always the fear of the undesirable—the straining away from it and the straining toward the desirable."

If we are indeed trapped in an illusion of duality, what lies beyond the limits of what we think of as "just the way it is"? What is the unified principle? This is where we run into problems. This is where elaborate mythologies and complicated techniques are created to explain the unexplainable. When Jesus spoke of the unified Trinity of the Father, the Son, and the Holy Spirit; when the Buddha taught about nondiscrimination;

when Krishna met Arjuna on the battlefield to talk about karma and liberation—all of these teachers were attempting to lead seekers into an experience of unity. Instead, clunky religious doctrines grew up around the simple yet indescribable truth of unity consciousness.

The unified principle cannot be fully described. Language is a system of expression created within duality. Words attract their opposite and distort the unified principle. The best I can do is to remind you that everything in this book is intended to lead one to an experience of unity. And only experience can release us from the trap and the illusion of duality. Whether we know it or not, each one of us longs to awaken from the illusion. We "remember" unity consciousness, a state of being where all things are so deeply connected that they are no longer experienced as opposites, and therefore are not in conflict, but rather hold together in a meaningful and creative unfolding. A landscape where things aren't all-or-nothing, black-or-white, right-or-wrong. A state of grace where we hold the opposite tendencies in a light embrace of unity. Somewhere deep within we know about this other way of being; we know about unity; we remember God. And we long to return to this experience of truth. And so we search for it, but are handicapped by our own dualistic means of searching. It's as if we were trying to cross an ocean on a bicycle. No matter how hard we pedal, we won't make it. We're using the wrong vehicle. "Man strives for the fulfillment of his deep longing to transcend and find, deep with himself, a new state of consciousness in which all is one," says Pierrakos. "When he seeks this on a plane where all is divided, not only can he never find what he seeks, but he must despair and split himself further apart in conflict, because illusion creates duality."

The story of the Buddha's enlightenment is a powerful example of the pitfalls and the possibilities in our quest for unity. The Buddha, before he was the Buddha, was a prince who had been sheltered from the painful realities of life and death by his overprotective parents. It wasn't until he was a young man in his twenties, with a wife and son, and a palace replete with dancing girls and the like, that he strayed beyond the gates of the royal complex and saw with his own eyes suffering, illness, old age, and death. Stung by his discoveries, he was unable to continue his former life. He left the palace and his family, determined to understand the cause of suffering and perhaps to discover a way to inner peace and happiness.

Many of us—if we grew up in the relative protection of our parents' caretaking, innocent of the full extent of the world's pathos—can identify with the Buddha's story line thus far. It traces a common mythic journey. The innocent child grows into the young adult who discovers his own naivete. He looks more clearly at his family, starts to participate directly with human society, and experiences the pain and confusion of life in the world. Adolescence is like that stage in the Buddha's life when he feels the sting of suffering invade the cocoon of his innocence.

So overwhelmed was the Buddha by the disparity between his former life and the reality he had discovered, he spent six years as a monk, fasting and practicing the Yogic meditations of the day. In his resolve to understand suffering and death, he denied his body any source of pleasure, practically starving himself to death in the process. But it wasn't until he abandoned all extremes—first his hedonistic life in the palace, and then his severe asceticism in the forest—that he found what he was looking for. He called it the "middle way." The middle way is not either/or; it is both, and more.

It is said that the Buddha reached enlightenment upon accepting a bowl of rice and milk after a life-threatening fast. He had fully experienced the extremes of life, both self-indulgence and self-denial. From his own experimentation he slowly came to realize that in between our misperceptions (either/or consciousness) is a state of perfect balance (both), and within that balance, peace and happiness (more). Upon awakening to the truth, he uttered, "How wonderful. How wonderful. All things are enlightened exactly as they are."

The big difference between the Buddha and ourselves is what he did to achieve enlightenment. He did not only read about it or go to a few workshops or to church once a week. He took his own radical path into the wilderness of his mind and feelings and kept traveling until he was free. His goal was freedom from duality consciousness and therefore he rejected anything that kept him in an illusion of separateness. This is the model that he wanted us to follow when he devoted the rest of his life to teaching. He, and the awakened prophets before and after him, never set out to tell us what to do. Their message was to awaken from the dream of a world that is full of conflict and suffering into a different consciousness, one whose reality we can barely imagine. Many years later, in a different land, and from a different religion, C. S. Lewis spoke from Buddha's point of view when he said, "Heaven will solve our problems, but not, I think, by showing us subtle reconciliations between all our apparently contradictory notions. The notions will all be knocked from under our feet. We shall see that there never was any problem. And, more than once, that impression which I can't describe except by saying that it's like the sound of a chuckle in the darkness. The sense that some shattering and disarming simplicity is the real answer."

Teilhard de Chardin said that people who journeyed long enough on the spiritual path would discover ". . . the supreme happiness of finding themselves face to face with a unified universe." But don't make the mistake that because unity consciousness is the supreme happiness, our sense of individuality is wrong or will make us suffer. Our task as human souls is to live as individual beings in connection with others and all things. We can become more and more the individual we were made to be even as we become less and less attached to our sense of specialness. We can be unique without being better than anyone else, without being special. The dancer Martha Graham said, "There is a vitality, a life force that is translated through you into action. And because there is only one of you in all time, this expression is unique, and if you block it, it will never exist through any other medium and be lost." This is true. We can live with a passionate devotion to our uniqueness and at the same time take our place in a unified field with others and all of life. Then we will have found unity within duality—the supreme happiness.

When we discover the supreme happiness of unity within ourselves we reconcile what once seemed unreconcilable. Opposites become partners. Our longing for stability in a constantly changing world becomes humorous. Our desire for connection and our troubles with intimacy become grist for the spiritual mill. We allow diversity to flourish within the context of unity. We understand that the unadulterated, pure, singleness of feeling we long for can be experienced only when we allow all feelings to live in peace within our hearts. "Feeling," said Hazrat Inayat Khan, "is life and death at the same time." That is what enlightenment is finally about. And from that comes a fearless sort of living that allows us to delight in the koan of human existence. We stop fearing the opposite of happiness, or the opposite of success, or the opposite of love, because we no longer believe in opposites. Unity within duality reduces the sense of drama and tragedy of daily life. It cleanses the ego from its frantic search for specialness. It leaves one clean and sober, noble and happy in a broad kind of way.

When we marry the opposites, we still live passionately here on earth, we still suffer, and wonder, and grieve, but we also live somewhere else, on top of the mountain, beyond suffering. As the religious scholar Eknath

Easwaran says, "Once we enter the unitive state, our passport is good in both worlds."

The supreme happiness of unity is a hard-won treasure. Its realization and integration take patience and devotion. Although we can never really secure its illuminating presence, the more we enter its grace, the more it pervades our experience. Easwaran says, "In the unitive experience, every trace of separateness disappears; life is a seamless whole. But the body cannot remain in this state for long. After a while, awareness of mind and body returns, and then the conventional world of multiplicity rushes in again with such vigor and vividness that the memory of unity, though stamped with reality, seems as distant as a dream. The unitive state has to be entered over and over until a person is established in it. But once established, even in the midst of ordinary life, he sees the One underlying the many, the Eternal beneath the ephemeral."

KARMA AND FAITH

I yearn to understand some measure of thy truth which my heart believes and loves. For I do not seek to understand in order to have faith but I have faith in order to understand. For I believe ever this: I shall not understand unless I have faith.
—ANSELM

Karma is an Eastern term; *faith* is a Western one. In my understanding, acceptance of karma and an attitude of faith both spring from the same source, and lead to the same freedom. Both tell us that whatever happens to us happens for a reason—not a magical, mystical reason, but a rational, meaningful, and workable reason. When we view life through the lens of karma, nothing is random; everything is connected; nothing is wasted; everything has a reason and a purpose. When we have faith in the "rightness" of everything in our life, even our problems make sense and can be used. Karmic understanding leads to a faith in life. Faith is the ultimate spiritual gift; it lets us lean back and rest in the perfection of God's plan.

Karma has been misunderstood in its journey from the East to the West. It is not an occult science of predestiny. It is not exotic. Karma is really quite simple and rational: it is about action and consequences. It lays out before us a map of "what ifs" and we get to choose how we want to live. If I act with ignorance, the consequences will be painful and will create future ignorance; if I act with understanding, the consequences will be harmonious and I will feel that river flowing within, that joy of being aligned with my soul. Jesus was describing the law of karma when he said, "As ye sow, so shall ye reap." It is nothing more complex than that, except that for a Hindu or a Buddhist, the sowing part extends back eons into past lives. You don't have to believe in reincarnation to appreciate karma, although an understanding of karma makes the idea of reincarnation more believable.

One of my favorite contemporary Indian scholars and Hindu mystics is Eknath Easwaran, a brilliant interpreter of Hindu and other religious texts. Easwaran came to America as a Fulbright scholar in 1959, and later, at the University of California at Berkeley, taught the first academic course on meditation offered for credit at a major American University. His many books are well suited for the American reader and I recommend them for anyone interested in a better understanding of the law of karma and other Eastern concepts. The following passage is taken from Easwaran's translation of the Bhagavad-Gita:

> Every act or thought has consequences, which themselves will have consequences; life is the most intricate web of interconnections. This is the law of karma, one of the most important and least understood ideas in ancient Indian thought. The law of karma states simply that every event is both a cause and an effect. Every act has consequences of a similar kind, which in turn have further consequences and so on; and every act, every karma, is also the consequence of some previous karma. . . . Baldly put, the law of karma says that whatever you do will come back to you. If Joe hits Bob, and later Ralph hits Joe, that is Joe's karma coming back to him. This sounds occult because we do not see all the connections; but the connections are there, and the law of karma is no more occult than the law of gravitation. It states that that blow has to have consequences; it cannot end with Bob getting a black eye. It makes an impression on Bob's consciousness—predictably, he gets furious—and it makes an impression on Joe's consciousness as well. . . . Most people have no idea how many others are affected by their behavior and example. It gives us some idea of how complex the web of karma actually is. No one, of course, has the omniscience to see this picture fully. But the idea of a network of such connections, far from being occult, is natural and plausible. The law of karma states unequivocally that although we cannot see the connections, we can be sure that everything that happens to us, good and bad, originated once in something we did or thought. We ourselves are responsible for what happens to us, whether or not we can understand how. It follows that we can

change what happens to us by changing ourselves; we can take our destiny into our own hands. . . .

Karma is sometimes considered punitive, a matter of getting one's just deserts. This is accurate enough, but it is much more illuminating to consider karma an educative force whose purpose is to teach the individual to act in harmony with *dharma* (spiritual laws or principles)—not to pursue selfish interests at the expense of others, but to contribute to life and consider the welfare of the whole. In this sense life is like a school; one can learn, one can graduate, one can skip a grade or stay behind. As long as a debt of karma remains, however, a person has to keep coming back for further education. That is the basis of *samsara,* the cycle of birth and death.

Understanding karma motivates us to take responsibility for our actions. We begin to see that whatever happens in our life is the result of a chain of previous actions within the infinite web of all creation. Therefore, bemoaning what is happening or, conversely, being attached to what is happening is an erroneous way to live. We are not victims in an arbitrary universe, but rather participants in an intelligent and interconnected web of cause and effect. It's not just your personal karma. That's a mistaken concept. It is multiple karmas, subtly acting on each other, in an eternal dance. Scientists explain the action of multiple karmas by a theory called the "butterfly affect," whereby a butterfly flapping its delicate wings in South America can ultimately affect the weather in Japan. Similarly, your actions, as they meet up with the actions and reactions of others, create human weather systems of great consequence.

To be in touch with the multiple karmic patterns of life is the way to freedom. It allows you two things: first, it helps you understand that everything that happens to you is part of an interwoven, ever-evolving, enormous, and eternal tapestry. This understanding liberates you from pettiness. It makes it more difficult to assume victim consciousness—self-pity, resentment, anger, or vindictiveness. Second, if you train yourself to read the strands of karma, you begin to choose actions and reactions that spawn happiness and freedom as opposed to more suffering.

Karma puts the concept of destiny in a different light. As opposed to a belief that an event was destined to happen because of divine intervention, karma tells you that we can predict anything by following it back to its root action. It's the difference between things being magically fated and things happening because the awesome and intricate levels of cause and effect finally bore fruit in a certain, specific way. I used to tell my children that if something occurred it was meant to happen that way, that there was a reason for everything if they would only look below the surface of their emotional reactions. But when they became teenagers they found that explanation stupid and used all sorts of scientific theories to dispute what they considered to be my wishful way of thinking. They were completely unimpressed with my attempts to paraphrase the laws of karma.

I've discovered if you can describe how you think about complex and deep issues to your own teenagers then you must have hit upon something worth repeating. I had long ago given up using the "it was meant to happen" line with them, when my father died. Soon afterward I was with Daniel, my youngest son, at the Vermont farmhouse that had been my family home for years. Standing on the banks of a beautiful little pond that my father had dug, Daniel and I wondered why he had died so suddenly.

"Well, I guess it was meant to happen," I mused, forgetting in my grief that this was not a shared ideology.

"What do you mean, 'meant to happen'?" Daniel asked, with that familiar annoyed tone of voice. "You mean God meant it to happen so he just upped and made it happen? I don't buy that."

"No," I said wearily. I had been through this before, and was in no mood on this day to defend my beliefs to an argumentative seventeen-year-old. I sighed and looked across the pond to my father's fields. It was early spring, just before a rain, and the air smelled like that of so many walks I had taken with my father. I bent down and picked up a little stone and threw it into the still waters of the pond. The ripples spread out from the impact until the water lapped up on the banks where we stood and touched the tips of Daniel's sneakers. Suddenly I knew how to describe karma, and why I had said, "It was meant to happen."

"See the way the water changed when I threw in the rock?" I asked. "See how each ripple created another ripple, and another and another until the water hit the shore? And see how the water is calm again but your shoe is wet?"

"Yeah."

"That last ripple was meant to touch your shoe. Not because of some occult plan, but because it was written into the movement of my hand and the choice of stone and even the conversation we were having. Everything stacked up perfectly so that the ripple would touch your shoe. Everything we did this morning and everything we did yesterday affected us standing here at this pond and conspired together to create this ripple touching your shoe. In that way it was meant to happen."

"So Grandpa died last week because that's what everything he did led up to?"

"Yes. Everything we do sends out ripples. Those ripples move, intersect with other ripples, and end exactly where they were meant to—in direct proportion to the force of the initial impact. If I had thrown that rock with less force it wouldn't have touched your shoe. Something else would have happened."

"So if Grandpa had lived differently, or hadn't married Grandma, or whatever, he wouldn't have died last week. So that's all you mean?"

"Well, it's more than that. Grandpa's whole life was a rippling outward from some initial creative impact. Something threw a stone called Grandpa into the pool of the universe and ever since then Grandpa's soul has been rippling out right according to plan. The plan was written into the creative source, which extends back through his parents, his ancestors, maybe through other lifetimes. Grandpa's soul has been rippling out for I don't know how long. I happen to believe that all of our lives issued forth from the same impulse and that the ripples go on forever. And that everything that happens to us finds its cause and its meaning in that initial force. That's God, and that's karma, and that's what I mean by 'it was meant to happen.' "

Daniel didn't say anything. Being the thoughtful person that he is, though, I knew that he was digesting the information. A few days later I heard him on the phone with a friend using the ripple image to explain something he was going through. I was satisfied that he understood.

The laws of karma tell us that all actions have a reaction and that all things in the phenomenal world are connected through their overlapping karmic ripples. Once understood and embraced, karma makes us want to choose actions that lead to happiness and freedom. Instead of acting unconsciously and then suffering guilt or recrimination, we train ourselves to avoid further suffering by acting with karma in mind—by acting soulfully. There's a big difference between a prudish attitude toward life, one born of fear or imposed morality, and soulful action. Soulful action does not mean we are dry and boring people who take no risks. Rather it signifies a wide-awake understanding of reality; a conscious, moment-to-moment choosing of how we want to experience life. We can now look at past situations and see how they were affected by our own actions, by the actions of others, and by the unseen forces of karma.

Karma describes; it does not judge. Reality, just as it is, is a living description of all that came before it, all that influenced it. Within the description is not only a picture of the past influences, but also a message about how to act in the future. If we understand the law of karma we can no longer take the victim's stance. When trouble befalls us we can look for the patterns that led us to wherever we are today. We can try to follow the ripples in the pool back to the moment when the rock hit the water's surface. Even when we can't find our way back, we can trust that there is a pattern, one too intricate for our minds to follow.

Thich Nhat Hanh says that "nothing exists by itself alone. Everything has to inter-be with everything else in the cosmos. For example, if you look deeply into a flower you will also see the sun, the clouds, the seeds, the soil. Every flower is made up of these non-flower elements." This is another way to understand karma. Karma says that all actions inter-be with all other actions and therefore all things are part of each other. Everything we do affects everything. Do we want our actions to create peace and love and harmony or do we want them to contribute to more suffering? We have that choice at every moment of our lives.

It may sound like a life lived by the laws of karma is serious, interminable work. But in actuality, the most wonderful thing that can happen to us is to be saved from a life of guilt and blame by karma. When we live by the laws of karma and faith, our lives work better. We find it easier and easier to enter unity consciousness and a life of balance. Karma and faith make us both sober and lighthearted, practical and carefree. It is a great relief to stop playing the victim, to put down the useless emotions of guilt and blame, to forgive ourselves, others, and life itself.

BEAUTIFUL PROBLEMS

Ruth Dennison, an American teacher of Buddhist meditation, explains karma like this: "Karma means you don't get away with nothin'." Nothin' includes everything you do and think and intend. If you do something but your intention is not aligned with the action, you will create a problem that will reveal itself in direct proportion to the intention. For example, if you begrudgingly help someone at work but all the while you are resentful and later you speak behind his back, your begrudging attitude will have as powerful an effect as your actual deed. Both your deed and your attitude will create future karma. In this way, karma isn't about being good or bad. It's about the excellent structure of life. Whatever you do, whatever you intend, will take form in some way that you may or may not recognize later on. Therefore, if you observe closely what is happening in your daily life, you can find your own handiwork everywhere. If you don't like what is happening, you can figure out how and when you created it. You can change what you are doing now to affect the present and the future. This is good news since it is impossible to change what someone else is doing.

Our problems are descriptions of past actions. If we move beyond self-pity or self-recrimination and observe our problems as messages about our past actions, then problems become our greatest teachers. They reveal to us how to lessen our own suffering and the suffering of others. A therapist friend of mine has her clients speak to her about their "beautiful problems." She explains that each problem a client shares with her has its own story to tell and its own wisdom to reveal. Far from something to run away from, or to glibly pass over, or to be ashamed or afraid of, a problem can be tenderly and fearlessly used to end our suffering. In this way, a problem is beautiful.

I'll tell you a story about a friend of mine—Karen—whose problems did not seem at all beautiful to her. In her world, problems lived in enemy territory and were best left unexplored. I met Karen when she was in her early twenties, when she came to work on Omega's staff. An exceptionally intelligent young woman, she always seemed upbeat, healthy, and active. She loved nature and animals. She hiked and kayaked and rock climbed. During all the years that Karen worked with me, I rarely saw her in a bad mood. She was the kind of person whose sunny disposition and good health make you feel good, but also a little uneasy. Sometimes being around Karen would make me wonder about myself: "How come I'm not always in a good mood?"

I lost touch with Karen after she left Omega. When we reconnected, six years later, I could hardly believe she was the same person. She called and asked if she could visit; she said she was in a crisis and had been so for a while, but had been too ashamed to contact me, or, for that matter, any of her friends. For more than a year she had been completely alone, afraid to be with other people socially because she was depressed, overweight, and unhealthy. It seemed to her that she had lost touch with who she had once been, that she had gone from being always happy and together to being always unhappy and a mess. Before, she had never had problems, she said; now that's all she had.

When we met I asked her what had happened. She said that she had backed herself into a life situation that was impossible to escape from, yet equally impossible to stay within. Recently graduated from chiropractor school, she was working at a large health clinic to pay off the student loans and the credit cards that had kept her afloat while in school. From the beginning, she had been unhappy in the job. The way she was expected to treat her patients—quickly, and with little follow-up—went against everything she believed in. Two years into the job, she was still in debt. What was left of her salary after she paid her rent and food and car payments went to her mother, who was also ill and in debt. Her health began to deteriorate under the stress of working extra hours. She had no time to exercise or eat well or be with friends.

But this story didn't seem to explain the dramatic change in Karen—in her appearance, her attitude, her health. In passing, just as she was leaving, she told me that her father had died six years earlier, and within the same week her boyfriend also died in a freak river rafting accident. Soon afterward Karen had entered chiropractor school. I asked her how she had dealt with these losses. She said that basically she blamed herself for her boyfriend's death because they had recently separated, and she felt that she had never lived up to her father's expectations and felt vaguely guilty about his death too. But she hadn't put too much thought into these things; she had been too busy. I suggested that if she followed her life back to these events, she could probably learn a lot about her present state of affairs. Had she ever considered therapy? But Karen felt she had no time or money to spare on herself. She just needed to work harder, to "get it together."

One evening Karen ended up in the emergency room with a racing heart, and was diagnosed with a thyroid condition that required medication and rest. Her boss made it clear that if she took more days off he would have to let her go. Karen called me in the kind of panic where no matter what I said to her, all conversations led back to the same place of unworkability. If she took off from work so she could rest and heal, she would be fired and would lose her car and her apartment. What would she do then? If she stayed on at work, she would remain sick, even get worse. She hated her job, she said. "That's probably why I got sick in the first place. But there's no way I can quit now." Nothing I said of a practical nature seemed to help. We went round and round in a circle of despair and fear. After a while I stopped trying to rescue her and I just listened.

Finally, she said, "Can you give me some inspiration? I need something to hang on to or I'm afraid I'm going to go under." I took a deep breath and closed my eyes and said the first thing that came to me: "Lean back. Just take a deep breath and lean back into God's arms. Something greater than your fear is holding you now and will keep holding you. You can rest in that embrace. You have to have that faith. You have to lean back and rest in that faith."

On the other end of the phone line I heard my friend crying. Her voice had wavered a few times previously in the conversation, but now she broke down. "I don't deserve to lean on God," she wept. "I got myself into this stupid situation. I'll have to use my own smarts to get myself out of it. I'm the one who's so untogether. I must have done something pretty bad to deserve this mess. That's what scares me. I'm about to lose my job, and then I'll have to give up my home and my car. What about my dog? Who will help my mother? I'm going to lose everything because I blew it. This is punishment; this is karma."

"That's a very unhelpful, unkind voice to listen to," I told her. "And it's only going to lead you into a deeper mess. This is definitely karma, but karma is not punishment. Karma tells you how you ended up where you are. It's not blame. It's just information. Some of the situation you're in came from your own choices and actions; some came from your boss's actions; some from your parents' actions, and even from people's actions you don't know. How can you blame yourself for such a big mess?

"Take a deep breath," I said, taking one myself, "try to let go of blaming yourself, and lean back. A few times every day when you feel your heart racing and your panic rising, just stop thinking and worrying, and literally lean back into God's embrace. Imagine yourself being held. Trust that everything will be all right, that it already is all right, that nothing is an impossible situation. No mess is too big to get through. Rest in that faith and then see what happens next."

"I don't think that's such a good idea," Karen said. "I have to keep my wits about me; I have to figure this out. I can't just stop thinking and have faith that everything is going to turn out."

"You can lean back and have faith, *and* you can be smart about how to proceed. It's not either/or. But if you don't lean back first, you're going to keep spinning your wheels and clouding your mind with blame and fear. You can have faith or you can have fear, and I can assure you that faith is a lot more helpful than fear."

My friend reluctantly agreed to try this, careful to point out to me that she couldn't trust too much, that she had to stay alert or things might fall apart. I assured her that she could do both, that trust and vigilance were not mutually exclusive. "Remember what the Sufis say," I told her. "Trust in God, but tie your camel."

Some people mistake faith for magical thinking or for a lack of intelligence. But faith is really the ultimate intelligence, because it is an acknowledgment of the truth: we don't really know how to get ourselves out of our biggest messes, or even how we got ourselves into them. At a certain point even the smartest person cannot figure out how to handle life's most complex issues. Faith is giving over to a greater intelligence—aligning our intelligence with the mind of God—and praying for the strength to trust.

A few weeks later Karen called me again. Things had gone from bad to worse. She had been diagnosed with Graves' disease—a serious autoimmune condition that affects the thyroid—and had been told that if she didn't pursue immediate treatment with radiation therapy she could die. By this time, she was no longer working and could barely get out of bed. Her rent was due; her car payments were overdue. She had no medical insurance.

She asked me, "Is this what faith in God gets you?"

"Do you have faith in God?" I asked her.

"I feel too sick and scared to have faith in anything. I don't want to have radiation treatment. I'll have to be on unnatural hormones and medication for the rest of my life. I believe in natural medicine." We had entered the circle of fear again.

"What's more natural," I asked, "dying from Graves' disease or receiving radiation treatment? And where do you think the radioactive iodine comes from anyway—Mars? It comes from here, planet earth, the same place that brings you herbs and organic food and vitamins. Maybe God is offering you, in the form of medical science, a chance to heal and live, a chance to get strong again and help others heal. You have no other choice now than to accept that you have a serious disease. You need radical treatment or you'll die. Your karma has led you right here to this beautiful problem. You can't go back. But you can go forward in a new way. You can learn from your past actions and reactions and begin to create something different. First you have to line yourself up with reality; you have to accept where you are and trust that even in the midst of your confusion and pain there is wisdom to be gained. You can use what you have been handed for the kind of inner growth that will make your life happier and more meaningful."

Talking with Karen over the next few days, I came up with a six-step process that she could use to get her through the next difficult weeks:

The Karma and Faith Process

1. Quiet your mind.
2. Forgive yourself, others, and God.
3. Ask for help.
4. Lean back.
5. Listen to your beautiful problems.
6. Give back to others.

First, I asked her to practice *quiet mind.* "Every time a thought of anger or anxiety comes to the surface—like 'Why did this happen to me?' or 'How will I pay the rent?'—take a cleansing breath and imagine your mind as a calm pool of water," I told her. "Just do that over and over and see what happens."

Next I asked her to do the second step: to *practice forgiveness*—forgiveness of herself and of God. "Forgive yourself for whatever you did to get Graves' disease, and forgive God for whatever you didn't do—for the overlapping karmic actions of others; for environmental factors; for your parents' genes. Breathe in a gentle breeze of forgiveness toward yourself, and breathe out a gentle breeze of forgiveness toward God. Feel yourself surrounded by the warmth of forgiveness."

I told Karen to spend the next couple of days practicing quiet mind and forgiveness of self and others. With a quiet mind and an open heart, step number three, *Ask for help,* comes more easily. I had already suggested that Karen call on friends for financial and logistical help, and for emotional support. She said she felt too ashamed of her health and helplessness to reach out. I told Karen that once she had let the tiniest bit of forgiveness into her heart, her shame and guilt would lessen. Forgiveness is a mighty tonic. It neutralizes self-blame and blame of others. It's easier to see into what you need and how to go about getting your needs met if you aren't blaming yourself or others for your problems. You can then reach out and ask others to help you get through a difficult time. You can ask God to help you too. You'll see that you're not alone, that others have suffered too, and that compassionate friends and a compassionate God are there for you to lean on.

I told Karen, "Call your sister and see if she will front you a month's rent. Call your neighbor and ask him to watch your dog while you recover. Call your friends and ask one of them to drive you to the hospital. Pray to God for peace of mind and strength of heart to get through these dark days."

Step number four is to *Lean back* into God's perfect plan with willingness and faith. "You can practice this," I told Karen, "by sitting on the edge of your bed, spreading your arms wide open, closing your eyes, and imagining that you are surrendering to whatever God has in store for you. Assume that God is there to catch you, just as sure as the bed is there to catch you. Now actually lean back slowly until you are resting on the bed. As you lean back, let your fear and helplessness go; trust that you will be held. Then lie on your back with your arms spread open, feeling the bed supporting you. Whenever you feel anxious during the day, take a few minutes to practice leaning back on the bed. You may think otherwise, but I assure you that the wisest action comes after you have practiced quiet mind and forgiveness, and when you are leaning back into God's perfect plan."

It's when we are leaning back and resting gently in faith that we can ask our beautiful problems to speak to us and to teach us about ourselves. If we try to listen to our problems when we are anxious and fearful we will only beget more problems. Step number five—*Listen to your beautiful problems*—won't work if you're full of self-blame and worry. In Karen's case, there was no use considering the deeper problems (the death of her father, the death of her boyfriend, her shame and isolation) before she came to terms with her immediate anxieties and fears around her illness and treatment. So I told Karen to make some progress with the first four steps before she entered into dialogue with the full range of her beautiful problem. She would know when she had the presence of heart and mind to begin step number five.

Karen listened intently to my "karma and faith process." She had come to the end of the line—she realized that her resistance to facing reality could actually cause her to die. Fortunately, this shook her up; she knew she had to do something different. Before we got off the phone Karen said to me, "You said it was a six-step process. What's the sixth step?" I told her that I would tell her the last step after her radiation treatment and after she was feeling better. A few weeks later she called me again. She had gone through the treatment. It had been a difficult and frightening time. But she was already feeling stronger, and she was also feeling strangely expanded and more alive than she had in years. She had used the five steps and learned a lot about herself in the process. "Like what?" I asked her.

"Well, I learned about my lack of self-forgiveness and how that cuts me off from life and other people. I learned that ever since my father and my boyfriend died I have been running away from myself. The farther I ran, the more lost I became. If I wasn't running, I was beating myself up. I just never had the courage to stop and look at my problems head-on. You'd call them my beautiful problems. I understand that now. I understand a lot of what you meant, I think. Like that my fears were keeping me from the truth, that faith is more helpful than fear. And one last thing—I learned about how wonderful the doctors and nurses in the hospital are. I am very grateful to them. I'm actually grateful to my Graves' disease, if you can believe that. I've grown so much through all of this. I don't think I ever would have learned about beautiful problems, about karma and faith without this crisis. And I don't think you can really live a happy life without looking squarely at your problems, and without some kind of faith. I want to give some of this back to other people. I want to help other people going through this kind of stuff. So many people helped me."

"Remember that sixth step you were wondering about?" I asked Karen.
"Yeah?"
"Well, you figured it out yourself. It's giving back. It's being so filled with trust in God's plan that you want others to have that same kind of peace. The sixth step is giving back."

After Karen had healed and stabilized, she decided to become the kind of chiropractor who does more than crack bones. She wants to use her gifts to help people really heal, to help them use their health crises as beautiful problems, to show them how to lean back into God's perfect plan. Now that her health is better, she is going back to school for more training.

Following the trail of karma leads to the full and true picture of reality. It's a demanding trail to follow, but it leads to the heart of the matter: truth. "Truth is what you're meant to be, but haven't yet perhaps become," I heard the British Catholic nun Sister Wendy say in an interview with Bill Moyers. Many people know Sister Wendy from her televised art history series. But Sister Wendy is much more than an eccentric art historian. She is also a genuine, open-minded seeker of spiritual truth, and a generous teacher and guide. "Truth is what God made you to be," she says, "all your qualities fulfilled, no dead sections that you are afraid to work with ahead of you, no areas of negligence that you just didn't bother to take seriously. . . . To be human means we have to be open all the time to experience, to receive it, to grow by it, to use it. One of the things that I most hope when I die is that God won't say, 'Well, I sent you a lot of experiences and you just lived through them; you didn't use them.' Which is the easy thing to do: just to endure them, to let them pass, to suffer or to enjoy . . . but, not to have used them, not to have grown by them. It's demanding to be human."

In the next chapter—"A Soulfulness Toolbox"—I offer means and methods for the demanding work of being human. The journey to the Landscape of the Soul leads us back into the world, where we can test the genuineness of our spiritual experiences. What is the proof that our experiments with different states of consciousness have "worked"? How do we know if we have really communed with God? The best proof is if our "I am" experiences are actually useful. Why have religions always set down commandments of moral, just, and loving behavior? Why have they told us to forgive and to serve each other? Because this is what communion with God does: it expands our sense of self to include others; it expands our capacities to love. A genuine experience of God makes us want to give, to share, to care, to commune with others in the ways in which we have communed with God. An experience of the sacred naturally evokes the kind of moral behavior that religions try to enforce—not immediately, but eventually, and radically. We become radicals, extremists—the kind of extremists that Joan of Arc, Gandhi, and Martin Luther King, Jr., became. Our actions come not from what we've been told to do, but from within.

In "Letter from Birmingham Jail," Martin Luther King wrote, "Though I was initially disappointed at being categorized as an extremist, as I continued to think about the matter, I eventually gained a measure of satisfaction from the label. Was not Jesus an extremist for love? 'Love your enemies, bless them that curse you.' Was not Amos an extremist for justice? 'Let justice roll down like waters, and righteousness like an ever flowing stream.' Will we be extremists for hate or for love?" In the last chapter we bring our experience of soulfulness into the Landscape of the World. We take up the challenge of becoming "extremists for love."

16 | A Soulfulness Toolbox

What struck me most was the silence. It was a great silence, unlike any I have en-
countered on Earth, so vast and deep that I began to hear my own body: my heart
beating, my blood vessels pulsing, even the rustle of my muscles moving over each
other seemed audible. There were more stars in the sky than I had expected. The sky
was deep black, yet at the same time bright with sunlight. The Earth was small, light
blue, and so touchingly alone, our home that must be defended like a holy relic. The
Earth was absolutely round. I believe I never knew what the word "round" meant
until I saw Earth from space.
    —ALEKSEI LEONOV

The journey through the Landscape of the Soul changes one's perspective
in the same way that the Russian astronaut Aleksei Leonov meant when he
said, "I believe I never knew what the word 'round' meant until I saw
Earth from space." Seeing ourselves and the world from the heights of
spiritual insight makes everything more *real*. It's not so much that anything changes; rather, things become more fully what they already are. We
don't transform ourselves; we become ourselves. And the more fully we
step into reality, the more we want to defend the earth like a "holy relic,"
the more we want to become, in Dr. King's words, "extremists for love."

   We journey into the Landscape of the Soul so that our life here in the
world might reflect the unity and love we touched on in our communion

with God. We don't go to the Landscape of the Soul to escape, just as the astronauts didn't leave earth with the hope of never coming back. Wherever we go on our spiritual journey, all roads lead back to our humanness—to the body, to the mind, to relationships, to our purpose in the world. The poet Wallace Stevens wrote, "The way through the world is more difficult to find than the way beyond it." In this chapter we look at some ways to help us go "through the world."

Perhaps the most valuable gift we bring back with us from the Landscape of the Soul is the knowledge of duality consciousness and unity consciousness. Every experience I have had of unity consciousness—whether through meditation and prayer, long retreats, and other consciousness-expanding practices, or through occasions of grace in nature and with people—has increased my ability to enjoy life in the world. An experience of unity consciousness does two things: it makes us fearless regarding death, and it makes us appreciative of life. If we know that duality consciousness is not the full picture of our soul's reality, but rather an interesting, temporary, creative experiment, we can relax more on this stage of the soul's journey. If we know that in duality consciousness we have a choice at all times—to experience suffering or freedom, pain or pleasure, hate or love, alienation or connection—we begin to want to choose actions that generate goodness and happiness. If we understand that the whole point of the dualistic realm is to teach our souls to work wisely with karma, life in the world loses its sense of painful drama and begins to feel more like a fascinating education.

A deep understanding of duality consciousness and a genuine experience of unity consciousness open our eyes to the ways of the world. We are touched just as the Russian astronaut was touched by seeing the earth from space. The ways of the world—including the violence and cruelty and ugliness of human actions—no longer confuse us; rather, human behavior—our own and others'—touches our hearts and makes us want to choose goodness in our own lives and to help others do the same in theirs. An experience of unity consciousness leads us to the same moral behavior that religions dictate for their followers. The difference is that when we ourselves choose, from the depth of experience, goodness over evil, we *become* good. If, instead, we do merely what we are told, we layer goodness over unhealed parts of ourselves. This rarely has the desired effect of making peace—inner peace or peace in the world.

Real peacemakers do not hate the hatred in others; they do not make war in their hearts against war. Real peacemakers start with an understanding of the nature of life. Understanding leads organically to a far-reaching and healing sense of forgiveness—forgiveness of one's own imperfections, and of the imperfections of others, and of the world.

FORGIVENESS

*To understand all
is to forgive all.*
  —VOLTAIRE

Once I heard the Vietnamese Zen monk Thich Nhat Hanh say, "*Le paradis est maintenant ou jamais,*" which, in French, as you may know, is "Paradise is now or never." On this occasion I observed him sitting under a maple tree on a perfect autumn day, leading a meditation for a small group of Vietnam War veterans. Thich Nhat Hanh, called Thay by his students, has a poignant voice: it is soft and wise, but it is also playful. It is tinged with sadness, and it is profoundly peaceful. *Le paradis est maintenant ou jamais.* Thay repeated this phrase a few times and then instructed the veterans to sit in silence. Looking around me at the carpet of blazing leaves and the clear blue sky, it was not hard to understand the concept. Here in paradise it was obvious that what stood between myself and happiness was the content of my own mind and heart.

But what about people whose suffering is greater than mine? I wondered. What about people who aren't sitting in a maple grove, well fed physically and spiritually? What about those who must endure war and poverty and abuse? How do *they* reconcile their karma? As I meditated on these thoughts, I opened my eyes and looked straight into the eyes of Thich Nhat Hanh. He was smiling at me, answering my questions with his smile. Thay had witnessed the kind of brutality I could only imagine, and he was smiling. Born in Vietnam in 1926, he became a Buddhist monk at the age of sixteen, and lived through years of war that ravaged his country and his people. Throughout those years he devoted his life to helping victims of war cope with overwhelming suffering. He lost family members, witnessed torture, and risked his own life as he tried to exert political pressure through peaceful resistance. Exiled from Vietnam for his leadership of the Vietnamese Buddhist Peace Delegation, he was nominated by Martin Luther King, Jr., for a Nobel Peace Prize.

Thich Nhat Hanh has never stopped working for peace—peace in the world, and peace within the hearts and minds of people. His personal history makes his present demeanor even more remarkable, for he is the most peaceful person I have ever encountered. His infrequent visits to America attract thousands of people who want merely to sit in the presence of a small, quiet man who practices what he calls "being peace."

Le paradis est maintenant ou jamais. Paradise is now or never. When Thay smiled at me I understood what this means. Humans are just inches away from paradise, but that last inch is as wide as an ocean. That inch is forgiveness. Who should know this more than Thich Nhat Hanh? People like Thay—Gandhi, Martin Luther King, Mother Teresa, the Dalai Lama—have crossed the ocean-wide inch by forgiving. That is why their words are so moving and why we want to be in their midst. Their presence teaches us how to be in paradise. Dag Hammarskjöld, who won the Nobel Peace Prize for his work as the secretary-general of the United Nations, said, "Forgiveness is a miracle by which what is broken is made whole and what is soiled is again made clean." Someone who was successful at making peace between nations should know what works and what doesn't work.

Voltaire said, "To understand all is to forgive all." The more we understand how our karma intersects with the karma of others, and how all karma exists in a web of meaningfulness, the easier it becomes to forgive ourselves and others. But forgiveness is an action, not an idea. We *understand* karma; we *practice* forgiveness. Like any difficult task we undertake, forgiveness requires both understanding and skill. And like any skill, it takes time and practice to strengthen our ability to forgive.

At a recent retreat with Stephen and Ondrea Levine, I participated in the following forgiveness meditation. I had heard Stephen lead this meditation before, but now he added something that struck me as particularly wise. As usual, he helped us relax and then guided us to invite into our awareness a person we wanted to forgive. This time he added a warning. "Don't invite in the 'three-hundred-pound weight,'" he said. "If you were just starting out in weight training at the gym, would you try to lift three hundred pounds? If you want to learn how to forgive, don't start out with Hitler or your uncle who sexually abused you."

Many of us assume that if we start with the big guys, then later we'll be able to forgive anyone. If the Dalai Lama can forgive the Chinese, if Martin Luther King could forgive the white bigots, well, then, I should be able to forgive Hitler. Instead, what happens is that without building up our forgiveness muscle, we just strain our hearts and end up feeling like a failure, or that the whole idea of forgiveness is preposterous. "To rush healing," Stephen said at this retreat, "is to do violence to the self." Instead, he suggested inviting someone into our meditation who is more easily forgivable—the bus driver who wouldn't stop this morning in the pouring rain; the person in the car in front of us driving 35 mph and not letting us pass; the rude waitress; the pushy guy who broke in line.

That's a good idea, I thought, as I slipped into a calm, meditative awareness. "Now invite into your consciousness the person you want to forgive," Stephen said. And, of course, even though he had just warned against the three-hundred-pound weight, I invited in my ex-husband—certainly not a Hitler, but one of the weightier people in my life, nonetheless. As the meditation proceeded, I struggled with three hundred pounds of history, barely hearing anything that Stephen said. "I should be able to handle this," I kept telling myself. "Why waste this precious retreat on a lightweight?" But soon I was sinking, pulled downward into old grievances and familiar ways of resisting forgiveness: "What he did was *wrong*! He doesn't deserve forgiveness. He needs to ask *me* for forgiveness, etc., etc."

As I stewed in my uncharitable feelings, I heard Stephen Levine say, as if in whisper, "*It is so painful to put someone out of your heart.*" Yes, I could viscerally feel that right now. So, I took Stephen's original advice. I let my ex-husband go from my consciousness for the time being, and picked up a situation that weighed a lot less. I focused on one of my sons' teachers toward whom I had harbored resentment for what I believed to be unfair treatment. I brought this person into my heart as Stephen led the following meditation.

A FORGIVENESS MEDITATION
From **Healing into Life and Death,**
Stephen and Ondrea Levine
(To be read slowly to a friend or silently to oneself.)

Begin to reflect for a moment on what the word "forgiveness" might mean. What is forgiveness? What might it be to bring forgiveness into one's life, into one's mind?

Begin by slowly bringing into your mind, into your heart, the image of someone

for whom you have some resentment. Gently allow a picture, a feeling, a sense of them to gather there. Gently now invite them into your heart just for this moment.

Notice whatever fear or anger may arise to limit or deny their entrance and soften gently all about it. No force. Just an experiment in truth which invites this person in.

And silently in your heart say to this person, "I forgive you."

Open to a sense of their presence and say, "I forgive you for whatever pain you may have caused me in the past, intentionally or unintentionally, through your words, your thoughts, your actions. However you may have caused me pain in the past, I forgive you."

Feel for even a moment the spaciousness relating to that person with the possibility of forgiveness.

Let go of those walls, those curtains of resentment, so that your heart may be free. So that your life may be lighter.

"I forgive you for whatever you may have done that caused me pain, intentionally or unintentionally, through your actions, through your words, even through your thoughts, through whatever you did. Through whatever you didn't do. However the pain came to me through you, I forgive you. I forgive you."

It is so painful to put someone out of your heart. Let go of that pain. Let them be touched for this moment at least with the warmth of your forgiveness.

Allow that person to just be there in the stillness, in the warmth and patience of the heart. Let them be forgiven. Let the distance between you dissolve in mercy and compassion.

Let it be so.

Now, having finished so much business, dissolved in forgiveness, allow that being to go on their way. Not pushing or pulling them from the heart, but simply letting them be on their own way, touched by a blessing and the possibility of your forgiveness. . . ."

When people shared after the meditation was over, it was easy to see why Stephen had warned against tackling the three-hundred-pounder. It seems that most of the participants in the room were as impatient as I had been and had invited into their hearts the heaviest of their burdens. Those who shared were tied up in mental knots, having used the period of meditation to wrestle with situations way too complex and heavy for their abilities. One woman had indeed tried to forgive Hitler and engaged the group in a long argument against forgiveness.

It was later, the night after the retreat, that the fruits of my work were served to me in a dream. That night, at home in my own bed, I dreamed that I was with my ex-husband and a group of people who were all involved in the same work project. Several people were attempting to lead the group, and one after the other proved to be ineffective, even destructive. Finally my ex-husband rose and took up the task and a sense of relief was felt throughout the group. We all saw his goodness and trusted him. Suddenly a wave of loving forgiveness overtook me. Why had I hardened myself to his inner goodness all these years? Did I really need to keep the iron curtain drawn between us? In the dream I went up to him and took his hands. I looked into his eyes and said, "I forgive you. I forgive you." A new and profound feeling of letting go washed over me.

Then I asked him, "Will you forgive me?"

He looked surprised and answered, "Yes, I will." Then we hugged, and I saw, as if in a movie clip, vignettes from our life together: riding the bus in New York City and reading aloud to each other; watching his beautiful hands touch the translucent skin of a newborn's face; appreciating his quick mind and his courageous leadership; sharing our love and concern for our children. I saw all of this, but none of the shadows that I usually chose to focus on.

That was the dream. For days afterward I felt that my heart had grown more spacious. The feeling of letting go of an anger and resentment that I carried for so many years was sweet and liberating. The dream had said it all—a hard heart that keeps a vigilant eye on the past cannot see the truth of the present. Resistance to forgiveness will not change what has already happened, and more important, it won't contribute to change now—in yourself or in those you won't forgive. Forgiveness is a healing balm and also a truth sayer. When forgiveness melts the heart, and when the turbulent waters settle and clear, you are left with the truth of the matter. You are aligned with karma, in touch with the whole story—the light and the shadow. Now you can choose how to be and act in ways that make your life work better. Forgiveness is a very rational act.

The process of forgiving that I began first in the Levines' workshop, and then in the dream, had lasting effects in daily life. From these imaginative activities—a meditation and a dream—a struggle that had been dominating my life for more than ten years began to shift. I had tried to forgive my ex-husband before, tackling my resistance as if I were a fighter in the ring. But I wasn't ready. I hadn't developed my forgiveness muscles sufficiently. You will be greatly rewarded on the spiritual path by forgiveness, but only if you take it step by step. Start with self-forgiveness, then build up slowly.

Some of you may have been deeply wounded in life by cruel and unjust people. You may need to take the tiniest steps toward forgiveness. "Please don't invite in the three-hundred-pounder—the rapist, the abuser, the cruel, the unjust—when the practice is in its infancy," Stephen Levine advises. "Let the practice build over time to eventually touch these profound wounds with the deepest possible mercy."

Forgiveness of others starts with self-forgiveness. Jung said this: "That I feed the hungry, that I forgive an insult, that I love my enemy in the name of Christ—all these are undoubtedly great virtues. What I do unto the least of my brethren, that I do unto Christ. But what if I should discover that the least among them all, the poorest of all the beggars, the most imprudent of all offenders, the very enemy himself—that these are within me, and I myself stand in the need of the alms of my own kindness—that I am the enemy who must be loved—what then?"

What then? Self-forgiveness is difficult for many people. We are so hard on ourselves, so unforgiving of our human imperfections. It's no wonder that it is difficult for us to give alms of kindness to others, to forgive others for their imperfect acts. We are in the need of the alms of our own kindness. You can use the Levines' meditation with yourself. It is a powerful exercise to invite yourself back into your own heart. Instead of beating yourself up, instead of feeling guilty, instead of hardening yourself to the world, you let waves of merciful awareness wash over your heart. You see yourself for who you really are—imperfect, willing to learn from your mistakes, ever-evolving into who you were meant to be. Don't reject yourself. Admit your imperfections. Forgive yourself for being human. And then try again. Life is ever-forgiving.

WORKING WITH TEACHERS AND THERAPISTS

Furthermore we have not even to risk the adventure alone, for the heroes of all time have gone before us. The labyrinth is thoroughly known. We have only to follow the thread of the hero path, and where we had thought to find an abomination, we shall find a god. And where we had thought to slay another, we shall slay ourselves. Where we had thought to travel outward, we will come to the center of our own existence. And where we had thought to be alone, we will be with all the world.

—JOSEPH CAMPBELL

Here is some good news about the journey through the Landscape of the Soul and through all of the landscapes already explored in this book— the choppy waters of mindfulness, the paradoxical terrain of the heart, the primal territory of the body. You don't have to go it alone. There are guides for these journeys. Yes, once in the waters you are in your own boat, and on the land you walk your own path, but the voyage has been made before. "We have not even to risk the adventure alone," writes Joseph Campbell, "for the heroes of all time have gone before us." Learning from these heroes is one of the most splendid and challenging aspects of the spiritual path.

Once I invited an old friend who had no experience with meditation or spirituality to join a retreat at Omega led by Thich Nhat Hanh. For years I had hesitated to bring this friend to an Omega program. A high-strung, high-powered music producer from New York City, his cynicism and wit were on the level of a caustic stand-up comic. I just couldn't imagine him being able to handle the peace or the people at Omega. But recently my friend had been experiencing a serious stress-induced illness, and if anyone could reach him, I thought it was Thich Nhat Hanh.

More than eight hundred people had gathered at Omega to be with Thich Nhat Hanh this time—a splendid Indian summer weekend in October, the kind that makes living in the Northeast worth every other miserable, cold winter day. My friend reluctantly agreed to take part in the retreat, commenting that sitting still with a Vietnamese monk was probably deserved punishment for choosing to go to a rock concert instead of an anti-war march back in 1968. I stood in the parking lot waiting for him, drinking in the deep blue sky and the brilliant sunshine, the orange and brown leaves of the maples and oaks, the golden bees in the late flower gardens. Hovering with the autumnal beauty was a peacefulness that always gathers around people in a meditation retreat.

My friend arrived characteristically late, just as the program was about to begin. As he got out of his sleek black car and rushed to greet me, Thich Nhat Hanh was walking with a Vietnamese nun in the opposite direction toward the lecture hall. Monk and nun walked slowly and silently in their simple brown robes—two autumn leaves against the blue sky.

My friend stopped in his tracks, watched the two approach, and bowed his head as they passed, a very uncharacteristic move on his part. No words were shared. He turned and continued to observe Thich Nhat Hanh and the nun make their steady progress toward the hall. An American Zen teacher, Richard Baker Roshi, has described the way Thich Nhat

Hanh moves as "a cross between a cloud, a snail, and a piece of heavy machinery—a true religious presence."

When I reached him, my friend was still standing in the same spot, head slightly bowed. His hand was over his heart. "What was that?" he asked.

"That was not a what," I said. "That was Thich Nhat Hanh."

"Wow," he said. "That was weird. I felt as if I couldn't move. That guy was so, so . . . slow!" These were the only words he could find to describe the energy he felt coming from Thich Nhat Hanh. Perhaps it was the marked contrast of his own rushed drive from New York City; perhaps it was the visual impact of a Buddhist monk and nun walking through a glorious fall day; but whatever it was, my friend was never the same. He sat patiently in the lecture hall in silence, surrounded by people whom he usually would have torn to shreds with snide remarks. He listened intently to Thich Nhat Hanh's simple words. From that day on he began to change the pace and the texture of his life.

This is one of those conversion stories that can be misleading, and yet it is also a common one. Many people are moved to change their lives only through contact with another person who has indeed changed his or her own life. Had I given my friend one of Thich Nhat Hanh's books he probably would not have read it. Even if he had, and even if the book had inspired him to meditate, he would not have had the same powerful experience. The effect of Thich Nhat Hanh brushing by him was similar to what the Hindus call *shaktipat,* or "the touch of the Guru." It is really quite a simple thing—as simple, and as mysterious, as falling in love, and also as dangerous.

Whenever I am asked about my spiritual path, I find myself first speaking about my teachers, the men and women who have guided me on the journey, the ones who have taught me about self-discovery, heartfulness, and unity consciousness. Sometimes I have tried to leave them out of the story. I want the teachings to stand for themselves, to show up as the simple treasures that they are, unencumbered by confusing personalities and the all too human foibles of charismatic teachers, therapists, or religious masters. As an American, I am touchy about authority figures, especially spiritual leaders and the blind faith they engender. Yet I can't do justice to the complex simplicity of the spiritual journey without referring to the people who helped me chart my course.

Here, then, is one of the most treacherous paradoxes of the spiritual path: the purpose of the journey is to move beyond an ego-based reality;

to expand out of duality consciousness; to release our attachment to a limited sense of self so that the truth can bowl us over on a daily basis. Why then would we want to get messed up with someone else's ego, as surely we will if we engage with a living teacher? Why would we want to subject ourselves to the sticky mass-ego of a spiritual group, which usually congeals around a spiritual teacher? The answer is as mystifying as the answer to the perennial question about love: Why do we fall in love when romantic love leads to such grief? Because it's there? Because we can't know love without a lover?

Comparing a spiritual teacher or a psychotherapist with a beloved friend is more appropriate than comparing him or her with a mentor or a university teacher. For the relationship between a disciple and a student to bear fruits there has to be a level of intimacy, trust, and respect—the same emotional qualities that one usually brings to friendship or family relationships or romantic love. And herein lies one of the dangers of the student/teacher relationship. It takes a mature person to give his or her heart to a teacher without projecting all sorts of impossible needs onto that teacher. Yet most of us are not yet emotionally or spiritually mature when we seek a teacher. In fact, we engage with a teacher in order to become mature.

Psychology calls this fundamental problem *transference*. A good therapist is trained to deal with the inevitability of transference. She knows that a client sees her through the lens of his own needs and family history. She knows how to help the client understand the nature of transference and how it relates to larger issues of authority, responsibility, and self-respect. She may, for the sake of the therapy, allow the client to transfer his feelings about his parents or his siblings or his wife onto her, but eventually she will help the client free himself from the illusion of transference, and in doing so she will help him immeasurably in all of his relationships. Unfortunately, many therapists lack this skill. They may end up engaging in their own form of transference—called *countertransference*—where they project their own needs for adoration and acceptance onto the client.

While transference and countertransference are common in the therapeutic relationship, they are rampant in the disciple/teacher relationship. Spiritual teachers and religious leaders are not properly trained to debunk the guru myth once it has developed. Religious literature doesn't say much about the psychology of disciples elevating their teachers to Godlike status, and teachers acting like God. Zen wisdom deals with the subject with this little ditty: "When you meet the Buddha on the road, kill him!" This is not easy! Especially when your Buddha figure is called Father or Mother, as is done in many of the religious traditions.

You might conclude, then, that it would be much safer to let lofty ideas and time-honored books be your guides on the spiritual path. But I disagree. From my own experience, and from observation of and discussions with many other spiritual seekers—those who chose a path similar to mine and those within traditional religious organizations—I have concluded that contact and study with an experienced spiritual guide is of such great value to the seeker that it ultimately outweighs the negatives. What I gained from my teachers did indeed come with a price. But it was worth it. Even though I have made a few dumb mistakes, even though I have been deeply disillusioned by the ways in which some of my teachers have lived their lives, even though the in-fighting and power plays of spiritual groups have made me wary of belonging to any church, I still believe that I got farther on the path through the guidance of my teachers than had I made the journey alone.

When I am stuck or depressed or scared, it's not the words I have read in a book that I turn to. I conjure up the memory of my teachers when I need a helping hand. I go back to moments spent in the presence of Pir Vilayat—singing under his direction in a choir; following his flights of fancy in a guided meditation; noticing how light seemed to emanate from him, and how his hands and his white beard and hair quivered with energy. I remember the soft and powerful voice of Marion Woodman, the Jungian analyst who taught me to cherish and trust my womanhood. I see myself sitting with Chögyam Trungpa Rinpoche and laughing at his preposterous heart and brilliant mind. I think back on the time when I went to therapy every week and was held in the healing embrace of my therapist's wisdom. I think about the kindness of my first Zen teacher; about the joy of being with a teacher as honest as Ram Dass; about a Yogi from India who didn't speak because he said words got him into trouble. I close my eyes and see him writing on the small chalkboard that he used to communicate. I remember the purity and power of his silence and the scratching sounds of the chalk, but not a word that he wrote. I remember looking into the ecstatic eyes of an Iranian dervish who taught me the ancient Sufi whirling practice; dancing on the tables with Rabbi Zalman Schachter; praying with Brother David Steindl-Rast, a Benedictine monk whose warmth and genuineness filled me with hope. Like a compass in my pocket, I keep the essence of my teachers with me always on the journey.

But please don't get all starry-eyed. Each one of my teachers was and is a real human being with many of the same faults that belong to me and you. In the early stages of my journey I recognized my teachers' short-comings only after the pedestal we cocreated shattered and fell. Later on, I approached teachers with more maturity. If we are mature, we'll enter into a relationship with a teacher with our eyes wide open to their human-ness. If we are naive, a disciple/teacher relationship will teach us many spiritual truths, but inevitably the most important lesson we'll learn is how to "kill the Buddha on the road"—or in less dramatic words, how to find the Buddha within ourselves.

The wisdom that teachers possess lives within each one of us. A wise man or woman does not have anything you yourself do not already have or cannot develop. You have probably heard this before. But these are not empty words. They are as true as the wisdom you may hope to gain from studying with a teacher. Often the only ingredient separating the teacher from the student is the ability to articulate wisdom, *not* the wisdom itself. A good teacher may indeed only be that: a good *teacher,* one who naturally possesses the quickness of mind to assimilate knowledge and the charm and theatrical sense necessary to transmit information. I am not slighting these skills. They are rare gifts. The mistake we all make is when we as-sume that a good spiritual teacher is therefore someone who practices everything he preaches, or whose whole life is exemplary.

It is difficult to tolerate the hypocrisy of a powerful person who does not demonstrate the same behavior that he prescribes—like celibacy, or generosity, or merely honest and loving conduct in daily life. The gap be-tween a teacher's words and his actions can be enormous and very dis-turbing. Just as in the old stories in which the cobbler's children go barefoot, and in the newer stories where the psychiatrist's kids are messed up, so too do many students feel betrayed by their spiritual teachers' in-ability to live what they teach. But the real roots of our disturbance is the misconception that we are the cobbler's children. If we enter into a rela-tionship with a teacher expecting to find a skillful and articulate friend, then we will be less disappointed when she or he exhibits common human failings. If we expect to find the mother or father we always wanted, we are destined for disappointment.

Teachers may talk with God, but they are not God. They may have walked farther up the path than you have, but they are not the path. They may have the kind of razor-sharp vision to peer through the mists of the mind and the heaviness of the heart, but they may not know how to put into practice the gifts of their knowledge. As a young student I found this hard to accept of my teachers. How could it be that my meditation teacher, Chögyam Trungpa Rinpoche, died from complications due to alcoholism? If his meditation techniques and philosophy really worked, then why did he need to drown his anxiety in drink? And why did Pir Vilayat, a master in a tradition that most reveres an open and loving heart, have problems sharing his heart with others? What about the stories of the TV evangelists who preach generosity and then pocket the faithful's donations, or the "celibate" monk who secretly has sex with his students?

Remember Esalen's Law from Chapter Thirteen? The author of this law, Richard Price, posted it at Esalen Institute as a warning for both teachers and students: *You always teach others what you most need to learn yourself. You are your own worst student.* Price learned about this law the hard way—as a cofounder of Esalen, he observed hundreds of spiritual teachers and psychologists tripping over their own words in their daily lives. As a cofounder of Omega I have been privy to the personal habits of some of the most highly respected religious leaders, psychologists, and best-selling authors in the world. I could probably sell stories to the tabloids about scenes I have witnessed—a revered monastic sneaking off to have sex with a student; a so-called enlightened guru with a greedy ego the size of a planet; a marriage expert cheating on her husband; a medical authority on stress and well-being exhibiting all the signs of an overwhelmed, unhealthy workaholic. There was a period of time when my disillusionment at work almost ended my career. Even though the majority of the teachers we brought to the institute were well within the bounds of integrity and professionalism, those who strayed into abject hypocrisy made me question the foundation of my work.

It was only after I myself began to teach that I gained some clarity, and some humility, about the issue. Fearing that I could turn into a monster, I watched myself closely as I taught. I noticed that I was drawn to teach the very things I was most confused about: my need to control life, my resistance to loss, my fear of death. I made sure I told my students—over and over—that what I knew came from my own life's lessons. I took great pains to make it clear that I was more like them than they cared to know. As a result, I have never been a great teacher. My style of teaching lacks the grandeur and authority that inspire and motivate people. Great teachers must walk a fine line between tremendous self-confidence and tremendous humility. It is not an easy line to walk; most people fall off in one direction or another. Great teachers are geniuses, and like geniuses of any ilk, they are rare.

Fortunately, good teachers are all we need. Teachers and therapists who are honest and who continue to work on their own shortcomings can be as helpful as the great teachers—the rare, enlightened beings whom we may be fortunate enough to meet. The subject of working with teachers—good and great teachers—is a complex one. For the sake of brevity and user-friendliness, I have broken it down into five frequently asked questions. In each section I use the word *teacher* to include any guide on the path: a spiritual teacher, a religious leader, a therapist, a mentor, or any other learned guide within the discipline of your choice.

Working with a Teacher

1. Do I need a teacher?
2. How do I find a teacher?
3. Should I choose a traditional path?
4. What kind of commitment should I make?
5. When have I finished my apprenticeship?

1. DO I NEED A TEACHER?

You do not *need* a teacher to walk the spiritual path, but you'll get farther along in a more efficient way with one. In many ways, the spiritual path is no different from any other learning process, be it music or sports or business. In the beginning it helps to have a teacher—just like it helped to have a piano teacher or a basketball coach when you were young. Even Mozart and Michael Jordan had teachers. A good teacher steeped in a wise and well-developed tradition of personal growth and spiritual transcendence is a blessing.

I find it offensive when someone who successfully engages in a religious or therapeutic discipline for many years turns around and blithely counsels others to take a "pathless" path. I have actually witnessed spiritual teachers, born and raised in intact religious cultures, and tutored from an early age in a rigorous tradition, espouse that since spirituality is all around us, all that is necessary is for each one of us to wake up and enjoy life. To me, that is like saying that since music is all around us, all one has to do is sit down at the piano and let it flow out through the fingers onto the keys.

I have also heard psychologists whose best-selling books were written after years of their own therapy tell people that therapy is a waste of time—that all one ends up discovering is "It wasn't your parents' fault after all." Don't listen to these people. They are suffering from amnesia. Indeed, we do discover—*after years of hard work*—that spirituality *is* all around us, and it *isn't* our parents' fault, but these are not small discoveries if we have learned them in the depth of our being.

2. HOW DO I FIND A TEACHER?

First determine what you want to learn. No one teacher will satisfy everything you are seeking. A psychotherapist will help you break through the psychological barriers that obstruct your experience of the sacred. A spiritual teacher can teach you how to meditate or pray or celebrate your way to other realms of consciousness. A religious master can explain to you a moral system to guide you through life and provide a community of seekers with whom to share the journey. Determine for yourself what stage of the journey you are on, and don't try to cram all your learning into one experience.

Sometimes we make the mistake of thinking that we can trust a therapist or a teacher just because she hangs a shingle from her office or he writes a best-selling book. Just because you see a plumber's name in the Yellow Pages doesn't mean he's a good plumber. Usually you ask around. You may even get estimates from several different plumbers before hiring one to do an important job. You can do the same thing with therapists and teachers. Once you have determined what you want to learn, it is a good idea to read, research, and ask others about a certain teacher or method. Be very clear about what you are getting yourself into before you start to work with a teacher. If you know up-front about the methods used, the kind of people attracted to the work, the price charged, the expected length of the training, you'll be less likely to feel ripped off or misled farther on down the path.

The best thing I learned in the famous Est training was to take responsibility for my spiritual education. Est was a personal growth system developed by Werner Erhart in the 1970s. The first order of business in the weekend training was for the teacher to get approval of the rules from the three hundred people in the room. We had been sent the rules of the Est training prior to the weekend, so they weren't exactly news. But as the teacher went around the room reiterating the rules, at least half of the people in the room found something to argue about: "I think it's ridiculous that you can't go to the bathroom whenever you want," or "Why can't I wear my watch? That seems like a rather controlling rule." The teacher's response was always the same: "Have you come to do the Est training or your own training? These are the rules of the Est training. If you don't like them, you can leave now and get your money back." The process was long and grueling. It took several exasperating hours to complete, but it was also fascinating and highly educational. It taught me that if I didn't like the system to start with, I'd be better off finding another one. It taught me not to waste my energy trying to fine-tune a system to match my every need. It taught me the value of commitment to a teaching, imperfections and all.

The following guidelines may be helpful for you to consider before engaging with a teacher or therapist:

What to Look for in a Teacher

1. *Does she try to walk her talk in the world?* Taking Esalen's Law into account, the key here is a willingness on the part of the teacher to show some humility, to reveal her struggles, and to attempt to make her life and her message congruent. She doesn't have to be perfect, but she'll be a better teacher if she is using her own life as a laboratory for her ideals and methods. The most superb teachers are the "wounded healers"—the ones whose wisdom is tested in reality. Good teachers are always learning themselves, adapting what they know to a world that keeps changing. There's nothing worse than listening to someone who has polished a personal growth speech or a spiritual sermon that remains static over the years. While religious or academic training, degrees, books, and previous teaching positions are credentials that may indicate a highly trained teacher or therapist, equally important are the ways in which this person continually tests her knowledge in the world around her. A teacher whose words sound more forgiving than judgmental, more open-minded than arrogant, more authentic than polished is probably growing along with her students.

2. *Does he demand excellence?* Spiritual practice leads to freedom but requires discipline. Spirituality cultivates a relaxed mind and an open heart through attention and self-restraint. As we grow we begin to abandon our anxieties, let go of defenses, and loosen up, but that is the goal, and not

necessarily the process. A good teacher expects excellence from his students. He requires commitment to the methods he teaches and rigor in the process of learning. When Pir Vilayat first came to America he was dismayed by his students' lack of self-discipline and set out to teach us impeccability, manners, and dedication. He had a hard job. It was 1968, California. His first request was that we sit up during meditation. The sight of young people, dressed in messy clothes and sprawled on the floor as he taught ancient and arduous practices of meditation, was more than he could bear. In return for his teachings he asked for certain behavior: no drugs, responsible work, diligent study. This felt austere to me in those days, but now I am grateful for the demands Pir Vilayat made. Nothing precious is gained without sacrifice; a spiritual teacher should teach you this.

3. *Can you have a regular, how's-the-weather conversation with her?* Look for a teacher who practices the "open secret," who enjoys the fact we're all in this together. If she is too busy with her own messianic complex, she won't have time to attend to your education. She can be noble, grand, detached, and powerful while also being down to earth and personal.

4. *Is he happy?* Spiritually happy people are kind people. Kindness and compassion are the trademarks of good and great teachers. This doesn't mean a teacher is always chipper or gentle or nice; sometimes compassion takes the form of a kick in the butt. A sure sign that a person is filled with compassion is if he also has a stable sense of joy about being alive. And a good sense of humor. While you don't want to reject a teacher because he can't tell a joke, it's best to work with someone who can readily see the humorous shadow lurking behind the seriousness of the work at hand.

Another Tibetan lama with whom I have studied, Gelek Rinpoche, tells this story to illustrate the power of loving-kindness and compassion in teachers. Gelek was born in Tibet into the family of the thirteenth Dalai Lama. Tibetan Buddhism is a complex religion—ornate, ritualistic, and demanding of hard work and study. It has a hierarchical structure that is maintained by a process of searching for and finding the reincarnation of a lama who has died. Gelek Rinpoche was recognized as an incarnated lama when he was just three years old, taken from his family, and raised as a monk at the largest monastic university in Tibet. As he describes it, he lived in a world that had changed little since the twelfth century until he was nineteen. The only form of travel was that on the back of a yak or a horse. "There were few wheels in the country," he says. During his years in the monastery Gelek was carefully tutored by some of the greatest living masters of Tibetan Buddhism. He and a handful of other monks were prepared to preserve most of the precious oral teachings of the Tibetan heritage.

In 1959, when Gelek turned nineteen, the Chinese Communists invaded Tibet, and Gelek, along with thousands of his fellow Tibetans, fled. Gelek did not leave only the country of Tibet when he fled to India. He also left the ancient ways of his culture and was thrust into the twentieth century and the 1960s. Handpicked to bring Tibetan Buddhism to the West, Gelek and several other young monks were sent to Western universities. Gelek tells the story like this: "Suddenly I had been 'liberated' by the Chinese! I was a young man in a new kind of world. I went to discotheques, drank gin, met women. I would return from university to visit my teachers in India and they would ask me, 'Are you finding liberation?' They would never scold me or even tell me what to do. They would only ask me if I was finding liberation. I would say, 'No.' But I would return to college and keep doing what I had been doing all along. When I would return to India my teachers again would ask the same thing. This went on for several years, until I realized that I was getting nothing from my behavior. Now I was ready to fulfill my mission: to find liberation and to teach Westerners. I had learned the Western culture, the good and bad parts. I knew the Western mind better than my masters. They had known what they were doing. It was their loving kindness and lack of judgement or moralizing that allowed me to learn."

5. *Is she experienced?* Has she developed mastery of her subject or tradition? Experience and mastery are precious commodities in a teacher or therapist. It has been said that just a glance from a spiritual master can wake us up. I wouldn't necessarily make that kind of mastery a requirement, but I would make sure that whomever I studied with had been around the block a few times, and I would be willing to make sacrifices—time, money, commitment—to study with someone who has mastery in her subject. A good teacher is steeped in the methods of a well-conceived tradition or school of thought. She may modify what she has studied into her own system, but she has behind her the lineage of her teachers and the wisdom of her experience.

My dentist told me a story that illustrates the preciousness of experience in a teacher. During dental school, my dentist studied with a "master" dentist, a man in his eighties who was still practicing. Because of the master dentist's years of experience, he was able to perform the most complex operations with the kind of grace and speed that made his work look easy. He warned the younger dentists not to mistake his speed for carelessness, but rather as a sign of experience. One day when my dentist was observing the master, a woman came into the old dentist's office for a complex procedure—a root canal, or some other torture—and was surprised when the job took the dentist just a half hour to perform. When she was handed the bill she was even more surprised. "Seven hundred dollars! This usually takes my other dentist much longer. You want me to pay seven hundred dollars for less than an hour of your time?" the woman complained. The old dentist answered, "Would you rather that I work slower?"

What to Avoid in a Teacher

1. *The "Crazy Wisdom" Excuse:* Crazy wisdom is a term some teachers use to condone outrageous, harmful behavior. The idea behind this excuse is that even crazy actions on the part of the teacher can lead the student to healing or enlightenment. If a teacher and the group around the teacher glibly explain away emotional or sexual abuse, financial shenanigans, or any other questionable behavior as "just part of the teachings," take a good, hard look behind the Wizard's curtain.

2. *A Lack of Boundaries:* Psychologists use the word "boundaries" to describe the kind of limit setting that comes from a healthy sense of self-worth. When we love ourselves—our body, mind, and soul—we know how to love others without excessive domination or submission. We know when to say no; we know how to ask for what we need; we know how to respond to the needs of others. We know how to set appropriate boundaries for ourselves and how to respect the boundaries of others. A lack of healthy boundaries leads to abusive relationships of domination or submission, control or resignation.

A teacher who doesn't create an environment with healthy boundaries creates problems. Without boundaries any relationship suffers. But the student/teacher relationship or the client/therapist relationship is especially susceptible to wounding when the teacher has not set healthy boundaries. On the spiritual path, we aim to loosen the boundaries between ourselves and the sacred. We want to become more open, less guarded, less identified with a small sense of self. A spiritual teacher or a therapist can easily take advantage of this situation.

How do you know if someone has set healthy boundaries? Use common sense here. Blatant abuses of power are a sure sign of a lack of boundaries. A subtler sign is when you get the feeling that your teacher needs as much from you as you do from him. The first therapist I went to told me, after our second or third session, that I intimidated him. He wondered aloud if I was smarter than he was and if he could handle that. I knew very little about therapy at the time and so I continued to work with him. In the subsequent sessions I found myself trying hard to take care of the therapist. Eventually I realized that the therapy wasn't working and I left. In retrospect I see that I should have left the minute the therapist told me I intimidated him. If my plumber had told me that the pipes in my house intimidated him, that the job was probably too much for his training and intelligence, would I hire him again?

A good teacher needs only one thing from you: your commitment to the work. A good teacher will love you and protect your spiritual growth through thick and thin. He doesn't need your love and protection in return. Your gift to a teacher is your gradual awakening into freedom. It may take you a long time, but a good teacher is patient. He's been there before you and he has faith in the process.

3. *Claims of Perfection:* Don't trust a teacher who imperiously claims her own perfection or the superiority of her tradition. Some teachers feel they must appear unblemished as evidence of the legitimacy of their beliefs. Those who claim perfection expect adoration. The teacher who holds herself up to inhuman standards is a stern taskmaster; she makes unnecessary rules and demands arcane behavior. When no one around the teacher ever seems to have fun, or when everyone practices squeaky-clean, holier-than-thou spirituality, question authority. Everyone is bound to crash when a teacher espouses perfection.

4. *Hiding Out:* Some spiritual paths are steeped in such ornate ritual or complex theory that a teacher can hide behind the facade of the tradition. A teacher may look the part, sound the part, act the part, but she may not really *be* the part. Bring some healthy skepticism along with you whenever you approach a foreign tradition. Don't be seduced by a beautiful language or the color of the monks' robes. And bring that same skepticism to homegrown spiritual teachers who hide behind their ability to entertain. A good teacher is often entertaining, but a good entertainer is not necessarily a good teacher.

3. SHOULD I CHOOSE A TRADITIONAL PATH?

America is the world capital of the hybrid. We're used to a medley of foods, music, peoples. Does it work to mix and match religions? Or should we stick to one tried-and-true path? These are good questions without easy answers.

I know adults who are coming back to the religion of their childhood, ready for the first time to approach the tradition with maturity and commitment. I know others who have left a long engagement with a teacher or a path who are bitter and turned off to religion. I know people who shun any organized path, blaming religions for the ills of the world. Religions are like any organization; they can be glorious examples of human creativity and harmony, or they can demonstrate the worst of our species' behavior. I always say that whenever two or more of us are gathered in any name, there is trouble. But there also is support, tradition, and community, and these are rich and wonderful aspects of the spiritual search.

The English word *religion* comes from the Latin *religare,* meaning "to bind back to the source." This is what religion is for—to connect us to the source of life. One important role religion plays in a seeker's life is to create spiritual community—the kind where people feel connected to each other and to "the source." If there is anything lacking in the new American spirituality, it is the strong sense of community that organized religions provide their followers. If you choose to join a traditional religious group—or any organized group of seekers—you will partake in the blessings of community. But it's a trade-off, because if you join a religious tradition, you will also encounter the shadow side of spiritual community—the rigidity, exclusivity, and political structures that can contaminate the rest of the spiritual quest.

On a formal path you will also come face-to-face with your unfinished issues with authority figures. If the group you join has a rigid patriarchal structure, and if you were raised in a similar kind of household, no doubt you will confront unresolved feelings about power, control, will, and surrender. Or, conversely, if you choose a path with loose boundaries and a chaotic teaching style, you may find yourself regressing into familiar childhood patterns. It is not necessarily detrimental to confront old authority issues on the spiritual path. If the path you have chosen is psychologically savvy, you will be able to grow spiritually as you mend psychologically. If it isn't, you may advance in one landscape, but your journey will be hindered in others.

For myself, commitment to one formal discipline in my early years as a seeker was both a blessing and a hindrance on the path. I am grateful for the Sufi practices that are now second nature to me; to the community of friends who will always be my spiritual brothers and sisters; and to the silent lineage of teachers and fellow seekers who stand behind me. I am also glad that I left the group of followers and the rules and regulations of the organization when I did. I am glad that I journeyed onward to learn new skills from a variety of disciplines and that I added different viewpoints from other traditions to my spiritual path.

Ultimately, the decision to join a traditional religion is one of personal preference. If becoming a Christian or a Jew or a Muslim or a Hindu or a Buddhist helps you become one with God, then you will have the blessing of a glorious tradition and a supportive community. If you find that kind of association too limiting, then make sure you don't become a professional dabbler. Even if you don't become a formal member of a particular faith, you still can benefit from the power of commitment by engaging in long, serious study and practice in one tradition before adding it to your string of beads.

4. WHAT KIND OF COMMITMENT SHOULD I MAKE?

Most religions ask for a commitment, which is understandable. Without commitment, engagement on a spiritual path loses its power. The same is true for therapy or any self-growth path. Jack Kornfield, an American Buddhist teacher, says that "there are two qualities that are most important to bring to our work with a spiritual teacher. They are our common sense and our sincere commitment." Your common sense will lead you to a path worth exploring. Your commitment will allow you to follow that path long and deeply enough to reap the benefits. Spiritual and psychological growth take time. Instant enlightenment is an oxymoron. Sometimes the darkest, most confused times on the path are the very ones we must stew in. If we rush the process, or give up before we've left the woods, we will find ourselves right back where we started. Commitment to a trusted path or teacher takes the guesswork out of these times. We can relax under the guidance of a veteran traveler. We can have faith in the ultimate wisdom of a religious tradition or a healing system.

Commitment doesn't necessarily mean a pledge of lifelong fidelity. It means that you bring all of yourself into your choice of teacher and teachings for as long as you choose to stay. If you decide to join a church or do a two-year training, or even a two-day workshop, you follow it through with all of your heart and soul. You give the methodology the chance to work. You trust your choice and therefore you trust the process. Commitment and common sense. At each moment, commit fully to what you are doing. And keep your common sense with you at every stage of the journey. It will tell you if your engagement with the path is still vibrant and helpful, or if it is time to move on.

5. WHEN HAVE I FINISHED MY APPRENTICESHIP?

The Dalai Lama says, "We can best tell if our practice is working after five, ten, twenty-five years." Americans, used to quick results, afraid of becoming dependent, and suspicious of being cheated, often misread the signs on the spiritual journey, grow impatient, and leave a path or quit therapy too soon. Don't let a short attention span rob you of the rewards of patience and faith.

When you feel the urge to leave a path, try to honestly assess if you are running away from hard work and self-confrontation, or if you have indeed completed what you came to do. Pray for guidance. When you do leave a teacher or a therapist or a group, make the break consciously and with kindness and good manners. Communicate your gratitude as well as your honest feedback. Use this prayer/poem by Robert Frost, "Reluctance," to help you with the inevitable feelings of loss that arise when you separate from a teacher and a community:

> To go with the drift of things,
> To yield with a grace to reason,
> And bow and accept the end
> Of a love or of a season.

Remember Buddha's dying words to his disciples: "Be a light unto yourself." Good and great teachers will help you become such a light. You may need to "follow the leader" for quite a while, but ultimately you should find yourself wondering what took you so long, and why you kept searching for something you had all the time. The great masters throughout the ages have always cautioned against their students becoming followers. In the Greek myth, Ariadne gives Theseus a ball of string to help him find his way out of a labyrinth. Teachers give us the Ariadne thread. We follow it toward the light, until we discover that the light is within us, and has been all along.

PRAYER

Normal consciousness is a state of stupor, in which sensibility to the wholly real and responsiveness to the stimuli of the spirit are reduced. The mystics, knowing that man is involved in a hidden history of the cosmos, endeavor to awake from the drowsiness and apathy and to regain the state of wakefulness for their enchanted souls.
—RABBI ABRAHAM HESCHEL

Sister Wendy says that "religion is a springboard. You're meant to spring on it, up into God. It's there for use. The spiritual is not there for use. The spiritual is there for blessing. The spiritual is given to you. You can't leap onto the spiritual and go up and do anything else, because it *is* everything else. You just can hold out your hands to receive it." When we engage in spiritual practice we are holding out our hands to receive spirit.

In this book I have given instructions in just a few ways to hold out our hands; I have shared with you spiritual practices that can, in Rabbi Heschel's word, awaken our enchanted souls. Meditation is such a practice; therapy is such a practice; body awareness is such a practice. But there are many more ways to search for and to experience God's presence. Ritual, retreat, chant, fasting, movement, breath, music, scholarship, silence—all of these and more are part of a large library of useful means for awakening. I have offered directions in mindfulness and heartfulness meditation because these practices have been my preferred methods. But I have also experienced the power of other methods, like group chanting and dance, and extended periods of prayer and silence.

Study with a teacher, or under the umbrella of a religious tradition, allows one to learn a variety of practices, some that require the guidance of an expert practitioner. I would love to be able to teach you here, in this book, some of the powerful practices I have learned from my teachers, and to share some of the visions I have had on extended retreats. But these experiences might appear like theater or exotic ritual in the written word.

They cannot be described without doing them injustice, or making them sound hokey or romantic, or without leading the practitioner into waters too tricky to navigate without a guide. If the more sophisticated practices of religious and therapeutic systems appeal to you, I recommend working with a qualified teacher. I certainly do not think that in order to live a spiritual life you must engage in such practices—that would be like saying that in order to take a walk in the glorious mountain air you have to learn how to scale the face of a cliff. You may want to be the equivalent of a rock climber—you may want to test yourself, reach beyond your limits, be a risk taker—but you don't have to, and it doesn't necessarily mean you are a more spiritual person if you do.

There *are* spiritual practices that can be adopted without fear of misuse or disrespect to a tradition. One such practice is prayer. Prayer is a way of engaging with daily life in a more open and optimistic way. Prayer does not have to take the form of kneeling by your bed with your hands folded. Saint John told his followers to "pray without ceasing," and Islam encourages its followers to engage in "ceaseless prayer to Allah." I learned about this kind of prayer from an Austrian Benedictine monk who visited us at the Abode community in 1979. His name was simply Brother David, and his teaching was as simple as his name. He said all spiritual practice added up in the end to being grateful. "What counts," said Brother David, "is prayerfulness, not prayers. And the fullness of prayer is grateful living."

I was quite pregnant with my second child when Brother David visited, and since he was staying in our house, I got to spend some private time with him. One morning the two of us sat drinking tea at my kitchen table—a slight man in a brown monk's habit, and an enormously pregnant woman. I asked Brother David why he had become a monk. A brilliant scholar steeped in the world's religions as well as history, physics, and biology, he was, nonetheless, a humble and funny man.

He looked across the table at me and asked, "Why did you become a mother?"

"Because I got pregnant." I laughed. "But really, it's because I love babies; I love children."

"I became a monk because I love God," Brother David said. "I love God the way you love your baby." He explained to me how the word *monk* comes from the Greek syllable *Monos*—"one." "The monk is a one-joy-man," he said. "Just like you are a one-joy-woman right now. You know how close your baby is to you, right there in your belly? That's how close the monk feels to God, and also that far away. Even though your baby is right in your belly, you can't see him, or hear him, or talk with him. You know he's in there, but you can't quite believe it. That's why monks pray all the time—God is right there in the monk, but the monk prays for God's presence to be delivered."

Brother David gave me the written text of a talk he had given to fellow monastics titled "Why a Man Becomes a Monk, by David, Monk of Mt. Savior." At the top he wrote in his lovely European handwriting, "For Elizabeth, with a grateful heart for the gift of sharing, Br. David," or at least that's what I think it says, because I dropped it in the bathtub once, during one of my many rereadings. Before I spent time with Brother David, I would never have said that I prayed. But to Brother David, prayer was not something to do, prayer was an attitude, a way of being. Prayer is an act of optimism. Even if we are unsure of to whom we are speaking, we can pray in a spirit of hopefulness. "For if despair is the ultimate locking up of pride within itself," Brother David writes in "Why a Man Becomes a Monk," "hope is the inner opening up of humble readiness to receive. The monk does not see beyond the horizon any more than any other man does. But he keeps his eyes steadfast on the horizon. . . . He is a wide open eye in the dark. His ultimate gesture is pure inner openness to receive and to be received."

To pray is to be "a wide open eye in the dark." When we are in a state of prayerfulness we create an atmosphere of openness and wonder. In this way, prayer is the creation of sacred space. Sacred space is not only found in a chapel. It is not only created by high ritual. A sacred space can be as ordinary as a living room; it can be created by the simple act of one person sitting quietly on a park bench as the sun sets. Prayer can be experienced in silence without any words spoken. In fact, silence is a mighty kind of prayer in itself; silence *is* sacred space.

Sacred space isn't always pretty or happy. Sometimes we pray because we are angry and hurt. The sacred space we create feels like the last resort, an act of throwing up our hands and saying, "You take over now, please." Sometimes it feels like a cry of hunger. Rumi says, "Don't look for water, be thirsty." Prayer is an expression of our thirst for connection, for peace, for compassion. It is our longing for God.

The Sufis say that our longing for God is God's longing for us. In this way, prayer is like a conversation between friends separated across time and space. *The Cloud of Unknowing,* considered by many the best book ever written on prayer, approaches prayer like this. *The Cloud,* as it is referred to by those who love it, was penned in the late fourteenth or early fifteenth century by an anonymous English Christian mystic. Here are his directions on prayer:

> This is what you are to do: Lift your heart up to the Lord, with a gentle stirring of love desiring him for his own sake and for his gifts. Center all your attention and desire on him and let this be the sole concern of your mind and heart. And so, diligently persevere until you feel joy in it. For in the beginning it is usual to feel nothing but a kind of darkness about your mind, or as it were, a cloud of unknowing. You will seem to know nothing and to feel nothing except a naked intent toward God in the depths of your being. Try as you might, this darkness and this cloud will remain between you and your God. You will feel frustrated, for your mind will be unable to grasp him, and your heart will not relish the delight of his love. But learn to be at home in this darkness. Return to it as often as you can, letting your spirit cry out to him whom you love. For, if, in this life, you hope to feel and see God as he is in himself it must be within this darkness and this cloud. But if you strive to fix your love on him forgetting all else, which is the work of contemplation I have urged you to begin, I am confident that God in his goodness will bring you to a deep experience of himself.

One of the reasons I love prayer is because it is an antidote to guilt and blame. If we are unhappy with the way we have acted or have been treated, instead of stewing in self-recrimination on the one hand, or harboring ill-will toward someone else on the other, prayer gives us a way out of the circle of guilt and blame. We bring our painful feelings to God and say, "I have done wrong," or "I have been wronged." And then we ask for forgiveness, or direction, or compassion, or patience. Prayer really does work; it does create miracles through the simple act of allowing us to voice the truth. Prayer moves the energy out. It releases the flow of the soul-river.

Sister Wendy says it like this: "I don't think being human has any place for guilt. Contrition, yes. Guilt, no. Contrition means you tell God you are sorry and you're not going to do it again and you start off afresh. All the damage you've done to yourself, put right. Guilt means you go on and on belaboring and having emotions and beating your breast and being ego-fixated. Guilt is a trap. People love guilt because they feel if they suffer enough guilt, they'll make up for what they've done. Whereas, in fact, they're just sitting in a puddle and splashing. Contrition, you move forward. It's over. You are willing to forgo the pleasures of guilt."

You can find prayers everywhere to free the soul-river, to stimulate conversations with God. Poetry and song, hymns and common prayers, your own articulated desires and dreams—all of these become prayer when used in sacred space. Here are a few prayers that I use because they express so well my own longings. Sometimes I repeat them verbatim, sometimes I use them to fashion my own prayers.

I keep this prayer by Thich Nhat Hanh on my bed stand and often I say it when I awaken in the morning:

> Waking up this morning, I smile,
> Twenty-four brand new hours are before me.
> I vow to live fully in each moment
> and to look at all beings with the eyes of compassion.

When I am worrying a lot, scared about things out of my control, like my children, or money, or the state of the world, I take a few minutes to slow down, breathe quietly, and silently repeat this prayer from Dame Julian of Norwich. I have already printed this prayer in the book, but because it serves me so well, I offer it again:

> All shall be well,
> And all shall be well,
> And all manner of things
> Shall be well.

This little portion of Psalm 19, from the Bible, is a constant prayer of mine:

> Clear thou me from hidden faults.

This is how I fashion it into a prayer of my own:

Dear God, please show me the hidden, dead spaces inside of myself, that I hide because of my own fear or selfishness or ignorance. Show me these dead spaces. Please guide me into full aliveness. Help me not to cheat on what you made me to be in any way. Show me in this quiet moment what I am afraid to see about myself. Clear thou me from hidden faults.

Here is a prayer from the Theosophist Annie Besant. I use it when I want to open my heart to other human beings; when I feel more kinship with trees than with people; when I am tired of humankind:

> O Hidden Life vibrant in every atom;
> O Hidden Light! Shining in every creature;
> O Hidden Love! Embracing all in Oneness;
> May each who feels himself as one with Thee,
> Know he is also one with every other.

I love this prayer from the Navaho Indians. I like to recite it in nature:

> The mountains, I become part of it.
> The herb, the fir tree, I become part of it.
> The morning mists, the clouds, the gathering waters,
> I become part of it.
> The wilderness, the dew drops, the pollen,
> I become part of it.

Prayer does not have to feel forced. The more we allow the "stimuli of the spirit" to touch our lives, the more prayer becomes a natural and personal response to grateful living. In *I Asked for Wonder,* a beautiful anthology of the writings of Rabbi Abraham Heschel, Heschel writes this about prayer: "To pray is to regain a sense of the mystery that animates all beings, the divine margin in all attainments. Prayer is our humble answer to the inconceivable surprise of living. It is all we can offer in return for the mystery by which we live. Who is worthy to be present at the constant unfolding of time? . . . Only one response can maintain us: gratefulness for witnessing the wonder, for the gift of our unearned right to serve, to adore, and to fulfill. It is gratefulness which makes the soul great."

COMMUNITY

Without ritual humans live in nostalgia.
—MALIDOMA SOME

I belong to a community chorus that sings classical music, sometimes with a local chamber group and at other times, combined with other choirs, with a philharmonic orchestra. Over the years we have performed a wide variety of music, from madrigals to requiem masses. For the thirtieth anniversary of Martin Luther King, Jr.'s death, my chorus got together with a local Baptist choir whose church had been burned by arsonists. The purpose of the concert was to celebrate Dr. King's message and to raise money for the building of a new sanctuary. We held our dress rehearsal at the temporary church—an open rehearsal for anyone in the congregation. My chorus sang a beautiful modern piece set to the words of Dr. King. The church choir sang several thrilling gospel songs from their repertoire. For the last piece of the program we all sang together a gospel song with the refrain, "The Jesus in me loves the Jesus in you." At the end of the song, members of both choirs went into the congregation and people hugged each other as we all sang, "It's so easy, it's so easy, when the Jesus in me loves the Jesus in you."

Most of us in my choir had never been to this church. And most of the congregation had never met any of us. But when we hugged and said that it was easy to love each other because it was Jesus doing the loving, and it was Jesus who was receiving the loving, barriers of awkwardness just melted away, and we were in the presence of God's love.

The most amazing thing that happened during this song was not the bridging of two communities, although that bridge was built. The real miracle was how members of my own chorus said aloud for the first time how much we cared for each other and how, together, we were celebrating the unspeakable mystery of creation. Many of us had sung together for more than twenty years, and in all that time we had never hugged each other, or looked into each other's eyes, or found a way to express our gratitude. We had never acknowledged that every time we rehearse and perform we create sacred space. Certainly we had shared many moments of joy, and even reverence. We had worked hard to make beautiful sounds in harmony with each other, but until this concert, we had not made it our expressed intention to use music to awaken our souls and to sow the seeds of love in the world.

How could we? While I imagine that most every member of my choir would say she or he walks a spiritual path, we are from different religious backgrounds, and many of us don't belong to a church or synagogue or other formal group. We're conditioned in America not to mix spirituality with anything but organized religion. It's considered offensive to some, and even illegal to others, to inject anything with spiritual undertones into community experiences. We've interpreted the constitutional edict to separate Church and State so rigidly that our culture suffers from a lack of meaningful community rituals. Even family gatherings—like birthday parties, or baby showers, or funerals—lack a touch of the sacred. So little of what we share together takes place within intentional sacred space. We may yearn for spiritual community in our lives, but few of us know how to create it.

Without planning on it, my choir created sacred space. We became, for a moment, a spiritual community engaged in a spiritual ritual. Ritual is nothing esoteric. It is merely a way to step out of normal consciousness and everyday relationship into sacred space. It is no coincidence that in every culture people have created rituals like the one my choir inadvertently participated in. Humans need ritual and community. Certainly every culture can also point to its hermits and monastics, but for the most part, the spiritual quest has always been supported by a community of seekers. We want to travel side by side on our spiritual journeys so that we can tell stories, pass on wisdom, celebrate life, mourn loss, and mark important changes.

Those pursuing a spiritual path are often drawn to solitary worship: meditation, retreats, silence. We figure that in solitude we have to deal only with ourselves, and often that's complex enough. In relationships we have to deal with two complex selves. In groups things can get pretty complex indeed. Yet it is in relationships and groups that we get to demonstrate our real spirituality—love and acceptance of ourselves, love and acceptance of others, and all the rich territory we must cover to learn how to love. There is strength in solitude, and there is sacredness in silence, but we are tested and rewarded most in relationship and communion. And when we consciously intend for a relationship or a community to find its purpose in the spiritual search, we help light up each other's path.

My relationship with members of my choir has changed since we sang soul to soul. I more readily see the Jesus in my singing partners—their goodness, their depth, their heights, their vastness—and it feels good to know that the Jesus in me is being seen by them. I think our singing is different too; we bring more soulfulness to our concerts. Our director wrote a letter to us a few weeks after the concert to share the exuberant responses she had received from audience members. She wrote,

> After every concert I receive many wonderful responses. This past concert went over the top. I will never forget the end of Saturday's concert as I

embraced audience members. The overwhelming reaction was, "thank you for doing this concert, thank you for this concert." The violinist was so moved by the event she returned part of her fee. As an event that bridged two communities, I knew we succeeded in a big way. What I didn't realize was what a musical triumph the concert was. We were extraordinary! Some of the best singing we have ever done. Wow! As a conductor, this concert took me into uncharted territory, and I must confess I stepped into it with some trepidation. But it powerfully confirmed my deep belief that music is a perfect vehicle to bridge the gap between peoples. We are indeed all one in this walk. We need to keep reaching out, *we need those hugs.* As the pastor of the church said after Sunday's concert, "We can't change the whole world, but we can do something about our part of it."

The magic of spiritual community is no secret to religious groups. Church communities of every faith have always endeavored to do their part of healing the world. But there is no reason why we can't create similar magic outside of organized religious settings. What would it be like if an office meeting were to start with a moment of silence, a few shared breaths of relaxation, and a commitment to hear the best intentions—the Jesus—in each other's words? What if we spent just a little time during a child's birthday party to honor the parents who are raising that child, to show respect to the grandparents, and to pray for a child's year of joy and awakening? What if we attended births and deaths with the sacred intention of welcoming the new babies and traveling just a little way with the departing friends? And what if we mourned well with updated rites of passage that healed our brokenness and helped everyone move on? What if we put aside our cynicism and embarrassment and joined each other in sacred space?

I can't tell you how to do this, except to say that it starts with the intention. Church-sanctioned rituals, even the most arcane and lavish ones, were created by people like you and me with the simple intent to invoke the presence of the sacred. You can make up your own sacred rituals with the people in your life to mark a transition, to celebrate your unity, to heal, to grieve. Of course there already is ritual in our culture, and some of it is meaningful and important: weddings, funerals, graduations, birthdays, religious holidays. As a people we often are lifted out of the everyday by events like a presidential inauguration or the Olympics—events that celebrate the best in human interaction. Sometimes our Thanksgivings and family gatherings take place on sacred ground. Those Americans who do worship together may feel satisfied by the rituals they engage in: Easter services, Passover Seders, First Communions, Bar Mitzvahs, and other commonly shared religious traditions. Yet many feel that even these rituals have lost their spiritual intention and are more like consumer holidays than sacred ceremonies.

When rituals become rigid, they lose their meaning and with it the ability to help us create dynamic community. To breathe new life into old rituals and to create new ones, all we have to do is go back to the basic reason for community and ritual. Not much has changed from ancient days: we are born; we mature through childhood and adolescence; we enter adulthood and choose a way of life; we age and die. Within each of these stages we pass through predictable thresholds. Ritual helps us move gracefully and with purpose through the inevitable stages of life.

I hosted a New Year's party at my house years ago that has turned into a ritual for our community of friends. For me, New Year's parties had long been only meaningless occasions to drink too much, so I decided to find a different way to usher out the old year and welcome in the new one. Over the years the party has evolved into an evening we all wait for—a chance to be together again in sacred space. Each year the same crowd of twenty or so friends gathers—give or take a few—to party in the standard way until one hour before midnight. After sharing food and drink, we gather in the living room around the fireplace. We meditate for a while and think about two things: First, what we want to accomplish in the next year, or how we want to advance spiritually, or any projected goal for the year ahead. Second, we think about what stands in the way of our achieving the goal, what we may have to let go of, what may need to die.

After each one of us has settled on our two goals—the new and the old—I pass around the circle a basket of pinecones. We each pick two cones and invest one with the old behavior that we want to let go, and one with the new goal that we want to bring forth. Then each person takes a turn and shares what he or she has invested in the pinecones. We listen to our friends, whose progress we have now observed over the years, and watch as they toss the cones into the fire—first with a prayer to release the old, and then with a prayer to be blessed by the new. By midnight we have all told the story of our pinecones and tossed them in the fire. As we toast the new year, a sense of release and promise pervades the room. And a deep sense of community.

Some years new friends join the circle. One year two friends shared their final New Year's ritual with us. Peter and Tim had been in the circle from the beginning; they were major players in our little community. Now they were both in the last stages of AIDS. We didn't know it that evening, but by March they would both be dead. My husband and I had gone to New York City the day before to bring them to their country home and to the New Year's ritual. It took a major act of will on both of their parts to make the trip, but they didn't want to miss what had become a sacred experience in all of our lives.

When it came time for Peter to tell us about his pinecones, he was tired and drawn, resting in a chaise lounge that we had pulled into the circle. Tim sat on the couch, wrapped in a blanket. Peter began to speak—ramble, rather—about life and death and everything else in between. We all listened patiently, more than patiently, because we knew that this might be the last New Year's Eve we would have with him. After fifteen minutes, though, Tim could take no more. He leaned over to Peter and snapped, "Just toss it!"

The New Year's ritual is now called the "Just Toss It" ritual, and we always throw two extra pinecones into the fire for Peter and Tim. It helps us to call their spirits into the circle once a year, to include them in the community.

Children especially need to be part of meaningful community ritual. Otherwise, they feel disconnected to a larger world and untethered to the deeper meaning of life. "Where ritual is absent, the young ones are restless or violent, there are no real elders, and the grown-ups are bewildered," writes Malidoma Some, an African medicine man who was raised in the ancestral tribal traditions of his native West Africa. Malidoma also holds three master's degrees and two Ph.D. degrees from the Sorbonne and Brandeis University, and has taught on the faculties of several American universities. He is a remarkable person for his ability to carry and combine the ways of tribal Africa and the ways of Western thought and psychology. I have heard Malidoma speak several times at Omega, and I participated in a workshop he led there around the time of my father's death. During the workshop he said something that was relevant to the upcoming memorial service I was planning for my father: "People who do not know how to weep together are people who cannot laugh together. People who know not the power of shedding their tears together are like a time bomb, dangerous to themselves and to the world around them. . . . We have to grieve. It is a duty like any other duty in life."

After I heard Malidoma speak I felt strengthened in my duty to make my father's memorial a meaningful grief ritual. The plan was to bring my father's ashes to one of his favorite spots on earth—the White Mountains in New Hampshire—and to sprinkle them on top of Mt. Washington. The whole family—my mother and sisters, our mates and kids, and a few uncles and aunts—were going to join my father's closest friends and hike up into Tuckerman's Ravine, a notorious gathering place for serious mountain climbers and alpine skiers. After the climb we were to eat dinner and sleep over at the rustic base camp. Beyond this, we had no other plans. No one really knew what to do and no one wanted to take responsibility for bringing the group together around our grief and gratitude. I think many families and groups find themselves in similar situations—with a desire to create sacred space and an inability or an embarrassment to do so.

Emboldened by my workshop with Malidoma Some, I decided to risk being ridiculed for being mushy, and take on creating a meaningful, participatory grief ritual. I sought out the help of one of my spiritual father figures, the Nigerian drummer and ceremonialist Baba Olatunji, who has taught at Omega for more than twenty years. I had seen him preside over memorial services before, so I figured he would be able to help me plan my father's ceremony. Baba explained to me that the elders in his village assume the role of surrogate father for those left fatherless. First he assured me that he would stand in for my father any time I wanted, then he asked me some about my father. Closing his eyes, he began to beat out a rhythm on the table where we sat. Then he said that in the Yoruba tradition the people believe that the soul of the loved one hangs on until the family sings his song to release him. "What is your father's song?" Baba asked as he drummed his fingers. "If you find his song, you can sing it to the winds and your father will hear it and it will tell him that all of you are happy for his freedom and are singing him into the next world. Do you know his song?"

Right away my father's song came to me. I laughed out loud, remembering the only song he ever hummed, or sometimes whistled. It was just a few notes, and if there were words, they usually were: *Da, da, dada, da, da, dada.* My sisters and I often sang this song to each other as a kind of code to indicate our frustrating yet loving relationship with the man. The song, like our father, was jaunty and efficient—a tune to be sung solo while tidying up around the yard or taking a brisk hike in the woods. It did the trick without much fanfare and with no waste.

I sang the song aloud to Baba and he drummed out its rhythm. There was something about this simple exchange that brought tears to my eyes, and that called forth the beauty of our multicultural, interwoven American lives. A wave of hopefulness spread over me—not just for my family and the upcoming memorial service, but also for the whole human family, and for the creation of new ways of celebrating our common spirituality.

After my meeting with Baba, I wrote to everyone who would be attending the memorial and asked them to be prepared to say or read something about my father—a memory, a story, or something inspirational about death and love. I then gathered my own stories and thoughts and wove my father's song into what I would say at the ceremony. The day came, and as if my father had planned it, the weather was terrible. My father enjoyed battling the elements; he had dragged the family on all sorts of adventures in extreme weather. We agreed he was laughing in delight as we assembled in the cold pouring rain to make the four-mile climb up the mountain. Even though it was mid-August, we were told there was snow on top of the mountain and that we should dress warmly. So there we were—kids, grown-ups, and a few elders in their seventies and eighties— dressed in sweaters and rain gear, carrying a cardboard box of ashes up Mt. Washington. After a half mile of dangerous hiking over slippery rocks, it became apparent that the youngest and oldest members of the group were not going to make it all the way to the top. So we stopped at a waterfall known and loved by my father and held the first part of the ceremony there.

Standing in a circle, I called on my father's spirit to join us. "We are here to honor you and to help you on your way," I told him. "All of us, your family and friends, and the sky itself, are weeping today. We want to remember you and to tell your stories so that afterward we can laugh again." Then I asked each person to come to the center of the circle, take some ashes from the now dissolving cardboard urn, say something to my father, and then toss the ashes into the waterfall. What followed was so moving, and so spontaneous, I was astounded. All of my reservations that a ritual would make this group feel uncomfortable disappeared with the first fistful of ashes thrown into the falls. Everyone, from the youngest grandchild to the oldest ski buddy, had prepared the most intimate and honest speech. The stories made us laugh and cry. The feelings expressed were real—no sentimentality, no holding back. The words spoken transformed the rain into healing water.

It was strange to stand there, with soggy ashes on our hands and in our hair, talking to my father, a New York advertising man, born and raised in Brooklyn, transplanted to Vermont, and now dead and gone. I looked around at our little group and felt the power of my father's life and the gifts he had given to each one of us. I felt the timeless nature of our ancestral connection and the promise of unending communion.

I said my piece last. I explained to everyone how Baba Olatunji had suggested we sing my father's song. "You may not know that a Jewish advertising man had a song," I said. "But he did. Does anyone know it?" And as if on cue, my sisters chimed in, "*Da, da, dada, da, da, dada.*"

"The unwritten meaning of this song is simple," I said. "It means, I am doing what I love to do and I'm having a good time doing it. That sums up my father to me. He knew what he loved and he did it as much as he could. What he loved was so readily attainable—nature, exercise, physical work, reading, eating—that he was usually a satisfied man. It seems to me that is rare in a human being. Yes, he could be impatient when something stood in his way. Sometimes that something was you and that was not always pleasant. But soon enough he would be out and about, humming his theme song. The world was good and he was out in it. Fortunately for us, my father's passion for what he loved was contagious. I feel blessed to know what I love and to have the gumption to go out and get it. I got that from my father. It is probably the greatest gift a father can give to a child. So, today let's sing my father's song to the winds of one of his stomping grounds. I am sure these trees have heard it before. May you be free to roam happily in the next world, Dad."

We all sang a few rounds of *Da, da, dada, da, da, dada.* And then the hardy among us continued up into Tuckerman's Ravine and scattered the rest of the ashes into the August snowfields. That night, tired and giddy, we sat around and played games, and laughed so raucously that the lodge owners had to ask us to please muffle our funeral party. We had grieved; we had fulfilled our duty. Now we could laugh.

Epilogue ┊ Signs of Progress

We shall not cease from exploration.
And the end of all our exploring
Will be to arrive where we started
And know the place for the first time.
—T. S. Eliot

When Bishop Desmond Tutu introduced Nelson Mandela at his inauguration as the new president of South Africa, he described him as being a man who had *Obuntubotho*. Obuntubotho, he said, "is the essence of being human. You know when it is there and when it is absent. It speaks about humanness, gentleness, putting yourself out on behalf of others, being vulnerable. It embraces compassion and toughness. It recognizes that my humanity is bound up in yours, for we can only be human together."

Obuntubotho is a sign of progress on the spiritual path. As you journey onward—with or without a teacher, in a group or alone, in virgin territory or on a well-worn path—you will be given signs and messages wherever you turn. The world will become a bank of messages. The more you travel onward, the more finely tuned you will become. You will see signs of spiritual progress everywhere, and you will hear messages of further direction always.

People put bumper stickers on their cars to announce their beliefs and preferences to the world. On the spiritual path you are the vehicle. You can wear a cross around your neck or a turban on your head, but others will know your true progress through your actions in the world. You will know how you are doing on the inside, and you will not need to announce it. But if you would like to wear a bumper sticker, perhaps you could have one of the following made up:

OBUNTUBOTHO   The Yiddish word for Obuntubotho is *mensch*. Spirituality makes you a mensch. A mensch is someone whom others want to be around because of a certain something—a kindness, a warmth, a quality of genuineness. A sign of progress on the path is the trust of other people.

THE TRUTH WORKS   A disciple once asked the Buddha how he would know the Truth if he found it. "You know the Truth, because the Truth works," the Buddha answered. When your life works better—when drama and chaos get tiresome, and goodness and peace are your preferred companions, then you are receiving messages from the Truth. When you are naturally happier, stronger, and more deeply engaged with people and place, you can assume you are touching on the Truth. Hazrat Inayat Khan said, "Truth alone can succeed; falsehood is a waste of time and loss of energy." When nothing feels wasted and when you are energized in body and mind, the Truth is making itself known.

IN TOUCH WITH REALITY   A sign of progress is when you no longer fight the nature of life. Instead, you work with it. You stop pretending that life is supposed to be a certain way and accept it on its own terms. You size up the human story and get on with living.

HONESTY IS AN APHRODISIAC   It does pay to be honest. It pays in rewarding relationships. It pays in unblocked energy. It pays in passion. To stand tall in who you are, unafraid to reveal what you want and need, kind enough to tell the truth, and brave enough to bear the consequences, is a telling sign of spiritual development.

SUFFERING IS OUR FEAR OF PAIN   There will always be pain in life. This is something we learn as we progress spiritually. We also learn that if we resist pain, if we fear it, then we create additional pain, called suffering. Our resistance to pain stands between us and full-bodied living; it keeps us at war with our problems and from making peace with life's dual nature. When pain arises in your life and you stand to greet it with calm curiosity, you will know that you are making progress on the path.

HOW CAN I HELP?   If you are spiritually happy you naturally want others to be happy. You can't help but help. Spirituality is the gift of love. Service to others is the discipline of love. If you reach out often to those in need, not because you should but because your heart leads you more and more deeply into the hearts of others, then keep on going.

DECLARATION OF INTERDEPENDENCE   John F. Kennedy said that "the supreme reality of our time is the vulnerability of our planet." Can you feel that? Are you becoming more and more aware of the interconnection of all beings, creatures, and elements? Can you sense how the karma of all things is connected in a delicate web? Do you hold as your own Jesus' words: "And whatsoever you do to the least of my brothers, you do to me"? Are you getting tired of the way our society celebrates the false ego's selfish and insatiable drive to acquire and use more and more? And does that make you want to be an agent of healing, an extremist for love? A declaration of life's interdependence is a sign of spiritual progress.

COMBINE LOVE AND LONELINESS   Chögyam Trungpa says that when the "spiritual warrior" progresses on the path, he "paradoxically, finds himself more alone. He is like an island sitting alone in the middle of a lake. . . . Although the warrior's life is dedicated to helping others, he realizes that he will never be able to completely share his experience with others. The fullness of his experience is his own, and he must live with his own truth. Yet he is more and more in love with the world. That combination of love affair and loneliness is what enables the warrior to constantly reach out to help others. By renouncing his private world the warrior discovers a greater universe and a fuller and fuller broken heart. This is not something to feel bad about: it is a cause for rejoicing."

THE ORDINARY IS EXTRAORDINARY   "Just to be is a blessing. Just to live is holy," said Rabbi Abraham Heschel. When we really feel this, without forcing, without trying too hard, then we know we're on the right track. When we see the marvelous structure of the universe in the mundane and when we love the whole world by loving our mates and children and coworkers, then we are making progress. When we don't need to be anyone special, but are pleased to be simply one of God's many creatures, then we will know the joy of the extra-ordinary. Our spiritual explorations may at first lead us away from the ordinary, but as we progress we come back to where we started and, in the words of T. S. Eliot, "know the place for the first time."

GOD IS OPTIMISTIC   Finally, look for these signs of progress on the spiritual path: a friendliness toward change and an optimistic vision of eternity.

My sister, after the death of my father, temporarily lost this kind of optimism. The sudden closeness of death threw her off balance. Her mood grew gloomy and her grief turned into depression. In this state she was too weary to attend a memorial service that my father's college buddies threw for him at New York University. So I went without her. Now, on top of grief and depression she added guilt. She left a message on my answering machine saying, "I feel so bad that I didn't go to New York. I just can't get out of this dark state of mind. What will tomorrow bring?" I answered her with this note: "The earth will turn, we will all be one day older, one day closer to the mystery where things like going to New York or staying home have no meaning. In that mysterious land beyond this one, we will all be united in a beautiful, clear light. I imagine it to be like swimming in white wine, lit with streams of sunlight. Golden. And we will all be together in a way that feels both intimate and vast. Time will be like a circle instead of a line. And we will all be thin."

It could have been the promise of being eternally thin that helped my sister, but I think it was the imagined dip in a healing, golden liquid. Spiritual optimism heals; it transforms our lives. Where before we saw adversity, now we sense adventure. Where we were impatient, now we are peaceful. Where we had fear, now we have faith.

Sometimes I know for sure that we swim forever through illumined white wine. Other times I'm not so certain. But I no longer need a guarantee. I have dipped into the wine enough times to let go of my fear. And so we end where we began, with fearlessness. In the beginning of this book I defined spirituality as fearlessness, as a way of looking boldly at life and death, as a brave search for the truth about existence.

May you be blessed on your brave search for the truth. May your soul lead you to pools and rivers and oceans of wine. May you drink and be intoxicated by love; may you swim and be strengthened by life. May you grow bolder and kinder. May you be grateful. May your body be charged with health and energy, and your life with purpose and passion. May you know the dignity of mindfulness, the openness of heartfulness, the freedom of soulfulness. May you remember who you are. May you awaken. May we all awaken.

Suggested Books, Audiotapes, and Music

The Joy of Sects: A Spirited Guide to the World's Religious Traditions, Peter Occhiogrosso
Everything you ever wanted to know about the panorama of humanity's spiritual quest, in a lively and intelligent resource book.

In a Different Voice: Psychological Theory and Women's Experiences, Carol Gilligan
The definitive work on the ways that women experience life, and how those ways have been negated and silenced in the culture. An empowering read for both women and men, it reshapes our vision of what it means to be human.

Conscious Femininity, Marion Woodman
An important and thought-provoking compilation of a Jungian analyst's interviews about the rise of feminine consciousness in our times. Women will find themselves more easily in the pages, but men will also benefit from the book.

Iron John, Robert Bly
Written primarily for men interested in their spiritual and psychological lives, this controversial, best-selling book about the male psyche helped me tremendously in my roles as a wife, as a mother of sons, and as a colleague of men.

He: Understanding Masculine Psychology and *She: Understanding Feminine Psychology,* Robert A. Johnson
Two slim volumes that explore masculine and feminine psychology through the retelling of ancient myths, and in a highly readable and affecting style.

The Marriages Between Zones Three, Four, and Five, Doris Lessing
One of my favorite novels in the form of a fable about the masculine and feminine archetypes, and about men and women, love and violence, ignorance and wisdom.

ALSO RECOMMENDED:

The Seven Storey Mountain, Thomas Merton
How I Believe and *The Phenomenon of Man,* Teilhard de Chardin
The Goddess Within, Jennifer Barker Woolger and Roger Woolger

SUGGESTED READING FOR BOOK II: THE LANDSCAPE OF THE MIND

Shambhala: The Sacred Path of the Warrior, Chögyam Trungpa
My favorite spiritual text, this book could be referenced in each of the landscapes, as it is much more than a meditation handbook. As a meditation guide, it is invaluable; as a guide for living, it is extraordinarily helpful.

The Miracle of Mindfulness: A Manual for Meditation, Thich Nhat Hanh
  A beautiful, lucid guide to Buddhist meditation that uses stories and exercises to reveal opportunities for being mindful, awake, and focused in the present moment.

How to Meditate, Lawrence LeShan
  This slim volume is a classic. It is simple and straightforward, written by a Westerner for Westerners who want to reap the rewards of meditation.

Zen Mind, Beginner's Mind, Shunryu Suzuki
  Another classic by one of the first Japanese Zen masters to bring Zen to America, in the form of informal talks on meditation and Zen practice.

The Three Pillars of Zen, Roshi Philip Kapleau
  An authoritative exploration of Zen meditation, yet also human, simple, wise, and full of life. For anyone seriously interested in meditation, this is a wonderful book.

When Things Fall Apart, Pema Chödrön
  I cannot imagine anyone who would not benefit from this book. It applies mindfulness philosophy and meditation to everyday difficulties, habitual patterns, and painful emotions.

Full Catastrophe Living: Using the Wisdom of the Body and Mind to Face Stress, Pain, and Illness, and *Wherever You Go, There You Are: Mindfulness Meditation in Everyday Life,* Jon Kabat-Zinn, Ph.D.
  Two books based on the research done at the Program of the Stress Reduction Clinic at the University of Massachusetts Medical Center, written by one of the wisest voices in the fields of stress, pain, and illness.

The Sun My Heart, Thich Nhat Hanh
  Further thoughts and instructions on mindfulness meditation using correlations between Buddhist psychology and contemporary physics.

ALSO RECOMMENDED:

Thoughts Without a Thinker, Mark Epstein, M.D.
Will and Spirit, Gerald May, M.D.
Worry, Edward M. Hallowell, M.D.
Time Shifting, Stephan Rechtschaffen, M.D.

SUGGESTED AUDIOTAPES

"The Present Moment," Thich Nhat Hanh
"The Inner Art of Meditation," Jack Kornfield
"The Insight Meditation Correspondence Course," Joseph Goldstein and Sharon Salzberg

"The Science of Enlightenment," Shinzen Young
"The Contemplative Journey," Father Thomas Keating
Tapes may be ordered from Sounds True, 800-333-9185

SUGGESTED READING FOR BOOK III: THE LANDSCAPE OF THE HEART

Emotional Intelligence, Daniel Goleman, Ph.D.
A summary of scientific evidence drawn from brain and behavioral research that returns human emotions to their proper place in any theory of human nature. The book offers a new vision of what it means to be "smart," one that includes self-awareness, zeal, altruism, social deftness, and compassion.

A Path with Heart, Jack Kornfield
A warm and friendly book, this classic on the spiritual life shows in detail and with humor and kindness the way to practice the Buddha's universal teachings here in the West. Filled with practical meditation techniques, psychological wisdom, and the author's own experiences, its subject matter includes classical Buddhist theory, as well as ways of healing relationships, dealing with addiction, and simplifying daily life.

Healing into Life and Death and *A Year to Live,* Stephen and Ondrea Levine
Full of stories about people with whom the Levines have worked, these books broach the subject of facing death as a way of living more fully.

Shambhala: The Sacred Path of the Warrior, Chögyam Trungpa Rinpoche
Although listed already in Book II, this book can serve as a primer for the Landscape of the Heart, and as a bridge between mindfulness and heartfulness.

Challenge of the Heart, John Welwood
A powerful, carefully selected collection of essays focusing on the challenges of love, sex, and intimacy in our times. Insightful commentary by the author weaves together the words of poets, psychologists, philosophers, and religious leaders.

Jung to Live By: A Guide to the Practical Application of Jungian Principles for Everyday Life, Eugene Pascal
A layperson's guide to Jungian principles that brings to life Carl Jung's theories on personality type, myth, dreams, and relationships.

The Power of Myth, Joseph Campbell with Bill Moyers
The brilliant collaborative effort of journalist Bill Moyers and Joseph Campbell, the world's preeminent scholar, teacher, and author on world mythology and its relevance to modern life. Written in a wise and warm conversational manner, at the end of Campbell's life, the book is a summing up of a huge body of work.

Meeting the Shadow: The Hidden Power of the Dark Side of Human Nature, edited
by Connie Zweig and Jeremiah Abrams
A collection of sixty-five wide-ranging articles that overview the dark side of
human nature and provide ways of working with the shadow as opposed to
disowning it. Tools for achieving self-acceptance, defusing negative emotions
that erupt in daily life, releasing guilt and shame associated with negativity,
and healing relationships through deeper authenticity.

A Little Book on the Human Shadow, Robert Bly
A lively, brilliant little book that uses mythology, pop culture, poetry, and personal story to encourage the reader to reclaim the disowned parts of the self.

Staying Well with Guided Imagery, Belleruth Naparstek
A blend of medical research, practical exercises, and actual imagery scripts for
harnessing the power of the imagination to improve physical, mental, and
emotional well-being—from curing headaches to strengthening the immune
system, and from encouraging emotional resiliency to creating heathy
boundaries.

The Artist's Way, Julia Cameron
For anyone who wants to be more creative—from practicing artists to those
whose creativity has been blocked for years—this excellent book is a participatory guide for releasing our most creative selves from fear of failure, guilt,
and other self-sabotaging beliefs about art and creativity.

ALSO RECOMMENDED:

Original Blessing, Matthew Fox
The Stormy Search for the Self, Stan and Christina Grof
The Soul's Code: In Search of Character and Calling, James Hillman
Goddesses in Every Woman and *Gods in Every Man,* Jean Shinoda Bolen
King, Warrior, Magician, Lover, Robert Moore
The Heroine's Journey, Maureen Murdock
Inner Work: Using Dreams and Active Imagination for Personal Growth, Robert A.
Johnson
Women Who Run with the Wolves, Clarissa Pinkola Estés
Healing Visualizations, Gerald Epstein, M.D.

POETRY ANTHOLOGIES

The Enlightened Heart, chosen by Stephen Mitchell
The Soul Is Here for Its Own Joy: Sacred Poems from Many Cultures, chosen by
Robert Bly

Women in Praise of the Sacred: 43 Centuries of Spiritual Poetry by Women, chosen by
    Jane Hirshfield
The Rag and Bone Shop of the Heart: An Anthology of Poems for Men, chosen by
    Robert Bly, James Hillman, and Michael Meade
The Essential Rumi, translated by Coleman Barks

SUGGESTED AUDIOTAPES

Health Journeys Audio Tape Series, Belleruth Naparstek (*order from 800-800-
    8661*)
"Noble Heart," Pema Chödrön
"The Second Half of Life," Angeles Arrien
"Warming the Stone Child," Clarissa Pinkola Estés
"Sitting by the Well," Marion Woodman
"Teachings on Love," Thich Nhat Hanh
"Coming Apart," Daphne Rose Kingma
"The Spiritual Advantages of a Painful Childhood," Wayne Muller
Tapes may be ordered from Sounds True, 800-333-9185

SUGGESTED MUSIC LISTENING

The following music can be used in heartfulness meditations and exercises:

To soften the heart:

Natives, Peter Kater and R. Carlos Nakai (Silverwave Records)
Requiem, John Rutter (Collegium Records)
Officium, Jan Garbarek and the Hilliard Ensemble (ECM)
Miserere, Allegri (Gimell)
Close Cover and *Whisper Me,* Wim Mertens (Windham Hill Records)
Stor Amhran, Noirin Ni Riain (Sounds True Audio)
Symphony No. 3, Henryk Gorecki (Elektra Nonesuch)
Vespers, Rachmaninoff (Telarc)

To awaken wonder:

The music of Bach and Mozart
The music of Van Morrison, especially: *No Guru, No Method, No Teacher; Poetic
    Champions Compose; Inarticulate Speech of the Heart; The Healing Game*
    (Polygram)
Exile and *Beat the Border,* Geoffrey Oryema (Real World Records)
The Cross of Changes, Enigma (Charisma Records)

Kundun, Philip Glass (Nonesuch)
The Best of Al Green, Al Green (The Right Stuff)

SUGGESTED READING FOR BOOK IV: THE LANDSCAPE OF THE BODY

The Human Body: Your Body and How It Works, Ruth Dowling Bruun, M.D.,
and Bertel Bruun, M.D.
Concise, lucid text accompanies full-color illustrations of the design, function, and interrelationships of all the working parts of the body.
The Relaxation Response and *Timeless Healing: The Power and Biology of Belief,*
Herbert Benson, M.D.
Both of these books skillfully marry the scientific and the spiritual, the med-
ical and the psychological. The first teaches a simple meditative technique for
fatigue, anxiety, and stress; the second overviews research done at Harvard
Medical School and offers examples and exercises on the power of faith and
prayer in health and healing.
The Enlightenment Process, Judith Blackstone
A rare book that combines the use of depth-psychology, bodywork, and en-
ergy exercises to help uncover authentic selfhood.
Spontaneous Healing, Andrew Weil, M.D.
A sound guide to creating a personal discipline that enhances the body's nat-
ural ability to heal and maintain health.
Addiction to Perfection, Marion Woodman
A groundbreaking book that shows how at the root of eating disorders, sub-
stance abuse, and other addictive and compulsive behaviors is a hunger for
spiritual fulfillment.
Feeding the Hungry Heart, Geneen Roth
A profoundly helpful book that shows how to work with the deep internal
hunger for self-respect and fulfillment that often translates into compulsive
eating and other unhealthy, unloving habits and behavior.
The Tibetan Book of Living and Dying, Sogyal Rinpoche
A manual for life and death and a magnificent source of inspiration from the
Tibetan tradition, this book is as practical as it is uplifting. It outlines the use
of meditation, the nature of the mind, karma and rebirth, the dying process,
and compassionate love and care for the dying.
Who Dies? Stephen and Ondrea Levine
An investigation of conscious living and conscious dying that presents a far
more humane psychological and spiritual milieu for those undergoing the
dying process now, those who work with death and dying, and those who
want to examine the death of the body and the life of the soul.

On Death and Dying, Elisabeth Kübler-Ross
> The pioneering book that brought death "out of the closet" in America and described predictable stages of grief.

Dancing at the Edge of Life: A Memoir, Gael Warner
> A brave and beautifully written journal of the last year of a young woman's life that unflinchingly looks at her illness, her cancer treatment, and her contradictory struggle to hang on to life, even while letting go of her attachment to it.

ALSO RECOMMENDED:

Women's Bodies, Women's Wisdom: Creating Physical and Emotional Health and Healing, Christiane Northrup, M.D.

The Road to Immunity, Kenneth Bock, M.D.

A Grief Observed, C. S. Lewis

Composing a Life, Mary Catherine Bateson

Heading Toward Omega: In Search of the Meaning of the Near-Death Experience, Kenneth Ring

A Letter of Consolation, Henri Nouwen

Life After Life, Raymond Moody

Embraced by the Light, Betty J. Eadie

SUGGESTED AUDIOTAPES

"Mobilizing the Life Force," Lawrence LeShan

"Creating Health," Christiane Northrup, M.D.

"Energy Anatomy," Caroline Myss

"Being with Dying," Joan Halifax

"Tibetan Wisdom for Living and Dying," Sogyal Rinpoche

"In the Heart Lies the Deathless," Stephen Levine

"Death Is Not an Outrage," Ram Dass

Tapes may be ordered from Sounds True, 800-333-9185

SUGGESTED READING FOR BOOK V: THE LANDSCAPE OF THE SOUL

The Bible, The Old and New Testaments (King James Version)
> Any modern traveler in the Landscape of the Soul will find the holy books of Judaism and Christianity helpful in two distinct ways. First, they explain the Western psyche and worldview; and second, they offer some of the most inspiring teachings and parables ever written.

Life Prayers and *Earth Prayers,* Elizabeth Roberts and Elias Amidon

Two small volumes that offer prayers, poems, and invocations that can be used to add depth and meaning to gatherings, celebrations, and ceremonies.

Gratefulness, The Heart of Prayer, Brother David Steindl-Rast

A thoughtful, joyful, and beautiful book about prayer, gratitude, and living life in its fullness.

The Cloud of Unknowing, Anonymous

An enduring classic of Christian mystical experience written in the fourteenth century that offers practical advice in prayer and contemplation that still has great relevance today.

I and Thou, Martin Buber

A landmark book on the mystical and social dimensions of the human personality by one of the most brilliant Jewish thinkers of the twentieth century.

Ordinary Magic: Everyday Life as Spiritual Path, edited by John Welwood

Thirty-five wide-ranging essays written by well-known spiritual teachers, therapists, and creative artists that show how spiritual practice and mystical awareness can contribute to better relationships with family, community, and the world at large.

Jewish Renewal: A Path of Healing and Transformation, Michael Lerner

A reinterpretation of Jewish tradition that will appeal to people of all faiths and to many who have given up on any faith at all. Part history, part hands-on instruction, the book is a profound encounter with the concerns of the modern spiritual life.

How Can I Help? Ram Dass and Paul Gorman

A how-to book in the form of stories, support, and inspiration for those who want to understand what really helps when we try to help one another—at home, at work, on the street, in the world.

Ritual: Power, Healing, and Community, Malidoma Some

A fascinating look at the uses of ritual in West Africa, and a helpful commentary on the lack of ritual and community in our own culture, by a man who lives in three worlds: the world of his African village, the world of the Ancestors, and the modern Western world, where he has received two doctorate degrees and taught at major universities.

The Passion of the Western Mind: Understanding the Ideas That Have Shaped Our World View, Richard Tarnas

What every Westerner should know about the history of Western thought in one big book that reads with the momentum of a novel.

Recovering the Soul: A Scientific and Spiritual Search, Larry Dossey, M.D.

A theory of mind and being independent of matter, time, and space presented from the experience of a medical doctor and from his research into the nexus of mysticism and healing, and religion and physics.

ALSO RECOMMENDED:

Silence, Simplicity, and Solitude, Rabbi David Cooper
World as Lover, World as Self, Joanna Macy
God in All Worlds, edited by Lucinda Vardey
A Thomas Merton Reader, edited by Thomas P. McDonnel
The Sufi Message of Hazrat Inayat Khan, Volumes 1–12, Hazrat Inayat Khan
Handbook for the Soul, edited by Richard Carlson and Benjamin Shield
Pathwork of Self-Transformation, Eva Pierrakos
The Pearl Beyond Price, A. H. Almaas

SUGGESTED AUDIOTAPES

"The Transpersonal Vision: The Healing Potential of Nonordinary States,"
   Stanislav Grof, M.D.
"Anam Cara: Wisdom from the Celtic World," John O'Donohue
"Kabbalah Meditation: Judaism's Ancient System for Mystical Exploration,"
   Rabbi David A. Cooper
"Son of Man: The Mystical Path to Christ," Andrew Harvey
"The Art of Forgiving: A Practical Path to Maturity and Inner Peace," Robin
   Casarjian

Tapes may be ordered from Sounds True, 800-333-9185

Acknowledgments

To the many teachers, scholars, artists, and practitioners whose wisdom has guided my journey, and especially those whose work I document and quote in the book, I offer gratitude for a deepened spiritual understanding and a richer and happier life.

Without the intelligence and kindness I received from my agent, Henry Dunow, this book may never have found its way into the world. The word *agent* is a misnomer for Henry; *shepherd* would be better, or maybe just *friend*, in the truest sense of the word. Ann Godoff, my editor at Random House, understood the intent of the book the minute we met, and has stood by me with warmth, trust, and astute direction every step of the way. I offer her and others at Random House—including Enrica Gadler, Robbin Schiff, Benjamin Dreyer, and J. K. Lambert—much gratitude. Several people read the manuscript as I was writing; their steadfastness and helpful criticism were invaluable. Thanks to Marcia Lesser, Joy Hopkins-Hausman, Tom Bullard, Kali Rosenblum, and Nancy Kantor Hodge. Thanks to James Kullander for literary camaraderie and loyal support.

A preponderance of the material I cover in this book comes from my experiences at Omega Institute. For more than twenty-two years I have worked with an exceptional staff at Omega; my friends and colleagues there—past and present—are too numerous to list. In mentioning just a few, I in no way mean to leave out those staff and faculty members whose friendship and support have meant so much to me. First and foremost, I thank Omega itself, which over the years has developed such a personality that I now relate to it more as a being than a place or an organization. I offer endless gratitude to my teacher and the founding inspiration of Omega, Pir Vilayat Inayat Khan, and the legacy of his father, Pir-O-Murshid Hazrat Inayat Khan, for the vision and the teachings that have made my life infinitely better. Stephan Rechtschaffen, with whom I cofounded Omega, deserves much of the credit for its success and vibrancy. I offer profound thanks to him not only for that, but also for being my former husband, my traveling partner through young adulthood, the father of my children, and a friend. To fellow founding member and soul-friend Tom Valente; to Steven and Lila Pague, Amina Eagle, and the rest of the early pioneers; and to the following staff members with whom I have worked for many years, I offer a deep bow of respect: James Kullander, Sarah Priestman, Marion Baker, Dinabandhu and Ila Sarley, Skip Backus, Kacie Drury, Kim Blisard, Harry Feinberg, Allan Vickers, Andrea Johnson, Linda Woznicki, Leëta Damon, Patrick Baily, Lois Guarino, John Berryhill, Michael Craft, Greg Zelonka, and so many other fine coworkers past and present. Your intelligence, boldness, and devotion to bringing beauty and healing into the world has been a source of happiness in my life. Board of directors members who have selflessly served Omega over the years include Don Altschuler, Mirabai Bush, Ram Dass, Joan Halifax, Tom Jackson, George Kaufman, Gary Krauthamer, Peter Roy, Arman Simone, and Gail Straub.

My fellow *mureeds* who studied with Pir Vilayat when I did—on the West Coast and at the Abode community—remain my spiritual brothers and sisters. I carry you all inside of my heart—a perpetual family meeting! A special thank you to Taj Inayat Glanz, beloved friend and teacher, A Few Good Friends, and my midwife sisters.

Those who have shared their lives and stories with me in my classes for staff and guests at Omega gave me inspiration and material for this book. Thank you for your courage to look within and grow. To those who have co-taught workshops with me, including my dear friend Saki Santorelli, my beautiful comrade Ila Sarley, and the generous-hearted Mirabai Bush, thank you for your insight and support.

For unwavering support, for deep companionship, and for growing together through the difficult transitions and the ordinary magic, I extend love and gratitude to my community of friends: Kali Rosenblum and Kevin Smith, Sil and Peter Reynolds, Moira and Bert Shaw (thank you, Bert), June and Phil Jackson, Gail Straub and David Gershon, Judith Gardten, Marion Cocose and Ken Bock, the memory of Peter Hendrickson and Tim Allen, and all of the other 50/50 Club members and New Year's Just Toss It pinecone throwers. I want to thank my children's friends and their parents for our shared adventures in the blessed territory of family life, and the Woodstock community at large, especially Gioa Timpanelli, Peter Occhiogrosso, Kathleen Tompkins, and Ars Choralis.

Along with my faith, my family is at the root of my strength and happiness. Love and gratitude go out to the following: my mother and my father, to whom this book is dedicated, and who raised me to pursue the truth, to love learning, and to care for the earth; my sisters, who are my dearest friends—Katy Lesser, Maggie Lake, and Joanne Finkel—and their families; and my sons—Rahm and Daniel, and my stepson, Michael—the loves of my life. Each has been a teacher and friend: Rahm, thank you for your wisdom in the Landscape of the Mind; Michael, thank you for your love in the Landscape of the Heart; and Daniel, thank you for your thunder in the Landscape of the Soul. Finally, I am grateful to my husband, Tom Bullard, for being a spiritual warrior—lighting up our path with humor, clear insight, and genuine kindness.

Index

ABOUT THE AUTHOR

ELIZABETH LESSER is the cofounder and senior adviser of Omega Institute (Rhinebeck, New York), recognized internationally for its workshops and professional trainings in holistic health, psychology, and cross-cultural arts and religion. Since 1977, when Omega was founded, she has helped direct the institute's organization and research, develop its programs, and train its staff. She has also been privileged to study and teach with leading thinkers and practitioners in the fields of human development and spiritual growth. Prior to her work at Omega, she was a midwife and childbirth educator. She attended Barnard College and San Francisco State University. She lives in the Hudson River Valley with her family.

ABOUT THE TYPE

This book was set in Bembo, a typeface based on an old-style Roman face that was used for Cardinal Bembo's tract *De Aetna* in 1495. Bembo was cut by Francisco Griffo in the early sixteenth century. The Lanston Monotype Machine Company of Philadelphia brought the well-proportioned letter forms of Bembo to the United States in the 1930s.